THE EURASIAN CENTURY

The EURASIAN CENTURY

Hot Wars, Cold Wars, and the Making of the Modern World

HAL BRANDS

W. W. NORTON & COMPANY
Independent Publishers Since 1923

For information about permission to reproduce selections from this book, write to
Permissions, W. W. Norton & Company, Inc., 500 Fifth Avenue, New York, NY 10110

For information about special discounts for bulk purchases, please contact
W. W. Norton Special Sales at specialsales@wwnorton.com or 800-233-4830

Manufacturing by Sheridan
Book design by Daniel Lagin
Production manager: Anna Oler

ISBN 978-1-324-03694-4

W. W. Norton & Company, Inc.
500 Fifth Avenue, New York, NY 10110
www.wwnorton.com

W. W. Norton & Company Ltd.
15 Carlisle Street, London W1D 3BS

1 2 3 4 5 6 7 8 9 0

To John Lewis Gaddis and Barton Bernstein

CONTENTS

INTRODUCTION

I t is January 1917, and the balance of power is breaking. A war that
started with the assassination of an archduke in Sarajevo has gone
global and will soon pull in nations from every inhabited continent.
Germany is on the verge of defeating Russia in the east, which will allow
it to plunder that dying empire's resources and make itself the master of
Europe from the North Sea to Ukraine. Germany's armies are exhaust-
ing France on the western front; its submarines seek to starve Britain
into surrender. If the U-boats don't deal London and the allies it subsi-
dizes a death-blow, bankruptcy might: The costs of war are bleeding the
British Empire dry.

Germany is on course to dominate the Old World, which would give
it a continental base to project power across the oceans and around the
globe. "If Germany won it would change the course of our civilization,"
the American president, Woodrow Wilson, has remarked; a world led
by an ascendant autocracy is not one in which even distant democracies
will be secure.[1]

It is December 1941, and humanity is slipping into an abyss. Hitler
already rules Europe from Brest to the Balkans; with German tanks just
outside Moscow, he believes he is close to defeating the Soviet Union

and crushing all resistance between the Atlantic and the Urals. In the Far East, imperial Japan is completing the totalitarian pincer movement. For years, Tokyo has been violently expanding its own empire into mainland Asia. In the wake of its attack on Pearl Harbor, the Japanese military is now embarked on a breathtaking advance that will give it control of territories from the Indian frontier to the International Date Line, from Manchuria to Australia's northern approaches.

Berlin and Tokyo are ruling their conquests with the homicidal cruelty one would expect from fascist states. Along with Italy, they have pledged to destroy the existing international system and build a dystopian "new order" atop its ruins. "The era of democracy is finished," Japan's foreign minister has declared. "Totalitarianism . . . will control the world."[2] In Washington, U.S. policymakers are terrified that the Axis powers will link up through the Indian Ocean and the Middle East, giving them command of the Eurasian landmass and the oceans around it. Should this occur, writes the brilliant strategist Nicholas Spykman, the Western Hemisphere will face "complete encirclement." It will be "impossible for us to preserve our independence and security."[3]

It is March 1947, and the world again hangs in the balance. World War II has destroyed two ruthless empires but empowered another. Soviet troops occupy territory deep within a prostrate Europe; Stalin and his allies are probing for advantage from Scandinavia and Greece to Iran and Korea. A bloody civil war will soon deliver the world's most populous country, China, into Stalin's camp; hunger and radicalism are creating ideal conditions for the spread of communist influence.

If hope, prosperity, and security cannot soon be restored in countries around the Soviet periphery, then Moscow—or its communist proxies—may sweep to power. If this happens, warn President Harry Truman's advisers, then a tyrant no less murderous than Hitler will have the resources of two continents at his disposal; the free world's prospects for survival will be slight.[4]

It is February 2022, and humanity is about to get a reminder that history rolls on. Vladimir Putin is preparing a quasi-genocidal war of conquest in Ukraine, a country that has figured centrally in every great-power contest for over a century. Putin's plan is a haunting echo of the programs of atrocity and aggrandizement perpetrated during World War II. It is also the culmination of a generation-long effort to make Russia great again, by restoring its primacy over a space from Central Asia to Eastern Europe.

Meanwhile, another aspiring emperor-for-life, Xi Jinping, is crushing all opposition at home and mobilizing Chinese society for expansion abroad. His regime is conducting the largest naval buildup since World War II in hopes of subduing Taiwan and making the western Pacific a Chinese lake. Xi is simultaneously trying to use economic and technological influence—as well as old-fashioned military muscle—to build a sphere of influence reaching deep into China's continental hinterland and beyond. Those who stand in China's path, Xi has declared, "will have their heads bashed bloody against a Great Wall of steel."[5]

A country that was, only decades ago, desperately poor is now seeking a hybrid hegemony on land and at sea. Xi and Putin have even sealed a new axis of authoritarians—an ambitious strategic partnership, with Iran as a third member, that aims to create a radically revised international order with an illiberal Asia at its core.

The struggle over the Eurasian landmass and the waters around it is the defining feature of global politics in the modern era. It is the crucible in which the contemporary world was forged. And that contest is raging, once again, today.

*

WE OFTEN THINK OF THE MODERN ERA AS THE AGE OF AMERICAN POWER. In reality, we're living in a long, violent Eurasian century. Since the early 1900s, Eurasia has been the cockpit of global rivalry. That isn't surprising, given how vast and valuable it is.

As the name implies, Eurasia consists of the combined expanse of those two Old World continents of the Northern Hemisphere, Europe and Asia. It includes the outlying islands of those continents, which are closely connected to them by Eurasia's marginal seas, as well as North Africa, which is as thoroughly linked to Europe by the Mediterranean as it is blocked from the rest of Africa by the Sahara. Eurasia thus runs from littoral Asia in the east to the Iberian Peninsula and the British Isles in the west, from the Arctic Ocean in the north to the Indian Ocean in the south.[6] This "world island," as geographer Halford Mackinder called it, is a space unlike any other.[7]

Comprising steppes, mountains, plains, deserts, jungles, and nearly every other topography, Eurasia accounts for more than one-third of the land on Earth. It possesses some 70 percent of the world's population as well as the bulk of its industrial might and military potential. It is the birthplace of all five of humanity's major religions and the cradle of many of the civilizations that shaped the world. Its inner seas, from the Mediterranean to the South China Sea, are conveyor belts for commerce; Eurasia also touches all of the great oceans that carry goods, fleets, and armies around the globe. In short, Eurasia represents a prize without equal; it is the strategic center of the world.

To be sure, the Eurasian landscape has never been static. For much of the modern era, Eurasia's powerhouse was Western Europe—until the post–World War II recovery of Japan, the breathtaking rise of China, and the development of Asia pulled the globe's economic center of gravity to the east. When the concept of Eurasia emerged, statesmen were just starting to grasp the strategic implications of oil and air power; by the 2020s, Eurasia and the world were entering a long, messy transition to a new energy regime and confronting the possibility of conflict in the digital domain. Eurasia's great maritime hot spot was once the North Sea, where Germany and Britain faced off; today, the most portentous waterways are the Taiwan Strait, the South China Sea, and other places where Chinese and U.S. power meet.

What *hasn't* changed, amid all this evolution and revolution, is that Eurasia is where the action is: where the bulk of the world's population lives and its economic activity occurs; where the globe's most powerful countries, America excepted, are found; and whose key regions and seas are home to the most intense, geopolitically defining rivalries. This is why the world has been repeatedly roiled, reshaped, and nearly destroyed by fateful clashes over the Eurasian supercontinent and its watery approaches.

Ambitious autocracies, from imperial Germany to the Soviet Union, have reached for dominance by seizing a commanding position in the world's strategic core. Offshore democracies, first the United Kingdom and later America, have partnered with onshore allies to preserve a world where freedom can flourish by keeping Eurasia divided. The greatest hot wars, cold wars, and proxy wars of the twentieth century were all part of this pattern. America's rivalries with a new set of challengers—China chief among them—are the next round in this geopolitical game.

*

ADMITTEDLY, THE WORD "EURASIA" MAY SOUND UNFAMILIAR TO AMERI-cans. But that's only because they've had the luxury of forgetting about it in an anomalous age of post–Cold War peace. The term itself dates back to the late nineteenth century, when geographers and strategists began to think of the two neighboring continents as a single, unified theater. As the twentieth century came to be defined by confrontations over that mega-region, the phrase became commonplace among intellectuals, political leaders, and military planners alike.

During the run-up to World War II, figures as varied as an American president and Nazi intellectuals fixated on Eurasia as a fount of unparalleled resources and power. At the outset of the Cold War, top-secret U.S. planning documents were littered with references to the Eurasian landmass—the critical area Washington could not allow any rival to rule. The concept even pervaded the most famous political litera-ture of the twentieth century. In *1984*, the classic novel George Orwell published in 1949, Eurasia was a totalitarian behemoth engaged in per-petual war, a reference that hardly had to be explained at all.

For generations, everyone familiar with global affairs knew that Eurasia was the shatter-zone where empires collided. That concept is making a comeback, as Eurasia becomes the epicenter of competition and conflict anew.

———
*

WHAT, THOUGH, DISTINGUISHES THE EURASIAN CENTURY FROM ANY other era? The physical features of the Earth didn't change suddenly in 1900. The twentieth century was hardly the first time Eurasia was an object of vicious dispute. As historian John Darwin emphasizes, the likes of Attila, Genghis Khan, and Tamerlane sought, long ago, to bring huge chunks of Eurasia under their sway.[8] Even compared to more recent history, war and rivalry are nothing new. In Europe, the centuries prior to 1900 saw terrible conflicts, such as the Thirty Years' War and the wars that followed the French Revolution. Contrary to contemporary Chinese propaganda, the history of Asia was scarcely more placid.

Yet the period following roughly 1900 was different; it was distinguished by the frequency, ferocity, and scope of its struggles. World War I and World War II were truly global conflicts, which featured combat from one end of Eurasia to the other and spread into lands and seas far beyond. They were two of the deadliest interstate wars in history (perhaps *the* two deadliest interstate wars in history, depending on how one counts) and played a starring role in what historian Matthew White has aptly called the hemoclysm, the unmatched torrent of bloodshed that characterized the twentieth century.[9] The Cold War was less violent, at least for the superpowers. But it was plenty gruesome in the developing regions, where millions died in the "small" wars that stood in for another world war.[10] And it was no less globally encompassing than the hot wars that preceded it; key battles occurred from Berlin to Sinai, from Angola to the Korean peninsula, from Southeast Asia to Central America.

These conflicts were fought for the highest stakes. They were what political scientists call hegemonic struggles, which determine who rules the international system and shapes the future of humanity. Not least, these clashes occurred rapid-fire, in historical terms: two world wars and the onset of a multi-generation Cold War in just over thirty years. The twentieth century saw desperate, repeated fights for global supremacy—fights that were often shocking in their intensity, global in their sprawl, epic in their stakes, and that all had Eurasia as their focal point.

Indeed, this Eurasian century was defined by epochal changes and outrageous extremes.[11] It was a time when great-power wars and rivalries expanded uncontrollably, engulfing, like raging fires, everything they touched. It was an era in which new, terrible forms of tyranny perpetrated unprecedented crimes at home and abroad. It was an age in which technological breakthroughs, from railroads to nuclear weapons, upended global politics. It was a century shaped by America's rise as a global superpower, which occurred largely in response to repeated crises of Eurasian security. Above all, it was a period whose unmatched carnage eventually produced—paradoxically—a modern system more peaceful, prosperous, and democratic than anything humanity had known before. The Eurasian century was unique in the destruction it sowed and the creation it spurred.

In many ways, Eurasian struggles made our modern world. To understand why this was the case—why a particular area became the engine of history at a particular moment—requires acquainting ourselves with the man whose life and work were at the center of this extraordinary age.

*

SIR HALFORD MACKINDER ISN'T A HOUSEHOLD NAME. A BRITISH POLYmath who lived from 1861 to 1947, Mackinder is remembered, not always fondly, by academics who study international relations. He has been forgotten by nearly everyone else.[12] Though passionately committed to the British Empire, Mackinder was never fully part of its policymaking elite. His foray into high-level statecraft, as British High Commissioner for South Russia after World War I, ended with failure and a fair bit of humiliation. He served out the twilight of his career in meaningful if somewhat obscure posts, such as the chairmanship of the Imperial Shipping Committee.

Yet influence comes in many forms, and Mackinder left a shadow longer than those cast by many politicians, diplomats, and generals.

Mackinder was one of the most interesting people of his era—at various times a mountaineer and an explorer, a member of Parliament, and a professor at prestigious academic institutions. He wrote prolifically, on a wider array of subjects than most intellectuals would now attempt to master. Mackinder was no dilettante, though; he largely founded geography as a proper academic discipline. He is also considered the father of its sister field, geopolitics—the study of how the physical features of the Earth interact with the struggle for influence and power. Beginning with a lecture delivered at the Royal Geographic Society in London in 1904, Mackinder provided as prescient a warning as any about what the next century would bring.

Mackinder's talk, titled "The Geographic Pivot of History," was a bracing work of analysis.[13] Mackinder explained how the march of technology, particularly railroads, was shrinking Eurasia's geography and potentially allowing a single power to control that vital landmass. The closing-off of the strategic safety valve provided by easy colonial expansion during the nineteenth century was now turning the great powers against one another in the twentieth. Politics and geopolitics were interacting in explosive ways; a theme that was mostly implicit in Mackinder's original lecture, but loomed larger later, was that illiberal regimes now had modern industrial economies at their disposal, a factor that could only enable new programs of repression and conquest.[14]

All of this, Mackinder predicted, would precipitate titanic clashes. A country or coalition that marshaled the land power needed to control Eurasia would become a global menace, for it would then command the resources required to build sea power without rival. So the pattern of world politics would be one in which assertive continental states pushed for Eurasian—and perhaps global—primacy, while their enemies, both the sea powers located off Eurasia's coasts and the vulnerable states situated at the edge of the landmass, labored to hem them in.

Mackinder got plenty wrong, which is why he spent the next four decades tinkering with his thesis. But he got the big themes of the young century right. His ideas became a touchstone for leaders who sought to overthrow the Eurasian balance and also for those who sought to preserve it—even when those leaders had never heard of Mackinder, let alone read his work. Some of the most important diplomats and strategists of the twentieth century, such as Eyre Crowe, the longtime British Foreign Office official who warned of a coming conflict with imperial Germany, and George Kennan, the American diplomat who authored his country's approach to the Cold War, drew heavily on Mackinder's thinking. It is a testament to Mackinder's enduring influence that we can trace the history of the Eurasian century through analyses he composed in real time.

Mackinder wasn't alone, of course. The Eurasian century spotlighted an international cohort of geopolitical thinkers who made intellectual waves by making sense of the emerging era. In the 1890s and early 1900s, the U.S. naval officer Alfred Thayer Mahan wrote incessantly about the role of sea power in a world of intensifying rivalry. His message was that the oceans were no longer moats protecting America but highways connecting it to a volatile world. Nicholas Spykman, the Dutch American sociologist-turned-strategist at Yale University, would challenge and adapt Mackinder's concepts during World War II. Karl Haushofer, the most prominent German geopolitician of the interwar era, helped the Nazi Party put Mackinder's ideas to awful purposes—a role Russian intellectuals close to the Kremlin have more recently reprised. They are exemplars of an authoritarian school of geopolitics that has both borrowed from, and threatened the very purposes of, its democratic counterpart. By revisiting the debates between these great (and not-so-great) intellectuals, we can better understand what happened in a tumultuous twentieth century and what is happening today.

Yet ideas don't translate themselves into action; the course of the Eurasian century was charted by some of posterity's most famous, and infamous, leaders. The protagonists included, on the one side, notorious tyrants who launched destructive grabs for greatness. Kaiser Wilhelm II, Adolf Hitler, Tojo Hideki and his coterie of Japanese militarists, and Joseph Stalin fused repression at home with aggression abroad; Xi

Jinping and Vladimir Putin are their most notable present-day successors. Opposing them were democratic statesmen who rallied coalitions
to turn back these authoritarian challenges: among them, Woodrow
Wilson, Winston Churchill, and Franklin Roosevelt during the world
wars, as well as Harry Truman, Dean Acheson, and their transatlantic
contemporaries during the Cold War.

World politics are messy, and so, at times, was the line between
these categories. Stalin helped Hitler touch off World War II, before
helping to defeat him, before confronting the West once again in the
Cold War. China helped the free world win that contest, before becoming its most potent rival today. The Eurasian century is fascinating for
the shifting alliances it produced—and because it demonstrates how
history is made at the intersection of structural forces, big ideas, and the
critical choices leaders make.

------
*

THIS BOOK TELLS THE STORY OF THE EURASIAN CENTURY. IT FEATURES
research in the papers and archives of many countries that clashed in Eurasia's prior contests; it draws on my travels to nations from Japan to India,
Australia to the United Kingdom. It uses these materials to explore the
tectonic shifts—the revolutions in technology and warfare, the rise of
vicious totalitarian regimes and toxic ideologies of conquest, and others—
that made Eurasia the central theater of twentieth-century geopolitics. It
recounts the epic fights the Eurasian century produced. And it shows how
the desperate struggles of the twentieth century ultimately birthed a thriving liberal order that is being threatened today. There are many reasons for
revisiting this story; two are most important.

First, fights for Eurasian primacy are fights over the fate of the world
and the future of human freedom. That claim may sound extravagant.
It isn't.

Eurasia is the fulcrum of world order: A country or group of countries that dominates its vital regions would have unmatched resources,
wealth, and global reach. If an aggressive autocracy or alliance of autocra-

cies became preeminent within Eurasia, it could fundamentally reshape world order and coerce its rivals around the globe. Even if this hegemon could not physically conquer the surviving overseas democracies, it could force them into such continual, piercing insecurity that they might struggle to preserve their safety and their freedoms simultaneously.

This was the nightmare of the great democratic leaders of the twentieth century. The same specter would haunt the democratic world if an autocratic China, or an autocratic axis, gained primacy within that landmass and its adjoining oceans today. The arc of this century, like the arc of the last one, will be determined by the outcome of Eurasian rivalry. The means and methods of Eurasian challenges may change over time; the stakes do not.

Second, how well America and other democracies fare in a second Eurasian century depends on how firmly they grasp the lessons of the first. It is easy to come away from this story with a sense of geographical determinism. After all, every country that reached for Eurasian hegemony was crushed in the end, because its ambitions brought down the collective force of an overwhelming enemy coalition. Imperial Japan, Germany (twice), and the Soviet Union all suffered this fate. Today's autocratic allies are encountering this danger anew. This is the dilemma Eurasian powers face: in growing strong enough to overpower their neighbors, they grow strong enough to earn the enmity of the world.

Yet the struggles of the twentieth century didn't have to turn out this way. As historian Richard Overy points out, the results of decisive battles can hinge on how accurately a few pilots drop a few bombs at a pivotal moment.[15] Both world wars and the Cold War might have had different endings had key leaders pursued different strategies at crucial junctures. Likewise, the outcomes of today's contests will hinge on the quality of leaders and the choices they make—and thus, on the degree to which those leaders harvest the insights the past 120 years have to offer. Not least of the reasons for studying the Eurasian century is that there is no better way of girding ourselves for the upheaval ahead.

THE EURASIAN CENTURY

1

MACKINDER'S WORLD

The Trans-Siberian Railway is a steel belt that binds two continents. Its nearly 6,000 miles of track link Moscow to Vladivostok; connecting lines run across Europe and down Asia's eastern edge. For more than a century, the Trans-Siberian has attracted travelers who want to journey through some of the world's most remote, and sometimes beautiful, territory: the Ural Mountains, the shores of Lake Baikal, the stunning isolation of the Russian steppe. But when it was completed in 1904, the Trans-Siberian Railway was the stuff of imperial dreams and geopolitical nightmares.[1]

The tsarist government built the railway—a monumentally expensive, debt-funded project—with glory in mind. The track was meant to open huge, resource-rich Siberia to settlement and industrialization. It would enable the Russian Empire to strengthen its influence in Manchuria, Korea, and throughout the Far East. The railway, argued its champion, Count Sergei Witte, would catalyze foreign expansion and domestic consolidation; it "would not only bring about the opening of Siberia, but would revolutionize world trade, supersede the Suez Canal as the leading route to China, enable Russia to flood the Chinese market with textiles and metal goods, and secure political control of northern China."[2]

The Trans-Siberian Railway changed the world, just not as Witte intended. Japan, Russia's rival in the region, understood exactly what was coming. Trains can carry troops, so strengthened transportation links to Northeast Asia would allow the tsarist empire to impose itself in Tokyo's backyard. "The day the Trans-Siberian Railroad is completed will be the day that crisis comes to Korea," one Japanese commander predicted, "and when crisis comes to Korea, all the Orient will face upheaval."[3] Tokyo wasn't about to let that happen. Just months before the final section of track was completed, Japan launched a surprise attack on the Russian fleet at Port Arthur, starting the first greatpower war of the twentieth century—a fight for imperial supremacy in Northeast Asia.

It was a portent of things to come. The Trans-Siberian Railway was a flashpoint throughout the bloody epoch that followed.

The modernization of the Russian rail network, with the Trans-Siberian as its backbone, helped bring on World War I by convincing German officials that a lumbering Russian steamroller would soon be able to mobilize with modern speed. "The big Russian railway constructions," Kaiser Wilhelm II brooded, were "preparations for a great war."[4] Rival Russian factions battled over the railroad during the civil war that World War I set off; concern that the Bolsheviks—or Germans—might control the tracks then motivated a hapless intervention by Washington and other powers. State Department officials left little doubt about the goal of that expedition; "the maintenance, operation and control of the Trans-Siberian Railroad" was its "initial and preeminently important step."[5]

The same railway had a starring role in the next world war. Between 1939 and 1941, the Trans-Siberian was an economic highway between the Axis powers, with the Soviet Union—then effectively allied to Germany—as the intermediary. By spring 1941, the railroad was carrying 300 vital tons of rubber from Japan's growing empire to Germany each day.[6] After Hitler turned on Stalin in June 1941, the railroad helped seal the alliance that ensured Germany's defeat. Huge quantities of American Lend-Lease aid traveled the Trans-Siberian from Vladivostok to

Stalin's European front.[7] And decades later, as Vladimir Putin was getting ready to invade Ukraine, the railway set the stage for another gruesome showdown.

During a slow, menacing buildup for Europe's largest conflict since World War II, Putin used the Trans-Siberian to shuttle military assets from one side of Eurasia to the other. Military trains carried tanks, trucks, infantry, and missile launchers from the Russian Far East to the Ukrainian border. One unit that made the trip, the 64th Separate Motorized Rifle Brigade, partook in the rape, torture, and murder of civilians in Bucha, the suburb of Kyiv whose name became synonymous with Russian depravity.[8] "There are maniacs who enjoy killing a man," one member of that unit acknowledged. "Such maniacs turned up there."[9] In 1891, Tsar Alexander III had declared, "Let a railroad be built." Over 130 years later, the Trans-Siberian was still a conduit for conflict.[10]

There's a good reason for this. Geography is stubborn; barring expansion or contraction, a country is where it is. Developments that alter geography, or ease the constraints it imposes, can thus profoundly change world affairs. The digging of the Suez Canal turbocharged the building of European empires in Asia and Africa by slashing travel times between metropole and periphery. The construction of a transcontinental railroad in the nineteenth century helped make the United States a global superpower in the twentieth, by giving it mastery of North America from coast to coast. The Trans-Siberian Railway made it possible to move armies rapidly across Eurasia; it previewed technological revolutions that would enable bids for conquest vaster still. So the completion of the Trans-Siberian augured an era of violent collisions on a global scale.

Sir Halford Mackinder saw that era coming, in a lecture he delivered when it was just about to begin. Mackinder's ideas previewed the basic patterns of conflict in the coming century. They thrust him into a grand debate, spanning countries and decades, over geopolitics and strategy in the modern age. And they had a lasting impact on those who sought to preserve a world fit for human freedom—as well as those who sought to destroy it. All the greatest wars and rivalries of the Eurasian century were contests to rule Mackinder's world.

*

"PRACTICAL MEN WHO BELIEVE THEMSELVES TO BE QUITE EXEMPT FROM any intellectual influence, are usually the slaves of some defunct economist," John Maynard Keynes once wrote. "Madmen in authority, who hear voices in the air, are distilling their frenzy from some academic scribbler of a few years back."[11] Keynes was saying that ideas precede policy, even if policy-makers don't realize it. That's a good way to understand the life and legacy of Halford Mackinder.

In fairness, Mackinder was no obscure scribbler. Born in 1861 in Gainsborough, in the English midlands, he would live until 1947—a period encompassing the apogee of European imperialism and British power, the descent into two world wars, and the onset of decolonization and the Cold War. As a boy, Mackinder read the news that Bismarck's Prussia had thrashed France and unified Germany, and wondered what the consolidation of a rising empire in the heart of Europe would bring. It was a remarkable time to be alive, and over a professional life spanning six decades, Mackinder did remarkable things.[12]

He was well equipped for ambitious and adventurous pursuits. The son of a doctor, Mackinder was educated at boarding school and then Oxford. He had a talent for languages, learning French and German, and a passion for exploration that would take him—physically or intellectually—around the globe. Mackinder may have been, as he put it, "rather a lonely boy" with an affinity for books and maps, but he was strong, athletic, and intellectually mature.[13] At university in the early 1880s, he cultivated his passions for geology and history, for public speaking and intellectual debate at the Oxford Union, and for service to the British Empire, through the Oxford Army Volunteer Reserve and the University Rifle Corps. After graduation, Mackinder first sought to become a lawyer, before beating a less conventional path.

Having taken to lecturing on geography for extra money, Mackinder turned his side hustle into an Oxford professorship at the age of twenty-five, on the strength of a talk that helped establish that subject as an academic discipline. He would play an important role in launching a series of prestigious academic institutions—the Oxford School of Geography, Reading University, and the London School of Economics—and he became a public intellectual who wrote on subjects ranging from tariff policy to the causes of war and peace. Mackinder then pivoted into politics, representing the Camlachie district of Glasgow in the House of Commons from 1910 to 1922. After World War I, he tried his hand at statecraft, serving as British High Commissioner for South Russia and attempting to sort out the chaos sown by war and revolution.

After losing his seat in Parliament in 1922, Mackinder threw himself back into public service, chairing unsexy but important bodies such as the Imperial Shipping Committee, meant to knit the British Empire together even as centrifugal forces were tearing it apart. For good measure, Mackinder was an accomplished mountaineer who led the first successful ascent of Mount Kenya. That climb was "a really serious mountaineering feat," a contemporary noted—even if it was also a deadly misadventure, marred by rumors (never proven) that Mackinder was involved in the murder of mutinous African porters.[14]

Mackinder was a classic polymath; he had several careers wrapped into one. "I do not admit to having been a rolling stone, because I have generally known where I was going," he remarked, "but I have certainly gathered no moss."[15]

He had, alas, known disappointment. Mackinder didn't accomplish all he intended. His highest aspiration was to be a heavy hitter in British policy—a man of ideas who was also a man of action. "If he got his foot on the ladder he might go far towards the top," one observer predicted in 1902, "especially as there is an absence of able young men."[16] Climbing Mount Kenya proved easy by comparison.

Mackinder was not a natural politician, in part because of his abstract intellectual style. He never became a member of the Cabinet or otherwise really broke into the highest levels of the policy elite. His stint as High Commissioner was short and inglorious; his most comprehensive statement on foreign policy, a book titled *Democratic Ideals and Reality*, was mostly ignored for a generation after it was published. Mackinder, wrote his friend Leo Amery, had a "more forceful personality and a more powerful brain" than his higher-flying colleagues. But he "never quite made the mark once expected by him."[17]

Yet if Mackinder failed to get his hands firmly on the levers of power, he still left a lasting imprint. Mackinder prided himself on his ability to think big—to see beyond the present crisis and grasp the historical forces at work. It was essential, he wrote, that leaders of a democracy "be able easily and happily to roam in thought over the surface of the world, thinking in millions, thinking in ages."[18] Those who heard him speak on the subjects he knew best never doubted his ability; decades later, one colleague recalled how Mackinder, so "tall, erect, distinguished," would enrapture his students by delivering, "in his sonorous voice, without ever a note, a perfectly argued and presented synthesis."[19] Where Mackinder most excelled was in explaining geopolitics, a discipline focused on the relationship between geographical realities and political power.[20]

In his field-defining lecture, "On the Scope and Methods of Geography," Mackinder insisted that the discipline involved more than the mere cataloguing of physical facts; such a dry endeavor "must always fail to attract minds of an amplitude fitting them to be rulers of men."[21] Mackinder's version of geography—*political* geography—involved studying how the earth's features affected the behavior of peoples and societies across the long arc of history, and how their behavior, in turn, reshaped the physical environment. This required imagination and sweep: "Humdrum detail is the greater part of every science, but no science can satisfy the mind which does not allow of the building of palaces out of its bricks."[22] Few built mental palaces more majestic than Mackinder's.

One of his most-read books showed how Britain's geography and geology—the combination of its resource endowments and position off Europe's coast—had turned a small island nation into a wealthy, liberal sea power with a peerless empire. Another volume explained how the features of the Rhine River Valley had influenced the long contest to rule Central Europe.[23] The vital theme of Mackinder's work was that geography profoundly shaped the timeless struggle for power: It wasn't quite destiny, but it was a reality no good strategist could ignore. "Man and not nature initiates," he asserted, "but nature in large measure controls."[24] Which meant that training its people and leaders in a geographical way of thinking was essential for Britain to thrive, especially as the world began to change in epochal ways.

*

THE WORLD OF MACKINDER'S UPBRINGING WAS A WORLD OF UBIQUI- tous British power. London was the global hegemon of the nineteenth century; its influence reached into every inhabited continent. The Royal Navy patrolled the seas, allowing commerce to boom and an age of globalization to ignite. Indeed, London presided over what we would now call a liberal international order; the first great international expansion of democracy happened when British-style representative institutions took hold amid British primacy.[25] Notwithstanding some nasty but mostly localized wars, Europe was enjoying its long post-Napoleonic peace, allowing London to avoid continental entanglements and bask in "splendid isolation." The symbolic apex of British splendor was Queen Victoria's Diamond Jubilee in 1897, which showcased the world's best warships and imperial troops from around the globe. The atmosphere, recalled historian Arnold Toynbee, was, "Well, here we are on top of the world, and we have arrived at this peak to stay there—forever!"[26]

In reality, British power—and international stability—were slipping away. Britain had lost one crucial pillar of its hegemony; by 1890, it no longer had the world's largest economy. A cohort of rising powers— Prussia (later Germany), America, and Japan—were asserting their interests and reordering their regions through short, sharp wars. France and Britain almost came to blows in 1898 over imperial visions that collided in Sudan; by 1899, London was embroiled in an ugly colonial scrap against the Boers in southern Africa. Russia, Britain's long-standing rival along fault lines from Eastern Europe to South Asia, was building up its economy and military. The British Empire was beset by crises everywhere. As Colonial Secretary Joseph Chamberlain put it, "The weary Titan staggers under the too vast orb of his fate."[27]

Geopolitical upheaval went hand in hand with sharpening ideological conflict. Clashes between opposing ideas, between competing systems of government, are as old as history. Such clashes had, however, temporarily subsided after the ideological flames ignited by the French Revolution were finally extinguished. The countries that defeated Napoleon and established the Concert of Europe in 1814–15 had shared a preference for order, which trumped, for a time, their different conceptions of justice.[28] As the Concert broke down in the late nineteenth century, ideological tensions flared anew.

The Great Game was not just a rivalry between voracious empires; the stark and widening gap between a democratizing Britain and a despotic Russia made that contest one of values, too. "We are not of the same make," the British minister in Tehran wrote. "We differ as our governments differ."[29] The leaders of another British rival, Germany, had committed themselves to seeking greatness through autocracy and coercion. Germany's chancellor, Otto von Bismarck, had once declared that history would be made not "by speeches or majority decisions" but "by blood and iron." Prussia had become strong, he explained, "not through liberalism and free-thinking" but through the guidance of resolute authoritarians who acted with "ruthless courage."[30] A key question of the twentieth century, Mackinder and many contemporaries believed, was whether liberal states or their illiberal challengers would set the rules of the road.

Even war itself had changed. Gone were the languid, desultory conflicts that Europe's cash-strapped monarchies had waged in an earlier era. The French Revolution had opened an era of total war—contests in which modern states, driven by fierce nationalism and boasting sophisticated bureaucratic and financial capabilities, harnessed society's energies to seek the outright destruction of their foes. In the 1860s, the

U.S. Civil War had demonstrated how combatants could mobilize man-power, money, and industrial muscle on a scale previously unheard of, to fight wars longer, more destructive, and more consuming than before. Even the smaller, shorter wars that followed—the wars of German uni-fication, the Sino-Japanese war, the Boer War—displayed the devastat-ing effects of modern firepower and mass-produced weapons. As the international system grew more disordered, great-power collisions grew more devastating.[31]

Finally, by the dawn of the twentieth century the world was getting more crowded, claustrophobic. Progress was partly to blame; steam-ships, railroads, and telegraphs were thrusting people and continents together. Conquest was another culprit. The rapid-fire European impe-rial aggrandizement of the late nineteenth century, what one foreign minister called a "veritable steeplechase for colonial acquisitions," had created mega-empires—with Britain's the largest—that covered the globe. Influenced by social Darwinism and the notion that only the fit-test would survive, strategists throughout Europe and beyond insisted that countries must expand, engorging themselves with lands and resources, or be devoured by their rivals. Strong states "assert themselves in the universal economy of nature," wrote one retired German general. "The weaker succumb."[32] Mackinder's world was becoming a tinderbox intellectually as well as politically.

The opening decade of the 1900s was a moment of tectonic change in world politics—even if it was, understandably, difficult for contempo-rary observers to make out just what was happening and why. That was Mackinder's task when he visited the Royal Geographic Society on the evening of January 25, 1904, to deliver a lecture called "The Geographic Pivot of History."

---

*

FEW STRATEGIC TEXTS OF THE MODERN ERA WERE MORE SEMINAL; MACK-inder's lecture influenced generations of military, diplomatic, and political leaders. Yet you might not have guessed it at the time.

The talk wasn't an immediate hit; one attendee "looked with regret on some of the space which is unoccupied here."[33] Perhaps that was because it was a frigid January night. Or perhaps it was because Mackinder's lecture combined vague abstraction, meandering narration, distant history, and mountains of geographical detail. The talk featured a long, if graceful, discussion of rivers, steppes, peaks, and monsoon lands; it was full of concepts ("Pivot Area," "Inner Crescent," "Outer Crescent") that then probably seemed obscure. Mackinder asked a lot of his listeners. He also delivered a lot, for the analytical heart of his lecture was a penetrating discussion of the forces producing a Eurasian century.

First was the end of what Mackinder termed the "Columbian epoch"—that 400-year age of European exploration and conquest that began with the discovery of the Americas. "Whereas mediaeval Christendom was pent into a narrow region and threatened by external barbarism," Mackinder explained, the Columbian epoch had seen "the expansion of Europe against almost negligible resistances."[34] The major European states had mapped and divided the globe; the process had accelerated in the nineteenth century as advances in firepower, medicine, and transportation drove imperial penetrations deep into Africa and Asia. Not long after Mackinder spoke, Britain would control an empire of 31 million square kilometers; the French empire, at 12.5 million square kilometers, was twenty times larger than France itself.[35] Yet now the Columbian epoch was ending, a victim of catastrophic success.

There were no more worlds to conquer. Africa and much of Asia had been subjugated; the "new Europes" of Australia, Canada, and New Zealand were part of the British Empire. There was "scarcely a region left for the pegging out of a claim of ownership, unless the result of a war between civilized or half-civilized powers," Mackinder said.[36] Britain had gained the most from this orgy of aggrandizement, but the implications were ominous nevertheless.

The European powers had, since Napoleon's demise, mostly avoided all-out conflict, in part because expansion directed their aggression outward; a "long war" against less developed societies facilitated a "long peace" among the empires themselves.[37] Now this safety valve was closed. "Every explosion of social forces, instead of being dissipated in a circuit of unknown space and barbaric chaos, will be sharply re-echoed from the far side of the globe." A "closed political system" would be vicious; great-power relations were becoming zero-sum.[38]

Tensions were also rising for a second reason: technology was remaking geography. "Mobility upon the ocean," Mackinder remarked, was "the natural rival of horse and camel mobility" on land. In the Columbian epoch, sea power had outpaced land power, thanks to revolutions in sail and then steam. The discovery or creation of shortcuts—the Suez Canal and the route around the Cape of Good Hope—had accentuated the advantage, endowing "Christendom with the widest possible mobility of power."[39] The great seafaring states, namely Britain, had encircled Eurasia, grabbing footholds in the Middle East, India, and China. They could also negate the advantages that major land powers, namely Russia, derived from occupying a central position on the world's largest landmass.

The classic example was the Crimean War, fought between 1853 and 1856. Russia possessed interior lines—comparatively short axes of movement and communication—when it fought France, Britain, and a declining Ottoman Empire. It hardly mattered. Britain and France used command of the seas to enlarge the battlefield, threatening Russia on fronts from the Black Sea to the Baltic. Russia's abysmal transportation infrastructure—the empire lacked railways south of Moscow—prevented it from concentrating its forces effectively. It took three weeks for allied troops to deploy from their home countries to the Crimean Peninsula; it took three months for Russian troops stationed near Moscow to move south. An allied naval blockade strangled Russian grain exports and sent the government spiraling toward bankruptcy.[40] The inferior mobility of land power sealed Russia's humiliation, just as the superior mobility of sea power had enabled Britain's global expansion.

Now, however, the pendulum was swinging back. The wars of German unification, from 1864 to 1871, had revealed how a dense network of railways could enable battlefield victory and geopolitical revolution. Prussia, guided by Bismarck and the vaunted General Staff, had expertly used its railway system to defeat its enemies by rapidly assembling overwhelming concentrations of force.[41] The Trans-Siberian Railway, nearly finished when Mackinder delivered his lecture, might make it possible to move armies and supplies on a far larger scale.

"True, that the Trans-Siberian railway is still a single and precarious line of communication," Mackinder allowed, "but the century will not be old before all Asia is covered with railways."[42] Nor would it be long before Russia was ready to rumble. A once-backward empire was now propelling itself forward; in 1900, Russia produced fifty times as much coal and 2,000 times as much steel as it had in 1860.[43] It was tightening its grip on areas from the Caucasus to Central Asia to Siberia. "The spaces within the Russian Empire and Mongolia are so vast, and their potentialities in population, wheat, cotton, fuel, and metals so incalculably great," said Mackinder, "that it is inevitable a vast economic world, more or less apart, will there develop."[44]

All of which raised the possibility that a mighty, centrally located state could grab control of the Eurasian landmass. "The Pivot region of the world's politics," Mackinder hypothesized, was "that vast area of Euro-Asia which is inaccessible to ships, but in antiquity lay open to the horse-riding nomads, and is today about to be covered with a network of railways."[45] Whereas Genghis Khan's armies had used horses to sweep across Eurasia, a new generation of conquerors would ride the iron horse to glory.

Any Eurasian hegemony was likely to be dark and brutal, thanks to a third development: the modernization of tyranny. Tyrannies had always existed, indeed predominated, but the twentieth century saw something more pernicious: a coterie of countries that fused extreme repression, industrial dynamism, and violent expansion. There were hints of this in 1904; Mackinder was chiefly concerned about a Russian Empire that clung to illiberalism and monarchy even as it modernized economically, followed by a Germany that fused an imperial autocracy with competent bureaucracy and industrial heft. Yet it would be the Bolshevik regime, after it seized power in 1917, that provided Mackinder with a clearer glimpse of the future: a remorseless, well-organized police state that pursued messianic projects at home and abroad.[46] That revolution showed, as would the fascist powers of the 1930s and 1940s, how the most horrific forms of political violence and the most fantastic dreams of Eurasian expansion were parts of the same totalitarian whole.

The consequences of such expansion would be not regional but global. The consolidation of Eurasia under a hostile power could threaten even countries protected by oceanic moats.

Eurasia, Mackinder pointed out, was three times the size of North America. In the early 1900s, it possessed two-thirds of the world's population and most of its industrial power. A country or group of countries that dominated Eurasia would be far stronger than any rival; it would be invulnerable to blockade or attack from the sea. Dominant land power would then make for dominant sea power; freed from threats on its borders, a Eurasian behemoth could build navies without match. "The oversetting of the balance of power" within Eurasia, warned Mackinder, would fatally threaten the balance of power beyond it, for this "would permit of the use of vast continental resources for fleet-building, and the empire of the world would then be in sight."[47] Or, as Mackinder would later reformulate his thesis: "Who rules the Heartland rules the World-Island; whoever rules the World-Island commands the World."[48]

Thus Mackinder's final insight: that the main event in global politics would henceforth be fateful fights between onshore aggressors and offshore balancers. Continental powers—here Mackinder eyed Russia, perhaps in league with Germany—would seek to rule the great Pivot Area as well as the "Inner Crescent," that ring of countries, from China to India to Western Europe, around the Eurasian core. Offshore maritime powers making up an "Outer Crescent" would try to hold the balance by supporting Eurasian "bridge heads," such as France and Korea, and harassing an aspiring hegemon on land and at sea.[49] As Eurasian powers pushed outward, enemies within and beyond that continent would struggle to pen them in.

In many ways, Mackinder was predicting a grim future, one in which the Eurasian rim was once again threatened by a "widespread despotism" emanating from the center. Yet there was, at least, a suggestion that such struggles might be constructive. A "repellant personality" had the benefit of energizing and uniting his enemies; a strong, vibrant Europe had been forged between the rival pressures exerted by "Asiatic nomads," or Mongols, pressing from the east and "pirates of the sea," or Vikings, circling to the north and west. "Neither pressure was overwhelming," Mackinder said, "and both therefore were stimulative."[50] Perhaps new Eurasian pressures could unleash new forms of creation.

*

MACKINDER'S ARGUMENT WASN'T CUT FROM WHOLE CLOTH. AN UNAPOLO-getic synthesizer, he borrowed from contemporaries such as Lord Curzon, a future British foreign secretary, and the writer H. G. Wells.[51] The lecture was a product of its time in another way; Mackinder ended by warning that the Chinese might constitute the "yellow peril to the world's freedom" if their territory were ever effectively administered by someone else. Whether or not they objected to his racism, those who encountered his thesis, either that night or later, did probe his ideas.[52]

Hadn't the Columbian epoch seen its own runs at European supremacy, from Philip II, Louis XIV, and Napoleon? Might air power—the Wright brothers had made their famous flight the year before—someday overshadow land and sea power alike? Was poverty-stricken Central Asia, a key part of the Pivot area, some great strategic prize? Was Russia, a late-developing country seething with political instability, the next geopolitical juggernaut?[53]

The critics had a point, for the moment, about Russia. The completion of the Trans-Siberian Railway did cause a clash with an offshore rival; the Russo-Japanese War began weeks after Mackinder spoke. But if the start of that conflict made Mackinder look prescient, the ending didn't. Russia suffered a crushing defeat, which precipitated an unsuccessful revolution that previewed a successful one. The railway, it turned out, was enough to provoke a war but not to win it; its single track could not adequately reinforce the tsar's battered armies in the Far East.[54] When Russia tried, instead, to send its Baltic fleet around Eurasia, those fatigued, barnacle-encrusted ships were slaughtered in the Tsushima Strait. For two generations thereafter, attempts at Eurasian domination came not from a Pivot state pushing outward but from Crescent powers—Germany and Japan—that struck into the Eurasian Heartland while also striking across the neighboring seas.

Yet if Mackinder had his share of misfires, his central argument was a hit. His lecture was an example of what Prussian military theorist Carl von Clausewitz called *coup d'oeil*, or "stroke of an eye"—the ability to glance at a chaotic battlefield and discern its vital rhythms.[55] Eurasia and the adjoining waters were about to become killing fields for many of the reasons Mackinder enumerated. Helping to hold the line, ironically, would be a country that had accomplished what he feared.

*

MACKINDER WASN'T THE ONLY BIG BRAIN TRYING TO MAKE SENSE OF A turbulent age. His lecture was part of a larger debate over strategy and survival in the contemporary world. That debate played out over decades; it unfolded on both sides of the Atlantic. It also intersected with another storyline of the Eurasian century—the rise of a New World superpower committed to preventing consolidation of the Old.

Mackinder had alluded to this possibility in 1904 but he hadn't done more than that, perhaps because he was ambivalent about the United States. Yes, America had grown rich and strong in a world London stabilized; British capital built the railroads, ranches, and factories that made the United States an economic heavyweight. Cultural, religious, and linguistic ties ran deep. It was common, then, for prominent Britons of Mackinder's day to hope that a maturing Washington would join London in defending a global order that benefited them both. Americans were a "powerful and generous nation," Joseph Chamberlain had remarked. "They speak our language, they are bred of our race. Their laws, their literature, their standing upon every question are the same as ours; their feeling, their interest in the cause of humanity and the peaceful development of the world are identical with ours."[56] Americans didn't always see it the same way.

The Anglo-American special relationship was a product of the twentieth century; it did not exist in the nineteenth. American nationalism had been forged in two wars against the British Empire; war scares and diplomatic disputes were commonplace for generations thereafter. If twisting the lion's tail was popular among U.S. politicians, that's because large swaths of the population—especially Irish Americans—disliked Britain so much. As the United States grew stronger, its belligerence was often aimed squarely at London and its lingering presence in the Western Hemisphere; in 1894–95, Washington nearly fought a war against a global superpower over an arcane boundary dispute in South America. "The United States," Secretary of State Richard Olney thundered, "is practically sovereign on this continent, and its fiat is law upon the subjects to which it confines its interposition." In other words, "Dear Britain: Get out."[57]

No surprise, then, that Mackinder sometimes worried that America's rise might mean Britain's fall. The critical thing was to keep the United States from swallowing Canada, he wrote in 1908. For "if all North America were a single Power Britain would, indeed, be dwarfed"; the new colossus would "take from us the command of the ocean" as well.[58] Dominant land power would lead to dominant sea power. If that sounds familiar, it's because America had largely managed to accomplish on one vast continent what Mackinder aimed to avoid on another.

The United States originated, wrote historian George Dangerfield, as a "grimy republican thumbprint" in a monarchical world.[59] Far from enjoying blissful isolation, it was ringed by hostile tribes and empires. Yet it did have powerful advantages: a rapidly growing population swollen by immigrants; a territory rich with timber, minerals, and other resources; an abundance of sparsely populated space to the west; an ideology of liberty that could be as appealing to foreign peoples as it was terrifying to their rulers; an experiment in republican government that was just effective enough to exploit these other benefits. Crucially, the United States was also located across an ocean from Europe, giving it home-field advantage in the struggle for the Western Hemisphere. Not least, America possessed an intense national ambition; it was "destined by God and nature to be the most populous and most powerful people ever combined under one social compact," future president and secretary of state John Quincy Adams wrote.[60]

By Mackinder's time, Adams looked prophetic. The United States had expanded from the Atlantic to the Pacific. It had connected that huge territory by building a transcontinental railroad and grabbing the route for the Panama Canal. American gross domestic product (GDP) had expanded *forty-fold* over the course of the nineteenth century; the United States had zipped past Britain as the world's economic leader. By 1913, America's manufacturing output—the primary marker of economic sophistication and power in the industrial age—was more than that of Britain and Germany combined. "What was a bleak and barren wilderness a hundred and some years ago," one foreign visitor marveled, "has quickly become this splendid and magnificent new world."[61]

This emerging behemoth was well on the way to dominating the hemisphere, making the Caribbean an American lake, and thereby vindicating the doctrine that Adams, under James Monroe's name, had promulgated. Having won supremacy regionally, the United States would soon start projecting influence globally, by seizing the Philippines from Spain and building the fleet of battleships that Theodore Roosevelt would send around the world. "Movement has been [the] dominant fact" of American life, historian Frederick Jackson Turner had observed in 1893. Now that Americans had conquered a continent, their "energy will continually demand a wider field for its exercise."[62]

When Mackinder worried about the future of the Old World, he may have had the recent history of the New World in mind. And as the

United States used its continental empire as a base for more distant excursions, it was developing an American school of geopolitics, with Captain Alfred Thayer Mahan as its dean.

*

MAHAN WASN'T AMERICA'S FIRST GREAT STRATEGIST. ALEXANDER HAMILton and John Quincy Adams had steered a young republic in a hostile world. Abraham Lincoln preserved the "last best hope of earth" by holding the union together during the Civil War. In 1860, the explorer, writer, and politician William Gilpin peered into the country's future, arguing that America's "intermediate geographical position between Asia and Europe ... invests her with the powers and duties of arbiter between them."[63] It was Mahan, though, who thought most systematically and wrote most prolifically about the purposes of American power on a global stage.

He was, like Mackinder, a rare creature—a naval officer who was miserable at sea. "Mahan couldn't handle [a ship] to save his life," a fellow officer scoffed.[64] Mahan seemed destined for mediocrity until he joined the faculty of the newly created Naval War College in 1885. The college's president, Rear Admiral Stephen Luce, wanted a sharp mind that could produce a science of sea power, akin to what military theorist Antoine-Henri Jomini had done for land warfare. Mahan was happy to try; naval warfare, he lamented, was a critical branch of "warfare in general" but its intellectual state was "exceedingly backward."[65] In a best-selling book, *The Influence of Sea Power upon History, 1660–1783*, published in 1890, and a torrent of publications over the next quarter century, Mahan used the naval rivalries of the past to seek timeless lessons about sea power and how it could best be employed.

It took a special mix of position, people, and politics to make a maritime power, Mahan believed. Sea power accrued to nations with favorable geography, in the form of long coastlines, natural harbors, and plentiful resources; favorable demography, in the form of a large population with an instinct for trade and sail; and favorable governance, in the form of a political system willing to shell out big bucks for a mer-

chant fleet and navy. Mahan, then, was an instinctive geopolitician, who
believed a country's "natural conditions" did much to make its strategy.[66]
Yet if Mackinder foresaw an age of land power supremacy, Mahanian
geopolitics held that those who ruled the waves ruled the world.[67]

Waterborne travel, he argued, was still the most efficient—and
global—mode of transportation. An ocean was not a barrier but a "great
highway . . . a wide common, over which men pass in all directions."[68]
Maritime trade was the lifeblood of national prosperity and power; a
country that controlled the seas could contain and immiserate its enemies on land. The British fleet, Mahan wrote by way of historical illus-
tration, had stymied Napoleon's bid for global empire by pinning him
within Europe and starving him of resources; its "storm-beaten ships,
upon which the Grand Army of Napoleon never looked, stood between
it and the dominion of the world."[69] The same was true in every age:
naval dominance would allow a country to sink the enemy's fleet, wreck
its commerce, and ruin its dreams. The essence of global influence, contended Mahan, was "the possession of that overbearing power on the
sea which drives the enemy's flag from it, or allows it to appear only as a
fugitive."[70] Or, more pithily, "Control of the sea, by maritime commerce
and naval supremacy, means predominant influence in the world."[71]

Mahan was a historian with a mission: he wanted Washington
to build, buy, or steal the sources of power in a ruthless world. "I am
frankly an imperialist," he acknowledged, "in the sense that I believe
that no nation, certainly no great nation, should henceforth maintain
the policy of isolation which fitted our early history."[72] He supported
the annexation of Hawaii, taking the Panama Canal route, and acquisition of coaling stations and colonies. He evangelized endlessly for a
blue-water navy, bristling with battleships, that would allow the United
States to defeat its enemies in decisive engagements far from its shores.
"War, once declared, must be waged offensively, aggressively," he wrote.
"The enemy must not be fended off, but smitten down."[73]

This was succor for the souls of sea power enthusiasts; Mahan's
work was celebrated by Theodore Roosevelt, Winston Churchill, and

Kaiser Wilhelm II. "The Emperor is familiar with all that Mahan has written," one journalist reported.[74] Critics scorned Mahan as a shill for imperialism and war. The doctrine of sea power, wrote journalist Norman Angell, was "a doctrine of savagery."[75] Mahan certainly doesn't seem enlightened by today's standards: he considered conflict a defining aspect of human behavior; his works were full of ideas that now feel toxic. Even so, Mahan was a fairly forward-thinking sort.

Mahan sought a stable, relatively open maritime system characterized by trade and interdependence, even as he recognized that the search for wealth could be a source of rivalry.[76] He thought sea power superior to land power because the former favored freedom; armies were easily turned against the populace, but navies that couldn't "extend coercive force inland" presented "no menace to the liberties of a people."[77] Mahan was an early proponent of the idea that democracies made better choices, over the long run, than autocracies, even as he worried that societies that honored "the freedom and rights of the individual" faced a growing danger from those that practiced "the subordination of the individual to the state."[78] And if Mahan was an unrepentant nationalist, his solution to the intensifying rivalries of his era was a new level of international cooperation to keep Eurasia safe for the world.

*

THAT STRATEGY STARTED TO COALESCE IN *THE PROBLEM OF ASIA*, A BOOK published in 1900. The world's largest continent, Mahan posited, was really three distinct regions: a northern zone (Russia and northern China) where cold weather and land power predominated; a southern zone (Egypt, the Arabian Peninsula, South and Southeast Asia) with warm weather and good sea lines of communication; and a "debated and debatable" zone (the Near East, Persia, Central Asia, central China) between. That zone was "debated" because it was a political disaster, populated by a decaying China and other feeble states. Strength would prey on weakness; a hulking Russia would try to blast through en route to warmer waters and longer coastlines. The "vast, uninterrupted mass of the Russian Empire" would then have hegemony from the Levant to the Pacific; it would possess a path to the world's oceans with all the resulting influence. "Her tendency necessarily must be to advance," Mahan wrote, "and it is already sufficiently pronounced to be suggestive of ultimate aims."[79]

Repelling this bid would require the grandest alliance humanity had seen. A coalition of powers around the Eurasian periphery and beyond must throttle Russia's effort to control Asian markets and trade, to deny it the wealth that would underwrite geopolitical supremacy. That alliance must also exert steady pressure on Asia's maritime flanks—the Mediterranean, the Indian and Pacific Oceans, even China's great rivers—as a way of supporting local, land-based resistance to Russian advances. "The land power will try to reach the sea and utilize it for its own ends," Mahan stated, "while the sea power must obtain support on land, through the motives it can bring to bear upon the inhabitants."[80] Controlling the waters around Eurasia, Mahan believed, was the key to denying a dangerous hegemony there.

The Russian threat faded after 1905, but the basic problem did not. Japan was playing the Mahanian game; it had thrashed Russia at sea on the way to expanding its continental empire. If Tokyo ran the table in the Far East, it might turn its attention to the open Pacific. "Should war with Japan come before the Panama Canal is finished," warned Mahan, "the Philippines and Hawaii might fall before we could get there."[81]

Mahan was also eyeing Germany. Berlin "was likely to give us something to think about seriously on this side of the water" if it ever got a free hand in Europe, he had written in 1897.[82] Britain might currently "hold Germany . . . in check," he later explained, but should Britain falter, "the world would again see a predominant fleet backed by a predominant army," in the hands of a German state that had not sated itself with colonies—and was thus all the hungrier for them.[83]

So how should America respond? By going global in its statecraft. The Monroe Doctrine was no longer enough; Washington must practice a forward defense in overseas regions. Its objective, Mahan wrote, "should be political and military equipoise, not predominance."[84] The

United States could no more tolerate a Russia, or Japan, that overawed the eastern half of Eurasia than it could tolerate a Germany that over-awed the western half: A hostile hegemony in either place would turn the adjoining oceans into vectors for insecurity. Official Washington was starting to agree. In 1899, the Open Door Note announced U.S. opposition to any power that would seek to dominate China economically or politically. What all this implied, for Mahan, was that America's geopolitical future lay in alignment with British power.

Both countries needed the great maritime highway to remain open to their commerce. Both countries had a vital interest in preserving a world not fatally unbalanced by the aggregation of despotic power at its core. The two great ocean-going democracies must therefore work together to police the seas and sustain a global system in which their shared traditions of liberty could thrive. Once Americans appreciated their "duties to the world at large," Mahan asserted, "we shall stretch out our hands to Great Britain, realizing that in unity of heart among the English-speaking races lies the best hope of humanity in the doubtful days ahead."[85]

Mahan's analysis wasn't always perfect. He was downright dog-matic in arguing that the "massed fleet of line-of-battle ships" was the only true form of sea power.[86] Critics in continental Europe rejoined that commerce raiding could choke off an enemy's trade without requir-ing a climactic engagement of battleships; German submarines proved the point by nearly starving Britain into submission in World War I.[87] Mahan's history was also sometimes slipshod; a great fleet may have saved Britain from Napoleonic invasion, but the master of Europe was ultimately beaten on land. Sea power alone was never enough, Mahan's rival, the British naval strategist Julian Corbett, pointed out. "Since men live upon the land and not upon the sea," wars were typically decided "by what your army can do against your enemy's territory" or by "fear of what the fleet makes it possible for your army to do."[88] Corbett was onto something. Winning global wars in the coming century would require coordinated operations in multiple domains.

What Mahan grasped, though, was that struggles for primacy in Eurasia would be profoundly influenced by struggles for control of its adjoining oceans. Moreover, the divergence between Mahan and Corbett obscured the convergence between their nations. Mahan was building an American school of strategy rooted in a doctrine of hegemonic denial. He was also laying the intellectual groundwork for an alliance that would have seemed improbable in the nineteenth century—and would repeatedly save the day in the twentieth.

*

MAHAN WAS AHEAD OF HIS COUNTRYMEN IN FORESEEING AN ANGLO-American global order. He was also a forerunner of a larger, more professional community of strategists in the United States. Mahan was a self-trained scholar who used history, geography, and other subjects to divine the proper uses of U.S. power.[89] This was the goal of an entire academic discipline, strategic studies, that emerged in the first half of the twentieth century as America's influence grew—and the world repeatedly collapsed around it. It took serial breakdowns of international order for America to build up the intellectual sinews of a superpower. At the heart of that endeavor was the question of what new technologies and new forms of tyranny meant for the world.[90]

The study of international order is often a response to its absence; the study of strategy flourishes after its failure. In the transatlantic community, the modern academic field of international relations arose in response to World War I and the abortive peace that followed. Writers such as the British diplomat-turned-scholar E. H. Carr produced books that purported to offer a new, scientific approach to global affairs. Think tanks and graduate schools of international studies popped up to educate the elites of today and tomorrow. And amid a new "epidemic of world lawlessness," as Franklin Roosevelt called it in 1937, there arose a new discipline dedicated to seeking security despite surging global chaos.[91]

Strategic studies married brains and money: It linked institutions of higher learning, such as Yale and the Institute for Advanced Study in Princeton, to philanthropies endowed by the likes of Rockefeller and Carnegie. It was a composite discipline, blending geography, history, economics, and political science; it brought the study of military issues into America's civilian institutions.[92] As violence engulfed Europe and Asia, the field's leading scholars pondered what it would take for democracies to survive when their existence seemed threatened as never before. Totalitarian states were exerting "relentless pressure," wrote IAS scholar Edward Mead Earle. It seemed doubtful that "the cherished heritage of Anglo-Saxon political freedom can be maintained in a world so thoroughly dominated by war."[93]

Technology and ideology had created a fundamentally new situation, Earle wrote in 1941. "The speed, range, and destructiveness of modern aircraft—particularly the bomber—have revolutionized warfare." Meanwhile, all-powerful states were waging all-consuming conflict. "Total war is not new," he acknowledged. "What is new is its terrifying potentialities when waged by a totalitarian government of imagination and daring, motivated by boundless ambition and fanatical nationalism, and possessed of all the technical resources of modern science and industry."[94] Democracies needed their intellectuals, no less than their soldiers, to answer the call to arms.

Earle practiced what he preached. His weekly seminar at the IAS helped birth some of the field's defining works, such as Bernard Brodie's *A Layman's Guide to Naval Strategy*. Earle spearheaded the writing of *Makers of Modern Strategy: Military Thought from Machiavelli to Hitler*, a pathbreaking book that enlisted nearly twenty scholars—including refugees from Hitler's Europe—to educate Americans in military realities.[95] During World War II, Earle put his mind at the disposal of the Office of Strategic Services and the Allied bombing campaign; he wrote directly to President Roosevelt on how to fight Japan in the Pacific.[96] Earle's ultimate ambition was to produce a "unified concept of Grand Strategy"—an integrated, comprehensive approach to securing America's interests in war and peace.[97] Yet the person who came closest to doing so was Earle's rival for primacy in the strategic studies pantheon: Nicholas Spykman.

*

SPYKMAN MADE HIS REPUTATION AS FOUNDING DIRECTOR OF YALE'S Institute for International Studies—a body created, in 1935, partly because the university's students were overwhelmingly isolationist.[98] Born in Amsterdam and having worked as a journalist in the Middle East and Asia, Spykman was no provincial. "The murder of an Austrian Archduke brought a million soldiers to Europe, and the failure of an Austrian credit institution closed all the banks in the United States," he commented; the world was interested in America, even if America was not interested in the world.[99] Having begun his academic career as a sociologist studying the centrality of power in domestic society, Spykman would refocus, amid the collapse of international society, on the centrality of power in global affairs.

Power, indeed, was Spykman's obsession—which makes sense, given that he wrote at a time when the most ruthless countries were running roughshod over their neighbors. The world, Spykman explained in a series of influential writings, was "a society without a central authority"—there was no police department to call when order broke down. States, then, had no choice but to seek power at one another's expense. Talk about the brotherhood of man was empty piety; morality would be tossed aside when it clashed with the quest for security. In an anarchic world, "states can survive only by constant devotion to power politics."[100] And of the factors that shaped the struggle for power, Spykman argued, geography "is the most fundamentally conditioning . . . because it is the most permanent. Ministers come and ministers go, even dictators die, but mountain ranges stand unperturbed."[101]

America's geography had long made it "the most favored state in the world."[102] Its temperate climate, enormous size, abundant resources, and dense network of internal waterways had propelled it to economic primacy. Its comparatively benign surroundings—oceans and weak or friendly neighbors—allowed it to dominate its neighborhood with "power to spare for activities outside the New World."[103] Now, however, technology was redefining distance; hostile states with modern air power could reach out and touch their rivals in devastating ways. If the railway preoccupied Mackinder, and the steamship transfixed Mahan, the shadow of the long-range bomber informed Spykman's seminal works during World War II.

"The world is again in flames," Spykman wrote in *America's Strategy in World Politics*, a national bestseller released in 1942. "Advanced technology has created bigger and better engines for mass murder; devastation and destruction is again the ultimate purpose to which the energy of nations is being geared."[104] Written after the fall of France had rocked the European equilibrium, the book was an urgent inquiry into whether the United States could preserve "an independent national life within the Western Hemisphere" if the Axis powers were able to "crush all resistance in the Old World."[105] The answer, for Spykman, was no. Mackinder had *asserted* that a Eurasian hegemon would threaten democracies everywhere. Spykman set out, in nearly 500 pages of careful analysis, to *prove* the point beyond doubt.

There was nothing limited about the Axis design, he argued. Germany aimed to conquer "the European land mass from the North Sea to the Ural Mountains." Tokyo sought "hegemony over the Western Pacific rimland from Siberia to Tasmania." If they succeeded, the Western Hemisphere would be "surrounded by two gigantic empires controlling huge war potentials." America's position between two hostile continents would become a deadly trap, as Axis air power and sea power squeezed the New World from both sides. For isolationists who pointed out, correctly, that Hitler had never said he planned to invade America, Spykman had an answer: any country ambitious and brutal enough to conquer half the world would not long tolerate the existence of a powerful enemy in the other half. "There is nothing in the history of international relations or in the nature of power politics," he wrote, to suggest that once Eurasian hegemony was achieved, "the struggle for power would automatically cease."[106]

Yet Spykman made a sophisticated case for intervention. He acknowledged that something like "continental defense," a strategy based on protecting only the Western Hemisphere, was viable for a while. Even against a hostile Eurasia, a fully mobilized United States could control strategic islands in the Atlantic and the Pacific; it could harass approaching invasion fleets with naval forces and land-based air power; a massive army could defend the country's coasts. It was impossible, former president Herbert Hoover declared, for Germany to "attack 130,000,000 people 3,000 miles overseas, who have a capacity of 10,000,000 soldiers and 25,000 aircraft."[107] The problem was that this strategy had a shelf life, because the United States couldn't actually hold all of the Western Hemisphere.

The Southern Cone—where most of South America's population, agriculture, and resources were located—was separated from the rest of that continent by mountains and jungles. Thanks to the bulge of Brazil, it was farther by sea from New York than from France; it was beyond the reach of even America's most formidable bombers. So as the Axis powers used their air and naval forces to control the Atlantic and Pacific sea lanes, America would lose its grip on events below the Amazon. It would have to make a "last stand" in a more confined "quarter-sphere" encompassing most of North America, the Caribbean, and South America above the bulge.[108] That quarter-sphere was fatally vulnerable to strangulation and eventual destruction.

Here Spykman showed himself to be a *grand* strategist, because his argument involved economic and political factors as much as military ones. In 1945, economist Albert Hirschman would publish a trenchant book, *National Power and the Structure of Foreign Trade*, showing how totalitarian states used predatory trade tactics to pull smaller countries into their grasp. An up-to-date version of Machiavelli, Hirschman wrote, would include "extensive new sections" on "quotas, exchange controls, capital investment, and other instruments of economic warfare."[109] Spykman was ahead of him, showing how Germany would wield Eurasia's resources, trade, and capital to force South American countries into economic and political subservience. The Axis nations would simultaneously use propaganda, subversion, and ideological warfare to bring proxy forces to power. They would gradually turn South America into a hostile redoubt, while using blockades and embargoes to cut the United States off from tin, copper, and other vital materials. "Military warfare in all periods of history has been accompanied by political action," Spykman wrote. Once America was so weakened that it could not defend the quarter-sphere, its enemies would close in for the kill.[110]

The implications were stark: indifference to the fate of distant countries could jeopardize the survival of America itself. The world was not divided into "water-tight compartments," Spykman wrote. "Only statesmen who can do their political and strategic thinking in terms of a round earth and a three-dimensional warfare can save their countries from being outmaneuvered on distant flanks." The United States must defeat the Axis powers before they gained unstoppable momentum—and then undertake a permanent campaign to keep Eurasia fragmented. Washington might even have to revive a defeated Germany to prevent the Soviet Union from taking its place: "A Russian state from the Urals to the North Sea can be no great improvement over a German state from the North Sea to the Urals."[111] Geopolitics was not a task for the morally squeamish or sentimental. The enduring requirements of U.S. security were preponderant power in the Western Hemisphere and a balance of power everywhere else.

*

BUT WHICH PARTS OF EURASIA MATTERED MOST? THIS WAS A LONG-running point of contention. Mackinder had imagined a peerless land power using the Pivot area as a springboard. Mahan saw sea power as real power and focused on the struggle for the Pacific and Indian Oceans. Spykman offered his own twist, in a book, *The Geography of the Peace*, that appeared after his life was cut short by illness, in 1943. The real danger, he suggested, came not from a Pivot covered with permafrost. It came from the Eurasian Rimland, that "vast buffer zone of conflict" where sea power and land power met head-on.[112]

"Siberia is practically empty of people while the Rimland sections in Europe, India, and China are crowded," Spykman wrote. "History tells us that it is in these latter regions rather than in the former that great civilizations and world-powerful states have existed." These areas, roughly equivalent to Mackinder's Inner Crescent, were home to Eurasia's most economically dynamic, densely populated countries. They were adjacent to its vital "inner seas"—bodies such as the Mediterranean, South China Sea, and East China Sea. These waterways and not the open oceans carried most of the world's seaborne trade, Spykman argued; they controlled maritime access to Eurasia itself. It was no coincidence that two world wars had seen Germany and Japan, two Rimland powers, seek mastery of the industry-rich peripheries of Eurasia, while also reaching into the adjoining waters. Nor would Spykman have found it odd that today's U.S.–China rivalry is playing out primarily in the interior waterways—the East China Sea, the South China Sea, the Taiwan Strait—of the most economically important region.

Spykman's most famous contribution was thus a partial inversion of Mackinder. The Mackinder Doctrine was that control of the Heartland led to control of the world. The Spykman Corollary was that "who controls the Rimland rules Eurasia; who rules Eurasia controls the destinies of the world."[113]

This point had implications for military strategy and the long-running land power–sea power debate. Since the Rimland was accessible by both water and land, fights for dominance there would not be straight-up battles between maritime powers and continental powers. They would be clashes of an amphibious nature. Offshore powers needed sea and air control just to reach Eurasia, but they also needed powerful armies on land to beat down their enemies there. "Sea and air power," wrote Spykman, echoing Corbett, were "the instrumentalities to achieve decisions on land."[114]

Spykman wasn't for everyone. His unrelenting focus on power was dark; his apparent amorality could be striking. Spykman's work, wrote Earle in one sour review, was sometimes savaged as "a primer for a new

American Prussianism." Earle didn't go that far, but he was appalled by Spykman's suggestion that the best guarantee of American security was a Eurasia forever mired in division. "At the end of the war the only choice we may face is that between a more stable organization and the end of all organization, between some sort of order and complete anarchy," he wrote. "The balance of power may well land us all in a crematory."[115]

Yet Spykman was right that Washington would eventually use a de-Nazified Germany to contain Moscow. His wartime writings were visionary in other ways as well. Spykman provided the most nuanced case for why, exactly, a consolidated Eurasia could prove so deadly for even a strong and distant America—an argument that resonated with U.S. policymakers through World War II and the Cold War. He illustrated how totalitarian states were practicing a totalizing approach to warfare. When George Kennan, during the early Cold War, warned that such states would employ "varieties of skullduggery . . . as unlimited as human ingenuity itself, and just about as unpleasant," he was learning from Spykman.[116] Even the devil's morality Spykman preached wasn't quite what it appeared.

"All civilized life rests . . . in the last instance on power," he wrote; any society that ignored that reality was destined for oblivion.[117] The fundamental question of strategic studies was how democracies could maintain their way of life in a terrifying age of global war. Spykman's answer was, by playing geopolitics remorselessly—and persistently— enough to salvage a world in which liberal institutions might endure.

*

WHATEVER THEIR DIFFERENCES, MACKINDER, MAHAN, AND SPYKMAN were members of a democratic school of geopolitics. Their goal was to craft strategies that would allow free nations to flourish. Yet there was also an authoritarian school of geopolitics, which put the discipline to very different ends. For these thinkers, Mackinder's vision—a world with a tyrannical Eurasia at its center—was not a nightmare to be averted. It was a dream to be achieved.

Maritime powers, writes historian S. C. M. Paine, have the option of basing their security on economic prosperity, which allows them to pursue positive-sum strategies rooted in trade and cooperation. Continental powers exist in cramped, cutthroat conditions, where the surest route to safety may be vivisecting their neighbors. For similar reasons, democracy was historically more likely to take root in insular (or effectively insular) countries that didn't need large armies than in continental states that did. Oceans promoted economic and political openness; cramped landmasses were laboratories for aggression and tyranny.[118] So it makes sense that the democratic school of geopolitics was an Anglo-American creation, while the authoritarian school arose in continental Europe.

This latter school was, in some respects, the original: the term "geopolitics" was first associated with Swedish intellectual Rudolf Kjellén and German geographer Friedrich Ratzel in the late nineteenth and early twentieth centuries. These thinkers were deeply influenced by social Darwinism; they saw nations as living organisms that must expand or die, and they defined nationhood in racial terms. The resulting form of geopolitics, writes one scholar, was "vindictive and expansionist." It prioritized the coercive quest for *lebensraum*, or "living space," a term Ratzel coined; it blossomed in countries, such as imperial Germany, where expansionist visions and illiberal values went hand in hand.[119] Geopolitics tempered by democracy was stark but rarely evil. Geopolitics with an autocratic bent was poison, pure and simple.

The epitome of this approach was the "Munich school," led by General Karl Haushofer. Haushofer had been an artillery commander in World War I. After Germany's defeat, he participated in right-wing paramilitary organizations while starting a new career as an academic. By the late 1920s, Haushofer's magazine on geopolitics was selling up to 500,000 copies annually; monthly radio broadcasts amplified his message.[120] The general was more prolific than penetrating; he wrote some forty books and 400 articles, many of which were rambling, repetitive, and mutually contradictory. His message, though, was well matched to a country that felt humiliated by the Versailles settlement—and to a Nazi leadership seeking intellectual legitimacy for revolutionary designs.

For Haushofer, geopolitics *was* expansion. Germany, thanks to its "ordeal of ruthless mutilation" after World War I, had been pinned into intolerable confines. Its only response was to "emerge out of the narrowness of her present living space into the freedom of the world." Germany must carve out an autarkic imperium encompassing Europe and Africa. Other oppressed, have-not countries—especially the Soviet Union and Japan—would do likewise across the remainder of Eurasia and the Pacific. Only by consolidating such "pan-regions" could the ravenous revisionist states overmatch their enemies, namely the United Kingdom; only by working together could they prevent Britain from playing divide-and-conquer. "Never again," wrote Haushofer in 1939, should Germany and Russia let "ideological conflicts" set them against each other. The goal of Haushofer's geopolitics was a Eurasia ruled by an autocratic alliance.[121]

There was no chance, and no pretension, this could be accomplished without murder and mayhem. The world, wrote Haushofer, needed "a general political clearing up, a redistribution of power." The young Eastern European countries lying athwart Germany's path were "state fragments" that "have no longer a right to exist."[122] Haushofer would endorse German aggression in the late 1930s and early 1940s, even as it became clear that this involved killing millions in the "living space" Berlin desired.

Haushofer's writings seem like an upside-down version of Mackinder, because that's exactly what they were. Mackinder had worried that a continental hegemon could outpace Great Britain; Haushofer wanted to accomplish exactly that. Haushofer carefully read and liberally borrowed from Mackinder's works; he even explicitly credited the idea of a Nazi–Soviet alliance to Mackinder, who as early as 1904 had worried that such a combination might be the ruin of the world. "Where does world history say that one may not learn from the enemy?" Haushofer crowed in 1939. "Russia and Germany both lost the [last] war because they fought on opposite sides. It took . . . a much longer time than Sir

Halford Mackinder had expected, for the Germans and Russians to find that out."[123] Mackinder, it turned out, was the "academic scribbler" influencing Haushofer, who influenced none other than Adolf Hitler.

*

TO BE SURE, HAUSHOFER'S INFLUENCE ON HITLER HAS SOMETIMES BEEN exaggerated. After World War II, U.S. war crimes prosecutors alleged that the former was the latter's "intellectual godfather," with Hitler "only a symbol and a rabble-rousing mouthpiece."[124] During the war, the OSS described Haushofer as the man who had "transformed the study of Geopolitics . . . into an instrument of German aggression on a world scale."[125] In reality, Haushofer's relationship to the Nazi regime was more ambivalent, in part because he was an old-school German conservative rather than a radical National Socialist, and in part because his wife was half-Jewish. Haushofer had misgivings about Hitler's eventual decision to attack the Soviet Union; his son would ultimately join the anti-Hitler resistance and pay for that decision with his life. Even so, Haushofer was present at the creation of Nazi geopolitics.[126]

The connection was Rudolf Hess, Haushofer's former aide and Hitler's prison-mate after the failed Beer Hall Putsch of 1923. Haushofer introduced Hitler to his theories of geopolitics during visits to Landsberg prison. "It is a pleasure, after a full soldier's life, to function as an old academic," he wrote, "even if the young eagles remain behind bars for a while."[127] As the Nazis gained influence, Haushofer maintained close contact with Hess, who became Deputy Führer; he saw Hitler as the vessel through which his intellectual rantings could become reality. Haushofer's son, Albrecht, described his father's views: "Whether we like it or not, they are now in the saddle; we cannot simply throw them out; thus we have the damned duty and obligation to put our shoulder to the wheel so that they will quickly lose their childhood ailments and learn to accept the right teachings."[128]

Those teachings left a mark. Haushofer may not have written Hitler's infamous treatise, *Mein Kampf*, but he certainly influenced it. Central arguments—the supposed illogic of Germany's interwar borders, the imperative to find living space in the east, the importance of eliminating European rivals—were "pure Haushofer," historian Holger Herwig writes.[129] "Only an adequately large space on this earth assures a nation of freedom of existence," Hitler asserted in one passage. "Hence, the German nation can defend its future only as a world power."[130] Hitler's later advocacy of a continental empire as an answer to British and American power also echoed his mentor's ideas. As the geopolitical theorist Robert Strausz-Hupé observed, "Hitler found in *Geopolitik* a coherent explanation as to how world powers had developed in the past and how Germany could assume her place in the historic procession of great states."[131] Haushofer cheered loudly from the sidelines as annexations, invasions, and atrocities followed. The Führer, he proclaimed, was "a Charlemagne," a practitioner of "geopolitical mastery."[132]

It didn't end any better for the old academic than for the young eagle. By 1940, Haushofer realized that he had encouraged forces he could hardly control. Karl and Albrecht quietly sent out feelers to acquaintances in England about ending the war Hitler had started.[133] Those failed, and the Haushofers lost influence when Hess fled Germany for Scotland on a one-man peace mission in 1941. The father quietly grew more alienated; the son, having conspired to assassinate Hitler in 1944, was executed by the Führer's henchmen as defeat impended. Karl Haushofer then killed himself while under investigation for war crimes by the Allies. "I want to forget and to be forgotten," his suicide note read.[134]

Haushofer wasn't quickly forgotten; his legacy was to tar the very idea of geopolitics and the reputation of its foremost practitioners. Mackinder, alleged one writer in 1947, was "the man behind the man behind Hitler." He added, not as a compliment, that "there is hardly a man or woman or child in these times whose past and future is not in some degree touched by the ideas for which Mackinder stood."[135] This was terribly unfair to Mackinder, who abhorred Hitler and all he represented. But it was true that there were darker elements to geopolitics—the emphasis on power and the permanency of struggle, the willingness to make moral compromises—that aggressive autocrats would not hesitate to weaponize.

That, too, would become a venerable tradition of the Eurasian century. Even today, when tyrants and their acolytes use geopolitical principles to justify radical expansion, they are following in Haushofer's tradition—and they are, perversely, channeling Mackinder as well.

*

CONSIDER ALEKSANDR DUGIN, AN INTELLECTUAL WHO MADE A NAME FOR himself as an ideologue of Russian resurrection. Like Haushofer, he was an intellectual disciple of Mackinder. After the collapse of the Soviet Union, Dugin used Mackinder's theories to explain how a new empire could arise from the ashes of the old.

Russia, Dugin argued, was existentially threatened by an American-led "Atlanticist" coalition seeking to implant its degraded liberal values everywhere. Moscow's best answer was to restore a "great-continental Eurasian future for Russia with our own hands." By reasserting control of the former Soviet republics, by forging alliances with other dissatisfied states, Russia could build a bloc formidable enough to frustrate a superpower. "The heartland of Russia" was the "staging area of a new anti-bourgeois, anti-American revolution," he wrote. "The Eurasian Empire will be constructed on the fundamental principle of the common enemy: the rejection of Atlanticism, strategic control of the USA, and the refusal to allow liberal values to dominate us."[136]

Beginning in the 1990s, Dugin became hugely influential within the Russian military establishment, where his geopolitical tracts were required reading. He seemed also a bit of a madman; after his daughter died a fiery death in 2022, in a car bombing presumably conducted by Ukrainian intelligence assets and meant for Dugin himself, he claimed that "our empire" was one of her first phrases as a child.[137] Few would say the same of Andrew Marshall, the quietly brilliant Pentagon strategist who had a reputation for looking farther into the future than his peers. Yet in 2002, Marshall tapped into the same body of thought that animated Dugin. A rising China could soon test the existing order, he warned. Washington must brace "for a long term competition . . . for influence and position within the Eurasian continent and the Pacific Rimland."[138]

The great geopolitics debate of Mackinder's era cast a long shadow; a century later, both enemies and friends of a liberal world order were still using it as a guide.[139] Mackinder and his contemporaries achieved a certain immortality. Their writings shaped the hopes and fears of statesmen through the generations that followed.

Each of these thinkers contributed something essential. Mahan was a prophet of the Anglo-American alliance, because he understood the role that sea control would play in struggles for dominance on land. Spykman showed that the Rimland could be just as menacing as the Heartland, and that geographic isolation was no guarantee of safety in a globalized age. Haushofer revealed how geopolitics, when divorced from democratic scruples, could be a recipe for iniquity. But above all, it was Mackinder's era. Eurasia became a geopolitical hothouse due to dynamics he identified.

The closing-off of strategic safety valves thrust the great powers against one another. The march of technology shrank Eurasia's epic geography. The emergence of totalitarian states with industrial economies fueled aggression and conquest. All this served to pit a series of potential Eurasian hegemons against liberal superpowers whose freedom and security depended on dashing those designs. The brutal clarity of Mackinder's thesis was that the stars were aligning for persistent, high-stakes struggle over Eurasia and the larger world. The brutal history of the Eurasian century would show how right he was.

THE GREAT BLACK TORNADO

E yre Crowe may have had Mackinder in mind on New Year's Day 1907, when he completed one of the most famous—and longest—state papers of the twentieth century. Crowe was an unusual member of the British diplomatic firmament. Born in Leipzig to a British diplomat and a German mother, he was raised in the very country he spent his professional life trying to thwart. Unlike most of the well-bred men who joined the Foreign Office, Crowe didn't attend public school or elite university in England. He wasn't even fluent in English when he started cramming for his entry exam. Crowe's colleagues deemed his mind as Germanic as his accent; he was a relentlessly logical thinker who didn't suffer fools gladly, even when those fools were the foreign secretaries or prime ministers he served. Crowe, wrote one contemporary, was "a dowdy, meticulous, conscientious agnostic with small faith in anything but his brain and his Britain."[1]

Despite and because of those characteristics, Crowe had an impressive career. He oversaw the blockade of Germany during World War I and helped shape British policy at the postwar peace conference. From 1920 until his death in 1925, he was permanent undersecretary of state for foreign affairs, Britain's highest-ranking career diplomat. "Crowe and the Foreign Office," a colleague recalled, "were one and indivisible."[2] But in 1907, Crowe was still making his way in the diplomatic world, with an unsolicited 16,000-word memorandum on why the country of his birth, tied to Britain by lucrative trade and royal blood, was challenging London's interests at every turn.

The catalyst was a colonial crisis in Morocco in 1905–06, when Germany picked a diplomatic row with France and then sought to bully Paris into submission. "By a direct threat of war, for which France was known to be unprepared," Crowe wrote, "she was to be compelled to capitulate unconditionally."[3] Yet it was the larger arc of German conduct—and capabilities—that really worried him.

Under Kaiser Wilhelm II, Germany was spoiling for trouble. Berlin was seeking colonies and imperial prerogatives from the South Pacific to South America; it was expanding its influence in the Balkans, the Mediterranean, the Middle East. Already boasting Europe's best army, Germany was now building a mighty battle fleet. And German leaders, having assembled their empire with "blood and iron," were once again speaking in bellicose tones. "In the coming century," foreign secretary Bernhard von Bülow had declared in 1899, "the German nation will be either the hammer or the anvil."[4] It was all enough to make Crowe fear that imperial Germany was not a country with reasonable ambitions and insecurities but a revolutionary state bent on upending the world.

Crowe admitted that it was hard to say precisely where Berlin was headed; it was possible the Germans themselves did not know. But Germany's pattern of provocation, and its growing military muscle, made it too dangerous for Britain to just hope for the best.

For centuries, London had sought security by exercising a comparatively benign preeminence at sea and opposing the "political dictatorship" of any state within Europe. Now, the Kaiser's statecraft was weakening both pillars of British policy. It seemed that Germany was aiming "at a general political hegemony and maritime ascendancy, threatening the independence of her neighbors and ultimately the existence of England."

The Kaiser was seeking to dominate Europe and become master of the oceans—which, Crowe asserted, would mean trouble for everyone.

German preeminence on the continent could only be built upon "the wreckage of the liberties of Europe." A "German maritime supremacy" would fatally endanger a British Empire dependent on global sea lanes and test America's Monroe Doctrine. In the end, "the union of the greatest military with the greatest naval Power in one State would compel the world to combine for the riddance of such an incubus."[5] Crowe wasn't far off the mark. His gloomy prophecy came true in World War I, the first great conflict of the Eurasian century, and one that showed just how terrible and totalizing those fights would be.

*

WORLD WAR I WAS SIMPLY EPIC. A STRUGGLE THAT STARTED WITH AN assassin's bullet in Sarajevo spilled across continents and oceans; it showed the staggering potential for mass slaughter in the industrial age. The fighting claimed 20 million lives and four empires; it set off revolutions from Central Europe to China. It incubated ideologies and resentments that would soon cause new horrors; it ended an era of globalization and started an era of global carnage. World War I, Theodore Roosevelt observed, was a "great black tornado" that swept up everything in its path.[6]

For that reason, the war is often considered the epitome of a futile slugfest, one that started for no good reason and ended with no good result. Yet World War I was hardly pointless. It was a struggle over whether an illiberal Germany could set the tone for the twentieth century by winning the dual hegemony Mackinder had feared.

Germany wasn't the country that most worried Mackinder in 1904, but it should have been. After unification in 1871, that empire took off like a rocket. By World War I, Germany had Europe's largest economy. It produced twice as much steel as Britain and had twice as much railroad track; its industries and universities were among the world's finest. Economic dynamism underwrote military dynamism; from 1880 to 1914, defense spending grew more than fivefold. Germany, one Briton

remarked, had once been "a cluster of insignificant states under insignificant princelings."[7] Now it was an industrial and military force in the
center of Europe—with the potential to expand into the Heartland, to
the Atlantic rim, and farther still.

It undoubtedly had the motivation. Bismarck had seen German
unification as an end point and followed rapid-fire aggression with a
generation of shrewd restraint. His less inhibited, and less capable, successors viewed unification as a stepping stone to other triumphs. Expansionists in Berlin lusted after a huge economic and political sphere of
influence—a *Mitteleuropa*—that would make Germany preeminent
on the continent. Via an expansive "world policy," or *Weltpolitik*, Germany sought global markets and resources; it seized imperial holdings in
China and eyed others in the Pacific, Africa, and Latin America. "Hundreds of thousands of Chinamen," thundered Kaiser Wilhelm II, "will
tremble when they feel the fist of the German Empire heavy on their
necks."[8] The time had come, announced Bülow in 1897, for Germany to
claim its "place in the sun."[9]

These designs flowed from a worldview that combined soaring ambitions and dark premonitions of disaster. Social Darwinism and extreme
nationalism suffused the German mentality. Intellectuals and strategists
worried that their late-rising country would be dwarfed by Europe's massive empires. In a vicious, anarchic world, where power and economic
security rested on industrial and agricultural prowess, they believed that
a country that could not expand—that could not grab land, resources,
and markets—would surely succumb. Contra Bismarck, who counseled
that Germany's central location on a crowded continent compelled caution, his successors believed that bold moves were necessary to escape
the vise. "Weltpolitik must . . . be pursued," diplomat Kurt Riezler wrote
before World War I. "German policy must escape the *circulus vitiosus*
[vicious circle]."[10] Two prominent expansionists had put it starkly: "If
Germany does not rule the world . . . it will disappear from the map."[11]

Visions of aggrandizement went hand in hand with cutting-edge
capabilities. Long a formidable land power, Germany built a massive,

highly trained army that could thrash any single European competitor. Never before a sea power, Germany invested in a blue-water navy, whose projected sixty battleships would intimidate Britain into passivity as Berlin pursued gains in Europe and farther afield. England's maritime mastery, the Kaiser gloated, was "going onto the dust-heap!"[12] Germany's behavior was consistent with the growing ambition of a surging power—and with the personality of its ruler and political system, too.

*

"I'M ABSOLUTELY CERTAIN NOW, WE'RE ALL IN FOR IT," SAID THEODORE Roosevelt after meeting Kaiser Wilhelm II, one of history's more tragically curious figures.[13] Wilhelm II was a cousin of the kings of Russia and England, two countries he fought in World War I. Disabled from birth, he compensated with absurd martial pageantry—"We are currently . . . occupied with the 37th change of uniforms since the accession to the throne!" one officer complained—and a geopolitical aggressiveness compounded by violent mood swings.[14] His specialty was bombastic pronouncements and impulsive policies that alarmed other powers, when quiet prudence would have better served his state. "What can I do to make myself popular [in England]?" the Kaiser once asked British imperialist Cecil Rhodes. "Suppose you just try doing nothing," Rhodes replied.[15]

Wilhelm's flaws were compounded by a system in which the emperor reigned but chaos ruled. Germany's hybrid political structure featured a democratically elected Reichstag, but gave the Kaiser and his offensive-minded military aides enormous authority in foreign affairs. The armed forces were revered above all other elements of society; the German General Staff was known as one of Europe's "five perfect institutions," the others being the Roman curia, the British parliament, the Russian ballet, and the French Opera.[16] Yet there was no cabinet to coordinate policy or adjudicate between factions—army and navy; industrialists and financiers—whose competing agendas drove expansion in multiple directions. Germany's practice, lamented Chancellor Theobald von Bethmann-Hollweg, was to "challenge everybody, get in everyone's way and actually, in the course of all this, weaken nobody."[17] And as agitation from trade unions, socialists, and other forces mounted, conservatives saw conflict abroad—ideally a short, victorious clash—as a way of reasserting control at home.[18]

Germany's raucous rise produced a revolution in European diplomacy. Berlin's push for influence in the Balkans and the Near East threatened Russia; its army existentially challenged France; its fleet menaced Britain's global empire and home islands. Germany's rivals thus settled disputes among themselves; they gradually coalesced into interlinking bilateral partnerships and finally, in 1907, a loose "Triple Entente." "The final struggle between the Slav and Germanic races finds the Anglo-Saxons on the side of the Slavs!" the Kaiser fumed.[19] He had only himself to blame. When Germany sought to break this ring, by challenging France and Russia in a series of crises between 1905 and 1912, it simply encouraged its foes to stand firm—and stand together—in the future.[20] As Bismarck had warned, a centrally located revisionist was making enemies all around.

Indeed, while historians have argued that systemic factors—Europe's interlocking alliances, its arms races and hair-trigger war plans—caused World War I, many of those factors traced back to the root problem of a powerful, pushy Germany. Berlin's behavior had split the continent into hostile blocs—the Triple Entente on one side; Germany, a declining, internally riven Austria-Hungary, and an unreliable Italy on the other—and made every crisis a high-stakes affair. Germany's military buildup had intensified arms races on land and at sea.[21] And while nearly all the great powers had offense-oriented war plans, Germany's Schlieffen Plan was extreme: it envisioned a lightning strike through neutral Belgium to defeat France in six weeks, followed by a mad dash to meet Russian armies in the east.

That plan was meant to address the two-front challenge Germany's position and policies had precipitated. But it promised to short-circuit diplomacy in a crisis by giving Berlin an overriding incentive to go fast and first. By envisioning the conquest of Belgium and northeastern France—the critical real estate from which any invasion of Britain would be launched—the Schlieffen Plan threatened to bring yet another enemy into any European war. Not least, its emphasis on exquisite timing made leaders in Berlin acutely sensitive to shifts in the military balance.[22]

It was, therefore, a problem that by 1914 Germany was on the verge of losing the European arms race. Britain was building two new battleships for every one constructed by Germany. France and Russia were dramatically expanding their armies; St. Petersburg was using 2.5 billion French francs to add thousands of miles of railroad tracks and slash its mobilization time. Germany faced no threat of unprovoked invasion: "If we do not conjure up a war into being, no one else certainly will do so," one of its top diplomats had admitted.[23] Before long, however, Berlin would be outgunned by its enemies; world power and *Mitteleuropa* would slip away.

So, a now-or-never mindset took hold. Talk of *Weltkrieg*, or world war, became common; leaders steeped in an expand-or-die mentality were tempted by high-risk gambits. Berlin must "defeat the enemy while we still stand a chance of victory," said Helmuth von Moltke in 1914, even at risk of "provoking a war in the near future."[24] It was the worst possible mindset with which to enter the European crisis that erupted that year.

*

"SOPHERL, SOPHERL, DON'T DIE ON ME. LIVE FOR OUR CHILDREN," A HEMorrhaging Archduke Franz Ferdinand implored his mortally wounded wife.[25] The pair had been struck by the bullets of a Serbian terrorist, Gavrilo Princip, during their visit to Sarajevo on June 28; they were in his gunsights thanks to a chauffeur who made history's most fateful wrong turn. Before that, nothing had gone right for Princip's band of radicals, who missed several chances to bag their prey. Afterward, nothing would be the same.

Germany didn't cause the July crisis; it was provoked by the murder of Franz Ferdinand, the crown prince of an unstable empire in an unstable region. In fact, the Balkans were the ambit of two declining multinational empires, the Austro-Hungarian Empire and the Ottoman Empire, as well as a rising state, Serbia, that was harnessing south Slavic nationalism to challenge them.[26] The region was Europe's gateway to the Middle East, the Eastern Mediterranean, and the Suez Canal, which meant that Balkan quarrels easily became international crises. Franz Ferdinand's killing tossed a match into this flammable material. And as the tension built in July 1914, it took multiple decisions, in multiple capitals, to turn that crisis into World War I.

Austria-Hungary sought to smash Serbia and shore up its deteriorating position. "The monarchy had been seized by the throat," said Austria's top general, and couldn't let itself "be strangled."[27] Paris and St. Petersburg did not want war, but neither would they stand aside as Austria-Hungary, backed by Germany, crushed a Russian client state and humiliated Russia. Britain waffled when firmness was needed. Yet in sorting out why a Balkan spat went global, two points are essential.

First, events in that region were ensnared in the tangle of tensions associated with Germany. The Kaiser and his aides worried that not backing Austria-Hungary against Serbia would seal the fate of that empire, leaving Germany alone against its enemies. Leaders in Paris and especially St. Petersburg feared that an Austro-Hungarian victory over Serbia would clear the way for Germany, the senior partner in that alliance, to spread its tentacles throughout the Balkans and the decrepit Ottoman Empire—perhaps even controlling the Dardanelles and the Bosporus, those narrow, vital waterways that connected the Black Sea to the Aegean and the Russian economy to the world. Wilhelm, characteristically, had recently stoked that anxiety, by dispatching a German officer to modernize the Ottoman army and declaring that "German flags will soon fly over the fortifications of the Bosporus." "Now you stick a Prussian garrison under our noses!" Russia's foreign minister had complained.[28]

Second, in July 1914 Berlin did almost nothing but provoke and instigate. The government secretly prodded Austria-Hungary to attack Serbia, pledging to back the Dual Monarchy even if that meant fighting

Russia and France. Germany then batted away proposals for a peaceful settlement, despite warnings from its ambassador in London that this was "the only way to avoid a world war."[29] As the crisis intensified, the military prepared to initiate the Schlieffen Plan, even though violating Belgian neutrality—and destroying French power—risked causing British intervention. German leaders differed on whether they actually expected war or simply wanted to shatter the Entente through coercive diplomacy; Wilhelm hoped his royal cousins, George V and Nicholas II, would stand aside rather than fight "on the side of regicides."[30] But his government took step after step that risked an all-out conflagration. "Yes, My God . . . it was a preventive war," Bethmann-Hollweg acknowledged, motivated by the view that "today war is still possible without defeat, but not in two years!"[31]

Britain's failure was one of deterrence, not de-escalation. Wilhelmine Germany was rash, but not suicidal. While many in Berlin were willing to risk a continental war against France and Russia, the one thing that might have sobered them was a prompt, definitive statement that London would also fight—and do so with a large, capable army that could spoil the Schlieffen Plan. "There is still the chance that she can be made to hesitate," Crowe wrote, "if she can be induced to apprehend that the war will find England by the side of France and Russia."[32] Britain's foreign secretary, Lord Grey, understood the stakes: "If Germany wins . . . she will dominate the whole of Western Europe."[33] Yet no such British policy was pursued, because no such policy was possible.

In 1914, Britain was only halfway committed to the continent. The British Expeditionary Force numbered just six divisions; the commitment to France was a "moral bond," as Crowe put it, nothing etched in stone.[34] The British Cabinet was so divided that Grey couldn't even publicly support Paris until events, and German military preparations, had accumulated a fatal momentum. The Entente's basic problem, and a recurring dilemma of twentieth-century geopolitics, was that the full multilateral unity that might have deterred war materialized only *after* it was underway. Indeed, after a fit of confusion at the end of July, the

Kaiser allowed his military to push ahead, waiting just long enough to pin the blame on Russia for mobilizing first. "The government has succeeded very well in making us appear as the attacked," one official wrote.[35] Within a week, Europe was at war.

There was nothing modest about Germany's aims. In September 1914, the Foreign Ministry drafted a program to ensure "security for the German Reich in the west and east for all imaginable time." France was to be "so weakened as to make her revival as a great power impossible"; Russia was to be "thrust back as far as possible." Germany would annex Luxembourg and parts of France, make Belgium and Holland client states, and create an unbroken economic empire from Eastern Europe to the Low Countries.[36] "The aim of this war," Bethmann-Hollweg stated, was "the establishment of German hegemony in Europe."[37] More broadly, the program was animated by faith that the future belonged to Berlin. "The spiritual progress of mankind is only possible through Germany," said Moltke. "It is the only nation that can . . . take charge of leading mankind toward a higher destiny."[38] World War I was a quest for Germany mastery in geopolitical and ideological terms alike.

*

IN LATE 1914, THE EXPLORER ERNEST SHACKLETON DEPARTED FOR A HARrowing expedition across Antarctica. A year and a half later, he returned to civilization, on South Georgia Island in the South Atlantic, and asked the whalers there who had won the war. The answer shocked him: a conflict that had begun with visions of rapid victory was grinding mercilessly on.[39]

Like Shackleton, most European leaders expected a short war—the first offensives, if prosecuted aggressively, would be decisive. "You will be home before the leaves have fallen from the trees," Wilhelm told his departing soldiers.[40] It briefly looked like he was right. German forces beat Belgium and knifed into northeastern France. "We are going through 1870 again," Britain's war secretary, Lord Kitchener, remarked.[41] London contemplated withdrawing its forces from France almost as soon as they had arrived. The French government laid plans to evacuate Paris as German armies descended.

Yet the Schlieffen Plan fell short. Fierce Belgian resistance didn't save that country but did spoil Moltke's timing. An unexpectedly swift Russian offensive forced him to prematurely shift 100,000 troops eastward. The undersized BEF overperformed on the French left flank. And at the last minute, French reserves counterattacked in a gap between exhausted, overextended German armies outside Paris. This "miracle on the Marne" was a triumph of improvisation: without enough trains to shuttle French soldiers to the front, General Joseph Gallieni threw the city's taxis into the breach. During late 1914, the two sides then sought to outflank each other in battles from the English Channel nearly to the Swiss border, before settling into a war of entrenchment. Having lost his "battle without a tomorrow," Moltke also lost his nerve and his job.[42]

If Germany's short-war strategy failed, so did the Entente's. While some observers had argued before 1914 that the interdependence of nations made conflict futile, Britain saw interdependence as a war-winning weapon. Prior to the conflict, London had secretly planned to use its leverage in global trade and finance—its control of banks, insurers, shipping, and communications cables—to detach Germany from the world and bring its economy down. Alas, interdependence was a two-edged sword; the war nearly precipitated a *global* economic meltdown, by shutting stock markets and causing a massive liquidity crunch. So London downshifted, settling for a more traditional—but less decisive—maritime blockade, meant, as Britain's top naval officer remarked, to slowly "starve and cripple" the enemy.[43]

By late 1914, the war had taken a pattern Mackinder surely recognized: a land-based, aspiring hegemon confronted an amphibious coalition. On one side were the Central Powers: Germany, Austria-Hungary, the Ottoman Empire. Germany was undisputed master of this coalition, as the other members had militaries better suited to imperial policing than interstate conflict. Only Germany, moreover, had a real blue-water navy. Its High Seas Fleet was strong enough to worry the Royal Navy but not to defeat it, so Berlin's surface ships mostly stayed close to home, the major exception being a bloody draw in the North Sea in 1916. What the aptly named Central Powers did have was control of an imposing and, from late 1915 onward, unbroken swath of land from Belgium to the Middle East.[44] So this coalition exerted pressure outward, against Serbia in the Balkans, against Russia in the Heartland, against London in the Middle East, and against France and Britain on Europe's Atlantic periphery.

Opposing them were the Allies—the Entente countries plus, later, Italy and others—that ringed the Central Powers and used both land power and sea power to pen them in. On land, French and Russian armies made heartbreaking sacrifices to keep tactically superior German forces at bay. At sea, the British fleet anchored the blockade, while securing lines of communication that connected the Allies to their empires, one another, and the world. Sea power also allowed the Allies to probe the flanks of the Central Powers, through operations in the Dardanelles, the Balkans, and the Middle East, in hopes of knocking out Germany's partners or luring new friends into the fight. Faced with impressive German power at the center, the Allies used global mobility to seek advantage at the periphery.

Yet neither side could break through, because neither could make its greatest asset fully count. The British Navy could not win the war on the Western front. The Kaiser's armies were peerless, but two of Germany's enemies were at least partially beyond their reach—Russia because of its tremendous spaces, Britain because of its channel and its navy. England was "the soul of the entire opposition," Admiral Henning von Holtzendorff wrote, and "she . . . cannot be conquered on land."[45] The ugly reality, U.S. ambassador to England Walter Page had lamented, was that "no end is in sight."[46] Every war is a revelation, and World War I revealed how expansive and destructive modern conflict had become.

*

FOR ONE THING, THE FRUITS OF CREATION HAD BECOME THE FOUNTS OF destruction—the technological progress that had propelled civilization upward now brought humanity spiraling down. The emergence of twentieth-century firepower, manifested in machine guns, mobile heavy artillery, and flamethrowers, multiplied the killing potential of individual soldiers and units. Modern defenses, such as trenches protected by concrete, barbed wire, and a torrent of bullets and shells, made offense more difficult. Combined with the persistence of nineteenth-century tactics, namely head-on advances by large, unprotected formations of troops, these innovations produced jaw-dropping losses. "There could never before in war have been a more perfect target than this solid wall of khaki men," one German soldier wrote.[47]

Austria-Hungary and France both suffered over one million dead, wounded, and missing by the end of 1914.[48] Single battles yielded casualty lists that eclipsed those of major wars in earlier eras—900,000 at Verdun, more than one million at the Somme, and 1.4 million in Russia's summer offensive, all in 1916.[49] Submarines, airplanes, tanks, and poison gas provided new means of slaughter, which governments enlisted their scientific and industrial communities to mass-produce. "This is not war," one Indian soldier wrote, "it is the ending of the world."[50]

How long could it go on? Quite a long time, due to a second factor: modern states capable of extraordinary destruction were also capable of extraordinary endurance.

Governments used compulsion and nationalism to generate huge pools of money, manpower, and materiel. France mobilized 7.9 million soldiers during the war; the British Empire, 8.4 million; Germany, 13.2 million; Russia, 15.8 million.[51] Napoleon had marshaled 7 percent of the French population for military service; Germany and France hit 20 percent in World War I.[52] Industry kicked into gear for a long war. The British fired 170,385,295 rounds of artillery on the Western front; by 1918, France was producing 200,000 shells *per day*.[53] The warring governments created new ministries to oversee mobilization, ration consumer goods, and monitor dissent; they used taxation and borrowing to spend prodigiously. The war persisted because states were able to push societies to their very limit.

Over the long term, this dynamic transformed the belligerents' political systems. Democracies that demanded more of their citizens had to repay them with expanded rights and benefits. Autocracies collapsed because of the privations inflicted upon their populations. Even before that, contemporary observers marveled at the sacrifices made to avoid defeat. "Generations will have to come and go" before Britain could recover, gasped former foreign secretary Lord Lansdowne.[54]

Lansdowne was one of many statesmen who tried to stop the bleeding by proposing, at one point or another, a compromise peace. But the events of 1914 had left peacemaking nearly impossible. Germany held most of Belgium and France's richest industrial areas, including 40 percent of its coal and nearly all its iron ore.[55] By late 1915, Germany also controlled much of Poland and the Baltic. The Allies couldn't accept a settlement on that basis without locking in Berlin's continental dominance; as British officials wrote, "Germany would have in her hands all, or nearly all, that she seeks from the war."[56] Germany could not relinquish those gains without admitting it had all been for naught. So both sides opted to escalate, by committing more resources and enlisting more allies, while enlarging war aims to make the suffering worthwhile.

Thus a third dynamic: conflict that was all-encompassing societally became all-encompassing spatially. World War I was the first war fought in three dimensions and three domains: on land, at sea, and in the air. Airplanes and zeppelins bombed cities far behind the lines; submarines created new options for contesting control of the seas. Wireless communications and spotter airplanes gradually enhanced command and control over long distances; railways rapidly moved large armies from place to place.[57] Modern technology was extending the battlefield, even as it shrank the scope for maneuver upon it. This was one reason the conflict so rapidly went global.

A fracas in the Balkans immediately ensnared most of Europe's powers, with more soon to follow. This clash between empires inevitably spilled into other regions. Japan and Australia seized German possessions in China and the Pacific; the Royal Navy chased German ships in the Indian Ocean and the South Atlantic; the blockade wrenched trade and investment patterns everywhere. German U-boats prowled the Atlantic and the Mediterranean; German spies tried to spark anti-British uprisings in Egypt and India. "If we are to be bled to death, England shall at least lose India," Wilhelm decreed.[58] Warfare engulfed chunks of Africa; the entry of the Ottoman Empire ignited the Middle East. And as the war dragged on, the fighters took sustenance from their empires. Roughly 1.68 million Indians served the British war effort, from Singapore to Gallipoli; France recruited 500,000 colonial troops. Much of the world became a sprawling battlespace; in a modern, interconnected environment, there was nowhere to hide.[59]

Soon America was the only major power not at war, although it was playing a crucial role economically. And as the fighting spread, it took on a life of its own; many of the regional conflicts World War I triggered would rage on after the fighting in Europe ended. "One year and three days after the Armistice," commented the chief of Britain's Imperial General Staff, Henry Wilson, in 1919, "we have between 20 and 30 wars raging in different parts of the world."[60] World War I was remaking the globe economically, politically, and—a fourth dynamic— ideologically, as well.

World War I is typically seen as an amoral land-grab by self-interested empires, and there is some truth in this. Britain and France enlarged their imperial holdings after the war; during the contest, they preemptively divvied up their enemies' territories to lure allies in and keep the Russians from falling out.

Even so, many Western observers believed that the war was so fateful because it pitted democracy and the rule of law against tyranny and an ethos of atrocity. The invasion of neutral Belgium, which involved the rape and murder of innocent civilians, reinforced the impression that the Germans were the "throned Philistines of Europe," a people so dangerous because they combined great power with autocratic brutality.[61] Other crimes of the Central Powers—submarine warfare that drowned women and children, the use of slave labor from occupied nations, the killing of over one million Armenians by the Ottomans—encouraged a view that civilization was at stake. "Decades before Hitler was even heard of," George Orwell later wrote, "the word 'Prussian' had much the same significance in England as 'Nazi' has today."[62] No lasting peace with "Prussian militarism" was possible, French leaders agreed.[63]

True, the Allies committed atrocities. Their blockade killed as many as 400,000 Germans and Austro-Hungarians, and perhaps 500,000 in the Ottoman Empire.[64] They had the embarrassment of a repressive, dynastic ally, Russia. But if those factors muddled the morality of the conflict, they didn't make the Allies insincere in seeing the war as a struggle to prevent a fierce autocracy from running amok. "This World War has become a conflict between two systems of philosophy," one German officer wrote. "Our opponents honestly believe . . . that they are fighting for the right which has been trodden underfoot by might. They are absolutely convinced . . . that for this reason Germany's defeat is absolutely an essential condition to the healthy and happy development of the entire world."[65]

Many Germans agreed that the conflict was deeply ideological. They believed, writes historian Wolfgang Mommsen, that their country's political model was "immeasurably superior to that of the western democracies." German intellectuals derided the "all-powerful tyranny of individualism" and celebrated citizens who obeyed the "central will of government." They argued that "the idea of German organization, the people's cooperative of national socialism," entitled the country to a starring role in the world.[66] And if war created a sense of grim necessity everywhere, German leaders argued unapologetically that the quest for greatness justified atrocity. "We are fighting for our lives," Moltke wrote of the rape of Belgium, "and all who get in the way must take the consequences."[67] World War I was a contest of ideas as well as a contest of arms.

* * *

*

IT IS TEMPTING TO SEE THE OUTCOME AS A FOREGONE CONCLUSION: How could Germany ever have overcome a coalition that had it surrounded and outgunned? By 1918, after the United States intervened, the Allies accounted for 51.7 percent of world manufacturing, versus 19.2 percent for the Central Powers; they made twice as much steel; they massively outproduced the Germans in tanks and trucks.[68] Germany's key ally, Austria-Hungary, was a military burden and a political basket case; the Ottoman Empire wasn't much better. Before the war, Germany had found itself encircled by mighty empires committed to its containment; during the war, it faced an even grander coalition committed to its defeat. "German ambition backed by German diplomacy—which is the worst diplomacy in the world—has welded all these nations into one coalition determined to put down this world tyranny," said British prime minister David Lloyd George.[69] From this perspective, Germany's dash for greatness was a suicide run.

Yet things hardly seemed inevitable at the time. Moltke's armies were one battle away from Paris in 1914. At several points, Germany had victory nearly within reach. In 1917, Germany's submarine offensive was threatening to put Britain out of the war before America could get into it. "Our present policy," warned Britain's First Sea Lord, Admiral John Jellicoe, "is heading straight for disaster."[70] In 1918, Germany's final offensives again put Paris and the vital Channel ports in jeopardy. The Allies, said French marshal Ferdinand Foch, risked being "forced back to the Loire."[71]

For most of the war, it was *Allied* strategy that looked hopeless. In the east, well-trained German armies mauled brave but poorly supplied Russian forces. "The Germans expend metal," said one Russian general, "we expend life." By late 1915, Russia had suffered 4 million casualties, and only huge reserves of territory and manpower (plus the opportunity to beat up on an even more hapless Austria-Hungary) were keeping it in the fight.[72] In the West, British and French commanders slaughtered their own forces in fruitless offensives. "Out of approximately 19,500 square miles of France and Belgium in German hands," First Lord of the Admiralty Winston Churchill wrote in 1915, "we have recovered about 8."[73]

The peripheral strategy aimed to break the deadlock by defeating Germany's weaker allies. But efforts to open new fronts in the Balkans and Dardanelles were costly debacles; operations in the Middle East couldn't decisively affect the war. Making matters worse, most of the additional powers the Allies pulled into the war were liabilities. A militarily pathetic Italy consumed British and French resources, while Romania—which intervened to great fanfare in 1916—was promptly ravaged by German troops and made an economic vassal of the German state. Even the British blockade hardly slowed the Kaiser's war machine at first. As long as Germany had the edge on land, despaired Lloyd George, "economic exhaustion alone will not bring us a triumphant peace."[74]

In fact, Germany decisively won the war in the east in early 1918, by defeating a prostrate, post-revolutionary Russia and imposing a landmass-transforming peace. The Treaty of Brest-Litovsk liberated Russia of one-third of its population, plus "32 percent of its agricultural land, 73 percent of its iron ore, and 89 percent of its coal."[75] Germany now ruled lands from the Baltic nearly to the Caucasus. It had built a European empire, replete with energy, metals, foodstuffs, and other resources; it was positioned to push deeper into a chaotic Russia and pressure British positions from Iran to India. "One should not have any illusions," French officials reported. "A Germany obtaining economic domination over the Balkans, Russia, and all of Western Asia has won the war and become master of the Old World."[76] The door to an epochal strategic transformation had, albeit temporarily, opened wide.

*

HOW DID GERMANY COME SO CLOSE TO VICTORY? ONE FACTOR WAS PURE military prowess. Thanks to superior logistics, training, and organization, Germany's troops were the most lethally efficient in the business. Each death they inflicted cost Berlin and its allies $11,344.77, while the Allies paid thrice that.[77] The General Staff produced tactically gifted, if ideologically fanatical, commanders such as General Erich Ludendorff. The Germans didn't fight flawlessly, by any means; their failed offensive at Verdun, a strategically meaningless French fortress town, in 1916 incurred a blood price the outnumbered Germans could hardly afford. Even so, Berlin came closest to cracking the code of World War I.

In the west, Germany—having seized positions in France early on—eventually mastered defense-in-depth. After Verdun, German forces built the 300-mile Siegfried Line, featuring multiple rows of trenches, concrete blockhouses and barbed wire, all the firepower needed to mow down Allied attackers, and large masses of defenders held in reserve. They then conducted a tactical withdrawal to that line, utterly despoiling the territory they evacuated. Recalled one German lieutenant, "Every village was reduced to rubble, every tree felled, every street mined, every well poisoned, every creek dammed up, every cellar blown up or studded with hidden bombs, all metals and supplies taken back to our lines, every rail tie unscrewed, all telephone wire rolled up, all combustible material burned; in short, we transformed the land into which the enemy would advance into a wasteland."[78]

The Germans also learned, quicker than their adversaries, how to take the offensive in a defense-dominant war. They used short but fierce artillery bombardments that stunned the enemy without totally surrendering surprise, sent small units of shock troops to penetrate the front lines, and then rapidly reinforced any advances; they synchronized artillery, air power, and infantry in ways that presaged World War II. These tactics, previewed by both sides in 1916–17, would allow Germany to break the western stalemate in 1918. "Basically, this war comes down simply to killing one another," said Ludendorff, and Germany did it better than anyone else.[79]

Second, being surrounded wasn't all bad, because Germany made a virtue of its central position. A dense, sophisticated railway system allowed Germany to realize Mackinder's vision of land power made mobile. At the Battle of Tannenberg in September 1914, the Germans blunted, enveloped, and destroyed advancing Russian armies by using railway transport to move and concentrate their troops. Throughout the war, Berlin shifted forces nimbly between theaters, once moving a full army from front to front within a week.[80] There was power in contiguity, as well. Germany repeatedly reinforced and rescued its allies on fronts from Galicia to the Piave River; the resources of a continent-sized bloc undermined the efficacy of the British blockade. "The economic unit from Arras to Mesopotamia cannot be crushed," boasted Bethmann-Hollweg.[81]

Third, World War I showed how much power a ruthless, radical-ized state could generate. Germany was initially little more prepared for a long war than the Allies; all tax receipts for 1913 would have funded only two months of fighting in 1915.[82] But Germany harnessed its resources more quickly and completely than its rivals.

From 1915 to 1916, German production of heavy artillery increased tenfold. An Office of Resources and Materials for War set up cartels to buy manganese, iron ore, and other materials. German industry cre-ated synthetic goods and "ersatz" food to deal with shortages caused by the blockade.[83] Simple domination and theft helped, too. Germany stripped coal, food, and labor from occupied territories, sometimes leav-ing the inhabitants to starve. It rationalized the Central Powers' war effort by taking control of Austria-Hungary's army and then much of its economy: railways, roads, factories, and more.[84] After 1916, when Ludendorff and his fellow general Paul von Hindenburg marginalized the civilians and created a de facto military dictatorship, they waged total war in search of total victory.

The regime worked the population to the bone in a bid to build ever more weapons. It adjusted to the blockade by feeding laborers and soldiers ahead of the sick and elderly. It rallied the population with hysterical warnings about the "world-destroying activities" of Jews and communists, invocations of German racial superiority, and promises of victory and plunder.[85] "War is the highest expression of the racial will of life," declared Ludendorff; Germany must throw everything into its struggle for greatness and survival.[86] This total-war strategy would ulti-mately wreck the economy and tip the country into revolution, but not before Germany pushed the Allies to the brink.

Finally, Germany offset spatial dilemmas through creative strategy.

Land warfare alone couldn't defeat Russia, but land warfare plus political warfare could. The first Russian revolution of 1917 occurred when the war overburdened a still rickety railway system, causing terrible food shortages and bringing to a boil simmering resentment at incompetent elites. After a relatively liberal Provisional Government tried, catastrophically, to keep fighting, the country suffered a second, totalitarian revolution under Vladimir Lenin.

That revolution had powerful supporters. German agents had backed the Provisional Government's most radical enemies, shipped Lenin back into the country from exile in Switzerland, and funded his political agitation. "The Bolshevik movement could never have attained the scale of the influence which it has today without our continual support," German leaders wrote.[87] It was a devil's bargain, given that Lenin hated capitalists everywhere. But Lenin had come to power calling for "land, bread, and peace"; he was willing, under Germany's suffocating military pressure, to sign away Ukraine, Belarus, Poland, the Baltic provinces, and other parts of the tsarist state at Brest-Litovsk. For Germany, then, supporting Lenin was a gamble worth taking. "If the Bolsheviks could destroy Russia as a great power," British intelligence wrote, "surely Germany could destroy the Bolsheviks in her own time."[88]

Germany almost dispatched another distant enemy, Britain, through submarine warfare. If Britain's empire and money gave it access to the world's resources, its island geography rendered it desperately vulnerable to blockade. When the war began, "four out of every five slices of bread consumed in the British Isles were made with imported flour."[89] The country that ruled the waves, alas, had no answer to aggression from below them.

Neither Britain nor Germany had paid much systematic attention to submarine warfare before the war. Germany possessed only twenty-one submarines, twelve of which were obsolete, in August 1914.[90] Yet high-stakes wars are hothouses of innovation.

With the German surface fleet mostly contained in port, a few submarine commanders took to sea to salvage some glory. On September 22, 1914, a single submarine—U-9, under Kapitänleutnant Otto Weddigen—spotted and sank the British cruiser HMS *Aboukir* in the North Sea. When two other cruisers stopped to rescue the survivors, U-9 sank them, too. The British lost 1,459 sailors; the Germans gained a new path to victory.

Germany's adoption of unrestricted submarine warfare in February 1915 changed the rules of combat at sea. To maximize surprise and self-protection, U-boats attacked without warning, sinking ships and drowning their passengers. The tactic also struck at the heart of Allied strategy. "There never was before in the history of the world such a situation as now obtains," the British Shipping Ministry wrote, "in which the destiny of all nations depends upon the maintenance of our communications with America and with our Allies."[91] The Admiralty struggled to cope with this challenge. During one humiliating week in September 1916, three U-boats operating in the English Channel evaded forty-nine destroyers, forty-eight torpedo boats, and 468 auxiliary ships to sink thirty Allied vessels.[92] The U-boat was such a revolutionary weapon because it threatened to upend the balance between a coalition dominant on land and one that relied on mastery at sea.

There was nothing inevitable about the outcome of World War I. That conflict was a case study in how achingly close an autocratic challenger could come to running the table and imposing its will on the world. In the end, the anti-German forces won, but only narrowly—and only by summoning unprecedented cooperation between democracies near and far.

*

COOPERATION OFTEN EMERGES FROM THE SHADOW OF CATASTROPHE, and in March 1918, catastrophe was stalking the Allies. Fresh off victory over Russia, Germany transferred half a million troops to France. In a win-the-war offensive, Ludendorff threw sixty-seven divisions, supported by over 1,000 aircraft and 2 million poison gas shells, at the Allies.[93] Exploiting penetrate-and-surge tactics refined on the eastern and Italian fronts,

Ludendorff cut a gash between the French and the British, threatening to overwhelm Paris and drive the BEF against the Channel. The Allies were reeling; the front was in disarray. Yet a moment of desperation produced a breakthrough in democratic unity.

At an emergency conference on March 26, British and French leaders—prime ministers David Lloyd George and Georges Clemenceau, generals Douglas Haig and Ferdinand Foch—agreed that their armies would stand shoulder to shoulder, whatever the cost. "With our backs to the wall, and believing in the justice of our cause, each one must fight on till the end," Haig announced. More critically, Clemenceau and Lloyd George named Foch supreme commander of Allied armies, providing a unity of direction that had previously been lacking. "Foch is now generalissimo and we must therefore obey his orders," one British general wrote.[94] National sovereignty came second to military survival.

Mackinder had predicted it would take a global village; "combinations of power" would thwart would-be hegemons.[95] Mahan had called for naval coalitions to keep aggressors in chains. Such countervailing alliances were nothing new. Power, when wielded irresponsibly, courts resistance. But World War I was different. A world war produced a worldwide anti-hegemonic alliance.

Staving off defeat had always required collective effort. The BEF had given its crucial support to France in 1914, while Russia's early offensive had diverted just enough German energy to help foil the Schlieffen Plan. Russia, Kitchener commented, had "saved us" by preventing a German "knock-out blow."[96] Japan, which fought mostly to expand its empire in Asia, helped sweep German ships from the Pacific. In September, the three key Allies—Britain, France, and Russia—agreed not to conclude a separate peace, in recognition that if they were divided, they would likely be conquered. Yet it took time and travail for the Allies to learn to fight as a team.

There was nothing like unified command in the west; into 1916, Haig explicitly refused instructions from his French counterpart, Joseph Joffre.[97] More broadly, wrote one British official, there was "no real cooperation between the Allies Powers on the various fronts."[98] This asymmetry of coordination offset the asymmetry of power Berlin faced. "The Entente Powers have more men, more guns, greater resources, and the whole world to draw upon," Lloyd George remarked, but could not win because "the German Emperor has secured complete control over the resources of all the Central Powers."[99]

The Allies struggled to coordinate for a fundamental reason: different geographies produced different strategic preferences. The French, with their most productive territory occupied by Germany, had to have decisive action in the west. "Every fighting man" who was not used there was simply "wasted," French General Headquarters believed.[100] The British, with their tradition of sea power and subsidies to allies, had dispatched the BEF to France but initially hoped to win without sending vast armies to the slaughter. British leaders preferred to menace the enemy's flanks and grind down its economy; they argued that operations in the Dardanelles were necessary to unlock Russian grain shipments and keep that country fighting.[101]

The result was a compromise that failed everywhere. Allied offensives in France in 1915 were thrown back with heavy losses. The Dardanelles campaign that year also stumbled, due to an inability to synchronize operations on land and at sea. British commanders failed to quickly bolster a naval task force that sought to force the straits by landing troops; they were then slow to reinforce the soldiers who eventually went ashore. The Allies bogged down and ultimately lost 250,000 men, many of whom died miserable deaths of disease. "There was not much sudden death," recalled one soldier, "but there was slow death everywhere."[102] And the operation only kept Russia going temporarily, until the revolution allowed Lenin to sign his separate peace. After that, the Allies found themselves diverting forces to Russia, to fight *against* a government now pledged to their destruction.

Nonetheless, if the threat that Germany might start a war had created the Triple Entente, the threat that it might *win* gradually created a more cohesive—and expansive—coalition.

Some of the most important cooperation was economic. The British Navy physically connected the Allies to each other and the world. "The territories of Britain and France," Mackinder later wrote, "were made one for the purpose of the war."[103] This unity allowed Britain to bring its economic heft to bear, producing much of the equipment, providing much of the money (some $6.7 billion in credit), and delivering from its empire much of the food the Allies needed. "Our finance is their very life-blood, without which they could not get on," noted Lloyd George.[104]

The Allies pulled closer over time, because wartime exigencies left them little choice. In 1915, the Entente powers pooled their gold reserves to bolster their ability to borrow and buy in America. While Britain and France initially took turns negotiating loans for the coalition, London carried the load once French creditworthiness was shot.[105] Shipping, meanwhile, was the linchpin of a strategy that drew men and goods from around the world, so the Allies created an Allied Maritime Transport Council to rationalize the use of scarce vessels and a Wheat Executive to manage food shipments. Recalled one participant, "No longer did empty Italian ships going west for American wheat and empty British ships going east for Australian wheat pass each other in the Mediterranean." The French put their railways at the disposal of the British, while British steel supported a French armaments industry that supplied Serbia, Russia, and eventually America.[106] None of this was glamorous, but all was essential. Winning a global war in the industrial age placed a premium on cooperation in trade, finance, production, and logistics.

It also required many hands to strangle Germany. Into 1915, Germany had remained resilient against a poorly coordinated British blockade, thanks in part to its ability to import through neutral European ports. In response, London empowered new administrative entities, such as the Ministry of Blockade, to streamline implementation; Eyre Crowe provided much of the bureaucratic energy. And as historian Nicholas Mulder shows, the Allies built a "transnational enterprise to master . . . the global trading system."[107] The British and French partnered to buy up global stocks of raw materials; they pressured banks in Allied and, later, neutral countries to cut off Germany; they exploited the fact that the Allies collectively controlled majority supplies of aluminum, hemp, nickel, rubber, and other commodities to draw the noose tighter. By late 1916, the blockade was humming, while the German economy was groaning. Daily rations were soon just 1,000 calories per person; calls for peace and political reform were growing louder.[108]

Finally, there was integration on land. To relieve the French, the British belatedly turned the BEF into a full-sized continental army. Although huge numbers of those troops died at the Somme in 1916, their sacrifice gave respite to French forces that were near cracking at Verdun. In 1917, Haig's forces made the primary effort while French armies were convulsed with malaise and mutiny. France had been "a real ally and a true comrade," Henry Wilson commented, "and we must pay her back in her own coin."[109]

Mistrust remained pervasive; Clemenceau believed London would "fight to the last Frenchman." But the Allies groped their way forward, with the creation of a Supreme War Council in 1917 and then the vital merging of command, supply, and logistics in 1918. By the fall, Allied personnel—not just British and French but also Belgian, Italian, Portuguese, and eventually American—were truly fighting together.[110] World War I saw the anti-German forces repeatedly stare defeat in the face, only to muster the solidarity to avert it in the end.

Even before that, Allied cooperation was making a crucial difference. As Berlin struggled with the blockade, as Austria-Hungary and the Ottomans faltered, as large British armies deployed to France, German commanders worried that time was slipping away. Germany was "continually opposed by old and new enemies" with imposing amounts of "man power, artillery, aircraft," Ludendorff and Hindenburg reported in August 1916. "Little by little," the blockade was causing "our exhaustion."[111] Their desperation was powerfully reinforced by the policies of a

country, and a leader, that had not yet joined the war. And that desperation would lure Germany into a lethal mistake.

*

IF WILHELM II WAS ONE OF HISTORY'S MORE DISASTROUSLY ECCENTRIC
figures, Woodrow Wilson was one of the most paradoxical. The twenty-
eighth president was a racist who stirred imaginations in Asia and Africa.
He was a scholar of congressional politics who failed, utterly, in his most
consequential attempt to navigate them. He spoke the language of high
morality but could be totally cold-blooded. Our lingering image of Wilson
is the starry-eyed idealist trying to remake a fallen world—"another Jesus
Christ," chided Clemenceau, "come upon the earth to reform men."[112] In
truth, Wilson oversaw America's first, albeit brief, emergence as a global
military heavyweight. And he understood, better than many of his countrymen, just how vital American power would be in the Eurasian age.[113]

Wilson hadn't wanted to take his country to war. America was an
economic juggernaut in 1914, but it remained a military afterthought.
The army was tiny; the navy had greater global aspiration than global
reach. There was no national security state to coordinate policy; the
federal government was small and weak. Americans still placed their
hopes for a peaceful world more in international law than in U.S. hegemony; American exceptionalism was still defined in terms of separation
from Europe rather than leadership of it.[114] So when the war started,
Wilson—like many Americans—viewed it as the product of a sick,
dying Europe, and believed his country's duty was to stay out. "We are
the only one of the great White nations that is free from war today," he
maintained into 1917, "and it would be a crime against civilization for
us to go in."[115]

Many of Wilson's advisers disagreed. From the outset, Colonel
Edward House contended that Germany represented "the unspeakable
tyranny of militarism for generations to come."[116] Robert Lansing, Wilson's secretary of state from 1915 onward, called the war a "struggle
between Autocracy and Democracy" and argued that "German impe-

rialist ambitions threaten free institutions everywhere." He admitted, though, that he had not "made any great impression" on Wilson, for the president feared that intervention in Europe would set America's immigrant communities against each other.[117] Wilson worried, also, that the war would lead to restrictions on speech and political protest, as well as greater government control of the economy. "War means autocracy," he warned.[118] Here was a recurring American debate of the modern era— whether democratic institutions were more likely to be endangered by abstention from Eurasian struggles or intervention in them. Wilson came around to the second view, but he initially adhered to the first.

For much of the war, Wilson's ire was directed at London as well as Berlin. By disrupting American trade, the British blockade created echoes of the events that had caused the War of 1812; the Foreign Office reported "a recrudescence of the traditional American sentiment about sea power when used against them."[119] And almost until America entered the war, Wilson's grandest aspiration was to end the madness by brokering a compromise settlement. After winning reelection in November 1916, Wilson called for "peace without victory" while temporarily constricting U.S. lending as a cudgel against the cash-strapped Allies. The British and French were saved, in this and other cases, by the fact that Germany refused to offer remotely acceptable terms.[120] Even so, his meddling reinforced London's view that a morally obtuse Wilson "wholly failed to grasp . . . the cause for which we and our Allies are fighting."[121]

If mediation was a dead end, so was neutrality. A country as powerful as America could not easily stay out of Europe; almost without trying, it became a central player there. And the war did not stay in Europe. It sprawled in ways that inevitably implicated the United States.

Because of the financial and economic ties that bound the United States to Britain, because the Royal Navy controlled the ocean's surface, and because Wilson was unwilling simply to cut off trade with the outside world, American neutrality was never really neutral. Whereas trade with Germany suffered due to the blockade, commerce with the Allies

boomed, as Washington sold them food, clothing, and munitions—
and lent them the money to buy it all. U.S. exports to Europe outpaced
imports by $500 million in 1914 and $3.5 billion in 1917; the American
government and U.S. banks lent the Allies over $9 billion during the
war.[122] This trade buoyed the Allies and bedeviled the Germans. One
British statesman admitted that London wouldn't last a month "if the
American supplies were shut down."[123] To Berlin, reported House, "it
seems that every German that is being killed or wounded is being killed
or wounded by an American rifle, bullet, or shell."[124]

Submarine warfare was intended to cut Britain's American lifeline.
It led unavoidably to American deaths at sea. "In God's name, how could
any nation calling itself civilized purpose so horrible a thing?" Wilson
gasped after a U-boat sank the contraband-carrying British ocean liner
Lusitania, killing 128 Americans, in May 1915.[125] The sinking precipitated the first of a series of crises in which Wilson threatened, somewhat
half-heartedly, to break with Berlin, causing the Germans to retreat just
enough to avoid making another enemy.[126] Yet this was a fragile equilibrium, because German leaders understood that American commerce
was sustaining the Allies—and submarine warfare was teaching American leaders about the implications of a German victory.

As Wilson's advisers and former president Theodore Roosevelt had
warned, a Germany that dominated Europe could roam free outside of
it; it might meddle in the Western Hemisphere and behave globally with
the same callous brutality it had already displayed.[127] In this climate of
pervasive insecurity, the United States would have to permanently militarize itself for protection—which might ultimately smother democracy
in America itself. In a world where "the military point of view" prevailed,
Wilson warned, America must be "ready for anything"; it would need
a "great standing army" and become "a mobilized nation."[128] "At last we
realized," he would later say, "that there was here nothing less than a
threat against the freedom of free men everywhere."[129] This is what Wilson meant when he eventually said that America must make the world
safe for democracy. He was *not* arguing that all autocracies must be

destroyed. He was saying that even distant countries would struggle to preserve their free institutions if powerful, aggressive tyrannies gained the upper hand.[130]

The rupture came in February and March 1917, when Berlin resumed unrestricted submarine warfare and began sinking U.S. ships. "There is no middle course," wrote Holtzendorff; only escalation could make "the whole world" respect German power.[131] Diplomats had warned that this was the road to ruin, writing that Germany would be treated "as a mad dog against whom the hand of every man will be raised."[132] Yet the government wagered that its new enemy would be slow to mobilize; Germany could starve England, Holtzendorff promised, "before a single American has set foot on the continent."[133] Not for the last time, everything hinged on whether Germany could win a European conflict before America could intervene decisively there. To improve the odds, the Kaiser also approved a scheme (promptly revealed by British intelligence) to lure Mexico into attacking the United States: Perhaps trouble on one continent could keep America out of another.

One wonders whether Germany, which feared it was losing the war, would have made the same wager had it realized how close it was to winning. In early 1917, the Allies were terribly weak. The collapse of tsarist Russia was approaching. France was at the limit of its endurance. A nearly bankrupt Britain—its poverty a state secret—was blowing through its assets and ability to borrow. The empire was "quickly drifting" toward insolvency, the Exchequer had warned; by June, London might have to accept any peace on offer.[134] Germany faced severe problems, but with a bit more patience it might have outlasted its enemies nonetheless.

Even after Germany made its choice, America made *its* choice reluctantly. Wilson was ambivalent: "If there is any alternative, for God's sake, let's take it."[135] Opposition was intense. Congressional critics charged that Wilson would plunge America into "the greatest holocaust the world has ever known."[136] Yet on April 2, Wilson called for—and received—a declaration of war on grounds that Germany's "submarine warfare against commerce" was also "a warfare against mankind." And he began to embrace the thesis that the war was really about what type of government would set the world's rules. The great "menace to . . . peace and freedom," he declared, lay in "the existence of autocratic governments backed by organized force."[137] What ultimately brought America into the war was the danger that instability and predation might spread uncontrollably from a Eurasia in illiberal hands.

*

IT WAS ALMOST TOO LATE. A GREAT DILEMMA OF GLOBAL STRATEGY IN the early twentieth century was that no Eurasian balance of power was possible without America, but America was located so far away that it often declined to intervene until that balance was nearly broken. Had Washington declared war two years earlier, after the *Lusitania* tragedy, Churchill later wrote, "what catastrophes would have been prevented; in how many million homes would an empty chair be occupied today; how different would be the shattered world in which victors and vanquished alike are condemned to live!"[138] Even after America joined the war, it wasn't ready.

There had been no joint planning with the Allies. U.S. ground forces numbered only 220,000 soldiers and marines, and many Americans did not realize that declaring war might mean dispatching them to Europe. "Good Lord! You're not going to send soldiers over there, are you?" one senator exclaimed. Nor did the United States have the ships to get those troops across the Atlantic, or the tanks, artillery, and planes needed to arm them.[139]

As a result, U.S. intervention didn't initially change much militarily, and the months thereafter were among the blackest yet. Relentless submarine warfare claimed over 800,000 tons of Allied shipping in April 1917; France and Britain soon had just weeks of wheat left.[140] Streams of U.S. money kept the Allies solvent, but the first year of America's war effort was primarily an exercise in mutual disappointment. The Allies rued America's military fecklessness; U.S. officials were stunned to discover how weak the Allies really were.

Yet U.S. intervention and Russian withdrawal did change things ideologically; the conflict was now much closer to a straight-up fight between democracies and autocracies. U.S. involvement also remade the war psychologically. The mere promise of support from the New World sustained resistance in the Old. If the Allies could wait for the gusher of American money and manpower, they would probably win—which meant that Germany, at the height of its conquests in early 1918, had no time to consolidate them. Berlin "could not wait" to "begin the decisive conflict in the west," Hindenburg remarked. "We had to keep the prospects of American intervention steadily before our eyes."[141]

Germany nearly won that race with its spring offensives; the commander of the American Expeditionary Force, General John Pershing, remarked that "the Allies are done for."[142] They might have been had not the Americans finally arrived in force.

American mobilization was slow, but when it gained momentum it was unstoppable. By mid-1918, nearly 10,000 U.S. troops were arriving in Europe per day. Pershing, who had earlier insisted on holding these forces back to serve in American-led units, agreed to feed some 200,000 troops into the beleaguered British and French ranks.[143] The appearance of fresh, well-fed U.S. soldiers bolstered the Allies while demoralizing the Germans; it provided the extra combat power that finally tipped the balance.

American forces fought tenaciously in defensive battles at Cantigny, Château-Thierry, and Belleau Wood. "Retreat? Hell, we just got here," one marine captain shouted when the combat became murderously tough.[144] In July, U.S. divisions helped blunt Germany's last-ditch assaults outside Paris at the Second Battle of the Marne. Foch then launched the counteroffensive that would deliver Allied victory. Most of the manpower was French, but the offensive could not have succeeded without the American contribution. "Allied forces are three times our strength and the damned Americans are sending fresh troops constantly," Ludendorff despaired.[145]

The Germans were beaten at sea, as well. A new strategy was vital;

the British belatedly adopted a convoying system that forced vulnerable submarines to take deadly risks by seeking out well-guarded merchant ships, rather than picking them off one by one. The U.S. Navy helped make the math work. By war's end, the United States had seventy-nine destroyers in European waters, working closely with the British.[146] Mahan's vision of a transatlantic naval alliance was realized; the submarine menace was vanquished.

By late 1918, a contest that had lasted longer than nearly anyone had initially predicted was ending more abruptly than nearly anyone had recently thought possible. In August, the Allies were still planning a decisive offensive for 1919; by September, Germany was falling apart. Ludendorff's offensives had broken the Germans rather than breaking the Allies; his exsanguinated armies were in danger of collapse. The Central Powers were dropping one by one, and Germany could no longer fill the gaps. "We cannot fight against the whole world," Ludendorff exclaimed.[147] The war was lost everywhere, including at home. Amid surging unrest, Ludendorff resigned, the Kaiser—long eclipsed by his own generals—abdicated, and a new, more liberal government sued for peace.

The coalition that beat Germany was a combination of power unlike anything in history. It included countries or colonies on all six inhabited continents; it accounted for more than half of the world's industrial production. At its core was a pathbreaking, transoceanic integration of capabilities, best symbolized by the deployment of 2 million U.S. troops to Europe, many of them armed with French weapons and transported in British ships.[148] And as nearly everyone understood at the time, U.S. power made the crucial difference.

"The hope of the Allies," Belgium's King Albert said, "was now entirely in America."[149] Absent U.S. involvement, the Allies would have struggled to break the deadlock in the west, let alone reverse Germany's victory in the east. The most likely outcome would have been a settlement leaving Germany dominant from Belgium to the Caucasus, with nearly all the resources—wheat, iron, oil, and many others—it needed for global power. If Germany's wartime practices were any indication, the areas its forces occupied would have been stripped of industry, raw materials, and food; they would have provided slave labor for German factories and land for German colonization. Ethnic cleansing and mass murder were real possibilities; in occupied Eastern Europe, German forces often "treated the inhabitants as barbarians, without rights or identity of their own."[150]

A German victory in World War I might not have been much better than a German victory in World War II. "Their plan," Wilson had said, "was to throw a broad belt of German military power and political control across the very center of Europe and beyond the Mediterranean into the heart of Asia." If Germany had succeeded, then "we and all the rest of the world must remain armed" and await "the next step in their aggression."[151] U.S. intervention saved the world from a cold war against a hyper-empowered Germany, in the best case, and from a German-dominated Eurasia, in the worst.

Meanwhile, America was starting to display the strength of a superpower. "Twentieth-century warfare," one American automaker remarked, "demands that the blood of the soldier must be mingled with from three to five parts of the sweat of the man in the factories, mills, mines, and fields of the nation in arms." Sure enough, government authority expanded, with the creation of new agencies and new federal powers for mobilization and production. By war's end, America's shipyards were outproducing the world. There were 4.8 million Americans in uniform, deployed from Siberia to France; the U.S. Navy was on pace to become the Earth's largest.[152] American intervention had transformed a great Eurasian struggle—and begun to transform America itself.

*

THE QUESTION WAS WHETHER THAT TRANSFORMATION WOULD endure—whether the war's end would produce a durable settlement, anchored by the same overbearing coalition, or simply bring, as Clemenceau feared, "a lull in the storm."[153] It was, unfortunately, the latter.

After the armistice, the victors gathered at Versailles to devise the grandest peace in history. A generation later, the world found itself staring into a totalitarian abyss.

The conventional wisdom remains that the peace was too harsh: a vengeful Versailles Treaty saddled Germany with reparations and humiliations, creating the spiral of resentment and radicalism that culminated in World War II.[154] It's true that Germany didn't get off easy. The Versailles Treaty undid the wartime settlements Berlin had imposed on Romania and Russia. It stripped Germany of 13 percent of its prewar land and 10 percent of its population. Berlin's colonies were confiscated. The Rhineland was demilitarized and temporarily occupied; France was given control of the coal-rich Saar for fifteen years. Germany had to surrender its navy, forgo an air force, and severely limit its army; it was handed a reparations bill of 132 billion gold marks and made to take moral responsibility for the war. "Germany renounces its existence," one of its delegates muttered.[155] Yet if Versailles wasn't a soft peace, it wasn't Carthaginian either.

France had wanted something far harsher. Clemenceau and Foch sought to dismember Germany territorially and cripple it economically. "To assure a durable peace for Europe," French diplomats asserted, "it is necessary to destroy Bismarck's work."[156] The peace was far more generous than those Germany had recently forced on Russia and Romania. Versailles left Germany mostly intact, ensuring that it would one day resurge as Europe's most powerful state. If anything, Germany came out of the war in a stronger position, as the breakup of Eastern Europe's empires meant that Germany's neighbors were now mostly small and weak. Even the reparations were not so crushing, because Germany ended up paying only 22 billion gold marks between 1918 and 1932.[157] In view of what Germany had done to the countries it occupied, and what it had planned to do if victorious, the peace was positively mild. So why did it fall apart?

Perhaps Germany wasn't treated roughly enough. Because the war had left Germany united, it hadn't solved the German problem—the inherent instability created by a country too assertive to settle for anything less than primacy in Europe, and too mighty to be constrained by its neighbors alone. And because the war had ended with German troops still occupying foreign soil, the reality of defeat was not carried home to the German people, as would happen during World War II. It was all too easy, then, for Germans to believe, and for unscrupulous leaders to tell them, that the country had not been beaten in the field and that *any* restrictions imposed upon it were illegitimate.

Then there was the difficulty of forging peace in a world still at war. World War I ended in November 1918, but the plethora of conflicts it ignited did not. Left- and right-wing groups were fighting it out from Central Europe to Siberia. Anticolonial agitation was rising; violence was roiling the Balkans, Asia Minor, and the Middle East. Famine and radicalism were spreading; a "social revolution," Lenin proclaimed, was "approaching for the whole world."[158] Lenin's Russia had become a fount of military aggression and ideological volatility; Great Britain, the long-time global stabilizer, was exhausted even as its empire expanded. "The world is on fire," Robert Lansing wrote; how could any settlement survive the flames?[159]

The most critical factor, though, was that the transoceanic unity that won the war began to fray before the peace was even signed. At Versailles, the British and French had divergent preferences, reflecting divergent strategic realities. The French, living in Germany's shadow, believed that country must be held down lest it rise and terrorize its neighbors again. "America is far away, protected by the ocean," Clemenceau explained. "Not even Napoleon himself could touch England. You are both sheltered; we are not."[160] The British had achieved their vital war aims with the surrender of the German fleet and the retreat of German power from Belgium. They wanted France, a once and perhaps future rival, to be secure but not dominant. So Lloyd George was willing to restore Germany for purposes of international trade and as a bulwark against communism; he sought a balance in Europe so Britain could be done with bloody commitments there. "The English would remain English," Clemenceau quipped, "and the French French."[161]

What about the Americans? In late 1918, U.S. power was staggering. Even friends, such as Australian prime minister Billy Hughes, feared being "dragged . . . behind the wheels of President Wilson's chariot."[162] Wilson himself had unrivaled influence. His advocacy for a peace that would remove the causes of war, that would protect the weak as well as the strong, had given him, in the words of the economist—and member of the British peace delegation—John Maynard Keynes, "a prestige and moral influence throughout the world unequalled in history."[163] Yet the peace Wilson envisioned was traditional and transformative at the same time.

Wilson favored a settlement tough enough to make clear that Germany had been defeated. In October 1918, he had even demanded—successfully—that Germany reject its military rulers before an armistice was granted. But Wilson also mistrusted Britain and France, and their imperial aspirations. He believed the old, Eurocentric model of international order had failed. "You have either got to have the old system, of which Germany was the perfect flower, or you have got to have a new system," he explained.[164]

The president had outlined that new system in his "Fourteen Points" speech of January 1918. He called for "open covenants of peace" in place of secret diplomacy, freedom of the seas and a relatively open international economy, the "adjustment of all colonial claims" with due heed to the wishes of the governed, and "a general association of nations" to protect its members' independence and territorial integrity. What America wanted, he said, was "that the world be made fit and safe to live in" for "every peace-loving nation."[165]

The lofty rhetoric exasperated some observers as much as it inspired others. Wilson had "no proposals that would bear the test of experience," Hughes scoffed.[166] Yet Wilson's preferences were not as idealistic as they might have seemed.

The reduction of economic barriers would break down British and French imperial advantages and give America greater access to global markets. "Open covenants, openly arrived at" suited a democracy that could hardly keep its commitments secret. Lest anyone doubt Wilson's realism, he made clear that any international organization must not interfere with the Monroe Doctrine, and he coupled calls for global cooperation with the threat of a naval buildup that would leave even Britain in America's wake.[167] Not least, Wilson understood that any peace had to be anchored by U.S. power—and this required navigating awkward politics at home.

This was the point of the League of Nations, which Wilson called "the most essential part of the peace settlement itself."[168] The heart of the League was its provision calling on all members to oppose "external aggression" against other members. The idea was to deter future violations of the peace by making clear that *America's* economic and perhaps military power could be brought to bear. "If you want to quiet the world," Wilson declared, "you have got to reassure the world, and the only way in which you can reassure it is to let it know that all the great fighting powers of the world are going to maintain that quiet."[169]

Yet the League had to play this role without emulating the practices—namely old-fashioned military alliances—that many Americans associated with Europe's tragic past. The world needed a "community of power," not a "balance of power," Wilson had said. So Wilson framed the League as a vehicle for global unity rather than as a tool of power politics. He refused to put U.S. armed forces directly under its control; he argued that the League, by enlisting American strength as a deterrent, would make it unnecessary to use that strength in a costly war again. "We cannot offer more than the condition of the world enables us to give," Wilson explained. There was no peace without American power, but American power could be enlisted only through creative indirection.[170]

What emerged from this tangle of preferences was a brutally contentious peace conference—Clemenceau labeled Wilson a "friend of Germany," while Wilson nearly went home in anger at Clemenceau—and a hybrid peace.[171] Germany was to be subdued and constrained, but only partially and temporarily. Self-determination prevailed in the creation

of an independent Poland, but not in the disposition of Europe's overseas colonies and empires. The conference created a League of Nations,
but one that featured only a loose commitment to aid victims of aggression, which then necessitated a separate offer of a U.S. and British security guarantee to France. "I like the League," Clemenceau said, "but I
do not believe in it."[172] Wilson spoke of a world transformed, but he
delivered something between the old and the new.

*

THE PROBLEMS WITH THE VERSAILLES SETTLEMENT WERE OBVIOUS. HOW
would a League that required unanimous decisions confront an aggressor
within its ranks? If the League was toothless, why should Americans support it? If it wasn't toothless, why the separate guarantee to France? These
flaws were inherent in the balancing act Wilson was attempting. Yet a durable peace might still have emerged, if—and only if—America embraced its
leading role.

As the 1920s would show, only America had the capital to rebuild
Europe economically. Only America could write down British and
French war debts, allowing them to forgo the reparations that embit-
tered Germany. Only America could provide France with the security
that would allow it to rehabilitate a fragile, democratic Germany rather
than trying, futilely, to keep it down. Only American involvement could
give the League credibility, allowing that body to become stronger over
time. Europe could not "put itself back in working order," Lloyd George
commented, "if the United States does not put oil in the machine."[173] Yet
this would require Wilson, who seemingly bestrode the world in 1918–
19, to convince his own citizens.

The Versailles settlement was bound to be controversial. If many
Europeans feared that the League would not sufficiently entangle America in the continent's quarrels, many Americans feared that it would.
Through Wilson's League, charged Senator William Borah, the U.S.
would "give back to George V what it took from George III."[174] And
now that the immediate threat had receded, why should not America,

the least vulnerable of all the powers, also pull back? Perhaps it was "too soon for the country to accept the League," Wilson remarked. America "may have to break the heart of the world."[175]

Perhaps, but the League was broadly popular with Americans in 1919, and Wilson lost the treaty fight due to politics as much as geopolitics. Republican "irreconcilables" opposed the League in almost any form. Republican internationalists supported—in fact, had originated—many of the ideas Wilson fought for at Versailles, but were loath to hand him a defining political victory. Henry Cabot Lodge, the Republican Senate Majority Leader, shrewdly adorned the League's covenant with amendments, meant to so weaken it that Wilson would ultimately reject the pact. Wilson played into Lodge's hands. When his prestige was high and he might have found a workable compromise, he refused to deal. "He has grown so accustomed to almost dictatorial powers," Wilson's adviser Colonel House had worried, "that it will go hard to give them up."[176] Wilson's obstinacy grew as his health declined, and he suffered a massive stroke during a speaking tour meant to sell the treaty. A broken Wilson instructed his supporters to vote against an amended treaty, which—along with U.S. membership in the League—went down to defeat.

During the 1920s, America remained economically engaged in Europe and Asia, without the strategic and political commitments to match. Rather than building an unrivaled navy to patrol the oceans, the United States sought to pacify the world through disarmament and outlawing war. Rather than leaving its troops in Europe, Washington brought them home, ignoring the pleas of the British and French. In essence, the United States sought to reap the benefits of a stable world, as it had during the nineteenth century—but in the twentieth century, that stability could come only from exertions it refused to make. When Washington withdrew economically from European affairs, during the Great Depression, it removed its last support for a troubled continent's tenuous peace. "Heaven knows how all of this will end," Lansing had written in 1919.[177] Absent U.S. leadership, it wouldn't end well at all.

*

MACKINDER HAD SEEN IT COMING. THE WORLD WOULD BLOW UP around him twice in the forty years after he published the Pivot paper. Mackinder took each explosion as a chance to revisit his thesis. America's "failure to share the burden of the victory" was "one of the great tragedies of the time," he said after Washington broke the heart of the world, although perhaps not surprising since Americans lived "so far from the peoples of Central Europe."[178] Even before that, Mackinder had weighed in on the geopolitics of the peace in a slim book, *Democratic Ideals and Reality*, published in 1919.

The title was the giveaway. Mackinder's book was an inquiry into what might make the postwar settlement stick, and he was skeptical that the League would do the trick. It was not enough to "lay down on paper good principles of conduct," he wrote. A stable peace had to be rooted in "the realities of time and space"—and an understanding of what had nearly befallen the world in the war.[179]

Mackinder misleadingly called that war a "straight duel between land-power and seapower," but he recognized that what won it was a fusing of the two. The marriage of British sea power and French manpower had held the enemy at bay. When French forces faltered, Britain's newly raised armies filled the gap; when Russia's defeat threatened to untie everything, another Atlantic democracy came to the rescue. "West Europe had to call in the help of America, for West Europe alone would not have been able to reverse the decision in the East."[180] Still, victory had been a near-run thing.

Germany's fatal mistake, Mackinder wrote, was its mix of ambition and indecision—its effort to conquer in two directions at once. "Had Germany elected to stand on the defensive on her short frontier towards France, and had she thrown her main strength against Russia," she could have won in the East and then settled in the West. "The world would be nominally at peace to-day, but overshadowed by a German East Europe in command of all the Heartland."[181]

World War I thus sharpened Mackinder's thinking in two respects. Like Wilson, he became more attuned to the ideological basis of great-power rivalry. On one side were the "organizers," who used autocratic methods to harness society's energy. Against them were "idealists," who cherished individualism and the rights of man. The fundamental question the war had raised was "which shall have the last word in the state," and in international society as well.[182]

Second, the Bolshevik revolution and Brest-Litovsk alerted Mackinder to a danger he had once noted in passing—that a tie-up between Germany and Russia would derange the world. A behemoth that ruled Europe and the Heartland might be unstoppable. It would combine industrial dynamism with agricultural riches. It could use artillery, airplanes, and submarines to control key maritime chokepoints, from Suez to the Skagerrak, while building fleets that could roam the globe. "What if the Great Continent . . . were at some future time to become a single and united base of sea-power?" Mackinder queried. Surely this was "the great ultimate threat to the world's liberty."[183] This, in turn, focused Mackinder on Eastern Europe—the one area where the Russian Heartland was not ringed by natural obstacles, whether ice-covered ocean to the north or mountains and deserts to the south, but instead abutted an open plain and Eurasia's Atlantic periphery beyond. This was the path an aggressive Germany might once again use to conquer Russia—or a messianic, Bolshevized Russia might travel to grab hold of Germany.

For Mackinder, then, the most critical feature of the peace was not the League of Nations. It was the creation of a cordon sanitaire between Russia and Germany—a "tier of independent states" that, in defending themselves, would keep Eurasia in balance.[184]

*

UNLIKE MOST INTELLECTUALS, MACKINDER WAS ABLE TO ROAD-TEST his theory. In 1919–20, the Russian Civil War was raging. The Bolsheviks were battling myriad enemies in a cruel, back-and-forth conflict that may have killed 9 million people; outside powers intervened for reasons ranging from wartime necessity to naked self-aggrandizement. Britain had initially come to prevent Germany from exploiting Lenin's revolution; it stayed, for a time, to stop communism and chaos from endangering Eastern Europe and the Middle East.

Enter Mackinder. In fall 1919, Britain's foreign secretary, Lord Curzon, named him High Commissioner to South Russia. Mackinder was to administer the territory controlled by one British-backed group of White Russian armies under General Anton Denikin, and to protect London's interests in a region aflame.[185]

It didn't go smoothly. Mackinder's departure was delayed by difficulties in hiring a staff, buying winter clothing, and sorting out lines of authority. After finally leaving England on December 4, he traveled through Paris, Warsaw, Bucharest, Sofia, and Constantinople, arriving at Novorossiysk on New Year's Day. "The journey was very slow, the conditions were barbaric," Mackinder griped.[186] By the time he arrived, Denikin's army—which had pushed within striking distance of Moscow months prior—was falling back toward the Black Sea in disarray. British intervention was collapsing before Mackinder's boots hit the ground.[187]

Mackinder wasn't deterred. He tried to cobble together an anticommunist alliance, by urging Denikin and the leaders of Poland—a country just created, in part, from fragments of tsarist Russia—to link arms. He then returned, via destroyer, to London on January 16 to propose an "all-round policy."[188]

History was on a knife's edge, Mackinder believed, because the Kaiser's autocratic challenge had given way to something more frightful. Lenin and Trotsky were creating "a centralized and bureaucratic" tyranny, one whose ethos was "Jacobin instead of aristocratic." Like the radicals of the French Revolution, they were uprooting domestic society while working to export their revolution. For now, the price was paid mainly by Russians; whenever the Bolsheviks found a village "without its proper complement of men the women and children would be killed." But the Bolshevik armies were adopting German military methods; there were hints of cooperation between these two outcast states. If "strong immediate measures" were not taken, Bolshevism might sweep "forward like a prairie fire," engulfing areas from India to Poland.[189]

Mackinder's solution was as grand as the problem. He proposed to "range up all the anti-Bolshevist States, from Finland to the Caucasus," training and arming them. The British must even be prepared to hold the Caspian Basin and the line from Baku to Batum themselves. This strategy would birth buffer states from Ukraine to the Baltic; the British government would fund the effort by regulating trade, collecting taxes, and economically administering non-Bolshevik Russia. A decisive effort might throw back communist forces "on a line extending from the Gulf of Finland to the Sea of Azov." But this success would merely "drive the Bolsheviks into Asia," so the "final remedy" was "to kill Bolshevism at its source."[190]

Like many big ideas, this one never had a chance. Britain was already phasing out aid to Russia's retreating White armies. London wanted to liquidate postwar commitments on the continent; it sought peace with the Bolsheviks to restart trade and avert famine in Europe. "This is obviously impossible," Curzon noted, "if military operations on a large scale are to continue for an indefinite period." Mackinder's proposal landed with a thud in the Cabinet. He soon resigned his position; Denikin's forces crumbled not long after.[191]

The episode was an embarrassment for Mackinder. But it did give him a clearer view of what lay ahead. The Soviet Union may not have immediately swept across Europe and Asia, yet Lenin did consolidate a state committed to global revolution, while forging a Faustian pact with Germany. From the early 1920s, the two sides secretly cooperated, militarily and technologically; in 1939, Hitler and Stalin agreed to divide Eastern Europe between them. The next world war broke out just where Mackinder had expected. The key actors were two radical revisionists who destroyed the system before trying to destroy each other.

3

THE TOTALITARIAN ABYSS

On December 11, 1941, four days after infamy, Adolf Hitler globalized World War II by declaring war on the United States. It was a curious, and ultimately suicidal, decision. In the two years prior, Hitler's armies had conquered Europe; by late 1941 they were banging on Moscow's gates. German submarines, again, had Britain on the brink. In the Pacific, Japan had just attacked Pearl Harbor—striking "like a bolt of lightning," German diplomats reported—and Tokyo might have absorbed America's rage alone had Hitler done nothing.[1] Yet Hitler picked a fight with the one country that could stymie his ambitions, because he understood, in his perverse way, the logic of the Eurasian century all too well.

Germany's drive for greatness would culminate in an epic "war of the continents," Hitler had long believed. Only a Europe ruled by Germany could "prevent the world hegemony" of North America.[2] Before December 1941, Hitler had focused on restoring German power and smashing his European rivals. But all this was prelude to the struggle with Washington—a clash, he believed, that was well underway.

Hitler had been dismissive of the United States when it crawled into a cocoon of isolation during the 1930s. Once America began to rearm and reengage, however, it haunted his decision-making. Germany had to settle all European scores quickly, Hitler resolved in December 1940, "because in 1942 the United States will be ready to intervene."[3] He invaded the Soviet Union in June 1941, in hopes that doing so would force Britain out of the conflict and keep America from getting in. The "swift defeat of the Soviet Union," Hitler's foreign ministry explained, "will be the best means for convincing the United States of the absolute senselessness of entering the war on the side of England, who will then be completely isolated and confronted by the mightiest combination in the world."[4] Hitler invaded one continent-sized power to avoid war with another.

In late 1941, though, the Soviet Union was still barely hanging on, and the Führer interpreted the menacing drift of U.S. policy—the provision of vital aid to London and Moscow, Franklin Roosevelt's undeclared war against German submarines, the promulgation of an Atlantic Charter anticipating the "final destruction of Nazi tyranny"—as proof that there was no use in waiting.[5] "The war with the U.S.," he said, "was sure to come sooner or later anyway."[6] So Hitler seized the initiative, and turned two raging regional storms into a single global maelstrom.

History, we like to think, is a story of progress. But the first half of the twentieth century was a progression from one nightmare to another. In 1918, a transatlantic alliance had strained to fend off one Eurasian challenge, only for a second, more malevolent and vicious, to arise. At the worst moments of World War II, the Axis powers dominated the Eurasian Rimlands, were enveloping the vital Heartland, and were menacing the island sanctuaries and oceanic supply routes keeping their opponents alive. They had united in an alliance to tear down the existing order and build empires of evil amid its ruins. By late 1941, the future of humanity again hinged on a deadly race. The Axis powers were rushing to consolidate control of Eurasia and prepare for conflict with America; their remaining enemies had to prevent them from harnessing the bounty of the supercontinent and loosing their full fury upon the world.

World War II was the nadir of the Eurasian century and the grimmest realization of Mackinder's vision. The run-up to conflict saw the rise of regimes that used the strengths of modern societies for expropriation, enslavement, and extermination. New technologies and new ways of war enabled supersized programs of conquest. Not least, the saga showed that the difficulties of blunting hegemonic gambits early could be severe, but the price of rolling them back later could be staggering. In all these respects, World War II delivered a searing education. It also gave Mackinder, having lived through two world wars that grimly vindicated his prophecies, the chance to offer a strategy for preventing a third.

*

THE MOST VEXING QUESTION ABOUT WORLD WAR II IS, "WHY?" WHY DID the Axis powers engage in some of history's most brazen land grabs? Why did advanced societies embrace a hideous barbarism? Why did they seek security in ways that denied it to everyone else? The answer illustrates the more chilling aspects of the modern era—and shows what entrepreneurs in villainy can achieve in a leaderless world.

World War II will always be associated with the cast of killers who started it. There was Benito Mussolini, a strategic bumbler who nonetheless set the tone for the era by pioneering fascist politics in the 1920s and helping to prove that aggression could pay a decade later. There were Tojo Hideki and other Japanese leaders who lunged for hegemony in Asia. There was Joseph Stalin, the arsonist who helped torch the world by allying with Hitler, before helping extinguish the blaze by defeating him. Above all, there was Hitler himself.

A bit of a loser for the first half of his life, Hitler became a fantastically talented demagogue in the second. "I have rarely listened to such a logical and fanatical man," a foreign military attaché observed in the 1920s. "His powers over the mob must be immense." Hitler mastered the politics of resentment to shatter German democracy. He then proceeded, through a mix of messianic ambition, pathological anti-Semitism, and brilliant opportunism, to shatter the world.[7]

These tyrants shaped their times as thoroughly as any leaders before or since. The experience with Hitler, wrote one British diplomat, had shown "how precarious is to-day the peace of the world when it rests in the hands of a single fanatical and unbalanced individual."[8] Yet people make history within a certain context. So why was a world that was meant to have been made safe for democracy so prone to political, and geopolitical, extremism?

It didn't have to be this way. For most of the 1920s, the liberal coalition that won World War I remained dominant. A solution to Europe's economic and security problems seemed possible; democracy still looked like the wave of the future. But that moment, like the decisive U.S. engagement that had enabled it, didn't last.

One problem was that World War I left so many potential troublemakers so aggrieved. Japan and Italy, two *winners* of that conflict, were angry that they had not reaped greater gains at the peace conference. A defeated Germany had lost its colonies, its prospects for European dominance, and its identity as a great power—a status not even the democratic leaders of the 1920s truly accepted. The Soviet Union was smarting from the detachment of Poland, Finland, and other parts of the Russian Empire; communist universalism and territorial revanchism would eventually make an explosive mix. The fundamental cleavage was between the haves and the have-nots—between those countries that seemed to rule the earth and those that felt deprived of their share of it.[9]

This cleavage was so profound because size and strength seemed to correlate closely in the twentieth century. Countries that controlled huge empires, or huge continents, could exploit their markets, resources, and population. Smaller powers would struggle to compete in a world where weakness could bring defeat, humiliation, and revolution. World War I had proven the point. Britain never could have prevailed without the sustenance provided by its empire, while the blockade of Germany had shown that physical control of food and resources was paramount. During the 1930s, Japan's leaders—who studied Germany's fate closely—began to lust after a "great economic bloc" in East Asia.[10] "There was a pronounced military weakness in those states which depended for their existence on foreign trade," Hitler agreed. "The only remedy" was "acquisition of greater living space."[11]

It wouldn't have been the *only* remedy in a better-led world. After World War II, the United States would create an international order in which states like Japan and Germany could achieve security and prosperity without expansion, because an open global economy provided markets and materials, while American-led alliances provided peace. Yet there was no one to play this role a generation earlier. A disengaged United States had the power but not the interest, while a depleted Britain had the interest but not the power. Mighty, insecure countries were left to their own devices—Japan's security, the government proclaimed in 1935, depended "entirely on the actual power of the empire"—which encouraged their most Hobbesian impulses.[12] A world between hegemons was a terribly brutish place.

Meanwhile, the breakdown of global trade during the Great Depression—another product of this vacuum of international leadership—made everything worse. Economic warfare augured military warfare; as markets slammed shut and tariffs rose, so did the premium on creating self-sustaining empires. Japan was the most extreme case. After Washington imposed the drastic Smoot–Hawley tariff in 1930, Japanese exports dropped by half, social and political conflict surged, extreme nationalism flourished, and peaceful expansion in China gave way to violent conquest.[13] "The more autarky is regarded as the goal," wrote E. H. Carr, "the larger the units must become."[14]

Most important, dreams of empire were informed by ideologies of conflict. Even before the Depression, an unstable postwar world birthed radicalism and resentment, with countries that had lost that struggle, or felt cheated by the peace, leading the way. Mussolini took Italy down the fascist path in the 1920s. As deprivation fueled desperation in the 1930s, Germany and Japan followed. "It is as though in the space of ten years we had slid back into the Stone Age," wrote Orwell in 1940. "Human types supposedly extinct for centuries, the dancing dervish, the robber chieftain, the Grand Inquisitor, have suddenly reappeared, not as inmates of lunatic asylums, but as the masters of the world."[15]

Because fascism was often so intertwined with racism, the Axis powers eventually would have torn each other to shreds. Even so, the fascist movements of the interwar era shared key characteristics. They subordinated individual rights to a collective will embodied by a visionary leader.[16] They pledged to preserve the racial purity of the nation while also equipping it for the rigors of modern rivalry. They sought to purge their societies of democratic weakness and decadence; they glorified cruelty and terror. "Words are a very beautiful thing," said Mussolini, "but rifles, machine-guns, ships, aeroplanes, and cannon are more beautiful still."[17] In the years before World War II, these countries undertook stunning arms buildups; in 1938, Hitler's Germany spent five times what Wilhelm's Germany had spent at the peak of its naval competition with Britain.[18] Not least, fascist leaders believed that revolution at home preceded revolution abroad. There was an "irreconcilable difference" between "the democracies and our two totalitarian countries," German foreign minister Joachim von Ribbentrop told Mussolini. "This was no accidental war but a question of the determination of one system to destroy the other."[19]

Indeed, if fascism featured a primitive barbarism, it was also a distinctly modern creation. Fascist governments responded to the dislocations of the interwar era by promising followers strength, cohesion, and purpose. Hitler and Mussolini skillfully used radio to expand their reach. Most important, totalitarian rule—"everything in the State, nothing outside the State, nothing against the State," as Mussolini put it—was only possible once governments could reach into every aspect of their citizens' lives.[20] The global horizons the fascist regimes then pursued showed what was possible when extremists took charge of advanced economies and capable states.

Mussolini employed modern methods to revive the "greatness of [the] past."[21] He envisioned a new Roman Empire in the Mediterranean, Middle East, and Africa, and used chemical weapons and terror bombing to subdue Abyssinia in 1935–36. Japan sought a "new order" in Asia, beginning its onslaught with the conquest of Manchuria in 1931 and intensifying it, in 1937, with a grinding, brutal war in China. Germany's vision was the most radical. Hitler sought "land for a hundred years" in the east, to crush or cow his democratic rivals in the west, to build an Old World empire that could overmatch America, and to remake the globe geopolitically and racially.[22] The Führer was "no random conqueror, without a plan," Ribbentrop declared. "He was sober in his calculations and was accustomed to think in terms of long periods of time."[23]

In 1940, the fascist powers would unite in the Tripartite Pact, an alliance of countries that hated both democracy and the international status quo. But even before that, the dictators created running room for one another. The success of Italy's Abyssinian campaign in 1935, and the impotence of the League of Nations in halting it, encouraged Hitler's remilitarization of the Rhineland in 1936. Mussolini then backed Hitler's annexations of Austria and Sudeten Czechoslovakia in 1938. Germany's subsequent tear through Europe encouraged Japanese revisionism in Asia. "So well have the aggressor nations mastered the tactics of aggression," U.S. treasury secretary Henry Morgenthau remarked, "that a victory in one part of the world is followed by outbursts of aggression elsewhere."[24]

A crucial reason the international order collapsed so completely is that revisionist powers assaulted it so comprehensively. Which raises another vexing question: Why didn't someone stop them before it was nearly too late?

*

ONE CLUE CAN BE FOUND IN A MEETING ON NOVEMBER 15, 1940. THE location was Berlin. The interlocutors were Hitler and Stalin's foreign minister, Vyacheslav Molotov. The subject was global domination. "Let's divide the whole world," Hitler proposed.[25]

Hitler and Stalin had already divided Europe. Their nonaggression

treaty, the Molotov–Ribbentrop Pact of August 1939, set off a continental war by allowing Germany to invade Poland without fear of Moscow getting in the way. His eastern flank secure, Hitler then turned
west, wiping out Denmark and Norway, the Low Countries, and France
between April and June 1940. Stalin, meanwhile, helped himself to half
of Poland, all three Baltic states, and parts of Finland and Romania,
while providing critical resources—oil, nickel, phosphates, manganese,
lumber, food—for the Nazi war machine. "All the isms," joked a British
official, "are now wasms."[26] Regimes from hostile ideological traditions,
fascism and communism, had found common cause in obliterating the
existing order. Molotov–Ribbentrop Eurasia was paradise for predators: Hitler and Stalin ruled from Siberia to the Atlantic. Hitler now
envisioned something grander.

Germany, Italy, and Japan had recently signed the Tripartite Pact.
Why shouldn't the Soviet Union, another advocate of global revolution,
join the party? If Germany and the Soviets fought "back to back," Hitler
told Molotov, "no power on earth" could beat them. Moscow should aid
the German war effort by pushing south, toward the Indian Ocean and
the Mediterranean. Hitler would focus on destroying Britain. "After the
conquest of England," he promised, its empire could be doled out as "a
gigantic world-wide estate in bankruptcy." A "world coalition" of totalitarian powers would own the earth.[27]

It wasn't to be. Stalin's price—a preponderant position from Finland
to Turkey—was too steep for Hitler, who was contemplating his own
conquests to the east.[28] For all the talk of alliance, Soviet–German tensions were already pulsating throughout the countries between them.
Seven months later, Hitler would launch Operation Barbarossa in a bid
to destroy the Soviet Union and create a totalitarian Eurasia by force.
Still, the Hitler–Molotov meeting indicates a fundamental weakness
of global order in the late 1930s: one of the countries that might have
pushed back against Hitler chose to ally with him instead.

World War I had shown that Eurasian concentrations would eventually meet global resistance. World War II revealed that "eventually"

could be an agonizingly long time. Britain and France didn't declare war on Hitler until September 1939, *after* he had shredded the Treaty of Versailles, taken Austria and the Sudetenland in bloodless coups, occupied the rest of Czechoslovakia, and then invaded Poland. The Grand Alliance that eventually defeated the Axis didn't coalesce until late 1941, *after* Hitler had conquered a continent and Japan was tearing through Asia and the Pacific. "They let us through the danger zone," Hitler's propaganda chief, Joseph Goebbels, later crowed. "And when we were done, and well armed, better than they, then they started the war."[29]

It's not like no one saw it coming. In 1935, the Soviet ambassador in London warned that German rearmament presaged "a new world war."[30] In 1937, amid fascist intervention in Spain and Japanese aggression in China, Franklin Roosevelt deplored a lawless world.[31] French premier Édouard Daladier put it sharply the following year: only the "blind," he told Britain's Neville Chamberlain, could not see that Germany intended to "destroy the equilibrium of Europe."[32]

There had also been opportunities to resist. The League of Nations might have humiliated Italy by imposing harsh economic sanctions during the Abyssinian crisis. Britain and France could have ruined Hitler when he rearmed Germany, marched into the Rhineland, or annexed Austria in 1938. "You might even now arrest this approaching war," declared Winston Churchill, then a backbench parliamentarian, if states threatened by aggression united in a "grand alliance."[33] The most grievous missed opportunity came later that year, at Munich.

Hitler provoked the Munich crisis by demanding a chunk of Czechoslovakia that was heavily populated by German speakers, and then insisting on terms that meant the destruction of the Czech state.[34] Had Britain and France fought, they probably would have won. Germany's vaunted air force, already so feared in Britain, was smaller and weaker than it looked; the awesome panzer armies that humbled France in 1940 did not yet exist. Berlin's finances, strained by Hitler's breakneck rearmament, were precarious. Nervous generals might have overthrown Hitler had he stumbled into war.[35]

Yet London and Paris caved at the last minute, allowing Hitler to annex the Sudetenland, seize its economic and military booty, browbeat other Eastern European states into submission, and give himself crucial advantages for the coming war. "If [Germany] succeeded in this," Daladier had earlier warned Chamberlain, "she would then set about realizing the dream of . . . a Mitteleuropa under German dominance."[36] Hitler himself gloated that the crisis had led to "an enormous improvement in the situation."[37]

Munich was the quintessential case of strategic dominos; the collapse of one position fatally compromised others. It also highlighted the factors that made timely balancing so difficult even as totalitarian pillage became so common.

Start with a failure of geopolitical imagination. Almost anyone could see that Hitler and his ilk were trouble, but who could have known, in 1936 or 1938, just how *much* trouble they would sow? Hitler masterfully exploited this problem by lying about his intentions—arguing that he was simply freeing Germany from an unjust peace, or making one last change to Europe's borders—which encouraged democratic statesmen to conclude that the uncertain consequences of appeasement were less terrible than the grim certainty of a war that resistance would bring. Chamberlain admitted that it made his "blood boil to see Germany getting away with it time after time." Even so, he "could not lightly enter into a conflict which might mean such frightful results."[38]

Related was the shadow of the past. World War I had been so searing that no democratic statesman wished to repeat it. The fact that the war had widely come to be seen, amid the failed peace that followed, as a terrible mistake, compounded that reluctance. Convinced that *nothing* could be worse than reliving World War I, the democracies focused as much on constraining themselves as they did on constraining their enemies. The prevailing view, Roosevelt would say, had been, "Do not do anything, it will mean a general war if you do it." The result was that "the desire for peace led to war."[39]

Additionally, with the status quo strained everywhere, it was hard to hold the line anywhere. By 1939, France had fascists on three frontiers: Germany, Italy, and Spain. Throughout the 1930s, an overstretched Britain—facing Japan in the Far East, Italy in the Mediterranean and Africa, and Germany in Europe—knew that war in one location would create gaping vulnerabilities in others.[40] The multiplicity of challenges empowered the revisionists and wrongfooted their rivals.

Most crippling was a final factor: division prevailed where unity was needed. The ravages of the Great Depression left the Western democracies ideologically polarized and strategically lethargic. The Soviet Union was suffering divisions of a different sort, as Stalin decimated his armed forces, starved his people, and violently purged his suspected enemies—behavior that made many democratic leaders fear Moscow as much as they feared Berlin.

Stalin had certainly killed more people during the 1930s than Hitler. He also shared Hitler's hostility to the European balance of power—which, he remarked, "had hitherto oppressed not only Germany but also the Soviet Union"—if not his urgency in destroying it.[41] His strategy was to make the Soviet Union a socialist superpower in preparation for the showdown with capitalism; his tactics were those of a ruthless opportunist willing to entertain the most improbable alliances until that moment came. Stalin knew Hitler was dangerous; he had waged a proxy conflict against him during Spain's civil war and considered fighting him during the Munich crisis. But after the latter fiasco he opted to buy time and space for a future conflict with Hitler by cutting a deal with Germany instead.[42] A Europe beset by one radicalism might have rallied against it. A Europe buffeted by two radicalisms, fascist and communist, could not keep its balance.

The overseas democracy hardly tried to help. The United States chose to act as though geography guaranteed its security for much of the 1930s, even though Roosevelt, having served as assistant secretary of the navy during World War I, knew it did not. "I have practically no power to make an American effort to prevent such a war from breaking out," he lamented.[43] The United States was militarily inconsequential for most of that decade, spending just 1.5 percent of national income on defense in 1937, as opposed to 28.2 percent by Japan, 23.5 percent by Germany, and 14.5 percent by Italy.[44] The total collapse of global order would eventually force America back into the arena, but only after worsening international conditions had initially convinced most Americans that it was wiser to stay out. So when London and Paris looked for help in the late 1930s, there was no one there. It was "always best and safest," Chamberlain scoffed, "to count on *nothing* from the Americans except words."[45]

The upshot was a cascading commitment problem. American isolation encouraged British appeasement, which left France isolated and made waffling Western democracies look like lousy partners to Stalin. The Germans, too, got the message: there were "no indications" America planned to intervene, Hitler's ambassador in Washington wrote.[46]

The balance of power is not automatic or self-regulating; it can fail catastrophically absent sufficient commitment and common purpose. Later generations would remember *that* lesson. Their tuition was a conflict whose dimensions, and depravity, were unforgettable.

*

HISTORY HAPPENS TWICE, WROTE KARL MARX: "ONCE AS TRAGEDY, AND again as farce." At first glance, World War II looked like a bad remake of World War I. Some of the battlefields were the same. Many of the players were the same. Hitler, as Daladier noted, was seeking Wilhelm's Mitteleuropa and then some. Germany was fighting France and Britain. One might have expected the second Eurasian war to have the same rhythm as the first. It didn't.

From the outset, World War II was distinguished by sheer speed and movement on the battlefield. In September 1939, Hitler thrashed Poland within weeks. After a brief winter respite, he took down most of Western Europe in just over two months; in 1941, he bagged Greece and Yugoslavia before invading the Soviet Union. By that point, Japan had conquered large tracts of mainland Asia; it added prizes from Wake Island to the Indian border in the months after December 1941.

Forces this big had never covered distances this great so quickly. At the high-water mark of the Axis, in early 1942, it seemed entirely possible that tyrannical regimes would rule the supercontinent and, perhaps, the globe. And if the first great war of the Eurasian century had displayed the destructiveness of modern warfare, the second showed the fragility of a world under totalitarian assault.

For one thing, the war revealed a radical compression of time and space. Technology, in shrinking distance, had supercharged aggression. In World War I, technological advances had increased the ferocity, but not the fluidity, of the battlefield. In World War II, new weapons, accompanied by new concepts, revolutionized the fight.

In the Far East, aircraft carrier warfare gave Japan incredible mobile striking power. The Imperial Japanese Navy's main carrier task force, the Kidō Butai, featured flat-topped ships that served as floating runways for deadly fighters, bombers, and torpedo planes. It posed a mortal threat to targets on land and at sea; it could move rapidly, and sometimes stealthily, from one end of an enormous theater to another. The implications became clear when Japan's carrier-based aviation ravaged the U.S. Pacific Fleet at Pearl Harbor, helped seize territories from Southeast Asia to the Central Pacific, bombed northern Australia, and then struck shipping and bases in the Indian Ocean—all in four months between December 1941 and April 1942.[47]

In Europe, blitzkrieg was the key that unlocked a continent. Germany wasn't the only country with tanks and dive bombers in 1940, and its forces weren't as high-tech as retrospective mythmaking has made it seem. What distinguished the Wehrmacht was a doctrine that used armor and air power creatively, to cut through the enemy's lines, ravage his rear, and break the back of his defenses. Mobile radios and a willingness to empower low-level commanders encouraged adaptation and initiative; other innovative approaches, such as airborne assaults, completed the package. Blitzkrieg was tailor-made to destroy enemies with limited strategic depth or an inability to cope with the chaos it sowed. France's formidable land force "has ceased to be an army," marveled one observer as Hitler's tanks rolled through that country. "It has been transformed into separate clots."[48]

To be sure, Hitler's conquests weren't inevitable. Great wars could still turn on the smallest things. Hitler's romp through Western Europe was such a shock because Germany was *not* obviously superior to the Allies; it had fewer tanks, aircraft, and divisions on the western front than Britain and France. What allowed the Wehrmacht to break French defenses, and the European balance of power, was a collection of contingent events: a heroic crossing of the Meuse River, under murderous fire, by a single German unit; the Allies' failure to bomb and strafe gridlocked German columns in the Ardennes Forest; the combination of bad luck and bad intelligence that allowed Hitler's armored spearhead to strike a weak spot in the French line, fatally unhinging Allied defenses and opening the road to Paris.[49]

The fall of France also revealed that conquest could be cumulative because aggression could pay. In 1937, Germany's top military officer, General Ludwig Beck, cautioned that "the Reich possessed neither the economic nor the military base to fight a major war."[50] Hitler solved that problem through smash-and-grab economics: dashing to rearm before his enemies, then robbing countries whose resources could be added to Germany's own. He used the annexation of Austria and Czechoslovakia to stave off economic disaster by seizing their money, raw materials, and labor. From Czechoslovakia, he also grabbed 1.5 million rifles, 2,000 field guns, 750 aircraft, and 600 tanks.[51]

That booty, combined with resources Hitler acquired from Stalin, helped create the military that terrorized Western Europe, which Germany then stripped bare through resource extraction, slave labor, and onerous occupation taxes. Said Hermann Göring, head of the Luftwaffe and then-chief of Hitler's war economy, "I intend to plunder, and plunder copiously."[52] This strategic Ponzi scheme couldn't work forever. But it worked well enough, for a time, to allow a single country to seize most of Western Eurasia.

Policies of extraction and exploitation illustrated something even darker, which was that a totalitarian Eurasia would be a strategic and moral cataclysm for the world. "The war of Greater East Asia is truly a war to destroy evil and to make justice manifest," declared Tojo.[53] Nothing was further from the truth.

When Japanese forces took Nanking in 1937, they murdered perhaps 200,000 civilians. Later, Tokyo implemented a "three-all" policy—kill all, burn all, destroy all—that depopulated parts of China by nearly half.[54] Sexual and economic enslavement, chemical and biological warfare, and the widespread murder of prisoners were pervasive in Japan's Asia, monuments to a policy that fused convictions of racial supremacy to visions of geopolitical splendor.

Germany outdid Japan. The killing of 6 million Jews and the enslavement of some 8 million "guest workers" showed how Hitler's Europe would be run. Hitler planned to wage a war of outright extermination against his erstwhile ally, the Soviet Union, by starving people in occupied areas. "Many tens of millions of people in this territory will become superfluous and will die or must emigrate to Siberia," German officials wrote.[55]

Genocide and geopolitics were evil cousins; policies of elimination would clear the living space Hitler wanted, while removing unwanted racial elements that might sap Germany's strength. "If there were no more Jews in Europe," said Hitler, "the unity of the European states would no longer be disrupted."[56] And given that most European Jews lived outside Germany, conquest was necessary to bring them into Hitler's grasp. These practices proved the potential for industrial-scale murder by a government that married efficiency to extremism. They were also a warning, said Churchill in 1941, of the horrors that would befall "all the continents of the globe" if Hitler triumphed.[57]

By this point, World War I had become an object lesson in how quickly moral constraints dropped away in a zone of total war. On the battlefield, the scale of conquest exposed areas—and populations—of unprecedented size to rampaging armies that aimed to destroy societies after defeating their military defenders. Above the battlefield, air power opened up new possibilities of laying waste to a nation's economy, and terrorizing its citizens, without ever controlling its territory. The Axis were first-movers; the bombing of major cities in Spain and China in the 1930s opened the age of aerial massacre. But the democracies, following the merciless logic of industrial war, soon became experts in delivering death from above.[58]

Finally, World War II demonstrated, even in its early years, how easily insecurity would shoot outward once the Eurasian balance was overturned. Having overrun Europe, Germany was threatening the United Kingdom, the Middle East, North Africa, and the Mediterranean. From French and Norwegian bases, German U-boats were waging a Battle of the Atlantic that left Britain struggling to survive. And after Germany absorbed its conquests, it could become a global superpower: "When we are masters of Europe," predicted Hitler, "we have a dominant position in the world."[59] Once Japan used its carrier-based air power to hit Hawaii in December 1941, it confirmed, not at all hypothetically, that Eurasian hegemony had become a platform for global expansion—and capped off a dizzying series of events that brought countries nearly everywhere into a frenzy of violence.

*

IN HINDSIGHT, THIS GLOBALIZATION OF THE WAR SEEMS INEVITABLE: countries that try to conquer the world end up fighting most of it. Yet if the Axis eventually provoked the grandest, most ideologically diverse, coalition in history, things didn't *have* to turn out this way.

The wartime alignments had shifted as dizzyingly as the battlefield between 1939 and 1941. What began as a conflict in which France and Britain faced Germany turned into a conflict in which Italy and Germany fought Britain after France fell, and then one in which the Soviet Union, America, and Britain fought the Axis—though Moscow abstained, until 1945, from fighting Japan. Different choices along the way might have yielded radically different outcomes.

In early 1940, Britain and France considered attacking the Soviet

Union, which had invaded democratic Finland and was effectively in league with Hitler. "We may very soon find ourselves at war with Russia," Britain's First Lord of the Admiralty wrote.[60] The Grand Alliance might never have formed had Britain surrendered later in 1940, thereby depriving the democracies of the base from which they would bust back into an occupied Europe. A year after that, two regional wars might not have merged had America not forced a showdown with Japan amid rising tensions with Germany—or had Hitler not then responded by declaring war on America. The globalization of the war wasn't just destiny. It demonstrates how key leaders and decisions shaped the geopolitics of a collapsing world.[61]

There was no guarantee that Britain would keep fighting once France collapsed; a faction led by the foreign secretary, Lord Halifax, favored exploring a compromise peace. After all, the threat of invasion was real; only an improvised evacuation from France had saved Britain's army. The U-boat war was intensifying, and Italy was attacking British supply lines in the Mediterranean. Britain confronted the "collapse of large-scale military opposition to Germany in continental Europe," wrote one minister, and "the prospect that . . . the full-fury of the German onslaught will be turned against these Islands."[62] Britain's survival hinged on geography, which placed its homeland beyond the immediate reach of Hitler's armies; naval superiority, which shielded those islands from invasion; technology, namely the advances in radar that helped the Royal Air Force control the skies above; and the personality of a new prime minister whose leadership amplified these advantages.[63]

Winston Churchill seemed ripped from an earlier era. He was "an adventurist on a historical scale," wrote one contemporary, "a romantic of British imperialism and war."[64] Yet Churchill was suited to his defining moment. Born to a British father and an American mother, he embodied the transatlantic unity that represented his country's best hope of salvation. His military ideas were sometimes amateurish, but his understanding of the war's stakes was acute. Not least, Churchill had a rare mix of eloquence and indefatigability. He was, wrote one colleague, "the man, and the only man we have, for this hour."[65]

His initial contribution was chiefly psychological. Churchill first rebuffed Halifax, pointing out that any peace with Hitler was merely a stay of execution. He subsequently declared that Britain would fight on, whatever the cost, until "the New World, with all its power and might, steps forth to the rescue and the liberation of the old"—a plea for American intervention, but also an assurance that London would not, by surrendering, squander any support Washington might extend.[66] Most of all, Churchill called forth British courage by explaining why resistance was essential—because otherwise the world would "sink into the abyss of a new Dark Age"—and by promising that, if Britain could avoid losing, it might eventually win. "Hitler knows that he will have to break us in this Island," Churchill declared, "or lose the war."[67]

Hitler did not break the British. Between July and October 1940, the Spitfires and Hurricanes of the RAF narrowly beat the Fokkers and Messerschmitts of the Luftwaffe in the Battle of Britain. German errors helped; Hitler's impulsive decision to shift his attacks from pounding the RAF to bombing cities terrorized Britain's population but gave its aerial defenders a badly needed respite.[68] That victory forestalled the immediate threat of invasion, and showed the world that Hitler was not invincible. Yet Britain was still at risk of running out of food, if Hitler's submarines cut its maritime lifelines, or running out of money. The threat of a "swift overwhelming blow," noted Churchill, had given way to a "long, gradually maturing danger."[69] There was also the unanswered question of how, exactly, Britain would claw its way back.

Securing allies was indispensable: without U.S. cooperation, British military chiefs wrote, "the hope of victory is remote."[70] More immediately, Churchill hoped that Stalin might betray Hitler, since the goals of one revolutionary, expansionist regime must eventually threaten the survival of another. In June 1940, Churchill even dashed off a message to Stalin, emphasizing the common threat—"the prospect of Germany establishing a hegemony over the Continent"—and proposing that London and Moscow, anchoring Europe's "extremities," crush Hitler in between them.[71]

Stalin, then profiting handsomely from his alliance with Hitler, made no reply. Yet Churchill was onto something. By late 1940, the gangsters' pact was unraveling, not least because Hitler, momentarily stymied by British resilience in the west, was seeking a solution in the east.

Hitler's invasion of the Soviet Union in June 1941 was a long time coming; it was part of his program to build a formidable empire by seizing immense lands and resources. "What India was for England," he said, "the territories of Russia will be for us."[72] Yet Hitler also believed that the road to London ran through Moscow, because the hope of Soviet intervention was keeping Britain in the war. "England has thus far always conducted her wars with help from the Continent," he told Mussolini.[73] Defeating Britain meant destroying the prospect of Soviet succor.

This gamble almost worked, in part because Stalin dismissed Churchill's warnings of impending attack as typical capitalist treachery. An unprepared Red Army, confronting a then-unrivaled Wehrmacht, lost millions of men; by late fall Hitler's tanks and troops occupied a line from Leningrad to Rostov. Only winter and a thrown-together defense of Moscow saved Stalin's regime, and this after Germany had lost crucial time due to Hitler's indecision about which axis of advance to emphasize. "The beginning of every war is like opening the door to a dark room," Hitler had said—and this invasion, indeed, had surprising effects.[74]

Stalin reinvented himself as a patriot and savior of the nation whose population he had terrorized. "The issue is whether the peoples of the Soviet Union shall remain free or fall into slavery," he declared.[75] The Soviet–British alliance went from an impossibility to a reality: "To crush Germany," Churchill had remarked, "I am prepared to enter into an alliance with anyone, even the devil!"[76] Most important, the Soviet stand outside Moscow had been aided by the timely delivery of tanks, trucks, fuel, and other supplies from Washington, revealing the extent to which America had, once again, become the arbiter of Europe's war.

*

NEARLY EVERYONE KNEW, BY MID-1941, THAT THE MOST DISTANT power was also, potentially, the most decisive. A U.S. declaration of war,

Stalin told American envoy Harry Hopkins, was "the one thing that could defeat Hitler, and perhaps without ever firing a shot."[77] Hitler, too, was watching Washington; his attack on the Soviet Union was meant to pre-empt the American threat. Yet if a successful assault might have deterred U.S. involvement, a failed assault hastened it.

Franklin Roosevelt was an unlikely war chief. His physical infirmi-ties, the result of adult-onset polio, caused others to underestimate him: Mussolini called Roosevelt a "paralytic who when he wants to go to the toilet or dinner must be assisted by other men."[78] But FDR, perhaps the shrewdest operator ever to occupy the Oval Office, never underes-timated *his* enemies, even when isolationist sentiment constrained him from confronting them. Roosevelt had long viewed Hitler as "a portent of evil"; he understood that regimes rooted in hatred and violence would export those miseries to the world.[79] "The Axis proclaims that there can be no ultimate peace between their ... philosophy of government and our philosophy of government," he said in 1940.[80] As the world caught fire, FDR sought to convince his countrymen that America couldn't just let it burn.

That education campaign gained urgency with the fall of France, which left Britain's fleet as the sole barrier between Germany and the Western Hemisphere. In speeches, fireside chats broadcast over the radio, and press conferences, FDR explained why regimes that had con-quered Eurasia would keep going: "It may be human nature for victors of that kind to say, 'I have taken two-thirds of the world and I am all armed and ready to go, why shouldn't I go the whole hog and control ... the last third of the world, the Americas?'"[81] He channeled Mackinder in argu-ing that primacy on land presaged primacy at sea: "If the world outside of the Americas falls under Axis domination," Germany's shipbuilding potential would be "two or three times greater" than that of the Western Hemisphere—"enough to win."[82] And he anticipated Spykman, argu-ing that Germany might use its newfound economic clout to handcuff South American countries to Berlin.[83]

In an Axis-led world, said FDR, the American people would be "lodged in prison, handcuffed, hungry, and fed through the bars from day to day by the contemptuous, unpitying masters of other continents."[84] Even if the country endured, its freedoms wouldn't: "To survive in such a world, we would have to convert ourselves permanently into a militaristic power on the basis of war economy."[85] A naked, friendless America might have to destroy itself to defend itself.

Many Americans disagreed. During the 1930s, Congress had legislated isolation in the guise of neutrality. Strict laws prohibited Washington from selling arms to belligerents or otherwise aiding countries at war. The start of World War II unleashed another angry domestic debate. Critics such as the aviator Charles Lindbergh warned that involvement in the "eternal wars in Europe" was pointless, and that America was being duped by desperate Jews and scheming Brits.[86] Leading intellectuals, as well as high-ranking military officials, argued that a properly prepared America could defend the Western Hemisphere against a hostile world, and that aiding Britain might squander tools Washington needed for itself.[87] Above all, anti-interventionists deemed a war to save democracy a contradiction in terms. Conscription and other coercive measures "will slit the throat of the last great democracy still living," thundered Senator Burton Wheeler. "It will accord to Hitler his greatest and cheapest victory."[88] It was another round in the great American debate—whether the country's way of life was more likely to be endangered by getting into Eurasia's wars or staying out of them.

Roosevelt's task, then, was to bring a divided country into a fragmenting world *before* Axis exploits made reentry prohibitive. His strategy involved moving opinion while never outrunning it. "It is a terrible thing to look over your shoulder when you are trying to lead," he said, "and find no one there."[89]

FDR framed his policies, such as loosening the Neutrality Acts to permit arms sales to the Allies, or rearming America through an unprecedented peacetime buildup, as ways to avoid war. He extended aid through unorthodox arrangements, such as trading a submarine-stricken Britain old American destroyers in exchange for rights to build

military bases on British possessions from Newfoundland to the Caribbean. Roosevelt's boldest idea was the Lend-Lease program, which simply gave arms and other supplies to a cash-strapped London and later
Moscow; his homely analogies made the radical seem commonsensical.
A man whose neighbor's house is burning doesn't sell him a hose, Roosevelt explained; he lets him use the hose lest his own home be consumed.
In the meantime, FDR secured an unprecedented third term, bending
the norms of democracy at home in hopes of preserving it in the world.[90]

By late 1941, the United States had become the "arsenal of
democracy"—a country not yet in the war, but influencing its course.
America was, once again, making itself a military superpower: in 1940,
FDR had authorized production of 50,000 airplanes per year, while the
U.S. Navy issued orders for 9 battleships, 11 aircraft carriers, 8 heavy
cruisers, 31 light cruisers, and 181 destroyers. The U.S. Navy was convoying merchant ships in the Atlantic; FDR had adopted a "shoot on
sight" policy toward Nazi submarines.[91] "Compliance with this order,"
wrote Admiral William Leahy, Roosevelt's chief of staff, "will undoubtedly result in a state of undeclared war with the Axis powers."[92] And if
FDR never moved fast enough to satisfy Churchill, he went far enough
to antagonize Hitler.

Roosevelt viewed Hitler "with fanatical hatred," wrote Germany's
ambassador in Washington.[93] Hitler himself termed Lend-Lease an "act
of war."[94] Washington and Berlin were on a collision course for the same
reason as in 1917: sustenance from across the seas was keeping Germany's foes alive. Yet neither Roosevelt nor Hitler was itching for a fight—
the former because most Americans still hoped to help *others* defeat
Germany, the latter because U.S. power had doomed Berlin before. So
even as incidents at sea accumulated, Hitler restrained his U-boat commanders in hopes of delaying America's intervention, while also trying
to distract it by goading another U.S. antagonist, on another side of the
world, to strike.[95]

U.S.–Japan relations had been deteriorating due to the war in
China. "Unless we are prepared . . . to withdraw bag and baggage" from

Asia, wrote U.S. ambassador Joseph Grew, "a head-on clash" was coming.[96] As in the Atlantic, though, neither side was eager to brawl. Tokyo understood it was dwarfed economically; by 1941, America's GNP was *twelve times* Japan's.[97] FDR knew that Hitler was the greater danger. "I simply have not got enough Navy to go round," he remarked.[98] So Roosevelt, through 1940, gave only limited aid to Chiang Kai-shek's government in China, imposed modest economic sanctions on Tokyo, and held in reserve weapons—namely an outright oil embargo—that would be more damaging but also more provocative.

Yet war occurred, thanks to a sequence of events that started in Europe, reverberated in Asia, and then came full circle. Hitler's victories of 1940 tempted Japan to ally with Germany and Italy, and to push south into Indochina at the expense of a defeated France, a desperate Britain, and a distracted America.[99] Yet if Japanese officials believed the Tripartite Pact would deter Washington, they miscalculated; it simply confirmed that Tokyo had joined the jackals that were ruining the world.[100] When Tokyo occupied southern Indochina in mid-1941, America responded with a full oil embargo and freeze of Japanese assets. The sanctions underscored that the resource-devouring war in China had, ironically, *deepened* Japan's dependence on American oil, scrap metal, and aviation fuel. So the embargo triggered a countdown to the immobilization of Japan's war machine—and to an offensive aimed at seizing the oil of Southeast Asia, while simultaneously neutralizing the U.S. fleet with an attack on Pearl Harbor.[101]

"What a reckless war that would be!" Emperor Hirohito had earlier exclaimed.[102] Admiral Yamamoto Isoroku, the architect of the Pearl Harbor attack, agreed: "Anyone who has seen the auto factories in Detroit and the oil fields in Texas knows that Japan lacks the national power for a naval race with America."[103] But Japanese leaders believed that the alternative to expansion was suffocation. They were unwilling to accept humiliation and retrenchment as the price of peace. Tokyo also had a window of military opportunity—it possessed ten aircraft carriers to Washington's three in the Pacific—which would slam shut as American industry churned out ships.[104] So Tokyo risked everything in a bid to smash U.S. naval power and then create a Fortress Pacific—an imposing set of island strongpoints—that an effete, democratic America would shrink from confronting head-on. It was a commentary on the country's political culture, and no less on the nature of twentieth-century geopolitics, that Japan preferred the possibility of national destruction to the loss of Asian empire.

What had FDR been thinking in bringing matters to a head? The fact that he pursued policies sure to provoke Japan while dealing with a greater threat from Germany horrified some of his own aides, most notably George Marshall, the army chief of staff.[105] Perhaps Roosevelt, the master of manipulation, was seeking a "back door" into war in Europe—which Hitler opened for him four days after Pearl Harbor. The reality, though, is simpler; FDR worried that the status quo had been shaken so thoroughly that further aggression, in any theater, might shatter it entirely.

"The hostilities in Europe, in Africa and in Asia are all parts of a single world conflict," Roosevelt believed; interlocking programs of regional aggrandizement were now destabilizing the globe.[106] He also feared that allowing China to be defeated would free Japanese forces to invade, and perhaps finish off, an already struggling Soviet Union. So Roosevelt drew the line, while leaving the final decision to Tokyo. He wanted Japan to fire "the first shot without allowing too much danger to ourselves."[107] The attack on Pearl Harbor, which eviscerated a napping Pacific Fleet—but fortuitously spared America's absent aircraft carriers—exceeded the cost Roosevelt had hoped to pay. But it did create instant consensus for war with Japan and, once Hitler made his move, with Germany as well.

The connections between theaters were profound, even if the trade-offs were real. Hitler's defeat of France had pushed Japan into the Tripartite Pact, Southeast Asia, and conflict with Washington. America had begun to rearm mostly due to gains by Germany, yet in doing so created a closing window of opportunity for Japan. Hitler sought to goad Tokyo into attacking America, then declared war once he believed Pearl

Harbor had achieved that effect. "This was a heavy blow for America and worse even for England," Ribbentrop exulted. "It represented the most important event . . . since the beginning of the war."[108] By December 1941, there were no purely regional crises. Events and choices ricocheted wildly in a conflict-plagued world.

*

AFTER PEARL HARBOR, CHURCHILL LATER WROTE, HE "SLEPT THE SLEEP of the saved and thankful." The war was over, except for the fighting: "Hitler's fate was sealed. Mussolini's fate was sealed. As for the Japanese, they would be ground to powder. All the rest was merely the proper application of overwhelming force."[109] Looking at the eventual production statistics, that seems right. By 1943, America's industrial output was four times Germany's; the Allies produced 151,000 planes to Germany's 43,000.[110] Hitler was now fighting a Grand Alliance featuring America, Russia, and Britain—"the greatest concentration of power," bragged Churchill, "that the world had ever seen."[111] Yet Churchill wasn't sleeping as soundly as he later claimed, because for a year after Pearl Harbor, the outcome was very much in doubt.

It wasn't so obvious at the time that the Axis powers were doomed economically. A Greater Germany encompassing most of Europe would have had a population and a GDP larger than that of the United States, and all the components—heavy industry, raw materials, abundant labor—of a "mighty economic bloc."[112] Japan was seizing the oil, rubber, and other resources of Southeast Asia. "Up to 1942," writes Richard Overy, "the balance favored the aggressor and might well have allowed them to win before American economic power could be placed in the scales."[113] The crucial question was whether the Axis could bar the doors to conquered regions before the Allies could push back in.

The answer was unclear in Europe and the Middle East. "Everything is terrible," Roosevelt wrote in late 1941.[114] The Soviets were barely surviving; renewed Nazi offensives in 1942 put Stalingrad and the indispensable Caucasus oil fields in peril. Germany controlled the eastern

Mediterranean after taking Greece in 1941 and Tobruk in 1942; Hitler sensed the "goddess of victory" as General Erwin Rommel's panzer armies advanced on Egypt.[115] Already relegated to the margins of Europe, the Allies were in danger of losing the surrounding outposts and supply lines they needed if they were ever to return.

They were also at risk of losing the Atlantic. Hitler's unconstrained U-boats prowled the waters of the Western Hemisphere; a pitifully unprepared America failed to take elementary steps such as blacking out cities on the East Coast. The slaughter in the sea lanes was unrelenting, and by December 1942, Britain had only two months of fuel left for its ships.[116] The situation in the Arctic was just as bad, as Nazi raiders and bombers operating out of Norway pulverized Allied convoys to Archangel. One of those convoys, PQ 17, lost 23 of its 34 ships, along with the 3,350 vehicles, 430 tanks, and 210 bombers aboard them. Superior power was no guarantee of victory if that power never reached the battlefield. Wrote Churchill to Roosevelt: "The oceans, which were your shield, threaten to become your cage."[117]

Then there was the Pacific. The Allies initially hoped merely to hold there, so they could focus on Germany. "The Japanese are not going to allow us to 'hold,'" Chief of Naval Operations Admiral Ernest King corrected, "but are going to drive and drive hard."[118] In four months after Pearl Harbor, Japan overran Singapore and the Philippines, Southeast Asia from Burma to New Guinea, and the Pacific almost to the International Date Line without losing a single major ship. "The whole world will revolve around our empire," one Japanese admiral exulted.[119] Hawaii and California's vital aircraft plants were vulnerable; Australia, the key base for any counteroffensive, was "beset grievously," that country's prime minister wrote.[120]

Victory in World War II was *not* just a matter of industrial arithmetic. The Grand Alliance had to blunt offensives by forces better trained, equipped, and seasoned than their own. They had to defend global supply lines and move forces across perilous watery expanses. They had to seize contested airspace above Europe and the Pacific; they had to conduct dozens of contested amphibious landings to reverse Axis gains and reach the heart of their enemies' power. "This war is a new kind of war," said Roosevelt. It encompassed "every continent, every island, every sea, every air-lane in the world." Yes, the Allies had "great reservoirs of power." But that wouldn't matter if they were "cut off from each other" or confounded by the challenges of global war.[121]

Making matters worse, America's supposedly limitless power was still quite finite. Into 1941, FDR hadn't even envisioned sending U.S. troops to Europe.[122] The United States lacked the shipping to carry armies to England or hostile beaches beyond. The armadas of bombers that would pulverize Japan and Germany were still being built. America had gargantuan military *potential*, Churchill noted, but limited military *power*: "We both of us have much to learn in the cruel art of war."[123]

That education might have been crueler had the Axis been smarter. Had Hitler accepted fascist Spain's offer to enter the war in mid-1940, the Axis might have taken Gibraltar, closed the Mediterranean, and routed Britain in North Africa.[124] Had Japan and Germany teamed up against the Soviet Union in 1941, the democracies might have faced a consolidated Eurasia. In December 1941, a modest Japanese force might have seized lightly defended Oahu, pushing America back to its West Coast.[125] None of these things happened; all were entirely conceivable.

The worst scenario involved an Axis thrust in the Middle East and the Indian Ocean. The Japanese panicked Churchill in April 1942 by unleashing their aircraft carriers in the Indian Ocean.[126] Around that time, Germany was approaching the Middle East through North Africa and the Caucasus. If the Wehrmacht punched through, FDR worried, that meant "joining hands between Germany and Japan and the probable loss of the Indian Ocean."[127] An Axis link-up would cut off Australia from Britain, sever links to China and the Soviet Union, deliver Middle Eastern oil into enemy hands, and effectively isolate the several theaters in which the Grand Alliance was fighting. Winning a global war required the ability to communicate and move worldwide—so the most dangerous enemy operations were those that might rip the Grand Alliance apart.

————

THE ALLIES DIDN'T AVERT THAT DANGER BY MUCH. IT WASN'T OVER-whelming force that allowed an outnumbered U.S. fleet, equipped with inferior aircraft, to win the Battle of Midway in June 1942, halting Japan's offensive and preserving the lifeline to Australia. Rather, the United States ambushed and sank four Japanese carriers thanks to codebreakers who pinpointed the coming attack and pilots who delivered their bombs with deadly accuracy at a crucial moment. "With a little ill-fortune the reverse might have taken place," said Marshall, and "the whole of the west coast of America" would have been exposed.[128]

The counterpart to Midway on the eastern front—the Battle of Stalingrad between mid-1942 and February 1943—wasn't a sure thing, either. The battle was part of Hitler's "win the war" thrust into the Caucasus. It culminated with intense combat in streets, houses, and factories; it devolved into a grueling death-match between undersup-plied, exhausted armies. It took tremendous courage from the defend-ers, sometimes fighting with knives and bayonets, to blunt Nazi attacks, infuriate a stubborn Hitler, and set the stage for the winter encircle-ment of Germany's Sixth Army—a reversal of fortunes that shifted the momentum of the eastern war. Yet if the margins at Stalingrad and Midway were narrow, these victories were part of a broader trend.

In crucial battles between mid-1942 and mid-1943—Coral Sea, Midway, and Guadalcanal in the Pacific, Stalingrad and Kursk on the eastern front, El-Alamein in Egypt and the U.S. landings in Morocco and Algeria, the struggle in the Atlantic, and others—the Allies held areas they could not do without and began offensive operations of their own. "The days of plugging holes are over," wrote British military lead-ers. The objective now was "victory, quickly and decisively."[129]

Victory wasn't quick, but it was decisive. In 1943–44, Allied operations—the island-hopping campaign toward Japan, the clearing of North Africa and the invasion of Italy, epic battles up and down the eastern front, and an intensifying war in the air—gradually tightened the noose. Finally, in 1944–45, the Allies converged on battered foes from multiple directions and domains. Berlin and Tokyo were crushed more thoroughly than the Central Powers had been a generation before; they surrendered after history's most total, most consuming conflict.

The task had been herculean. The Soviet Union mobilized over 30 million military personnel, first to defend a line stretching from Scandinavia to the Caucasus, and then to beat German armies all the way back to Berlin; the final offensive alone employed 6.7 million soldiers. To seize command of the oceans, the United States built 141 aircraft carriers, 807 cruisers, destroyers, and destroyer escorts, and 203 submarines, plus thousands of transport vessels, between 1940 and 1945. To win a multi-continent air war, it churned out 324,750 aircraft. Britain mobilized more than half of its population for military service or the war industries.[130] World War II was humanity's worst crime and greatest achievement. This mobilization of human and economic resources was unprecedented.

So was the geographical scale of the fighting. At the Battle of Kursk in 1943, some 7,000 German and Soviet tanks brawled in an area equivalent to half of England.[131] The Battle of the Philippine Sea in 1944 involved 24 U.S. and Japanese aircraft carriers, plus other forces that converged from the Philippines, Hawaii, and points beyond. The war itself created a "super-battlefield" that spanned four oceans, six continents, and nine major fronts.[132] All of this meant that feats of logistics, intelligence, and coalition management were as important as feats of arms.

The most iconic battle—the Allied assault on Normandy in June 1944—captures the enormity of the challenges. Over 130,000 troops from three nations hit five separate beaches, with more than 20,000 paratroopers preceding them, nearly 7,000 ships supporting the invasion, and 11,590 aircraft flying nearly 15,000 sorties to clear the way.[133] And Operation Overlord, the largest amphibious attack in history, was just the tip of a military, logistical, and economic iceberg.

The invasion was possible only after the Allies had routed the

Luftwaffe from the skies over France; after they had built up enormous fleets of warships and transports; after they had turned Britain into a giant base for armies and air forces; after they had secured Atlantic and Mediterranean sea lanes; after they had gained hard-earned experience in Africa and Italy; and after they had mounted one of the most intricate campaigns of deception in the annals of warfare. The invasion itself was synchronized with a huge Soviet offensive from Estonia to Romania; it presaged the flow of 2.5 million men, half a million vehicles, and 4 million tons of supplies across the Channel in the months that followed. Even the hard-to-impress Stalin admired the audacity: "The history of war had never seen such a grandiose operation," he said.[134]

The commander of Overlord, General Dwight Eisenhower, never thought its success was inevitable; he preemptively composed a message accepting blame for its failure. For a few agonizing hours on June 6, 1944, Ike's troops were at risk of being thrown back into the sea at Omaha Beach. The key battles of World War II were costly, contingent affairs. Yet the countries of the Grand Alliance won enough of them to turn the tide, close the ring, and pound their enemies into submission. So what allowed them to win a resounding victory just three years after they had stared defeat in the face?

*

SIZE DID MATTER. SO LONG AS THE ALLIES DIDN'T LOSE WHEN THEY WERE most vulnerable, they would probably win. The fact that the Axis had made enemies almost everywhere forced Berlin and Tokyo to disperse their forces rather than concentrating them decisively. It left them surrounded by foes committed to their destruction: if the Germans wanted a "war of extermination," Stalin declared, "they shall have it!"[135] It also brought them into an existential cage-match with America, a country whose unrivaled economy allowed it to singlehandedly outproduce its rivals, and whose geography made it nearly invulnerable to attack.

Hitler "did not yet know" how to beat America, he admitted after declaring war on that country.[136] He never figured it out. American production gradually got rolling, thanks to a system in which government generously funded and regulated the wartime economy, while also exploiting the magic of the market by mostly leaving industry in private hands.[137] Once U.S. industry hit overdrive, the Atlantic was secured, and Axis economies were being bludgeoned by bombs and blockades, the gap in power became unbridgeable.

In 1944, U.S. shipyards launched 2,247 naval vessels, more than every other country combined. By 1945, America's economic output was three times that of the entire Axis. American industry didn't just supply American forces; the U.S. shipped its allies, principally Britain and the Soviet Union, over 37,000 tanks and 792,000 trucks, 43,000 aircraft, food, fuel, artillery, and ammunition.[138] "The most important things in this war are machines," said Stalin. "The United States ... is a country of machines."[139]

Numerical superiority didn't guarantee victory, but it gave the Allies a margin for error that the Axis lacked. "I cannot understand these Americans," one German commander in Normandy lamented. "Each night we know that we have cut them to pieces, inflicted heavy casualties, mowed down their transport. But—in the morning, we are suddenly faced with fresh battalions, with complete replacements of men, machines, food, tools, and weapons."[140] It was the same story on battlefields around the world.

Yet it wasn't just the mass of the Grand Alliance that mattered; it was also the composition. The alliance had the total package: continental powers that could deny Germany and Japan a free hand within Eurasia, as well as offshore powers that could dominate the air and sea.

Today, most Americans don't know much about the Soviet role in World War II, but they should. The war in the east was incomprehensibly vicious—perhaps one in eight Soviet citizens died—and almost incomparably important. Stalin's armies tied down 75–80 percent of German manpower and inflicted 80 percent of German casualties; they consumed resources Hitler might have used to wage the Battle of the Atlantic or bolster Fortress Europe.[141] This is why Roosevelt placed such overriding priority on keeping the Red Army going. The United States delivered a quarter of the vehicles and much of the gas that helped Stalin's forces defend Moscow in December 1941; at Stalingrad, half of the vehicles Germany faced were made in the USA.[142] A communist army rode Dodges, Studebakers, Fords, and other monuments to American capitalism to victory. "Nothing would be worse than to have the Russians collapse," FDR explained. Only so long as Eurasia stayed divided could the democracies hope to win.[143]

Whereas World War II made the Soviet Union a land power without equal, a corrupt and divided China was no one's idea of a steamroller. But Chiang's regime anchored the Grand Alliance in Asia simply by refusing to die. China faced more Japanese forces than America did in all but one year of the war; its resistance, at a total cost of perhaps 14 million lives, kept Tokyo from pushing deeper into mainland Asia or pivoting more decisively to the Pacific. If "Russia's geographical and manpower position were . . . vital to the defeat of Germany," said King, "so China's geographical position and manpower were vital to the defeat of Japan."[144] FDR gave Chiang just enough support—a mere sliver of Lend-Lease aid—to keep him fighting, even when doing so required fraught, and often fatal, cargo flights from India across the Himalayas.

As those flights attested, land power meant little without air and maritime supremacy. A world war was a war of movement; it would be determined by which side could better project power, and deliver destruction, over unprecedented distances.[145] The Grand Alliance painstakingly won that freedom of movement, while denying it to the Axis. Air and sea dominance held a globe-spanning coalition together, while breaking its opponents apart.

In the Pacific, America waged a war of movement par excellence. Tokyo's theory of victory had been to wreck the U.S. fleet and then make the Pacific a Japanese lake guarded by impregnable strongpoints. Washington defeated that theory by surging back onto the offensive sooner than Tokyo anticipated, and by devising a strategy that bypassed the most heavily defended islands. That strategy, wrote General Douglas MacArthur, supreme Allied commander in the Southwest Pacific, was designed to "avoid the frontal attack with its terrible loss of life; to bypass Japanese strongpoints and neutralize them by cutting their lines of supply; to thus isolate their armies and starve them on the battlefield; to, as Willie Keeler used to say, 'hit 'em where they ain't.'"[146]

This island-hopping strategy showcased fast-carrier task forces—flat-decked behemoths ringed by cruisers, destroyers, submarines, and supply ships—that ranged the Pacific, raiding enemy bases, protecting amphibious landings, and smashing Japanese air and sea power. It exploited America's investments in logistics to get assault forces to their destinations and then turn freed islands into bases for the next assault—or for the long-range bombers that would raid Japan. U.S. submarines prowled the Pacific, devastating Japan's merchant fleet and putting the home islands on a starvation diet. By 1945, U.S. bombers were incinerating Japanese cities while mining the waters between the home islands. Japan ruled a large empire on the day it surrendered. But that empire was fatally weakened once it could not function as a strategic whole.[147]

The Allies accomplished something similar against Germany, which was remarkable given that Hitler's empire existed mostly on land. The first step was turning the Atlantic into a secure highway rather than a watery grave: "It is in shipping," Churchill had written, "and in the power to transport across the oceans . . . that the crunch of the whole war will be found."[148] As late as February 1943, Hitler's U-boats were winning. But the Allies got the upper hand through a furious fusion of efforts: codebreaking that ferreted out German submarines, development of better radar and sonar technology and more lethal sub-hunting techniques, the ability of U.S. industry to build ships faster than U-boats could sink them. The Allies also used the skies to control the seas. Long-range patrol aircraft closed the deadly "Mid-Atlantic Gap"; airplanes with miniaturized radar pounced on subs that surfaced; Allied bombers struck submarine pens and production plants in Europe; all as Allied convoys fought pitched battles with German wolf packs.[149] By mid-1943, the undersea hunters were dying in droves. America's industry could now determine the outcome on Europe's battlefields.

Meanwhile, the Allied bombing campaign was paralyzing Germany. That campaign was a long, bloody slog; of the 125,000 men who flew for RAF Bomber Command, over half were killed, wounded, or captured.[150] Yet American bombers flying by day and British bombers flying by night kept Hitler's Germany under round-the-clock duress. They severely disrupted German oil supplies and critical industries, and stretched scarce resources by forcing Hitler to defend territory far behind the front lines. By 1943, some 60 percent of Hitler's war economy was devoted to the air battle.[151] "*War has become vertical,*" declared U.S. Army Air Forces Chief General Henry "Hap" Arnold. "We are demonstrating daily that it is possible to descend from the skies into any part of the interior of any enemy nation and destroy its power to continue the conflict."[152] Indeed, the air war allowed the Allies to bring the battle deep into Germany even while they were excluded from Europe. Once they returned to that continent, it helped them win the war on land.

In theory, Hitler had interior lines; he could easily shuttle forces from one point to another. Yet by 1944–45, that wasn't the reality. U.S. and British planes tore up Europe's railroads and mined its rivers; they shredded coal and oil shipments to the front lines; they immobilized the panzer divisions Rommel needed in France after D-Day.[153] By war's end, Germany was struggling to move key units even a few hundred miles, to hold back U.S. forces that had arrived from half a world away. By grabbing "complete air superiority," General Alfred Jodl remarked, the Allies had "altogether decided the war."[154]

When all aspects of the Allied war effort came together, the effect was, quickly, decisive. Following D-Day, the democracies assailed Germany from the west and south, while the Russians chewed up Hitler's armies from the east and U.S. and British air power ground down the Nazi war machine from above. "In closing in on the wild beast," Churchill had exhorted, "all parts of the narrowing circle should be aflame with

Battle."[155] When the Allies did the same to Japan in mid-1945—with the Soviets joining the war in Asia as the United States battered Japan from air and sea—Tokyo surrendered. Modern war demanded the synergistic application of overwhelming power. This underscores another reason the Allies won—because one of the oddest coalitions in history was, somehow, one of the most productive.

*

COALITIONS AS GEOGRAPHICALLY DIVERSE AS THE ONES MACKINDER envisioned are bound to involve some weird combinations. It's not clear, though, that he foresaw anything quite like the Grand Alliance. The Soviet Union envisioned the eventual global triumph of communism, which meant that it was pledged to the destruction of its democratic allies as well as its fascist enemies. "The only bond of the victors," wrote Churchill, "is their common Hate."[156]

At the first meeting of the three key wartime leaders, in Tehran in 1943, Stalin horrified Churchill by proposing—jokingly, he claimed— that the Allies eliminate German militarism by simply murdering 50,000 or even 100,000 of its officers.[157] By their last meeting, at Yalta in 1945, there were abundant signs that Stalin intended to supplant Hitler's hegemony in Eastern Europe with his own. It's not surprising, then, that the Grand Alliance didn't outlast the conflict that birthed it. Its success in winning that conflict showed that survival in the Eurasian century required a mixture of deep solidarity and sordid compromise.

The solidarity was the province of the English-speaking democracies and was embodied by the Churchill–Roosevelt relationship. It wasn't a partnership of equals or even of similar personalities. "If either of them could be called a student of Machiavelli, it was Roosevelt," wrote one adviser; "if either was a bull in a china shop, it was Churchill."[158] Nor was the relationship entirely harmonious. Churchill was a passionate defender of the British Empire, which Roosevelt hoped to disassemble. But both leaders had a global outlook on the war; both saw the conflict, fundamentally, as a fight to preserve human liberty from the most ferocious enemies it had ever faced. And both understood that their countries were fated, in Churchill's words, to be "somewhat mixed-up together"—that maximizing the Allies' power required limiting their sovereignty.[159]

That process began with building an infrastructure of cooperation. During World War I, it took the Allies years to start working as a team. During World War II, it took a few weeks.

The U.S. and British military staffs had been planning (secretly) together even before America's war started. After Pearl Harbor, they created a Combined Chiefs of Staff to fuse consideration of strategy at the highest level, as well as combined bodies for planning, supply, mobilization, intelligence, and other issues. Unified commands were established for each theater; top U.S. and British military officials were in continual communication. "The Chiefs of Staff have been in intimate touch; they have lived in the same hotel," reflected Churchill. "Each man has become a definite personal friend of his opposite number on the other side."[160] That was an exaggeration; Anglophobia ran deep among Roosevelt's military chiefs. But the soldiers were merely following the lead of Roosevelt and Churchill, who met ten times during the war while carrying on a frank, and voluminous, exchange of letters.[161]

The most important result was a broad agreement on strategy—a Germany-first approach, because Hitler was the most dangerous enemy and the one all three key Allies were fighting, with substantial resources flowing to the Pacific so the Japanese couldn't dig in deeply enough that they would never be uprooted. "The defeat of Japan does not defeat Germany," FDR wrote. Once Germany was defeated, though, Japan's demise would be a matter of time.[162]

These strategic discussions produced fierce debates over the timing of a second front in Europe and the virtues of direct versus peripheral assault. The British, haunted by World War I, preferred to nibble around the continent's edges; the Americans, terrified that Hitler would harness Europe's resources, favored getting to the point. Yet these arguments produced a winning compromise: peripheral landings in North

Africa and Italy in 1942–43 that allowed the Allies to freely navigate the Mediterranean, amass shipping, and gain experience against softer targets, followed in 1944 by a more direct assault on the heart of German power.[163] We often think strategy is best made by a single leader. In this case, there was a wisdom of the crowd.

Indeed, America and Britain were "mixed up" at every level. They shared sensitive technology on radar, airplanes, and other capabilities. They pooled raw materials and basing facilities; through Lend-Lease, America was deeply enmeshed in the British economy. They allocated shipping and made other logistical choices together, in recognition that the availability—or lack thereof—of transports or tanks could mean the difference between victory and defeat. Intelligence, too, was essential to finding and killing the enemy on a global battlefield. So the democracies cooperated in breaking Axis codes and otherwise building as close an intelligence partnership as two great powers ever had.[164]

The Allies understood what the Axis never did: that the war would be decided not simply by how *much* power the rival coalitions possessed but by how efficiently, precisely, and symbiotically it was wielded. The proof was in how the Anglophone democracies dealt with some of the conflict's most daunting challenges.

The Battle of the Atlantic was a prime example, as the achievements of British codebreakers guided American B-24s and escort carriers to their prey. The air war was won in a similar way. The Allies could not invade Europe or break the German economy until they had defeated the Luftwaffe; they could not defeat the Luftwaffe until they had long-range fighter escorts for their bombers; they could not develop long-range escorts until they put British-made Rolls-Royce engines in U.S.-made P-51 fighters, which required agitation from innovators on both sides of the Atlantic as well as a personal appeal from Churchill to Roosevelt.[165] "When I saw your bombers over Berlin protected by your long-range fighters," Göring later said, he knew Germany had lost.[166] A global war was a contest in problem-solving, at which the Anglo-Americans succeeded like no one else.

That relationship worked because the two countries had compatible, if not identical, visions of global order; because they boasted democratic habits of compromise and dialogue; and because they grasped that any disagreements were trivial compared to their shared interest in defeating their enemies. Only the last applied to the Soviet Union, which made that relationship more tenuous and the trade-offs it necessitated more fundamental.

If Stalin and Hitler had forged one Faustian bargain to destroy Eurasian equilibrium, Stalin and the captains of global capitalism forged another to restore it. Mistrust, rooted in conflicting ideologies, suffused that relationship. "Churchill is the kind who, if you don't watch him, will slip a kopeck out of your pocket," remarked Stalin. "Roosevelt is not like that. He dips in his hand only for bigger coins."[167] Roosevelt, for his part, hoped that engagement would mellow the Soviet regime—that patterns of wartime cooperation might persist after victory. Yet the Bulgarian proverb he favored was less optimistic: "You can walk with the Devil as far as the bridge, but then you must leave him behind."[168] The fundamental test of the Grand Alliance, then, was whether it could get to Berlin and Tokyo in the first place.

Roosevelt and Churchill didn't spare any reasonable effort. Despite the perils of wartime travel, the Big Three met twice—at Tehran and Yalta—while Churchill went to Moscow on two other occasions. It is only a slight exaggeration to say that an ailing Roosevelt died for the Grand Alliance; the second of his long, grueling trips into Stalin's backyard probably helped finish him off in April 1945. "I am responsible for keeping the grand alliance together," he had said.[169]

That objective was the north star of FDR's statecraft. Decisions as fundamental as the Germany-first strategy and the demand for unconditional surrender were, at least partially, exercises in coalition management: They focused the Allies on the military objectives that united them while easing fears that any party would seek a compromise peace. True, Stalin chafed at the democracies' lethargy in opening a second front; Soviet blood, he pointed out, represented his asymmetric contribution to the cause. But

FDR was so generous with Lend-Lease aid and American technology because he understood that the Soviet Union was paying, dearly, in lives.[170]

This approach averted the nightmare scenario—an open breach that might allow Hitler to escape the Allied vise. It produced a partnership that rested, ironically, on the principle of comparative advantage: With the Soviet Union bearing the brunt of European fighting, the United States mobilized a relatively small army, just 90 divisions, so that its manpower could pour forth the machines that carried the entire alliance to victory.[171] The Grand Alliance also managed just enough direct coordination where it mattered most. Late in the war, Allied bombing tied up German traffic on the Danube and made it harder for Hitler to bolster a crumbling eastern front. And after the Allies invaded France in June 1944, the Soviets launched Operation Bagration, a major offensive that kept Hitler from rapidly shifting troops to the west.[172] It was symbolically fitting that Hitler committed suicide, the next April, as his rivals closed in from all sides.

This convergence wasn't cheap, morally or strategically. When America became an ally of the Soviet Union, it also became an accomplice of one of the worst tyrants on earth. No wonder FDR felt that he had to assiduously launder his new friend's image; Stalin, the bloody dictator who had murdered millions, became "Uncle Joe," the valiant member of the free world. The United States and Britain tolerated a great deal of Soviet wartime espionage. They also acquiesced, whether explicitly or tacitly, in the creation of a communist empire in Eastern Europe to replace the fascist one that crumbled with Hitler's defeat.[173] The more desperate the predicament, the more painful the compromises. Not for the last time, the only way to preserve human freedom was to link arms with some of its most awful foes.

*

WHAT ABOUT THE OTHER COALITION? EVEN AT THE ACME OF THEIR CONquests, Axis leaders knew their path to victory was narrow. "All the bowstrings of the Tripartite Pact community would have to be stretched taut," said Ribbentrop, "if the full potential of its power were to be realized."[174] In the end, though, many of the forces that drove this quest for global primacy hindered its prospects for success.

To be sure, the Axis had advantages. Germany and Japan pioneered creative military concepts; Berlin produced jet fighters, guided rockets, and other groundbreaking weapons. Once again, Berlin ruled in pure military effectiveness. According to one analysis, each German soldier was worth 1.2 American or British soldiers.[175] Ideological fanaticism was also a force-multiplier: in the Pacific, American military personnel were astonished at the ferocity of enemies who fought to the death. But every strength was counterbalanced by grave, even terminal, weaknesses.

One such weakness was decision-making. Each strategic mega-gamble—Hitler's double-cross of Stalin, Japan's move against Pearl Harbor—made a certain sense in the mental world Axis leaders inhabited. Taken together, they were a master class in self-harm. No matter how close the Axis came to victory, no matter how impressively their militaries preformed, there was something perverse about strategies that risked everything on a mad rush for hegemony—with strategic death as the consequence of failure. And if the decisions were perverse, so were the processes that yielded them.

Hitler's hyper-personalized regime had enabled his spree of successes from 1936 to 1941; an absolute ruler willing to make big bets ran off the ultimate geopolitical hot streak. Over time, though, that system magnified the flaws of the zealot who ran it.

In a regime that vested total authority in a single leader, there was little capacity to stress-test war plans or systematically vet strategy. "My true intentions you will never know," Hitler taunted his army chief of staff.[176] As the war turned, an isolated and paranoid Hitler refused to conserve vital manpower by allowing trapped forces to retreat. The absurdities climaxed when Rommel could not throw his reserves at Allied beachheads on D-Day because Hitler could not be awakened to give the okay.[177] The democracies produced imperfect leaders but created systems to sharpen their judgment. The autocracies had no such safeguards and paid a terrific price.

They also paid a price for their cruelty. Many Soviet citizens might have welcomed the Nazis as liberators, given their experience under Stalin; they changed their minds once they realized their choices were resistance or death. Tokyo might have had more eager collaborators in Asia had it not exploited those areas so nakedly. Goebbels summed up the Axis view of morality: "If we win, we shall have right on our side."[178] Perhaps so, but right helped determine who won in the first place. "There is not a single country which in its heart is following the Germans," said one Spanish official—which ensured that most countries that could oppose the Axis eventually did.[179]

Then there were the pathologies of Axis mobilization. No country had a perfect record here; Harry Truman, then a little-known senator from Missouri, made his national reputation by exposing waste in Washington. But no such exposés were possible in fascist states, where wartime dysfunction made America's model look quite good.

The Italian war effort was a joke, beset by corruption and cronyism. Japan conscripted virtually every household into its wartime mobilization, but never resolved crippling disputes between rival services, or between the military and civilians. Hitler waited too long to mobilize for total war, thanks to his faith in "blitzkrieg economics." Even as German industry picked up steam, Hitler's preference for administrative chaos allowed unending feuds and confusion.[180] Moreover, all the Axis powers neglected logistics and sustainment—a huge mistake in a war in which getting forces to the fight, and keeping them in the fight, was paramount, and one that reflected the indifference with which totalitarian rulers treated their own personnel.[181]

They didn't treat their allies any better. In principle, Axis leaders knew they must hang together. "Their weakness," said Hitler, "would be in allowing themselves to be defeated separately."[182] In practice, the fact that the Germans and Japanese considered each other subhuman—Hitler called Hirohito a "lacquered half-monkey"—condemned them to just that fate.[183]

Whereas Allied technological cooperation was transformative, Axis technological cooperation was trivial. The Axis never pursued coordinated operations in the Middle East and the Indian Ocean, or even exchanged basic information about their plans. Hitler didn't bother to tell Japan he planned to invade the Soviet Union; Mussolini had pulled the same trick on Hitler when he attacked Greece the year before. "Hitler always faces me with a *fait accompli*," he grumbled. "This time I am going to pay him back in his own coin."[184]

This fratricide took a toll. Germany and Italy competed to loot the resources of southeastern Europe. German soldiers stole supplies from their Romanian allies when things got desperate at Stalingrad.[185] If the Grand Alliance was sometimes more like a band of in-laws than a band of brothers, the Axis states hardly acted like allies at all.

Fascist leaders believed that decadent democracies could never muster the necessary commitment and sacrifice. "What is America but millionaires, beauty queens, stupid records and Hollywood?" Hitler had asked.[186] But in reality, fascist regimes rooted in the hard logic of domination struggled to master the softer skills that were indispensable in an endeavor as complex as World War II. The Grand Alliance fought a global conflict well, making choices and forging cooperation that put its power to good use. The Axis fought a war that was less than the sum of its parts.

*

"NOW I AM BECOME DEATH, THE DESTROYER OF WORLDS." THAT PHRASE, borrowed from Hindu scripture, occurred to the physicist J. Robert Oppenheimer when he witnessed the first atomic bomb test in July 1945.[187] Soon thereafter, American B-29s delivered death aplenty when they dropped atomic weapons on Hiroshima and Nagasaki. Scripture also came to mind for the new president who ordered those bombings. "We have discovered the most terrible bomb in the history of the world," wrote Truman. "It may be the fire destruction prophesied in the Euphrates Valley Era, after Noah and his fabulous Ark."[188]

Few events could have better ended World War II, because few events have so entwined creation and destruction. The atomic bombs themselves were a product of the prodigious scientific and industrial effort that gave America victory; the Manhattan Project featured a workforce and industrial base that rivaled the entire U.S. automotive industry.[189] Their delivery, from bases in the Mariana Islands, testified to epic feats of logistics and power projection. The strikes against Hiroshima and Nagasaki were the climax of a remorseless coercive campaign featuring the razing of Japanese cities, a blockade aptly named Operation Starvation, and the killing of hundreds of thousands of civilians.[190] Above all, the bombings affirmed a final lesson of World War II: how excruciatingly expensive it could be to repair a geopolitical balance once broken.

That price could be measured in the 60 million lives lost, or in the devastation of countries from Europe's Atlantic coast to the Asian littoral. It could be measured in the boundless crimes of the aggressors, but also in the moral transgressions of the democracies, whether the fire-bombing of enemy cities or the internment of Japanese-Americans in the United States. In this sense, the use of the atomic bomb simply confirmed how the war had normalized the slaughter of civilians. "You might have killed someone, sir," a police officer told Arthur Harris, the architect of Britain's bombing campaign, after stopping him for speeding. "Young man," Harris allegedly replied, "I kill thousands of people every night."[191] Not least, the war's cost could be measured in the strategic legacy it left behind.

The Soviet Union was, in FDR's words, "a dictatorship as absolute as any other dictatorship in the world."[192] It sought a global revolution just as complete, if more gradual, than Hitler's. When the war ended, Stalin's troops were occupying half of Europe; the Soviet Union had a commanding position at the heart of a shattered Eurasia. "The Soviet sphere," commented British foreign secretary Ernest Bevin, "extended from Lubeck to Port Arthur."[193] With Stalin pressing for gains from the Dardanelles to Manchuria, that sphere seemed likely to expand. "A future war with Soviet Russia," wrote Grew, "is as certain as anything in this world can be certain."[194] Whether humanity could survive such a war in the nuclear age seemed more doubtful.

The democracies weren't ready for the challenge. In fairness, Roosevelt had known what he wanted in the postwar world: a new international body, the United Nations, to replace Wilson's failed League; an open global economy to promote shared prosperity; a concert of great powers to keep the peace. But he hadn't devised any real formula for stability in Europe, much less a backup plan if the Allies' wartime comity gave way to postwar enmity.

The Allies should just "castrate the German people," FDR mused during the war.[195] He had approved a plan to permanently deindustrialize that country, thereby holding down one serial aggressor, but only by creating a power vacuum that might tempt others. And despite Churchill's concern that the rapid withdrawal of U.S. troops would leave Europe at Stalin's mercy, FDR had pledged, before his death, to do just that. "You really ought to bring up and discipline your own children," he airily told Churchill in 1944; Europe was not America's ward.[196] Others, fortunately, were grappling more seriously with the geopolitics of the peace.

*

MACKINDER, WHO TURNED EIGHTY IN 1941, HAD WATCHED THE WAR from Britain. He grasped the intimidating truth of Moscow's influence: "If the Soviet Union emerges from this war as conqueror of Germany," he wrote, "she must rank as the greatest land Power on the globe."[197] Like Roosevelt, he still hoped the Grand Alliance would endure and worried mostly about another German resurgence. Yet he also offered, in 1943, a strategy that would ultimately prevent *any* power from repeating Hitler's exploits.

Mackinder wrote at the invitation of Hamilton Fish Armstrong, the legendary editor of the journal *Foreign Affairs*. Armstrong encouraged Mackinder to refresh his earlier arguments, focusing on "the terrible danger . . . that would result from the political integration of Central Europe with the 'heartland' of Eurasia."[198] Mackinder obliged with an essay titled "The Round World and the Winning of the Peace."

The article was part autobiography: Mackinder explained the origins and evolution of his Pivot thesis, from the time when he had first

read about Prussia's triumph over France. It was part rejoinder to critics, such as Spykman, who had made names for themselves by claiming that Mackinder's Pivot wasn't so pivotal after all. Most of all, the
essay was Mackinder's final bid to make geopolitics the foundation of
a healthy world.

World War II showed that Eurasian challenges could succeed if the
global coalition was too slow to coalesce. Mackinder's solution was to
turn the wartime alliance into an enduring strategic community.

The community would consist of "a bridgehead in France, a moated
aerodrome in Britain, and a reserve of trained manpower, agriculture
and industries in the eastern United States and Canada." It would treat
the Atlantic not as a barrier but as a "Midland Ocean" connecting like-
minded countries on both sides. This transatlantic union was necessary to ensure that the countries of Europe would immediately—and
collectively—resist future aggression, rather than allowing themselves
to be picked off one by one. France was in the "key position," Mackinder
wrote privately while drafting the article, but would "lack courage unless
she has assured support of North America."[199] And this combination
was essential so that any Eurasian predator would face prompt pushback on land, in the air, and at sea.

All this meant there must not be another American disengagement.
Lasting peace required "lasting cooperation" by democratic societies.
Only such cooperation, Mackinder concluded, would ensure "a balanced
globe of human beings. And happy, because balanced and thus free."[200]

"I consider it one of the most interesting and important articles
which we have ever printed," Armstrong cabled.[201] Editorial puffery
aside, Mackinder's foresight wasn't any more infallible in this case than in
others. He still envisioned the Soviet Union helping to balance Germany,
rather than vice versa, in part because he doubted that "the conquering
democracies" would occupy the latter country long enough to "exorcise
the evil spirits."[202] Yet as Mackinder's entire career had illustrated, grand
concepts can be seminal even when supporting details are lacking.

The plan Mackinder proposed for containing a resurgent Germany wasn't far from the scheme the transatlantic democracies, including a reformed West Germany, would use to contain the Soviet Union. The geopolitical cage he intended to build for a future Hitler was the free world's response to Stalin instead. World War II had, tragically, created the conditions for another Eurasian struggle. It also gave rise to the strategy that would allow the West to prevail without fighting another global war.

| 4 |

THE GOLDEN AGE

"This world is at the end of its tether," wrote H. G. Wells before his death in 1946. "The end of everything we call life is close at hand."[1] Unless humanity changed its ways, Albert Einstein agreed, "we are doomed."[2] Einstein, who had introduced Roosevelt to the idea of the atomic bomb, was just as gloomy as Oppenheimer, who had masterminded its development. "If one is honest," Oppenheimer said in 1950, "the most probable view of the future is that of war, exploding atomic bombs, death, and the end of most freedom."[3] Some of the world's greatest minds were sure the next round of global rivalry would be the last.

It's easy to see why they thought so. The first half of the twentieth century was a tale of escalating carnage and chaos. The first two battles for Eurasia had consumed 80 million lives; history's most destructive war had ended with the use of history's most destructive weapon. That war hadn't even produced peace. The victors of World War II were now turning against each other, presaging a third global showdown that might end civilization.

Another clash for supremacy indeed followed; by 1950, it was raging everywhere from a divided Berlin to a divided Korea. This contest began in the endangered Rimlands around a Soviet-ruled Heartland; it spilled into rear and flanking theaters around the globe. Once again, a country that centralized authority at home sought to extend that control outward; once again, a coalition led by an offshore, liberal superpower conducted a desperate defense. Once again, there were times when the future looked black. "The way of life that we have known is literally in balance," George Marshall—now Truman's secretary of state—said in 1948. The "base of western civilization" was giving way.[4]

For two generations, terrifying crises, febrile arms races, and brutal proxy wars were the warp and woof of international politics. The threat of world-shattering violence was inescapable. The Cold War ultimately went longer and more global than either of the struggles that preceded it. The contenders had changed; the depressing patterns of geopolitics remained the same.

To a point, anyway. For all its atrocities and absurdities, the Cold War did not become another great-power hot war. It did not cause another Eurasian breakdown; it did not wreak atomic fury upon the globe. It resulted, rather, in the peaceful—relatively speaking—defeat of the Soviet Union and the rise of a world more prosperous, humane, and democratic than anything before. This time, Eurasian rivalry was not the cause of humanity's descent. It was the genesis of a golden age.[5]

This was a revolutionary departure from history, which required a revolutionary change in U.S. strategy. The Soviet Union looked a lot like Mackinder's original nightmare. The free world's answer looked a lot like his vision of a democratic security community that could break the cycle of violent conflict over Eurasia and, perhaps, the globe.

*

MACKINDER DIED, AGED EIGHTY-SIX, ON MARCH 6, 1947. HIS TIMING, TYPI-cally, was uncanny. Six days later, Truman addressed a joint session of Congress. "Nearly every nation must choose between alternative ways of life," he declared; America would "support free peoples who are resisting subjugation by armed minorities or by outside pressures."[6] Truman never mentioned Moscow: His ask was for aid to Greece and Turkey, two endangered outposts on the Mediterranean rim. Yet his speech was America's declaration of Cold War against a country that embodied the Heartland danger Mackinder had long foreseen.

Stalin's Soviet Union was a tyranny bent on transformation. At home, it had used brute-force modernization to make the country an industrial dynamo; its foreign policy combined the messianism of the communists with the imperialism of the tsars. The Soviet Union had emerged, during World War II, as a military heavyweight at the heart of Eurasia, a position that gave it access to the industrialized or resource-rich Crescent all around. Russia was becoming "by far the strongest nation in Europe and Asia," American intelligence analysts wrote—strong enough to dominate both continents "if the United States should stand aside."[7] Not least, the Soviet Union was led by a man who combined towering ambition with bottomless insecurity.

Stalin had ascended the Soviet system with a malevolence that unnerved even Lenin. He had secured his rule by killing millions of enemies, real or imagined. His long-term goal was the global triumph of socialism, ideally through the self-destruction of capitalism; his near-term goal was the survival and strengthening of the Soviet state. Having secured that aim in World War II, Stalin could pursue his medium-range goal: making the Soviet Union a superpower and its position unassailable. "Stalin believed that he was in the same position as Alexander I after the defeat of Napoleon," his successor, Nikita Khrushchev, recalled, and could "dictate the rules for all of Europe."[8]

To be clear, Stalin didn't *want* war. The Soviet Union had lost 20 million people in the last conflict; into 1946, Stalin still desired Western economic aid. But tactical flexibility couldn't obscure abiding hostility. "Today we are fighting in alliance with one faction against the other," he had said, "and in the future we will fight against this capitalist faction as well."[9] Stalin "looked at it this way," Molotov recalled: "World War I has wrested one country from capitalist slavery; World War II has created a socialist system; and the third will finish off imperialism forever."[10] Even short of that bloody climax, Stalin had opportunities to expand Soviet writ.

Following World War II, Stalin would stamp out resistance to Soviet power in Eastern Europe. He would then forge an alliance with China—and with it, a communist bloc from Germany to the Pacific—after Mao Zedong won that country's civil war. Meanwhile, he probed the margins of the non-communist world, supporting insurgencies, demanding concessions, or otherwise seeking advantage in Iran, Turkey, Greece, Scandinavia, Korea, and Libya. Stalin's appetite was enormous, his former foreign minister, Maxim Litvinov, explained, and his opportunism was relentless. Were the world to "give in and grant all Russian demands," it would then receive the "next series of demands."[11] And if Stalin refused to set limits on his expansion, there were few natural limits, either.

The Red Army was imposing, especially as a demobilizing U.S. military melted away. "The USSR has an overwhelming preponderance of immediately available power of the Eurasian continent," the Central Intelligence Agency reported. Or Stalin might stroll into the Rimlands without firing a shot.[12]

Postwar Asia was aflame with revolution, from the Indonesian archipelago to the Korean peninsula. Hunger and radicalism were stalking a broken Europe; communist parties were vying to rule France, Italy, and other countries. If these groups seized power or won it at the ballot box, they might hand Western Europe to Stalin and leave the remaining democracies in a situation just as desperate as in 1940.[13]

If America didn't act quickly, French officials predicted, "European economies will disintegrate" and the Soviets would "take over the Western European countries with their well-organized Communist Parties."[14] British leaders warned that stricken nations would be conquered, subverted, or intimidated into submission. The democratic world might relive "our experience with Hitler," said Bevin, suffering a "slow deterioration of our position" until war was the only option left.[15]

In the late 1940s, the possibility that Stalin might win an empire vaster than Hitler's was all too real. Yet that scenario didn't materialize, in part because Stalin was *not* Hitler, and in part because his enemies understood—on the basis of hard experience—that organizing to preserve the Eurasian balance now was better than scrambling to repair it later.

———

*

NOT ALL TOTALITARIAN REGIMES ARE IDENTICAL; NOT ALL PROGRAMS OF global revolution are equivalent. Stalin rivaled Hitler as a murderer, and his desired future, in which capitalist societies *everywhere* would be overthrown, was a "new order" as dystopian as what the Axis had envisioned. Yet because Stalin and his successors were more confident than Hitler, they were also more deterrable; their "scientific" certitude that Marxism-Leninism would *eventually* triumph made them wary of provoking war too soon. That wariness allowed a U.S. diplomat named George Kennan to propose a strategy that offered sharp, protracted rivalry as the key to *avoiding* cataclysmic war.

Kennan was, in some ways, America's Eyre Crowe. Like Crowe, Kennan was a career diplomat who wrote mammoth papers studded with insights. Like Crowe, Kennan clashed with superiors whose thinking he deemed inferior to his own. Unlike Crowe, Kennan was as fragile emotionally as he was formidable intellectually. Partly for that reason, he enjoyed a moment of historic influence followed by decades of painful dissent from the doctrine he had crafted.[16]

Kennan was part of a cohort of Russia hands trained by the State Department in the 1920s and 1930s. While stationed in Moscow before World War II, he had witnessed Stalin's rapacious cruelties firsthand. In 1945, he had predicted—probably after reading Mackinder—a "basic conflict" between "the interests of Atlantic sea-power, which demand the preservation of vigorous and independent political life on the European peninsula, and the interest of the jealous Eurasian land power, which must always seek to extend itself" as far as possible.[17] This was unwelcome counsel for a president trying to preserve the Grand Alliance. Yet the nosedive in U.S.–Soviet relations after V-J Day left Washington grasping for answers Kennan could provide.

In a series of seminal analyses written in 1946–47, Kennan killed off dreams of postwar cooperation. The hyper-suspicious Stalin was immune to reassurance: "Nothing short of complete disarmament, delivery of our air and naval forces to Russia and resigning of powers of government to American Communists" would ease his mind.[18] Moreover, the mix of Russia's exposed geography, which conditioned its rulers to seek protection through expansion, and its communist ideology made coexistence an illusion. Soviet leaders would "seek security only in patient but deadly struggle for total destruction of rival power."[19]

Yet if cooperation was impossible, conflict wasn't inevitable. The experience with Hitler had conditioned many observers to think that, when facing an aggressive absolutism, the only options were appeasement and war. Kennan outlined a middle path.[20]

Stalin might hate America, but he respected its power. After all, when World War II ended, America accounted for nearly half of global production.[21] And since capitalism was, in Stalin's mind, doomed, Moscow could be patient in awaiting its demise. The Soviet Union would press relentlessly for advantage; it might use force when conditions were right. But it would prudently retreat when it hit resistance. Soviet power, Kennan wrote, could be "contained by the adroit and vigilant application of counterforce."[22] Western strength could make war unnecessary— and make the clock the Kremlin's enemy.

Communists trumpeted the decrepitude of capitalism, but the Soviet Union had the more profound inner weaknesses: an inefficient command economy, a tired and tyrannized population, a political system that devoured its own. If non-communist countries blocked Soviet expansion, they could disarm the Kremlin of its most potent weapon— its sense of historical inevitability—and force Moscow to address its own contradictions instead. America, Kennan wrote, could "increase enormously the strains" on Soviet policy; it could achieve "the breakup or the gradual mellowing of Soviet power."[23] Washington, not Moscow, could win the next Eurasian struggle without firing a shot.

This would require America to do something unexpected: to build a thriving Western world. Stalin believed his triumph was certain because his enemies were hopeless. A new, postwar depression would tank capitalist economies; greedy imperialists would tear one another down. As Stalin put it, Germany and Japan would "rise to their feet again" and "smash" the United States; even Britain and France would join the fray.[24] When the collapse or conflict unavoidably came, the Soviet Union would collect the spoils.

"World communism is like [a] malignant parasite which feeds only on diseased tissue," Kennan wrote. Containing Soviet power required surrounding it with unity and strength.[25] This was Kennan's most prescient insight—and when he penned it, he had no clue what it would really mean.

*

NEITHER DID ANYONE ELSE. TRUE, U.S. OFFICIALS UNIVERSALLY AGREED that a return to isolation would be disastrous; they had no intention of letting depression and aggression consume the world again. Yet even as U.S.–Soviet tensions increased, Truman had no plan to rebuild continents, erect a global alliance network, or permanently accept the obligations of a superpower. The early Cold War was a time "of great obscurity to those who lived through it," the great American diplomat Dean Acheson later wrote. U.S. officials "hesitated long before grasping what now seems obvious."[26] What transformed containment from an idea into a strategy was a series of extraordinary crises that yielded extraordinary U.S. commitments. Acheson, as undersecretary of state and then secretary of state during the Truman years, was usually at the center of them.

Educated at Groton, Yale, and Harvard, Acheson seemed the very embodiment of America's Eastern elite. A skilled lawyer with a powerful mind, his intelligence could be as piercing as his arrogance. What truly distinguished Acheson was his quickness in perceiving the unique demands the postwar world placed on Washington—and his penchant for action *now* in meeting them. If Kennan was the sometimes-frustrated architect of containment, historian Wilson Miscamble has written, Acheson was its "master builder."[27]

The first of these crises was the collapse of British influence in the Mediterranean. Most U.S. officials assumed, in 1945–46, that London was still a global power. But if World War I had initiated British exhaustion, World War II completed it. In February 1947, British officials broke the news that they could no longer support Greece, which was battling a communist insurgency, or Turkey, which Stalin was seeking to intimidate into making concessions on control of the straits linking the Black Sea to the Mediterranean. Acheson, then undersecretary of state, grasped the import. The fall of these garrisons would "open three continents to Soviet penetration," while convincing tired, frightened countries everywhere that there was no stemming the red tide.[28] Washington's conclusion, reported one British diplomat, was that "no time must be lost in plucking the torch of world leadership from our chilling hands."[29]

Truman's response—first conceived by Acheson and his colleagues over a frantic weekend—was to ask Congress for $400 million in aid for Athens and Ankara, and to explain the stakes as starkly as possible. Truman warned that a world in which independent nations could be coerced and subverted would turn very nasty, very quickly. He framed the emerging Cold War as a struggle between liberty and tyranny. Most crucially, he argued that America must proactively invest in peace and stability, to avoid the unraveling that might necessitate greater, bloodier commitments later. Aid for Greece and Turkey "amounts to a little more than 1 tenth of 1 per cent" of what America had spent to win World War II, Truman said. Surely this modest commitment was warranted to avoid a slide into World War III.[30]

Congress approved the aid, but Truman's preventive ethos was tested weeks later when Western Europe neared the abyss. A frigid winter had exacerbated economic and political turmoil. George Marshall, Acheson's boss, had hoped to catalyze regional recovery by reviving the German economy, but hit a wall of opposition in Moscow; a weak, unstable Europe suited Stalin just fine. The situation in a divided Germany was hardly "tragic," he told Marshall in a midnight meeting at the Kremlin, while doodling wolves on a notepad in his habitually menacing way.[31]

Marshall was motivated, not intimidated: He understood what happened when vicious regimes controlled vital regions. "The patient is sinking while the doctors deliberate," he declared upon returning to America. "Action . . . must be taken without delay."[32]

Within weeks, Marshall's aides—notably Acheson, Kennan, and their colleague Will Clayton—had cobbled together a radical initiative called the European Recovery Program, soon dubbed the Marshall Plan. That multiyear, $13 billion aid project was "a lifeline to sinking men," Britain's Ernest Bevin gushed; America would use its wealth, technology, and know-how to bring a dying Europe back to life.[33] Washington undertook a similar policy toward Japan in 1948. Only by rebuilding two of the "greatest workshops of Europe and Asia," Acheson had explained, could the Rimlands be saved and Soviet expansion thwarted.[34]

The Marshall Plan invigorated a third aspect of U.S. policy—cultivating a free-world community united by democratic values. The plan itself used economic weapons to avert the death of democracy in the cradle of Western civilization. It was also part of a shift from punishing incorrigible tyrannies to reviving them as friendly democracies.

Japan became, in the words of American proconsul Douglas MacArthur, "the world's great laboratory for an experiment in the liberation of a people."[35] U.S. officials rewrote the country's constitution, dissolved its military, empowered elected leaders, and purged autocratic elites. In Germany, General Lucius Clay built a free press, instituted regular elections, and supported democratic reforms. In both cases, deindustrialization gave way to economic rejuvenation. Washington took this path because there was no stability in the world without prosperity in Japan and Germany—and because, as Acheson had argued, only deep political change could transform a "will to war" into a commitment to peace.[36]

Peace still seemed elusive in 1947–48, though, because the Marshall Plan triggered a grave crisis of European security. Implementing the plan meant firing Communist Party ministers from Western European governments; the left responded with mayhem and strikes. Rehabilitating western Germany was vital to European reconstruction, but it terrified the French and infuriated Stalin. The Soviet dictator responded, in June 1948, with a land blockade of West Berlin, in hopes of forcing the Western powers out of that divided city. Even before, he had reacted to America's propping up of Western Europe by clamping down on Eastern Europe; his proxies overthrew Czechoslovakia's democratic government in February. War was in the air and the region was in a panic. The Europeans, said Marshall, were "completely out of their skin, and sitting on their nerves."[37]

The solution came, this time, from the Europeans, who formed a defense union and then begged, cajoled, and persuaded Washington to join it. "For those who seek peace," Acheson—now secretary of state—declared in April 1949, this North Atlantic Treaty offered "refuge and strength." For those who contemplated aggression, it was a "warning" of "woe" to come.[38]

Much as Mackinder envisioned, the North Atlantic Treaty placed U.S. industrial muscle at the service of European security. The democracies of that region, said one State Department official, were backed by the "potential of Pittsburgh and Detroit."[39] Crucially, the treaty would suppress threats from within as well as from without; by protecting Hitler's former victims, it would allow them to build up the new West German state rather than holding it down. Most important, the pact reduced the paralyzing uncertainty that had encouraged European appeasement before. "If trouble did come," Bevin remarked, America's friends would not "be left waiting as in 1940."[40] The alliance would stiffen Europe against Soviet pressure—and allow America to shape Eurasia's strategic balance. After 150 years of abstention from peacetime alliances, the New World had made itself the arbiter of the geopolitics of the Old.

Yet the treaty hardly solved the free world's problems. At the start, the pact was only a paper alliance. It did not come with additional, standing deployments of U.S. troops to Europe. It did not portend the globalization of American security commitments; in Asia, Truman was abandoning Chiang's China and publicly writing off South Korea and Taiwan. The signing of the treaty followed a historic build-*down* of America's forces; military spending plummeted from $83 billion in 1945 to $9.1 billion in 1948.[41] The West was held together "with string, chewing gum, and safety pins," Acheson recalled.[42] It would take a final crisis to make containment real and take America's free-world project global.

The Korean War occurred because Stalin, stalemated in Europe, saw opportunity in Asia. North Korea's founding dictator, Kim Il Sung, had long sought Moscow's approval to crush the South. Stalin gave it only after Mao had conquered China, creating revolutionary momentum in Asia and uniting the two great communist giants; after Moscow's first atomic bomb test in August 1949 had strengthened his strategic position; and after Acheson had announced, accurately if unwisely, that Washington had no commitment to South Korea.[43] The Soviet leader wagered that America would not intervene; that if it did, U.S. forces would arrive too late; and that a successful invasion would rupture the geopolitical restraints being emplaced around him. He was wrong on every count.

The United States *could* thwart the North Korean assault, because it had occupation forces in Japan. Truman *did* fight because he remembered the 1930s all too well. If the democracies cut South Korea loose, he believed, "no small nation would have the courage to resist threats and aggression"; if the free world didn't push back now, it would only invite greater outrages in the future.[44] So the United States rushed forces into South Korea, holding a small perimeter near Pusan, then turning the tide with a landing behind enemy lines at Inchon. That stunning reversal led to disastrous *American* miscalculation—a rush to the Yalu River in hopes of liberating the entire peninsula—which triggered intervention by Mao's China and left Washington mired in a bloody quagmire.[45] But not before the war had electrifying effects.

"Korea saved us," Acheson said; it impelled a worldwide offensive that he, as Truman's preeminent adviser, directed.[46] The North Atlantic Treaty became the North Atlantic Treaty *Organization*, boasting a unified command structure with 25 divisions. Truman permanently committed additional U.S. forces to Europe; the allies ramped up military spending and agreed, in principle, to rearm a democratic West Germany. On Eurasia's other flank, Acheson negotiated a phalanx of security pacts with Japan, the Philippines, Australia, and New Zealand. Underpinning all this was a monumental military buildup.[47]

American defense spending tripled, reaching 14 percent of GDP; the U.S. nuclear arsenal and conventional forces more than doubled during the war. "Without superior aggregate military strength, in being and readily mobilizable," NSC-68, a top-secret document prepared under Acheson's supervision, had stated, "a policy of 'containment' . . . is no more than a policy of bluff."[48] Washington was now building, in Acheson's phrasing, "situations of strength" at both ends of Eurasia.[49] It was creating a security community spanning two oceans rather than one.

*

THE FORMATIVE YEARS OF CONTAINMENT WERE A PERIOD OF UNRELENT-ing crisis. The United States groped, and sometimes stumbled, for answers to jarring strategic shocks. By the early 1950s, however, Washington was creating a new world order. Because this program had taken shape amid such chaos, it was easy to miss how epochal it was.

Twice in recent decades, the world had fallen into violent anarchy. It seemed, as Eisenhower remarked, that "the nations of the West" were "blindly enacting parts in a drama that could have been written by Lenin."[50] After World War II, it could have all happened again. But instead there emerged, in Acheson's phrasing, "half a world, a free half" that would ultimately exert more pressure on Moscow than Moscow could exert on it.[51] Lenin hadn't scripted *that*. The crucial variable was a change in how an offshore superpower engaged the world's strategic core.

The United States would not allow, through inaction, another total-itarian sweep across Eurasia. It would build, in peacetime, the strategic linkages that might prevent a deadly imbalance from leading to war. Washington would revive moribund regions; it would foster a free world rooted in liberal values; it would deny Stalin easy expansion and forge the shield behind which the non-communist nations could flourish. America would "create strength instead of weakness," said Acheson, so Moscow would someday "recognize facts."[52]

This strategy blended high-minded ideals with ruthless geopolitics. The United States focused on denying Soviet expansion in Western Europe, the Near East, and East Asia—areas that had enough eco-nomic potential to tip the global balance, and that were strategically situated to block Kremlin access to the Atlantic, the open Pacific, and the Mediterranean. It contained a recent ally by working with recent enemies, while converting serial aggressors into reliable democracies. It created alliances that protected vulnerable nations, while also allow-ing America to harness their manpower, resources, and strategic geog-raphy. The United States pursued a generous, positive-sum vision of cooperation with allies, as part of a cutthroat, zero-sum strategy for competition with adversaries. In doing so, it changed the game in Eur-asia and beyond.

By banishing historical antagonisms within the Rimlands, Ameri-ca's alliance network helped those countries achieve historic teamwork against the Heartland threat. By underwriting a vibrant international economy, America removed the *need* for West Germany or Japan to go on homicidal rampages for resources and markets; by planting itself firmly in Europe and East Asia, it removed the *opportunity* for such revisionism. The combination of U.S. military protection, diplomatic leadership, and economic support would underwrite a degree of demo-cratic security and prosperity that eventually proved fatal to stagnating communism. And the creation of a non-communist bloc that spanned continents, and effectively encircled the Soviet Union, fostered a free-world overbalance that doomed Moscow in the end.

"Our alliance system," said Acheson's successor, John Foster Dulles, "has staked out the vital areas of the world" and fused them to Washington.[53] Before 1945, America had joined ad hoc coalitions in times of war. After 1945, it would anchor an enduring, transoceanic partnership to keep the peace.

Only America could play this role. Only America could decisively influence events at both extremities of a distant supercontinent. Only America was secure enough that it could focus on projecting its power outward, into Europe, East Asia, and the Middle East. And only America had the mixture of geography and ideology that made this power more reassuring than terrifying.

A faraway America was no threat to physically conquer and permanently rule Eurasian countries, which made it more attractive as an ally against predators nearby. A democratic America had traditions of consultation and compromise that made its power seem comparatively benign. By the 1950s, Washington was building a huge informal empire, and doing so mostly at the behest of the countries involved. "For an anti-Stalinist," observed French intellectual Raymond Aron, "there is no escape from the acceptance of American leadership."[54]

For America, there was no escaping the obligations leadership imposed. The legions never fully came home after World War II; in the early 1950s, Washington would have 900,000 military personnel in Europe and Asia. Aid to Europe and Japan approached 5 percent of U.S. GNP in 1948.[55] For decades thereafter, the United States had primary responsibility for lubricating the international economy and coordinating the free-world coalition. Those tasks could be taxing indeed.

There had never been anything like this system of globe-girdling, peacetime alliances; that diversity produced impressive strength and endless headaches. From the late 1940s onward, Washington brawled with its closest friends over issues from nuclear strategy to the international monetary system. During debates over German rearmament in the 1950s or the economic shocks of the 1970s, it seemed the free world might fall apart.

What held it together were the institutions, such as NATO, that encouraged day-to-day cooperation even amid diplomatic tension, the democratic values that provided a reservoir of mutual respect, and the fear of Soviet hegemony that made American hegemony bearable. Most of all, what sustained the free world was America's enlightened approach to leading it.

The United States opened its markets to allies before they opened theirs to it; it helped them regain their economic competitiveness even at the expense of its own. Washington always claimed the dominant voice on security issues, but invited the input and initiative of allies; it resisted, usually, the temptation to simply dictate to its friends. In short, America deliberately underutilized its power vis-à-vis allies, to maximize their collective strength against adversaries. For decades, Washington would bear unprecedented burdens in hopes of achieving unprecedented levels of free-world prosperity and peace.[56]

Were there better options, Acheson asked, "to stop Soviet expansion without a catastrophic war?" To "increase the power of the free world" by easing its internal frictions? Was there another way of building a "new world environment?"[57] The answer, Acheson's generation concluded, was no. Breaking the pattern of Eurasian anarchy required a radically new American approach.

*

IT WASN'T THAT EASY, OF COURSE. WHEN TRUMAN LEFT OFFICE IN 1953, almost no one outside of his administration thought the West was winning the Cold War. The Korean War was draining and demoralizing. Western economies were groaning under the weight of recovery and rearmament. Truman's successor, Dwight Eisenhower, warned that America was headed for disaster. "The Communist sweep over the world," he wrote, had been "much faster and much more relentless" than the authoritarian onslaught of the 1930s.[58] We may remember the Cold War as a time when the West built its barricades and waited for the enemy to collapse. In truth, the contest featured continual maneuvering and probing,

as Moscow tried to escape containment and the West confronted the
ensuing challenges.

One challenge involved the relationship between technology, geography, and military power. America built its strategy around alliances
that drew red lines against aggression while drawing the capitalist world
together. Yet red lines don't enforce themselves. Throughout the Cold
War, American officials worried that an imbalance of military strength
might allow Moscow to bust through the containment barrier, or simply
divide and demoralize U.S. allies.

These weren't just fevered nightmares. The man who won the deadly
power struggle after Stalin's death in 1953, Nikita Khrushchev, sometimes seemed *more* dangerous—because more volatile—than his predecessor. Khrushchev's "dearest dream," he once remarked, was to wedge
Washington apart from NATO. He raced to build long-range missiles
he could use for leverage in East–West face-offs. "Let this device hang
over the capitalists like the sword of Damocles," Khrushchev said.[59]
Keeping the free world together, and the Cold War cold, required running the most terrifying arms race in history.

That race was always influenced by an asymmetry: America's Eurasian allies were very close to the Soviet empire and very far from the
United States. This allowed Washington to manipulate the balance of
power on Moscow's doorstep. But it also gave the Soviet Union, the
world's greatest land power, overwhelming superiority along the East–
West divide.[60] The Korean War and the Western buildup that accompanied it had shown that the cost of matching Moscow tank for tank,
man for man, was intolerable. Washington, said Eisenhower, could not
defend "every spot in the world."[61] America would have to exploit other
asymmetries—superior technology, preponderant global reach, and,
not least, the willingness to start a nuclear war in order to avoid losing
a conventional one.

Every aspect of this endeavor was arduous. The Pentagon built a
network of bases around the Eurasian periphery, to conduct strikes
against the Soviet Union and project power into its backyard. It assidu-

ously prepared to defend Western Europe as far forward as possible—for no NATO ally wanted to be liberated if that required first being conquered—and rapidly move reinforcements across the Atlantic. These imperatives, in turn, created another: preserving the naval dominance necessary to keep Soviet fleets contained and the free world connected. In friendly hands, one NATO strategy document stated, the North Atlantic was "the most essential link" between America and Europe; in hostile hands, it was a highway "whereby the Warsaw Pact can extend a political and military presence world-wide."[62] So one of the Cold War's most important battles was the silent struggle between Soviet submarines trying to sneak through maritime chokepoints into the North Atlantic and U.S. submarines trying to pen them in.[63] The Cold War featured a multi-decade competition to shape the world by shaping the underlying military balance. Nowhere were the difficulties sharper and more shocking than in the nuclear realm.

From the outset, most U.S. policymakers considered nuclear war an absurdity. Eisenhower, who wrestled continually with the issue, said that after a thermonuclear conflict, "it would literally be a business of digging ourselves out of ashes, starting again."[64] The nuclear revolution had created weapons so powerful they might be unusable—yet there was no good alternative to putting them at the center of U.S. strategy.

Under Ike and after, America would build the ability to deliver unprecedented destruction with unprecedented speed over unprecedented distances, by developing a nuclear triad composed of long-range bombers, land-based missiles, and submarine-launched ballistic missiles. Planners crafted intricate theories of nuclear strategy; they calculated the percentage of Soviet industry America had to be able to destroy, and the number of people it had to be able to kill, to keep the Kremlin from contemplating aggression. One U.S. attack plan called for an all-out aerial assault that would leave the Soviet Union, in the words of one general, "a smoking, radiating ruin at the end of two hours." All the while, the American arsenal grew apace: from 1,169 warheads in 1953, it reached 32,400 by 1965.[65] Stripped of its euphemisms, the art of deterrence was the art of threatening mass annihilation. The challenges, ethical as well as strategic, were agonizing.

In search of strategic efficacy and economic efficiency, Eisenhower exploited America's early nuclear advantage—a roughly ten-to-one edge in deployed warheads—by threatening to punish communist aggression anywhere with a devastating strike against the Soviet Union itself. "Our only chance of victory," said Eisenhower, was "to paralyze the enemy at the outset of the war."[66] That strategy worked for a time, but unraveled as the Soviets developed their own intercontinental striking force, leading critics to worry that "massive retaliation" left the free world with only the choice between suicide and surrender.[67] The Kennedy administration shifted to "flexible response," which involved strengthened conventional defenses and more calibrated forms of nuclear escalation—only to find, in Vietnam, that the former was hideously expensive, and to realize, amid nerve-wracking crises, that the latter might prove impossible. "The line between non-nuclear war and nuclear war is distinct and observable," Secretary of Defense Robert McNamara admitted, but "once the momentous decision has been made to cross that line, everything becomes much more confused."[68]

For the rest of the Cold War, the United States would keep searching for options—limited nuclear strikes, strategies for protracted nuclear war—meant to make deterrence effective by making the use of civilization-shattering weapons plausible. Even as U.S. diplomats negotiated arms control deals with Moscow during the 1970s, the Pentagon invested in highly accurate missiles, penetrating bombers, and other tools meant to squeeze strategic advantage out of superior technology. It may have been, said one U.S. secretary of defense, that "large-scale nuclear war" could never be a "sensible, deliberate instrument" of statecraft.[69] But American presidents had to convince Moscow, and themselves, that it was, for a world in which nuclear weapons were unusable would be a world in which Eurasia was safe for Soviet aggression.

It wasn't foreordained that the United States would win this contest. By the 1970s, the Soviet Union had attained strategic nuclear parity, thanks to a determined buildup of long-range forces. Moscow was also deploying new intermediate-range missiles, the SS-20s, which could, said one Soviet general, "hold all of Europe hostage."[70] The Red Army was fielding new conventional capabilities—better tanks, logistics, and attack aircraft—to smash through NATO's defenses. At the same time, the Kremlin was realizing long-term investments in aircraft carriers, submarines, and other globe-ranging capabilities. "We have seen a massive power shift," said Secretary of Defense Donald Rumsfeld in 1976. The Soviet Union was "becoming a true superpower."[71]

The upshot, U.S. officials feared, would be to worsen NATO's conventional plight in Europe, neutralize Western nuclear response options, and allow Moscow to checkmate American power around the world. Whether or not the Kremlin used its waxing military might for aggression, it might well use it for intimidation—to coerce Western Europe into timidity and neutrality, by showing that U.S. defense guarantees were worthless. The danger, one French president later commented, was that "the Soviets would have picked off each Western European country without having to go to war."[72] The Western answer would involve a new round of the arms race in the 1980s.

That race often seemed like an exercise in insanity. "The United States is piling up armaments which it well knows will never provide for its ultimate safety," Eisenhower had said. "We are piling up these armaments because we do not know what else to do."[73] Yet as much as the arms race appalled Ike and his successors, the implications of military weakness appalled them more. The requirements of deterrence in the nuclear age weren't pretty. The failure of deterrence could be uglier still.

---

*

MANAGING THE ARMS RACE ALSO REQUIRED MEETING A SECOND challenge—being strong, but not stupid, in crises. The superpowers never fired their awesome nuclear arsenals. But they brandished them at each other in high-stakes showdowns along the East–West divide. The Soviet Union and its allies sought to use calibrated coercion—combined, in many cases, with geographic advantage—to crack containment. America had to push back without pushing too far.

The crisis capital of the Cold War was a divided Berlin—"the testicles of the West," in Khrushchev's idiom.[74] Berlin mattered symbolically because here, the two competing systems were on display; it was salient geographically because it was located deep in East Germany and surrounded by Soviet armies. When Moscow wanted to make a point, it "squeezed" West Berlin; when the Kremlin made gains in the arms race, Berlin was where it tried to translate military strength into diplomatic success.

In 1948, Stalin had blockaded West Berlin in hopes of aborting the new West German state. Between 1958 and 1961—after the Kremlin had developed a nascent, and much exaggerated, intercontinental missile force—Khrushchev started two more crises to force the West out of Berlin. Khrushchev threatened that the rockets would rain down if NATO resisted; he said Berlin was a question "of geography which he intended [to] make use of."[75]

Mao Zedong was trying something similar in the Taiwan Strait. Mao, more than Khrushchev, was Stalin's true successor, at least in the level of violence he inflicted on his own people. His cavalier approach to nuclear war—it might kill 300 million Chinese, he mused, but that would leave 300 million survivors—frightened even the Kremlin.[76] Mao had initially planned to seize Taiwan, ruled by Chiang Kai-shek's Nationalists, as a coda to the civil war. But once the Korean War started, the U.S. Navy saved Chiang by "neutralizing" the strait. So Mao settled, in 1954–55 and again in 1958, for shelling Taiwan's small offshore islands, located miles from the mainland. Those islands were a "noose" around America's neck, he said—a place where geographic proximity allowed Beijing to put exposed outposts under enormous stress.[77] Like Khrushchev, Mao was testing whether America would risk everything to protect positions in the shadow of Communist power.

The presidents Khrushchev and Mao confronted—Eisenhower and Kennedy—thought they had to try. Credibility appeared to be an all-

or-nothing proposition for a country whose commitments circled the globe. If America's allies saw that Washington was unwilling to defend one beleaguered bastion, why would they trust it to defend others? "If we were to leave West Berlin," speculated Kennedy, "Europe would be abandoned as well."[78] The only problem was that actually defending these bastions might invite the apocalypse. There was no way to save the Taiwanese offshore islands conventionally, U.S. planners reported; defeating Chinese attacks would require nuclear strikes against the mainland and perhaps "general nuclear war between the US and the USSR."[79] Nor could an isolated Berlin be defended without nuclear escalation, an idea that horrified, because it threatened to vaporize, the very allies it was meant to reassure.

Avoiding humiliation *and* annihilation required a balancing act. Washington would not retreat; the United States, said Ike, would "push its whole stack of chips into the pot" if necessary.[80] To make the threat real, American presidents also engaged in coercive signaling— what Dulles called "brinkmanship"—of their own. In 1955, Ike secured a congressional resolution authorizing military action in the Taiwan Strait. In 1961, Kennedy called up the reserves while having a subordinate publicly warn that, for all Khrushchev's rocket-rattling, a strategically superior America could still pulverize the Soviet Union.[81] The United States would hold the line, leaving the enemy to choose whether to keep testing it at the risk of global war.

But because there was something ridiculous about threatening nuclear conflict over access to Berlin or some specks off Asia's coast, both presidents offered de-escalatory off-ramps. In 1959, Ike agreed to a meeting of foreign ministers and then a summit with Khrushchev to defuse one Berlin crisis. In 1961, Kennedy acquiesced in the building of the Berlin Wall, which the East German government used to solve its crisis of legitimacy by simply imprisoning its fleeing citizens. "A wall," said Kennedy, "is a hell of a lot better than a war."[82]

America escaped these crises without catastrophic escalation or credibility-killing retreats. The balance of resolve was roughly equal in a divided Europe: Khrushchev didn't want to die for Berlin any more than Ike or Kennedy did. Even Mao, with his bloodcurdling comments about nuclear war, didn't actually want to find out how bad it could be. Kennan's thesis seemed vindicated: if the West was strong and resolved enough, it might not have to fight. Nonetheless, these episodes were frightening; at one point, Kennedy directed his aides to quietly study a surprise first strike against the Soviet Union.[83] Perhaps the heaviest burden of containment was its requirement to stare down the enemy over local stakes that hardly seemed worth global war.

So showed the Cold War's gravest crisis. The chain reaction that caused the Cuban Missile Crisis started when Fidel Castro seized power in 1959, steered that country toward socialism, and then, amid plummeting relations with Washington, moved closer to Moscow. The American response, a botched invasion by Cuban exiles, was strategic blowback exemplified; it led to a Soviet–Cuban military alliance and the secret deployment of Soviet missiles to Cuba.

Khrushchev was trying to achieve several things at once. He wanted to protect Castro's socialist revolution so that it could spread throughout Latin America. He wanted to rectify the strategic balance by placing his intermediate-range missiles where they could hit the United States. He wanted leverage for the next round of the Berlin crisis. The deployment threatened to flip the geography of the Cold War, by exposing America's soft southern underbelly and entrenching Soviet strategic power in Washington's backyard. The gambit was exposed by U.S. spy planes, however, leading to thirteen days of terror in October 1962.[84]

The crisis brought the superpowers "eyeball to eyeball," said Secretary of State Dean Rusk—and brought America face to face with the fundamental challenge of crisis management in the Cold War.[85] Kennedy never believed he could accept the Soviet deployment; doing so would give Moscow another vector to threaten America, while giving countries everywhere reason to doubt U.S. resolve. Yet Kennedy also realized that invading Cuba or bombing the missile sites risked rapid, uncontrolled escalation, starting in the Caribbean and spreading around the globe. In the nuclear age, he said, any choice for war was "one hell of a gamble."[86] So Kennedy dialed up the coercion by instituting a blockade of Cuba and visibly preparing for conflict, while also making concessions—a public pledge not to invade the island, a private promise to withdraw old U.S. missiles from Turkey—meant to avoid it.

The strategy worked, in part because America still had a seven-to-one nuclear advantage, along with—for once—conventional dominance in the Caribbean. "We do not want to unleash a war," Khrushchev admitted. "We wanted to intimidate and restrain the USA vis-à-vis Cuba."[87] If Moscow was going to fight, there could hardly be a worse time or a worse place. But the crisis was chastening for *everyone*, and the risk of war may have been higher than Khrushchev and Kennedy knew. Had one of several incidents—the shoot-down of a U.S. spy plane over Cuba, a confrontation between an American warship and a Soviet submarine, and others—gone differently, matters might have gotten out of hand.[88]

The missile crisis, then, had one constructive effect: it ended the most dangerous part of the Cold War. "There appear to be no differences between your views and mine regarding the need for eliminating war in this nuclear age," Kennedy wrote to Khrushchev. "Perhaps only those who have responsibility for controlling these weapons fully realize the awful destruction their use would bring."[89] In the years afterward, the two sides would reduce the chance of war through arms control treaties and agreements to accept an awkward status quo in Berlin and Cuba. They informally resolved *not* to shoot down each other's reconnaissance satellites, since fears of surprise attack risked creating a self-fulfilling prophecy.[90] Meanwhile, the Politburo had dumped the crisis-craving Khrushchev for the less blustery, if no less ambitious, Leonid Brezhnev.

The reward for hanging tough was a tamer Cold War; after 1962,

Moscow got more cautious about playing games of nuclear chicken. Elsewhere, alas, the Kremlin was only starting to fight.

*

THE CORE OF AMERICA'S COLD WAR STRATEGY WAS SIMPLE: BUILD SITUA-tions of strength in Eurasia's industrial Rimlands. A third challenge, how-ever, was that the Cold War metastasized rapidly, and thereby exposed a great deal of weakness.

The source of that weakness was a tsunami of change in the devel-oping world. In just a quarter century, the collapse of European empires would create almost 100 new countries. Ideological radicalism and anti-Western resentment coursed through this emerging global south; from Latin America to Southeast Asia, the potential for mischief seemed endless. "The Russians can defeat us," the journalist Walter Lippmann predicted, "by disorganizing states that are already disorganized, by dis-uniting peoples that are torn with civil strife and by inciting their dis-content which is already very great."[91]

An opportunistic enemy would try just that. Stalin hadn't initially seen much potential in countries which Marxist dogma deemed unready for revolution. "One cannot trifle with the laws of historical develop-ment," he sniffed.[92] But Mao's triumph in China convinced Soviet leaders that the vistas for expansion were greater at the vulnerable periphery of the international system than at the well-defended center. Khrushchev championed "national liberation" movements sweeping the developing regions; he predicted that decolonization would "bring imperialism to its knees."[93] If Moscow couldn't break through containment, perhaps it could turn the free world's flanks.

Washington, by contrast, would have preferred to steer clear of the global south. But even divided worlds can be interconnected, so separat-ing vital from non-vital theaters proved hard indeed.

Countries that didn't have industrial resources might still control geography along the supply lines to regions that did; poor nations might possess oil, rubber, and other materials rich nations needed. If the Kremlin penetrated Latin America, it might destroy the hemispheric immunity that made the United States a global power. And if the Soviets ran off a string of Third World victories, the perception that Moscow had the momentum might undermine more important regions as well. So the Cold War sprawled as uncontrollably as the hot wars before it. "The whole southern half of the globe," declared John Kennedy in 1961, was "the great battleground for the defense and expansion of freedom today."[94]

By this point, Washington was unmistakably on the defensive. Khrushchev had thrust Soviet power into the Middle East, by selling (through Prague) arms to Egyptian leader Gamal Abdel Nasser, and then threatening to incinerate Paris and London after Britain and France attacked Egypt in 1956 in response to Nasser's nationalization of the Suez Canal. He was building a Latin American beachhead in Cuba. In Southeast Asia, Chinese and Soviet aid had helped the Viet Minh defeat the French in 1954; support from Moscow and Beijing would sustain North Vietnam in its war against Washington. The Soviet Union, China, and Cuba all looked to expand their influence in Africa during the 1960s and 1970s, as superpower tensions set the global south alight.[95]

Here, the Cold War featured many hot wars—civil wars, major conventional wars in Korea, Vietnam, and the Middle East, proxy wars, and insurgencies by the dozen. The superpowers wooed friendly countries while subverting hostile ones; they battled for influence in places, whether Angola or Afghanistan, that were once hopelessly obscure. The potential for escalation was real. A seesawing war between Israel and its Arab enemies in October 1973 elicited a massive U.S. airlift to shore up the Jewish state, followed by threats of Soviet military intervention, followed by an American nuclear alert. And the viciousness of these struggles could be terrifying: 14 million people died in Asia's Cold War–era conflicts.[96] For America, the Third World was where containment evolved from an elegant, regionally focused strategy into something more limitless and morally messier.

It wasn't that Washington *wanted* thugs as partners; from Vietnam to Venezuela, it periodically tried to stabilize troubled societies through

audacious reforms. But sometimes, in polarized and profoundly *unsta-*
ble places, there just weren't good alternatives to working with the
impure. When stakes were high, dangers imminent, and options lousy,
U.S. leaders resorted to less admirable expedients: support for friendly
dictators, destabilization or attempted assassination of hostile rulers,
brutal counterinsurgency programs, even military intervention. Some
of these interventions, such as U.S.-backed coups in Iran in 1953, Gua-
temala in 1954, and Chile in 1973, delivered anti-communist stability
for a time. Others, such as the not-so-covert invasion of Cuba at the Bay
of Pigs, backfired immediately. All were based on the idea, explained one
U.S. official, that "there are degrees of evil": supporting bad actors might
be the price of containing worse ones.[97]

This wasn't mere rationalization. By keeping countries out of communist hands, the United States preserved the possibility that they
might eventually turn democratic, as many did during the 1970s and
1980s. In the meantime, though, this ethos courted moral overstretch:
corrupt means can undermine the worthiest ends. Fighting along a
nearly global perimeter would bring strategic overstretch, too.

The culmination of both problems came in Vietnam. America
brought to Vietnam the same outlandish ambition that had allowed
it to remake other regions. The task, Lyndon Johnson explained, was
not simply to defeat the communist insurgency but to "enrich the hopes
and existence of more than a hundred million people."[98] America was
motivated, also, by the same fear of falling dominos that had led it to
intervene in Greece, Turkey, and Korea. Elsewhere, these impulses had
worked wonders. Here, they invited tragedy.

South Vietnamese leaders were unwilling to undertake the reforms
that U.S. officials urged on them, because doing so might threaten their
own power. Washington's answer, in 1963, was to back a counterproduc-
tive, destabilizing coup against its own proxy, Ngo Dinh Diem. Despite
deploying over 500,000 troops to the South, and dropping over 643,000
tons of bombs on the North between 1965 and 1968, the Pentagon could
not break the will of committed enemies. "The North will not count the

cost," vowed General Secretary Le Duan.[99] Nor did Washington prudently cut its losses; the view, as Rusk had said, that victory "would be worth any amount" produced an epically expensive defeat.[100] All this allowed Moscow to make Vietnam a strategic bonanza, by using modest injections of aid—especially lethal air defense systems—to drain and defeat its greatest adversary, in a peripheral conflict with worldwide ramifications.

The Vietnam War pulled U.S. troops from Europe and caused a global surge of anti-Americanism. It distracted Washington from countering the Soviet strategic buildup or moves in other regions. Its human costs and moral agonies ruptured America's Cold War consensus; the war, wrote Henry Kissinger, was "a national nightmare that stimulated an attack on our entire postwar foreign policy."[101] Vietnam showed that overextension anywhere could weaken positions everywhere—leaving Washington ill-prepared for the coming Soviet offensive.

"The world was turning in our direction," one KGB official recalled. Imperialism's weakness was socialism's opportunity.[102] Soviet arms deliveries to Third World clients skyrocketed from $9.2 billion between 1966 and 1975 to $35.4 billion between 1978 and 1982.[103] Between 1975 and 1979, Marxist revolutionaries seized power in Afghanistan, Angola, Cambodia, Ethiopia, Grenada, Laos, Mozambique, Nicaragua, South Vietnam, and South Yemen. Moscow used airlifts of Soviet weapons and Cuban troops to decide conflicts in Angola and the Horn of Africa. Most strikingly, it sent 80,000 troops to invade Afghanistan in 1979. That operation put Soviet forces within striking distance of the Strait of Hormuz and the Persian Gulf oilfields. Combined with an Islamist, anti-American revolution in neighboring Iran, it thrust the region into turmoil.

By the early 1980s, Soviet troops and proxies were menacing chokepoints and sea lanes from the Horn to the Caribbean; U.S. officials feared that additional allies from southern Africa to Central America were facing defeat. "The Soviet Union," boasted KGB head Yuri Andropov, "is not merely talking about world revolution but is actually assisting it."[104] The Cold War was a struggle for position on a global battlefield. It might not matter that America held the industrial flanks of Eurasia if it faltered everywhere else.

*

THEN THERE WAS A FINAL DILEMMA: WHETHER AMERICA COULD WIN THE Cold War without losing itself. Most U.S. policymakers adhered to Roosevelt's dictum that America could not survive as an "oasis of liberty surrounded by a cruel desert of dictatorship."[105] If the Soviets ruled Eurasia, Truman believed, America would be cut off from markets and materials. A totalitarian bloc would exert crushing pressure on the scattered remnants of the free world. Then, "we would have to take defense measures which might really bankrupt our economy, and change our way of life so that we couldn't recognize it as American any longer."[106]

The road to the garrison state, in this scenario, ran through American defeat in the Cold War. As before, however, dissenters countered that the Cold War itself could destroy American democracy, by causing the country to regiment its economy and militarize its politics. "The greatest danger that can befall us," Kennan himself had written, "is that we allow ourselves to become like" the other side.[107] Kennan wasn't wrong to worry. The Cold War was a protracted struggle that wrought profound domestic change.

For the first time, America built a peacetime national security state—a huge standing military, an awesome intelligence apparatus, and other tools of global power—as well as a "military-industrial complex" that churned out weapons and lobbied for influence. It centralized power in the presidency—in a nuclear conflict, there might not be time to ask Congress's opinion. Presidents further hoarded authority through the use of covert action, arms sales, and other tactics of a twilight struggle; at times, they simply lied about what they were doing on America's behalf. "If . . . America is to become an empire," claimed Senator J. William Fulbright, "there is very little chance that it can avoid becoming a virtual dictatorship as well."[108]

Meanwhile, Red-baiting became a regular, repugnant part of American politics. Demagogues demonized social reformers as agents of subversion. McCarthyism, which ruined lives, ended careers, and constricted free speech, served up the saddest example of the damage anticommunist hysteria could cause. For a moment in the 1950s, in fact, the specter of the garrison state seemed very real.

As McCarthyism was running rampant during the Korean War, sky-high military spending was triggering taxes, price controls, and other economic distortions. Truman throttled back production of butter so that America could build more guns; when steel workers bucked his wartime wage restrictions, he nationalized the mills and threatened to draft the strikers. "We are embarked on a voyage," cried Senator Robert Taft, that "may wreck the greatest adventure in freedom the human race has ever known."[109]

Fortunately, America never destroyed what it was trying to defend. McCarthy eventually discredited himself with his wild allegations; Truman's economic program was so unpopular it helped end his presidency. Military spending fell below 10 percent of GDP under the cost-conscious Eisenhower, and never climbed back above it.[110] And for all the stresses exerted upon it, the country's democracy retained its equilibrium.

The Cold War orthodoxy of the 1950s gave way to the cultural and political upheaval of the 1960s. When presidents went too far, the courts, Congress, and civil society found ways of reining them in. A country whose streets and campuses filled up with activists protesting the Vietnam War or the arms race was clearly not a country that had sacrificed dissent. The Cold War even showed that Eurasian struggles could make America freer and stronger.

The Cold War certainly made America more equal. The fight for the Third World may have involved coups and counterinsurgencies— but it also inspired the federal government to help civil rights reformers break down the racial caste system at home. When the Supreme Court banned school segregation in 1954, it did so under a chief justice, Earl Warren, who believed that "our American system . . . is on trial both at home and abroad."[111] When Eisenhower forcibly integrated Little Rock schools in 1957, he acted because he worried that "our enemies" were "gloating" over America's domestic injustices.[112] When Lyndon Johnson finally killed Jim Crow by passing landmark voting and civil rights bills, he declared those breakthroughs "a triumph for freedom as huge as any victory that has ever been won on any battlefield."[113] The Cold War put *virtuous* pressure on the American system, by raising the price the country paid for failing to honor its ideals.

A Eurasian struggle transformed America in other ways. For the first time, the federal government made generational outlays in U.S. universities, to master the disciplines—from rocket science to regional studies—that were vital to victory. "Next to defense," one CIA report concluded, "education is the biggest business of the modern state."[114] The dictates of national security also produced groundbreaking infrastructure projects, such as modernization of the federal highway system.

Even the much-lamented military-industrial complex was overwhelmingly a good thing. Military spending poured money into a growing middle class; it turbocharged tech hubs like Silicon Valley and defense-heavy regions like Southern California. In 1959, nearly 85 percent of U.S. research and development in electronics was funded by government.[115]

These investments produced rockets and other world-destroying weapons that America needed to keep containment vibrant. They also impelled commercial spinoffs, from integrated circuits to the Internet, that propelled America into the information age. Fairchild Semiconductor, an early leader in that field, got its start by making computer chips for missiles. Production for the Pentagon then produced economies of scale that allowed the firm to reduce costs and market its chips commercially. Unprecedented peacetime military outlays, writes historian Diane Kunz, "made the affluent America of the Cold War possible."[116] No less critically, they helped America maintain its position of leadership as the world moved from a mass-manufacturing era to one in which dominance in digital innovation and advanced information technologies became the marker of economic and military prowess.

Throughout the twentieth century, Americans debated which was more dangerous to their freedoms: letting brutal forces dominate Eurasia or going all-out to stop them. The Cold War proved that American democracy could withstand, even profit from, the rigors of rivalry—so long as the free world could find a way of winning it.

*

DEEP INTO THE 1970S, THAT PART REMAINED UNCERTAIN. THE SOVIET Union was surging in the arms race and the global south. America was reeling after Vietnam and Watergate. The free world was in a funk, as soaring oil prices stunted the global economy. A "fundamental alteration in the correlation of forces," bragged Soviet defense minister Dmitri Ustinov, was underway.[117]

The diplomacy of détente—a series of summits and superpower agreements that temporarily de-escalated the Cold War—reinforced that impression. In the Strategic Arms Limitation Treaty, America acknowledged the Soviet Union as its nuclear peer, even as Moscow continued to build the world's largest missile force. In the Helsinki Accords, the West effectively recognized a Soviet sphere of influence in Eastern Europe. Détente also gave Moscow greater access to Western trade, technology, and financing, which it used to buttress Eastern-bloc economies and its own military-industrial complex.

American leaders, especially Richard Nixon and Henry Kissinger, had seen détente as containment, modified; they believed a mixture of rewards and restraints would moderate Soviet behavior even as Soviet power grew. The Soviets, however, saw détente as a great victory—and a chance to keep increasing their strength without risking global war. Détente, said Brezhnev, was "the way to create more favorable conditions" for communism's peaceful triumph.[118]

By 1980, though, détente was dead. So, within another decade, was the Soviet empire. The free world would ultimately win the Cold War, through remarkable commitment and continual innovation.

That endurance was itself remarkable. The Cold War lasted far longer than even Kennan had expected. From beginning to end, Americans on the left and right wondered whether it was worth waging. Containment, Lippmann had warned, was a "strategic monstrosity" that might break America before it broke the Soviet Union.[119] Eisenhower wondered when the United States could "sit back and relax somewhat."[120] There were moments, especially after Vietnam, when Americans seemed sick of containment's costs and challenges.

In every case, though, the United States came storming back. The Soviets helped here: whether by invading Afghanistan or deploying lethal missiles to Europe, the Kremlin had a knack for showing just how quickly global order might crumble if America gave up the fight. The Soviet Union, National Security Adviser Brent Scowcroft said, "periodically rescued us from ourselves."[121] And having seen the international system buckle before, most Americans were willing, albeit reluctantly, to pay the price of Cold War as insurance against something worse. That persistence more than repaid the investment, because it bought time for the free world's strengths, and Soviet weaknesses, to do their work.

As Kennan had argued, the two superpowers were never equal. At its peak, the Soviet economy was between one-third and one-sixth the size of the U.S. economy. Washington had the allegiance of Britain, West Germany, and Japan, while Moscow counted the likes of East Germany, Hungary, and North Korea as allies.[122] Once the lines in Europe and Northeast Asia stabilized, the Cold War became a battle between dynamic democracies and impoverished tyrannies. So long as the free world didn't crumble, the Kremlin could stay in the game only by straining to the limit.

The price of Moscow's military prowess was a defense industrial complex that devoured over 20 percent of GNP, a figure that helps explain why the Soviet Union was such a fearsome competitor—and why it fatally exhausted itself in the end.[123] In the same way, Moscow eventually developed the embellishments of a global superpower, including the network of overseas clients. Yet that "achievement" left Moscow underwriting regimes that were economically incompetent, brutally repressive, and prone to provoking revolutions *against* communist rule.

The invasion of Afghanistan was a case in point. Far from a strategic masterstroke, it was a last-ditch effort to prop up a clueless, savage regime, and it left Moscow fighting a protracted war that brought military attrition and international opprobrium. The Soviets, diplomat Anatoly Dobrynin later rued, had invited "patterns of imperial overextension" like those that had once plagued America—but with only a fraction of America's power.[124]

This wasn't the only way in which strategic lucre turned out to be fool's gold. The deployments of SS-20s and heavy ICBMs were meant to intimidate the West, but eventually roused it to re-intensify the arms race. The Helsinki Accords contained provisions on human rights that the Soviet-bloc regimes planned to ignore, but their long-repressed citizenry did not. Even something as anodyne as expanded East–West travel proved dangerous, as it revealed the degree to which the Cold War was creating a contrast that the Soviet system couldn't withstand.

The Soviet model hadn't looked so bad when capitalism was mired in depression and democracies couldn't deliver for their citizens. That all changed from mid-century onward. The Rimland democracies, cultivated and protected by Washington, became models of capitalist prosperity; by the 1980s, Western per capita GDP was *nine times* that of the Soviet bloc.[125] Capitalism was delivering on communism's promises. The Soviet-backed regimes in Eastern Europe, for their part, had proven so incapable of meeting the public's needs that repeated violent crackdowns were needed just to suppress the inevitable revolts. The disparity was humiliating for those communist elites who remained capable of humiliation. It would eventually cause them to start asking what had gone wrong.[126]

Admittedly, the shocks of the 1970s had made it possible to think that history was turning in Moscow's direction. No less an authority than Henry Kissinger worried about "fall of the Western world."[127] But resilient capitalist systems adapted; Western democracies summoned enough cooperation to keep the free-world economy intact. By the early 1980s, these countries were making the leap to information-age prosperity, while inflexible command systems were stumbling into terminal decline. "In the U.S., small children play with computers," Moscow's top general lamented. "Here, we don't even have computers in every office of the Ministry of Defense."[128] The Soviet Union could compete in an era defined by mass-production industrial economies. It was hopelessly backward in the emerging digital age.

By then, Moscow was feeling a final weakness, born of centralized power and central position. The one-two punch of geography and ideology blessed America, encouraging countries to bandwagon with a distant democracy. The Soviet Union was cursed by comparison. An overbearing land power located within Eurasia was an existential threat to nearby countries, even—especially—Moscow's mostly unwilling allies. Communist ideology, for its part, could be more repulsive than attractive; a movement that permitted only one true leader demanded more obedience than some followers were willing to give. Throughout the twentieth century, regimes that bid for dominance from within Eurasia had gotten themselves killed. This time, the Kremlin's fellow communists were among those holding the knives.

The stabbing started early. Yugoslavia's Tito broke with Stalin in 1948 and became a tacit Western ally; Stalin spent the rest of his life trying, fruitlessly, to end Tito's.[129] Stalin recovered from that split by sealing his alliance with Mao. Over the next two decades, Mao's China epitomized Leninist extremism: it waged not one but two undeclared wars against the United States, while killing perhaps 40 million *of its own people.* Yet as Beijing terrified Washington, it tormented Moscow; by the mid-1950s, the two communist allies were on the path to confrontation.

The core issue was ideology, chiefly who would lead international communism after Stalin's death. It was magnified by geography, since tensions between two continent-sized neighbors can easily turn violent. These effects were, in turn, compounded by a deceptively sophisticated

U.S. strategy, which kept China under "maximum pressure," as Dulles phrased it, to "compel them to make more demands on the USSR which the latter would be unable to meet."[130] The long-building explosion finally came with a border war along the Ussuri River in 1969, blowing up a Sino-Soviet alliance—and creating a Sino-American one.

The latter partnership, sealed with toasts in Beijing in 1972, was improbable; it paired the "original anti-Communist," as veteran Red-baiter Nixon described himself, with the "original communist," as he called Mao.[131] For Nixon, the new relationship would fragment the enemy bloc by exacerbating its rivalries: in a dispute between two Eurasian heavyweights, America must "tilt towards the weaker" to counter the stronger.[132] For Mao, reconciliation was rooted in recognition that China, too, could use the "far barbarians" to balance the "near barbarians."[133] Here was a logic of geopolitics that transcended ideology. Put differently, Washington would work with a monster to make the world safe for Chinese communism and American democracy.

If the morality was fraught, the strategy was transformative. Washington, Dobrynin fretted, was "building a new strategic alignment of forces in international politics": the Sino-American partnership left Moscow with colluding enemies on both sides.[134] The U.S.–China relationship also gave Mao's successor, Deng Xiaoping, a taste of capitalist abundance, letting Beijing access Western trade and technology that accelerated his free-market reforms. Within years, a U.S. president visiting Moscow could point to an increasingly prosperous China as proof that "the power of economic freedom" was "spreading around the world."[135] The Sino-American partnership hammered the Soviet Union in strategic and ideological terms alike.

As the 1970s ended, the Soviet Union looked formidable but was actually quite feeble. The foundations of Soviet power were crumbling; overreach had become acute. "Like an overanxious chess player," wrote CIA analysts, "Moscow . . . has exposed lines of attack to its adversary, placed advanced pawns in jeopardy and acquired positions that it must defend at high cost."[136] The rulers who had gotten the Kremlin into this fix couldn't get it out; a physically decaying Brezhnev, so unwell he had to be carried by bodyguards, embodied Soviet decline. Like Wilhelm's Germany in early 1918 or Hitler's Germany in late 1941, the Soviet Union had lunged for supremacy—and left itself open to a decisive counterthrust.

*

THAT COUNTEROFFENSIVE TOOK FORM OVER MANY YEARS AND HAD many authors. Yet the thinker who best articulated it was a quiet egghead named Andrew Marshall. The leader who applied it most effectively was a former actor named Ronald Reagan.

Marshall was a product of the Cold War. A defense intellectual by trade, he spent his first career at the RAND Corporation—the Pentagon's think tank—studying Soviet behavior and the arms race. His second career, as director of the Pentagon's secretive Office of Net Assessment, made him one of the most influential strategists most people had never heard of. Russian observers would later call Marshall the "Pentagon's Gray Cardinal"—and for good reason. During the 1970s, Marshall had formulated a theory of how America could regain the strategic edge, which Reagan then turned into a theory of Western victory in the Cold War.[137]

"The United States will have to out-think the Soviets," wrote Marshall in one paper, since it could no longer "outspend them substantially." In particular, America must apply its resources in ways that amplified its strengths and exacerbated Moscow's vulnerabilities. The purpose was to "induce Soviet costs to rise" and "complicate Soviet problems in maintaining its competitive position"—to make the Cold War unbearably expensive for the Kremlin. The key was finding "areas of U.S. comparative advantage" and "steering" the rivalry into those areas. Stability might be one goal of U.S. policy, but it wasn't the only goal. To reclaim the initiative, Washington had to take risks and knock its adversary off-balance.[138]

There were hints of such a strategy in the 1970s. To conserve resources and political will, the United States swore off heavy-footprint military interventions in the Third World; it began, tentatively, to turn the tables by supporting anti-communist rebels who were taking up arms against Moscow and its proxies. Jimmy Carter started to exploit another key asymmetry—an asymmetry of legitimacy—by drawing attention to how Soviet-bloc regimes systematically oppressed their citizens. The Pentagon, meanwhile, was cooking up an "offset strategy" that envisioned using cutting-edge technologies to make revolutionary gains in precision and lethality.[139] Yet it was only in the 1980s that these initiatives came together in a comprehensive assault.

Reagan was well suited to lead that offensive because he was unburdened by pessimism about Western prospects. Reagan did not fetishize stability in the superpower relationship; a perpetual nuclear stalemate, he commented, "could get us both killed."[140] Nor did Reagan think the Cold War would last forever. Moscow's "incompetent and ridiculous system" must change or die.[141] One of Reagan's advisers put it bluntly: "He really wants the totalitarian system to end, but not by war."[142] During the 1970s, Reagan the critic of détente had catalogued, in radio broadcasts and private letters, the worsening weaknesses of the Soviet system. During the 1980s, Reagan the president tried to make the Soviet Union retreat and reform by making the strain on its position unbearable.

Military power was the leading edge. Reagan oversaw the greatest U.S. military buildup since the Korean War, focused on concepts and capabilities that would "impose disproportionate costs" and be "difficult for the Soviets to counter."[143] The Pentagon poured money into precision-guided munitions that could eviscerate Soviet tank columns, revolutionary Stealth bombers that were invisible to Soviet air defenses, and sensors and strike capabilities that could wreak havoc in the enemy's rear. The army's Air–Land Battle and NATO's Follow-on Forces Attack envisioned using networks of shooters and sensors to break up Soviet forces before they reached the front lines. The navy's Maritime Strategy would use superior global striking power to threaten Moscow with worldwide escalation—targeting Soviet supply lines, client states, even Far Eastern territories—if it started a war in Europe. "For the first time in our conventional rivalry," assessed Marshall, America was "really moving toward gaining the upper hand."[144] Through technology and creativity, Washington was slicing away at the superiority Moscow had long derived from geography and mass.

The Soviets were losing the nuclear race as well. Following Carter's lead, Reagan invested in a new generation of terrifyingly accurate sea- and land-based missiles, whose precision multiplied their destructiveness. The United States responded to Moscow's deployment of SS-20s to Eastern Europe by deploying its own Pershing-IIs to Western Europe; now, most of the Soviet bloc was within range of missiles that took just minutes to strike their targets. Reagan also approved an aggressive nuclear doctrine that centered on using penetrating bombers and highly accurate missiles to devastate Soviet nuclear forces and command structures while attack submarines sank Soviet missile subs and electronic warfare crippled the Kremlin's early-warning networks.[145] The nuclear deadlock was giving way to renewed U.S. advantage. Then, in 1983, Reagan announced his most unorthodox idea: the Strategic Defense Initiative.

This moon shot was meant to use U.S. advances in sensors, computers, and other digital-age capabilities to make ballistic missiles, the heart of Soviet strategic power, "impotent and obsolete."[146] Critics ridiculed the idea, and it was true that SDI—like other Reagan-era military initiatives—wouldn't be ready anytime soon. But all of these investments sent the message that America was exploiting information-age superiority to put an impoverished, innovation-poor adversary in an impossible position. If the Soviets "want an arms race," said Reagan, they would have to "break their backs to keep up."[147]

The same was true in the global south. What had begun as an experiment under Carter became something more lethally ambitious under Reagan. The United States gave guns, money, and other support to anti-communist guerrillas in Afghanistan, Nicaragua, Cambodia, and Angola. It harnessed their asymmetry of motivation to impose an asymmetry of pain on Moscow. America would "do to the Soviets what they have been doing to us," said Reagan's aide Richard Pipes. "At a very low cost . . . we can make it very hard for them."[148] The centerpiece of this strategy was Afghanistan, where Washington worked with Pakistan, Saudi Arabia, and other partners to bleed and banish the occupying Soviets. But as Chief of the Soviet General Staff Nikolai Ogarkov admitted, "there are trouble spots on every continent."[149] America was making Moscow pay prohibitively to hold what it had.

Finally, Reagan attacked the vulnerable heart of Soviet power. He assailed the Kremlin rhetorically, condemning it as an "evil empire" that brutalized and betrayed its own people.[150] His administration flooded the Soviet bloc with subversive literature and radio broadcasts; it supported movements, especially Solidarity in Poland, that were challenging Eastern-bloc regimes. Reagan also ratcheted up the economic pain on the Warsaw Pact by imposing sanctions, discouraging loans, and shutting off sources of Western technology. "The Soviet Union is economically on the ropes," Reagan said. "This is the time to punish them."[151] Moscow's greatest weakness was the rottenness of its own system, so throwing the Kremlin back meant throwing that failing into relief.

Timing was crucial. Reagan's strategy wouldn't have worked a decade earlier. By the 1980s, though, an overburdened adversary was primed for punishment. In every region, in every aspect of the Cold War, the Kremlin was losing ground. "We will never be able to catch up with you in modern arms until we have an economic revolution," admitted Ogarkov. "And the question is whether we can have an economic revolution without a political revolution."[152] Acheson would have been proud: America had claimed a situation of strength in the third Eurasian struggle. There was still no guarantee of a happy ending.

In 1914, Germany had chosen the possibility of national destruction over the certainty of painful decline. In 1941, Japan had made the same choice. In the early 1980s, the Soviet Union didn't seem willing to just fade away. Quite the opposite: superpower tensions soared and East–West diplomacy faltered. "The leadership is convinced that the

Reagan Administration is out to bring their system down," said one Soviet observer; "therefore they have no choice but to hunker down and fight back."[153] War wasn't inconceivable; in late 1983, Soviet leaders may briefly have thought a hyper-aggressive Reagan was using a NATO war game as cover for a surprise attack. Reagan had broken the superpower stalemate. He had also created a more perilous Cold War.

*

THE WORLD, THANKFULLY, AVOIDED BOTH THE POLARITIES REAGAN HAD dreaded—the "hail of fiery atoms" and the "quiet, deadening accommodation with totalitarian evil."[154] The Cold War ended with the third outcome, which he, like Kennan, had hoped for—a Western victory, resounding and peaceful. By the late 1980s, the Soviet Union was giving up in the military competition and the Third World. It watched as its Eastern European empire crumbled. After a forty-year struggle, Moscow surrendered on every issue of dispute. "We have lost World War III," fumed one Soviet general, "without a shot being fired."[155]

He presumably blamed Mikhail Gorbachev, who presided over this wholesale retrenchment of Soviet power. Gorbachev had taken command in 1985 after the last, senescent remnants of the Brezhnev generation departed the scene. The contrast was immediately evident. Young, energetic, and intellectually adaptable, he was everything his predecessors were not. "Myths and taboos (including ideological ones) are nothing for him," wrote one adviser. "He could flatten any of them."[156] Having spent time in the West, Gorbachev realized how far behind his country had fallen. He understood that the Soviet Union, blocked abroad, must begin to heal itself at home. "We couldn't go on living like this," Gorbachev believed. Moscow had to "alleviate the pressure that had borne down on us."[157] Gorbachev was the leader Kennan had been waiting for; his rise was a product of containment's success.

Gorbachev did *not*, however, plan to call off the Cold War—much less liquidate the Soviet Union. He believed in communism, albeit a reformed version of it. He hoped that clever diplomacy, rather than

Khrushchevian histrionics, could pry apart Washington and NATO; he wanted a renewed détente that would deliver trade, technology, and other things that would reinvigorate Soviet power. Gorbachev "seeks to relax East–West hostility . . . not to suspend the competition but to put the USSR in an improved long-term position," the CIA assessed.[158] But he could get that détente only by giving up everything.

Gorbachev's inescapable problem was that Soviet power entered a death spiral on his watch, because "reform" proved fatal to a system rooted in Leninist repression. Gorbachev's economic tinkering only compounded the flaws of an obsolete command economy. When he began liberalizing politically to create space for more dramatic economic change, he destroyed the one thing that held a totalitarian empire together—the power of the Communist Party. These processes would fatally fracture the Soviet state. Along the way, they made Gorbachev ever more desperate to slash defense spending and find international stability amid domestic upheaval—which allowed Reagan, genially but remorselessly, to make the price of that stability exorbitant.[159]

Into the late 1980s, Reagan kept the heat on in Afghanistan. He took a hard line on arms control; he pushed Gorbachev to respect human rights and individual liberties in the Soviet Union itself; he demanded, in West Berlin, that the Kremlin "tear down this wall." His policy, he explained, involved "just hanging back until we get some of the things we want"—by which he meant fundamental changes in how Moscow did business at home and abroad.[160] By 1987, a frustrated but flexible Gorbachev grasped that the only deals would be deals on American terms. "U.S. policy is one of extorting more and more concessions," he griped. "I'm weeping for you," his interlocutor, Secretary of State George Shultz, replied.[161]

Yet Reagan's strategy succeeded because he tempered strength with subtlety. The president had always planned to engage the Soviets from a place of power.[162] After the war scare of 1983, he realized that a cornered, humiliated Kremlin might lash out rather than caving in, so he used conciliation to make coercion effective.

Reagan's diplomacy was tireless: he held five summits with Gor-

bachev between 1985 and 1988. He treated the Soviet leader respect-
fully; he promised to take no victory laps after Kremlin concessions.
"We would simply express our appreciation," he said.[163] And Reagan
made clear, in public and private, that the reward for a fundamentally
changed Soviet Union would be a fundamentally better relationship
with the world. Moscow could "win accolades from people of good will
everywhere" by leaving Afghanistan, he said in 1987. This "would be
viewed not as a retreat but as a courageous and positive step."[164]

This carrot-and-stick diplomacy was protracted, sometimes painful, and periodically dramatic, as when Reagan and Gorbachev nearly
negotiated away their nuclear arsenals entirely at the Reykjavik summit
in 1986. Over time, though, Reagan applied enough pressure to make
an out-of-options Gorbachev realize that retreat was necessary, while
providing enough reassurance to make retrenchment palatable. Moscow
was "doomed" to cooperate with Washington, Gorbachev explained.
"Our main problem is to remove the confrontation."[165] Over three short
years, a two-generation conflict would end with historic Soviet concessions disguised as diplomatic breakthroughs.

In December 1987, the superpowers signed the Intermediate-
Range Nuclear Forces Treaty, which eliminated ground-launched,
intermediate-range nuclear missiles from their arsenals. By proscribing
the feared SS-20s, the treaty effectively ended Moscow's long effort to
coerce and divide NATO. By junking four deployed Kremlin missiles
for each American one, the pact showed that the arms race was ending
with asymmetric Soviet accommodations.[166] The next year, Gorbachev
began withdrawing from Afghanistan, under face-saving agreements
crafted to conceal a Soviet defeat. In a speech at the United Nations in
December 1988, Gorbachev announced that he was slashing Soviet conventional forces, while promising "freedom of choice" for nations everywhere and waving the white flag ideologically by saying Moscow had no
claim to "the ultimate truth."[167]

By this point, Gorbachev was radically expanding civil and political
freedoms within the Soviet Union, while using Reagan's endorsement of

those reforms to hold his domestic enemies at bay.[168] Most dramatically, in 1989–90, Gorbachev allowed the implosion of the Warsaw Pact, the opening of the Berlin Wall, and the reunification of Germany within NATO— changes that would, one U.S. official remarked, "rip the heart out of the Soviet security system."[169] It was a stunning outcome, and it owed a great deal to the power, security, and attractiveness of the Western world.

Twice in the past century, worldwide cataclysms had occurred because revisionist powers believed they could use sharp, brilliant wars to escape the tightening noose. The late-stage Soviet Union had no such possibilities. It was ringed by free-world alliances that were backed by solemn U.S. commitments, decades of massive military outlays, and threats of nuclear escalation. These commitments, and the capabilities backing them, were all the more formidable thanks to the stark changes in the military balance during the 1980s. If the Kremlin went down peacefully, it was because America's situations of strength gave Moscow no chance of averting decline through war.

Yet the Kremlin could also concede because the Western world allowed it to do so comfortably. Gorbachev believed that a stagnating Soviet Union could become *more* prosperous by joining a vibrant Western economy. He did not fear that a retreating Soviet Union would be attacked by a vengeful Germany or a remilitarized Japan, because those countries were now satisfied democracies, lashed to the United States. "The presence of American troops can play a containing role," Gorbachev remarked; the U.S. security system made Eurasia safer for everyone, *including the Soviet Union.*[170] Moscow could quit the arms race altogether, adviser Anatoly Chernyaev admitted, "because no one will attack us even if we disarm totally."[171] Who could have said *that* in 1914 or 1941? The historic achievement of America's postwar project was creating a world in which its own worst enemy could feel secure in defeat.

* * *

*

THE COLD WAR ENDED WITH AN AVALANCHE OF MIRACLES: THE LIBERA- tion of Eastern Europe, the retreat of Kremlin influence across the global periphery, the breakup of the Soviet state. Even before that, the Cold War had remade the world.

The number of democracies increased from perhaps a dozen in the early 1940s to 76 by 1990 and 120 a decade later: The cultivation of free institutions at the core of the postwar system allowed them to spread, eventually, far into the periphery as well.[172] In a world made safe for trade by the U.S. dollar and the U.S. Navy, global wealth increased faster than in any prior era.[173] The prospect of wars between the major capitalist powers receded dramatically; the killing fields of Western Europe became a zone of prosperity and peace. The third struggle for Eurasia wrought changes as fundamental as those wrought by the first two, with only a fraction of the violence.

This isn't to trivialize the costs. The United States spent an average of 7.5 percent of GDP on defense during the Cold War, a figure unimaginable in any prior "peacetime" era.[174] It lost around 100,000 service members in the Cold War's "small wars." For other countries, the toll was steeper: some 20 million people died in all the wars of the Cold War era, although some of those conflicts were less closely tied to the superpower rivalry than others.[175] The nuclear arms race that terrified humanity, the atrocities committed by Pinochet, Suharto, and fellow brutalizers who sided with the West, and other tragedies and misdeeds further inflated the bill. There was no immaculate victory in a clash as epic as the Cold War. That conflict scarred every nation, every region it touched.

But the proper way of reckoning with those costs is to ask, compared to what? Was the Cold War worse than the two preceding hot wars, which set records for exsanguination and inhumanity? Was it worse than the prospect that another totalitarian evil might gain the ascendancy as the capitalist world tore itself apart? "If you want a picture of the future," wrote Orwell in the wake of World War II, "imagine a boot stamping on a human face—forever."[176] The idea that the East–West conflict was a catastrophe for the world and a Pyrrhic victory for Washington betrays a short historical memory and a real lack of imagination. Compared to what happened in the first half of the twentieth century and what could have happened in the second, the Cold War looks pretty good.

Nuclear weapons deserved some credit; as warfare became more apocalyptic, it became less useful as an instrument of policy. Yet nuclear deterrence didn't happen automatically. Histories of the twentieth century might not stress the stabilizing qualities of nuclear weapons had Hitler, Stalin, or Mao been the first to attain them. It mattered that the world's foremost nuclear power was a democracy that sought to prevent aggression rather than a tyranny that sought to profit from it. The structure of nuclear deterrence that took hold during the Cold War was part of a new structure of global politics, in which a mighty offshore superpower pledged itself to the defense of onshore friends. Technology once again shaped the Eurasian century, but in ways that were shaped by strategic choice.

The free-world security system also delivered a final benefit: stability that outlasted the superpower rivalry. No one had to lay the foundations of a new global order once the Cold War ended; those foundations had been tested long before. Germany and Japan did not, as some had feared, return to their bad old ways once the Soviet Union disintegrated; they had more to gain by remaining embedded within a liberal order led by the United States. The situation after 1991 was unprecedented in the modern era. For the first time in a century, no actor, or group of actors, could threaten to dominate Eurasia and make it a platform for global expansion.

Amid the euphoria that followed, it sometimes seemed that a horrible Eurasian century was over. Foreign affairs journals were filled with articles arguing that globalization had rendered geopolitics passé. After a dangerous Cold War, declared Secretary of State James Baker, America could now seek a world-spanning "democratic peace."[177] Mackinder was long dead when the Cold War concluded, and so, perhaps, was the relevance of his ideas.

But history hadn't ended, and neither had the Eurasian century. Fifty years earlier, in 1942, Spykman had warned that Japan wasn't the only scourge of stability in the Western Pacific: a "modern, vitalized, and militarized China" might one day dominate the region.[178] Thirty-eight years before *that*, Mackinder had closed his 1904 lecture with a similar prophecy: a China that expanded within Eurasia might pose the greatest threat "to the world's freedom," because it "would add an oceanic frontage to the resources of the great continent."[179] At the dawn of the post–Cold War era, that prospect seemed quite distant. Today, it looms large indeed.

THE SECOND EURASIAN
CENTURY

I t had the feel of a historical watershed. On February 4, 2022, the world's two top tyrants—Russia's Vladimir Putin and China's Xi Jinping—met in Beijing, just as the Winter Olympics were beginning there. The foreign diplomatic presence was lighter than usual at these "genocide games": China's unrelenting repression of its Uighur minority kept representatives of some democracies away. But the Eurasian dictators were marching in lockstep. During a ceremony at which Xi and Putin signaled their sartorial unity by sporting mauve ties, they signed a 6,000-word statement proclaiming their strategic resolve.

Beijing and Moscow pledged to defend their illiberal polities—which they, of course, termed "democracies"—against Western impositions. They condemned U.S. alliance blocs in Europe and Asia as Cold War relics; they touted Sino-Russian cooperation with "no limits" and "no forbidden areas."[1] The text was dense, yet the meaning was clear: the two Eurasian powers were, as Xi had said, fighting "back-to-back" against the oppressive hegemony of the liberal world.[2] It wasn't quite Molotov–Ribbentrop or the Tripartite Pact. But it was another call for a radically new system with an illiberal Eurasia at its core.

There had been hints of what that world might look like. In 2008 and

2014, Putin had revived the tradition of territorial conquest in Europe by dismembering Georgia and then Ukraine. Beijing had previewed a Sino-centric Asia by illegally claiming much of the South China Sea and picking fights from the Senkaku Islands to the Himalayas. Both countries carried out military buildups aimed at America and its allies; both embarked on Eurasian gambits to secure their continental hinterlands. Both regimes were veering into highly personalized, neo-totalitarian rule; both leaders were speaking the language of confrontation against foreign foes. Yet what made the Sino-Russian statement of February 2022 so memorable was not what had come before, but what came shortly after.

On February 24, Putin sent his armies crashing into Ukraine. The invasion was unabashedly eliminationist in its goals: Putin aimed to crush Ukraine's military, topple its government, and absorb its territory. The invasion was equally eliminationist in its methods: in the areas they occupied, Russian units raped Ukraine's women, stole its children, murdered its citizens, and otherwise sought to erase its national identity. Years earlier, Aleksandr Dugin, that hardline geopolitical thinker, had written that Russia must build a "great-continental Eurasian future ... with our own hands."[3] The war in Ukraine suggested those hands would be covered in blood.

Fortunately, if Putin's vision was grand, his execution was atrocious. The Kremlin ruler had sought a brief, brilliant victory; he got a long, tough slog that cost his country dearly instead. Even so, the events of February 2022 *were* a historic watershed. They served notice that a second Eurasian century was underway.

By early 2022, the democratic dominance of the post–Cold War era was fading. Key regions of Eurasia were awash with upheaval; from Ukraine to Taiwan, the air hung heavy with the threat of war. Global politics were more polarized than at any time in decades, as a cohort of autocracies within Eurasia confronted a free-world community on its margins. This contest, like every prior Eurasian conflict, features new technologies, new alignments, and new modes of rivalry. But the stakes and dangers are all too familiar. America and its allies must win a new cold war against a new axis of authoritarians—provided they can prevent a hot war that might rip the world apart.

*

THE POST–COLD WAR ERA WASN'T SUPPOSED TO END LIKE THIS. THE PAYoff from the free world's victory in the superpower struggle was an imbalance of power more marked than anything since the Pax Romana. America's goal, for the next quarter century, was to make that moment last.

The end of the Cold War transformed the international landscape: subtracting one superpower from a two-superpower system left a single, hyper-dominant coalition. America and its treaty allies accounted for roughly 70 percent of global GDP and 75 percent of world military spending.[4] Serious competitors were nowhere to be found. China was just rising to its feet, while post-Soviet Russia was flat on its back. When another would-be challenger, Saddam Hussein, sought to master the Middle East by invading Kuwait in 1990, the resulting "mother of all battles" turned into the mother of all beat-downs, which showed how outrageously superior America's information-age military was. The ideological mismatch was also severe; democracy, having vanquished communism, enjoyed a dearth of rivals and a surfeit of prestige.

America's first decision, in this environment, was not to throw it all away. Neo-isolationists argued that the end of the Cold War should mean the end of U.S. globalism; America, wrote one erstwhile hawk, could become "a normal country in a normal time."[5] Yet most U.S. officials in the 1990s and later understood that America's postwar project hadn't been solely about containing communism. It had also involved suppressing the strategic anarchy that had ravaged Eurasia twice before. That responsibility endured, even if the Soviet Union didn't. "Either we take hold of history," said James Baker, "or history will take hold of us."[6]

The return of history was the last thing Washington wanted. So the United States preserved its Cold War alliances as strategic circuitbreakers in key regions. It extended NATO deep into Eastern Europe, to enlarge the zone of stability that had arisen in the West. Under multiple administrations, America would maintain a globally dominant military, to keep its alliances credible and keep new threats in check. "The world order," one Pentagon document stated, "is ultimately backed by the U.S."[7]

Sure enough, when Saddam barged into Kuwait in 1990, a U.S.-led coalition kicked him out. When ethnic conflict engulfed the Balkans, Washington and its NATO allies extinguished the flames. When China coerced a democratizing Taiwan with missiles and military maneuvers in 1995–96, the White House sent two carrier strike groups to back Beijing down. China might be a "great military power," said Secretary of Defense William Perry, but "the premier—the strongest—military power in the western Pacific is the United States."[8]

American military hegemony would tame potential challengers until economic integration transformed them. The United States welcomed China and Russia into the World Trade Organization; it pulled them into a booming global economy. This was a classic "golden fetters" strategy: it would give Moscow and Beijing stakes in supporting the U.S.-led order, while encouraging economic reforms that would unleash pent-up desires for freedom among their people. America would turn would-be rivals into "responsible stakeholders," and perhaps even pacific democracies, before those countries could turn against the system that had made them rich.[9]

Finally, America would soothe the sources of international rivalry by spreading liberalism farther than ever before. After 1945, Eurasia's geopolitics changed once the politics of Germany and Japan changed—and once cutthroat mercantilism gave way to economic collaboration. The lesson, for the post–Cold War generation, was that strengthening human rights, promoting democratic reforms from Eastern Europe to Southeast Asia, and fostering trade and globalization would bring a freer, richer, safer world. "The successor to a doctrine of containment must be a strategy of enlargement," said Bill Clinton's national security adviser, Tony Lake—"enlargement of the world's free community of market democracies."[10]

This strategy was ambitious, but it wasn't especially radical. In the bipolar environment of the Cold War, America had promoted security, prosperity, and democracy within the free world. In the unipolar environment of the post–Cold War era, America took that project global. The goal, George W. Bush would explain, was to "build a world where great powers compete in peace instead of continually prepare for war"—to banish Eurasian rivalry by locking in liberal values and benign U.S. hegemony.[11] That's not, unfortunately, what happened—although the record of America's post–Cold War statecraft wasn't so bad, and the story of why it stumbled isn't as simple, as it may seem.

*

CONSIDER WHAT THAT PROJECT ACHIEVED. THE POST-COLD WAR ERA didn't have to be a comparatively peaceful, prosperous interlude between epochs of rivalry. It might just have been more of the same. A reunified Germany and a reinvigorated Japan might have bullied the countries around them. The specter of "German aggression, German tanks," still lingered, Polish leaders warned.[12] The world, political scientist John Mearsheimer predicted, was headed "back to the future," as the resumption of history freed geopolitical demons caged by the Cold War.[13] Instead, the post–Cold War era saw rising global incomes, record levels of democracy, and another quarter century of great-power peace. U.S. power was indispensable in every regard.[14]

Commerce rarely thrives in chaos. Post–Cold War globalization gained momentum in a climate of security provided by Washington, just as late-nineteenth-century globalization occurred on waves Britannia ruled. U.S. hegemony *was* mostly stabilizing: the extension of NATO into Eastern Europe smothered embers of conflict in that region by protecting smaller countries from their former tormentors. Germany and Japan remained within the bear hug of U.S. alliances that both protected and pacified them; before long, the worst one could say was that these nations spent *too little* on defense. And across Eurasia's regions, it was America that deterred violent revisionism and succored emerging democracies. "Why is Europe peaceful today?" Mearsheimer later conceded. Because Washington was a "night watchman" keeping the terrors away.[15]

So what went wrong? One problem was the catastrophic success of economic integration. After a disastrous post-collapse depression, Russia recovered; its real GDP doubled between 1998 and 2014, which allowed military spending to quadruple. China, now fully embarked on its post-Mao reforms, exploited global markets and technology to turbocharge development; GDP surged twelve-fold, and military spending tenfold, between 1990 and 2016.[16] The drones, submarines, and missiles this buildup featured were often made with technology procured, licitly or illicitly, from the democratic world.[17] None of this would have happened had Washington not pulled Russia and China into a thriving world economy—and given them the strength to unsettle the status quo.

This first problem wouldn't have hurt so much if not for a second: democracy was less irresistible than Washington hoped. Russia never completed its political transition. The structural residue of the Soviet system, the autocratic instincts of its elites, and the economic carnage of the 1990s cast the country back into strongman rule. Autocracy persisted in China; rather than being mellowed by economic integration, the Communist Party used the resulting prosperity to buy off the population and build the repressive capabilities of the state.[18] A thoroughly liberalized Eurasia might have become a "democratic zone of peace."[19] But in its two largest countries, illiberal leaders and legacies proved tenacious. Which related to a third problem: for the once-and-future great powers of Eurasia, American hegemony looked threatening indeed.

From the early 1990s onward, Russian leaders made clear that *they* didn't welcome U.S. influence in Eastern Europe. Russians, British diplomats reported in 1997, saw NATO enlargement as "a humiliating defeat."[20] Chinese officials made not-so-veiled nuclear threats when Clinton stuck up for Taiwan in 1996.[21] Beijing would later call the post–Cold War era a "period of incessant warfare" and strife.[22] Clearly, not everyone thought U.S. power so benign.

But what, exactly, was so threatening? No Kremlin leader ever seriously alleged that NATO, then racing to *reduce* its military capabilities, was going to conquer Russia.[23] Nor was there any chance of America invading China; if anything, the U.S. presence in Asia made Beijing safer by precluding an unconstrained, remilitarized Japan.[24] In some ways, Beijing and Moscow were actually the biggest beneficiaries of U.S. strategy. China grew rich and powerful in a world pacified by Washington. NATO expansion, much as Russia hated it, kept Germany contained and Eastern Europe—long the pathway for marauding armies—tranquilized. Yes, Moscow had lost its empire. But it had gained greater safety—more than in 1914 or 1941, certainly—from external attack.

The real problem was that safety from external attack isn't the only thing rulers want. They want glory, greatness, and empire; they want security not just for their nations but for themselves. *This* is where the conflict emerged.

By maintaining, even expanding, its sphere of influence, Washington was preventing Moscow and Beijing from creating their own. NATO expansion reduced the odds that a resurgent Russia might someday rebuild its empire. "Just give Europe to Russia," President Boris Yeltsin told Clinton. "I don't think the Europeans would like this very much," Clinton replied.[25] China, once Asia's premier power, couldn't even take Taiwan, with the U.S. Navy parked off its coast. The post–Cold War order might have given Russia and China what they needed. It certainly didn't give them what they desired.

That order also antagonized China, and later Russia, by menacing their regimes. The men who ran the Chinese Communist Party were not stupid. They knew Washington was using economic seduction to promote political evolution; they worried that an autocratic regime might not survive in a democratizing world. America, Chinese officials alleged, was waging a "smokeless World War III" against Beijing.[26] Similarly, once Russia's democratic experiment failed, an increasingly illiberal Vladimir Putin had to fear ideological contagion from post-Soviet states, such as Ukraine and Georgia, that *were* reforming and moving toward the West. "We should do everything necessary so that nothing similar ever happens in Russia," he remarked.[27] For the advanced democracies, U.S. influence was mostly reassuring. For autocracies, it was an existential threat.

Since U.S. policies generated more resistance than expected, preserving the peace would have taken more effort than Washington had planned to exert. Here, a final problem arose: America wanted all good things at once.

The United States claimed a "peace dividend" even as it increased its global ambition: defense spending fell from 6 percent of GDP in the 1980s to 3 percent as the 1990s ended.[28] That didn't matter much at first, because America's lead seemed insurmountable. But as the balance shifted, Washington found itself distracted and demoralized.

The distraction came after September 11, 2001. Those attacks were a by-product of America's effort to secure the Middle East by stationing troops in Saudi Arabia—which was a grievous insult to Osama bin Laden and his fanatical followers. The U.S. response to 9/11 was to seek a deeper peace in this least stable part of Eurasia by eliminating threats—from terrorists and rogue regimes—and implanting liberal values. Very little went as planned.

Two long, mismanaged wars claimed over 7,000 American lives. They consumed U.S. resources for more than a decade. Their disappointing outcomes, combined with the effects of the 2008 financial crisis, produced sharp cuts in U.S. defense spending. They also elicited a feeling, under both Barack Obama and Donald Trump, that "nation-building here at home" should displace order-building abroad.[29] America was feeling that old temptation of retrenchment. The handcuffs on history were being loosened just as fierce Eurasian forces were stirring, again.

* * *

*

THE FIERCEST CHALLENGE IS ALSO THE MOST NOVEL. XI'S CHINA IS A Leninist regime that professes adherence to socialism but practices an unequal, state-driven capitalism. It combines wealth and technological savvy with angry, atavistic nationalism. It strives for supremacy through old-school military coercion and new-age digital authoritarianism. Yet if China isn't quite like any prior world power, the thrust of its statecraft—its bid for hybrid hegemony—is nothing new. And if Mackinder saw this coming, it's because China's geography is both a blessing and a curse.

China has the Eurasian reach the Soviet Union enjoyed—one can travel halfway from Shanghai to the European Union without leaving its borders—as well as the usable oceanic frontage the Kremlin mostly lacked.[30] That position creates perpetual problems: China is ringed by some twenty countries, including four nuclear powers and many historic enemies. Its large, distant hinterland is populated by Tibetans, Mongols, and Uighurs who wish to escape Beijing's grip.[31] But that position also makes a strong, motivated China the scariest sort of power—one that can aspire to mastery in multiple domains.

Today, China is strong; the rocket-fueled ascent of the post-Mao era made it the world's workshop and top trading state. And China is motivated, thanks to a cocktail of power, history, ideology, and personality.

China is not so much a rising power as a risen power that wants its say in reshaping a system it did not create. It is a former empire that once controlled large tracts of Eurasia and held much of the Western Pacific in its sway; its leadership views a Sino-centric world as the norm to which history must revert. China is also a bitter, brooding revanchist that seeks to undo a "century of humiliation" by reclaiming territories— and respect—surrendered when the country was divided and weak. Finally, China is an illiberal state whose rulers fear the subversive norms of a liberal world.[32] And it has swerved, under Xi Jinping, back into a more personalized form of tyranny, with all the destabilizing potential that implies.

Xi did not create the assertive China we know today; that trend began under his predecessor, Hu Jintao. But after taking power in 2012, Xi systematically dismantled constraints on his authority at home and curbs on Chinese conduct abroad.[33] Over the following decade, the "chairman of everything" obliterated term limits, sidelined rivals, and grabbed more power than any leader since Mao. At the Communist Party Congress in October 2022, Xi manifested his dominance by having an aging Hu hustled away. The year after, he purged his country's foreign minister, defense minister, and the generals in charge of its nuclear forces within the space of a few months. And as Xi shook up the Chinese system, he staked his legacy on winning similarly sweeping changes in the wider world. "No force can stop the advance of the Chinese people and the Chinese nation," he declared in 2019.[34]

China undoubtedly seeks global primacy; Xi's "great rejuvenation of the Chinese nation" is a euphemism for Beijing retaking its perch atop the world. In Xi's desired future, one Sinologist explains, a "global network of partnerships centered on China would replace the U.S. system of treaty alliances, the international community would regard Beijing's authoritarian governance model as a superior alternative to Western electoral democracy, and the world would credit the Communist Party of China for developing a new path to peace, prosperity, and modernity that other countries can follow."[35]

This isn't some secret plan. Beijing is openly engaged in an omni-directional global offensive meant to win leadership in international institutions, create new economic and security relationships with developing countries, position itself at the center of world trade and technological networks, and gradually make the American-led order a thing of the past. For years, Xi has talked explicitly about "building a socialism that is superior to capitalism" and realizing "a future where we will win the initiative and have the dominant position."[36] The path to hegemony will be smoother if Beijing can first tame the regions it abuts.

China is imposing itself in East Asia and the Western Pacific, the earth's most economically vibrant region and Beijing's gateway to the world. Xi once loosely described this project as "Asia for Asians"; a region rid of U.S. power will fall under Chinese control.[37] Beijing claims nearly all of the marginal sea—the South China Sea—through which much of global commerce passes, strategically located features in the East China Sea to its north, as well as the critical island, Taiwan, between them. China cannot lose "even one inch" of this territory, Xi maintains.[38] China also seeks a larger, less formal, sphere of influence in which countries from South Korea to Australia must defer to its wishes. This program requires cutting the chain of U.S. alliances in the Western Pacific. Beijing will share that ocean, one Chinese admiral quipped, if the line is drawn at Hawaii.[39]

The methods of Chinese expansion are multiple. For decades, China has been pulling the region's economies into its orbit, so they will be, eventually, unable to escape its gravitational field. It corrupts and co-opts Asian elites; it sows disinformation and division in democratic societies. Beijing has used everything from paramilitaries sailing fishing vessels to the construction of artificial islands built atop coral reefs—a "great wall of sand," one U.S. admiral quipped—to secure the South China Sea.[40] The hard-power backstop for this activity is the biggest peacetime military buildup by any country, anywhere, since before World War II.

Since the 1990s, China has been amassing weapons—submarines, advanced air defenses, cruise and ballistic missiles—meant to keep U.S. ships and planes far away. Other capabilities, including advanced attack aircraft, heavily armed surface ships, and aircraft carriers, give China a power-projection capability of its own. Now, the People's Liberation Army is building hypersonic missiles, long-range bombers, an expanding strategic nuclear force, and other capabilities of global reach. The exact cost of China's modernization is shrouded in deception, but the scale and pace are astounding. China, once an afterthought for Pentagon planners, now boasts the world's largest missile force and navy by number of ships. The size of its nuclear arsenal doubled just between 2020 and 2023.[41] China is rapidly reaching the point where it can plausibly hope to hammer America's forces in the Western Pacific and then reorder the region to its liking. Or, perhaps, it can attack its neighbors and use the threat of nuclear escalation to keep Washington from intervening at all.

The focal point, for now, is Taiwan, where Xi has ordered the

People's Liberation Army to be ready for action by 2027.[42] Historical score-settling aside, Taiwan's centrality comes from a mixture of location and innovation. Technologically speaking, that island produces the vast majority of the world's highest-end semiconductors, the source of the computing power that drives our digital age. Geographically speaking, Taiwan commands the inner seas of the Western Pacific; it anchors the First Island Chain, which blocks Beijing from the waters beyond. A democratic Taiwan, writes one PLA analyst, is "a lock around the neck of a great dragon."[43] A Chinese-controlled Taiwan would open up the entire region.

Once Taiwan is taken, the Chinese navy could threaten Japan's life-giving supply lines. "If Taiwan falls, our southwestern islands are indefensible," one official in Tokyo told me. China could tighten its grip on the South China Sea and the countries, from India to Australia, whose economic lives depend on it; Beijing could play havoc with U.S. alliances across maritime Asia while freeing up resources for missions near and far.[44] For China, Taiwan is not a resting place. It is a springboard to regional dominance and global reach. China's destiny will not be fulfilled, says Xi, until the country is a "great maritime power."[45] Mahan would be proud.

*

MACKINDER ALSO ANIMATES CHINESE POLICY, AS BEIJING IS MAKING THE most of its continental centrality. Expansion eastward, into the Pacific, requires taking on strong U.S. positions, which makes western expansion more attractive: building—or, rather, rebuilding—an integrated Eurasia with China as its hub. These maritime and continental thrusts are two sides of the same coin; the more secure China is on one flank, the more attention it can devote to the other. So Xi's China has resolved, as a PLA general once recommended, to "seize for the center of the world."[46]

Xi announced as much in Kazakhstan in 2013, grandly unveiling his Belt and Road Initiative—a "project of the century," he would later say.[47] Under BRI and follow-on projects, China has been weaving webs of influence enmeshing countries from Southeast Asia to Southern Europe and beyond. Infrastructure projects in Pakistan, Sri Lanka, and Myanmar can help China encircle India and punch through to the Indian Ocean. Overland pipelines and transportation networks ease China's Malacca dilemma—the fact that much of its trade and energy flows through maritime chokepoints—by providing safer access to the Persian Gulf and Europe. Investment and loans-for-resources deals ensure supplies of critical minerals in Africa, Latin America, and Southeast Asia. The proliferation of 5G telecommunications networks and "smart cities" outfitted with Chinese surveillance gear propel Beijing's technological influence into the developing world.[48] Here, the flag follows trade: as China invests in a blue-water navy, it is eyeing a global network of bases along key waterways from the Gulf of Thailand to the Bab al-Mandeb, while using peacekeeping missions, training programs, anti-piracy operations, and paramilitary forces to beef up its security presence abroad.[49]

In the near term, these programs will improve China's access to resources needed for its development: fossil fuels for its industries, cobalt and nickel for green energy projects, digitized data for its artificial intelligence algorithms. In the longer term, the goal is to develop overwhelming strength vis-à-vis a Europe that is relegated to a democratic toehold in a Sino-centric supercontinent, or even an America pushed to the margins of a system managed by Beijing. "Access to Eurasia's resources, markets, and ports could transform China from an East Asian power to a global superpower," scholar Daniel Markey writes.[50] It would open up new horizons in Latin America and the Arctic, places where Chinese influence is already expanding fast. It would give Beijing greater capacity to influence—and coerce—worldwide.

It would also create, within Eurasia, a system totally unlike the one Americans have come to know. Democracy would become an endangered species in areas with heavy Chinese influence; just look at how Beijing and Moscow use their combined heft to crush "color revolutions" in Central Asia. Economically and technologically, all roads will lead to Beijing. In the year 2049, predicts the Sinologist Nadège Rolland, residents of Eurasia will "baidu" rather than "google," while getting their news from China Global Television Network, not CNN. They will navigate using Chinese alternatives to the Global Positioning System. They will have access to an autocratic Internet guarded by Beijing's "great firewall."[51]

Exaggerated or not, this scenario illustrates the many forms of Chinese power. Beijing may sometimes seek Eurasian influence by beating Indian soldiers to death along their shared Himalayan frontier.[52] Yet what makes the Chinese challenge so vexing is that it combines military muscle with subtler methods of control.

BRI itself has been somewhat downgraded since 2020, due to concerns about bad loans and "debt trap diplomacy." But Beijing is still carving out digital spheres of influence, as countries adopt its 5G technology and Beijing buys or builds data centers, fiber-optic cables, and other infrastructure of the Internet.[53] China is still using loans and investment as sources of attraction; it leverages its market power, as the top trading partner of more than half the world's countries, to manipulate their policy choices. It has debuted new projects, such as the Global Development Initiative and Global Security Initiative, that are meant to tie countries—particularly in the global south—more closely to China by offering alternatives to an economic and security architecture that has long been led by the United States. It uses police training programs, intelligence exchanges, and other such endeavors to protect corrupt or autocratic regimes against challenges from within. Not least, China is racing to dominate artificial intelligence, quantum computing, synthetic biology, and other high-tech industries, so that it can lead the world economy and reap the geopolitical advantages. "Under a situation of increasingly fierce international military competition," Xi avers, "only the innovators win."[54]

In Xi's Eurasian gambit, timeless aspirations meet cutting-edge capabilities. It is here, too, where China's internal and external politics most fully mesh.

The Chinese government threw between one and two million Uighurs into concentration camps in the half decade after 2017. It combined digital repression, in the form of pervasive cameras, biometric scanners, and DNA swabs, with physical repression, in the form of checkpoints, forced sterilization, and other atrocities, to make their home region, Xinjiang, a showcase for twenty-first-century totalitarianism.[55] The Chinese Communist Party must put the "organs of dictatorship" to work, Xi directed, and show "absolutely no mercy" toward its enemies.[56]

Geopolitics infuse this humanitarian catastrophe. Xinjiang sits astride transportation routes to Central Asia, Pakistan, and other Eurasian hot spots, so instability, let alone "subversion," there is intolerable.[57] As Beijing uses its sway with nearby countries to forcibly repatriate Uighurs who escape—or deploys its cash and surveillance gear to boost friendly tyrannies—it further previews the brutalities that will proliferate with Chinese power.

Alas, China isn't the only autocracy trying to rewire Eurasia and, with it, the world.

*

THE RITUALIZED HUMILIATION TOLD YOU A LOT ABOUT MODERN RUSSIA. The occasion was a televised meeting of the country's Security Council on February 21, 2022. Its members were being invited to ratify Putin's decision to recognize the independence of Kremlin-backed separatists in eastern Ukraine, a precursor to the full invasion that followed. But Putin's spy chief, Sergei Naryshkin, flubbed his lines and was publicly scolded—and visibly terrified—by his smirking boss. "Speak clearly," Putin taunted, the joke being that honesty, let alone dissent, might be a fatal mistake. In Putin's Russia, the prime directive is fealty to the tsar and his geopolitical games.[58]

Russia, unlike China, cannot aspire to global primacy, much less make itself the pivot of a new world order. Its economic power is too modest and its resource base too weak—statements that were true even before Putin started squandering the country's manpower, money, and materiel in Ukraine. But that doesn't mean Moscow will fade into irrelevance, much less that it is—as Barack Obama once taunted—a mere "regional power."[59] Russia's challenge has global implications, because Moscow can weaken the international order from one azimuth as China assails it from another. Putin's great goal, in fact, has been to tear down Europe's post–Cold War peace and build Russia's "great Eurasian future."

History happens at the nexus of impersonal forces and highly personal policy choices. Russia, writes historian Stephen Kotkin, has always seen itself as a "providential country with a special mission."[60] Lacking secure borders, it has long pursued that greatness at the expense of nearby states. If Putin took up this mantle so ardently, it's because the breakup of the previous Russian empire—the Soviet Union—affected him so viscerally.[61]

As a KGB officer stationed in East Germany in 1989, Putin lived the destruction of Stalin's legacy. He would later call the Soviet breakup the "greatest geopolitical tragedy" of a century with no shortage of them.[62] When Putin became president at the turn of the millennium, he ruled a state that had lost its Eastern European security belt, its global influence, and its dignity. As he consolidated power and snuffed out Russia's feeble democracy, he worried that liberalizing states on Russia's borders would become "slaves to America."[63] It wasn't long before Putin began devising a multi-pronged strategy of Russian restoration, one that grew bolder as his grip on power tightened.

The first prong involved renewing the foundations of empire by reclaiming primacy in the post-Soviet space. If China is the strongest of the revisionist powers, Russia has been the most violent. Long before the showdown with Kyiv, the history of Putin's rule was one of wars and lesser interventions—in Chechnya in 1999–2000, Georgia in 2008, Ukraine in 2014 and after, and Belarus and Kazakhstan from late 2020 to early 2022, to name a few—to reverse the contraction of Russian power. Those interventions showed off the conventional military that Putin rebuilt, as well as a modernized nuclear arsenal meant, among other things, to deter Western interference in his wars of Russian restoration.[64] Putin also used other tricks—electoral meddling, poisoning pro-Western politicians, promoting asymmetric trade agreements, corrupting local elites—to suborn and subordinate post-Soviet states. Breaking down these countries' sovereignty was the precursor to building up Russian-led institutions. The Eurasian Economic Union, Putin announced in 2011, would be "one of the poles of the modern world."[65]

The strength of that pole would depend, in part, on the weakness of the Western community. If Khrushchev's "dearest dream" was to split America from Europe, then Putin, too, strove to break the transatlantic bonds that constrain Russian power. Prior to invading Ukraine, Putin demanded, as his price for peace, a divided Europe in which NATO was effectively rolled back to its Cold War frontiers and half the continent was left exposed to Russian intimidation.[66] This was just saying the quiet part out loud.

From the late 2000s onward, Russia subverted NATO and the European Union through cyberattacks, electoral meddling, sabotage, and political warfare—the sort of tactics a former intelligence operative might favor. Putin tried to neuter European countries geopolitically by making them dependent on Russian oil and gas; the state-run energy giant Gazprom, he said, was "a powerful political and economic lever of influence over the rest of the world."[67] At the same time, Moscow cultivated disaffected illiberal states, such as Viktor Orbán's Hungary and Recep Tayyip Erdoğan's Turkey, as Trojan horses within NATO; he even sought to overthrow European governments that were moving toward Washington. Putin's intervention in America's presidential election in 2016 was part of this larger strategy; it aimed to enfeeble the West by polarizing and dividing its strongest state.[68]

Meanwhile, Putin revived another Cold War legacy by projecting Russian power into flanking theaters. His forces turned the tide of the Syrian civil war in 2015 and after, using air power and special forces to checkmate a U.S.-backed rebellion and—per Defense Minister Sergei Shoigu—thereby "break the chain of color revolutions" sweeping the post–Cold War world.[69] One intervention foretold another, this time in Libya's civil war, as well as use of paramilitary forces and destabilization tactics across Africa. Russia intensified military operations in the Arctic and North Atlantic; it sent security contractors to Venezuela in 2019 to shore up an embattled autocratic regime; it bolstered military rulers in the Sahel. If the initiatives seemed scattered, the common motives were to reestablish Moscow's global influence and distract Washington by forcing it to play defense around the world.[70]

But the crux of Putin's project was always Eurasian, because Russia's stature must forever be tenuous without a firm continental base. This made a fourth prong of Russian strategy—an autocratic entente with China—crucial. The Soviet Union lost the Cold War because it fought NATO and China simultaneously. Putin was set on avoiding that mistake.

Over a quarter century, the two countries drew closer: expanding arms sales and defense cooperation, supporting tyrannies in Central Asia, promoting illiberal views of human rights and Internet governance in international organizations. For years, China's record-breaking military buildup was facilitated by purchases of Russian aircraft, missiles, air defense systems, and other capabilities; Beijing helped keep Moscow's defense sector solvent by providing it with needed revenue. By 2019, U.S. intelligence reported that "China and Russia are more aligned than at any point since the 1950s," as their militaries carried out exercises in conflict zones from the Baltic to the South China Sea.[71] The two regimes were united by their shared opposition to U.S. power and liberal ideas, and no less by the strong personal relationship between Xi and the man he called his "best, most intimate friend."[72] As long as those rulers maintained peace along what was once the globe's most heavily militarized border, they could focus their energies outward, against the American-led world.

Admittedly, this campaign looked less coherent in real time than it does in hindsight; as late as 2009, Russia's top general paired China with NATO as "the most dangerous of our geopolitical rivals."[73] Even Putin's interventions were often improvised. He invaded Georgia in 2008 after NATO had unwittingly achieved maximum provocation with minimum deterrence, by declaring that Tbilisi would one day join the alliance but leaving it defenseless in the interim. The taking of Crimea in 2014 occurred amid confused circumstances following a popular revolt against a pro-Russian government in Kyiv; Putin grabbed a peninsula because he was losing a country.[74] But the basic outlines of Putin's project gradually became unmistakable, and they reflected a mixture of autocratic impulses and Eurasian ideas.

The link between Putin's regime and his policies was made clear enough by Russia's murderous, systematic cruelty during the invasion of Ukraine. But the link was always there.

A democratic Russia would not have viewed liberalizing, pro-Western neighbors with such dread, or so assiduously stoked external tensions to excuse internal abuses. "War helps justify domestic repression," writes one scholar, "and the fear of Western influence at home helps justify war."[75] Likewise, the point of roiling the politics of rival democracies was to make Putin's own illiberal system—"sovereign democracy"—look better by comparison. "The liberal idea," he declared in 2019, "has become obsolete."[76] A similar blend of ideology and geopolitics informs Putin's fascination with Eurasianism. The supercontinent, Putin remarked, is a haven for the "traditional values" decadent democracies have forsaken, and a source of "tremendous opportunities" Russia must pursue.[77] "We need to create a common zone . . . from Lisbon to Vladivostok," he declared in 2022.[78]

Russia's gambit thus intersects with China's: both are traversing Eurasian roads to a revised global order. And if there is long-term tension here—a China that truly bestrides Eurasia must have Russia as vassal or enemy—in the near and medium term, shared enmities keep them well aligned. The same goes for a third challenge, this one emanating from the Middle East.

*

PRIOR TO 10/7—HAMAS'S GRUESOME ATTACK ON ISRAEL IN OCTOBER 2023—many Americans probably saw the Middle East as a strategic backwater, a distraction from places that really matter. That says more about the intellectual hangover from America's post-9/11 wars than it does about the region itself.

The Middle East is the crossroads of three continents. It commands the narrow waterways that connect Asia to Europe by linking the Indian Ocean to the Mediterranean. Talk of any "green transition" aside, its resources will fuel the global economy for years to come. The Middle East is too valuable to be ignored, which is why Russia and China are giving it so much attention. As the life and death of Qasem Soleimani illustrates, homegrown powers are also vying for greatness there.

Between 1998 and 2020, Soleimani commanded the Quds Force, an elite wing of Iran's Islamic Revolutionary Guard Corps. That position combined the prerogatives of special operations czar, intelligence chief, and shadow secretary of state; it made him Iran's second most powerful man, after Supreme Leader Ali Khamenei. During his tenure, the charismatic Soleimani cultivated a foreign legion of proxies, from Hezbollah in Lebanon to Hamas in the Palestinian territories to the Huthis in Yemen, that may have totaled 200,000 troops. His forces spread Iranian influence from the Mediterranean to the Gulf of Aden; they made up an "axis of resistance" meant to surround and, one day, eliminate Israel. He also tangled, repeatedly, with Washington.[79]

Soleimani's men provided lethal mines that killed hundreds of Americans in Iraq between 2003 and 2011; no rival state has spilled more U.S. blood in the last quarter century than Iran. By late 2019, tensions with Washington were spiking again. The United States had quit the nuclear deal it signed with Iran in 2015 and piled on sanctions as part of a "maximum pressure" campaign. Tehran retaliated by using its asymmetric strengths—drones, missiles, commandos, proxies—to strike tankers in the Persian Gulf, Saudi oil refineries, and Americans stationed in Iraq.

In January 2020, Soleimani was planning something grander—a region-wide blitz of attacks. But as he made the rounds to rally his forces, U.S. intelligence was watching. Just after Soleimani touched down at

Baghdad International Airport, a Hellfire missile delivered by a U.S. drone blew him to pieces—and nearly ignited a war between Washington and the country that seeks to eject it from the Middle East.[80]

After the Cold War, most Americans saw Iran as a tin-pot tyranny, a "backlash" state fighting the tide of human affairs.[81] That's not how Iran's rulers see themselves.

Modern Iran is heir to a proud Persian civilization. Like China and Russia, it is an erstwhile empire that hopes to reclaim lost privileges and prestige. And if the Shah's Iran was an American ally, today's Iran is a revolutionary regime locked in confrontation with a superpower. The tactics of Iranian foreign policy do change; the regime has periodically pursued de-escalations with its neighbors and with the West. But those de-escalations have all ultimately been abortive, not least because the deeper aims of Iranian strategy have remained the same. "Since 1979," writes Karim Sadjadpour, "Iran has sought to expel the United States from the Middle East, replace Israel with Palestine, and remake the region in its image."[82]

Iran, of course, is a power-political pipsqueak compared to China or Russia. It cannot conquer the Middle East or create a Tehran-centric order in the traditional sense. Its ambitions are mostly a project in *disorder*, which the Middle East has had aplenty.

The chaos sown by the U.S. invasion of Iraq in 2003, the precipitous U.S. withdrawal from that country in 2011, and the Arab revolts that began that year created a region receptive to Iranian advances. "Our borders have spread," Soleimani declared. "We must witness victories in Egypt, Iraq, Lebanon, and Syria."[83] Iran has typically sought those victories through means creative and destructive in equal measure.

Iran weaponizes misery: it fuels civil wars, inflames sectarian tensions, and uses well-supplied proxies to gain leverage in the havoc. Under Iran's sponsorship, the Huthis built an arsenal of drones and missiles they could use to strike Saudi Arabia, create havoc in the Red Sea and the Gulf of Aden, or even engage in violent face-offs with the United States and Israel. Hezbollah became a formidable quasi-state actor with a stockpile of perhaps 150,000 deadly rockets. "As long as Iran has money, we have money," Hezbollah's leader, Hassan Nasrallah, bragged in 2016.[84] On the military front, Iran relies on special operations forces, missiles, drones, and other low-cost, high-impact tools—which, when provided to proxies, can be used to bloody enemies from behind a veil of deniability.

Or Iran can use those weapons itself. After Soleimani's killing, Tehran fired 22 missiles at U.S. troops in Iraq.[85] As this episode shows, Iran compensates for debility with daring; whether by taking American hostages or killing American troops, Tehran has repeatedly courted conflict with stronger, but presumably less committed, states. Likewise, after Israel killed high-ranking Iranian military officials in Syria in April 2024, Tehran struck back with a salvo comprising hundreds of drones and missiles. Not least, Iran has marched closer, over many years, to a more potent military equalizer—a nuclear capability that would secure the regime, deter U.S. or Israeli intervention, and give Iran freer rein to support its friends and coerce its foes.

As Soleimani discovered, the costs of this agenda have been severe. Iran's regional aspirations—and nuclear ambitions—have immiserated its own people, by sucking away resources and saddling the economy with sanctions. Partly for this reason, the regime's standing has grown more precarious; sustaining it has required recurring, bloody suppression of unrest. Iran's policies also brought it, more than once, to the brink of war with Washington; they produced smoldering, sometimes-deadly conflicts with Saudi Arabia and Israel, as well as expanding patterns of cooperation among Tehran's many Middle Eastern rivals.[86] One of the most remarkable regional trends of recent years—the thickening of economic, security, and political ties linking Israel to key Gulf states such as Saudi Arabia and the United Arab Emirates—is a testament to how fear of Iran unites the Jewish state and its onetime Arab enemies.

Indeed, balancing is a geopolitical compliment; it reveals how much Iran has achieved. By the late 2010s, Tehran had made itself the dominant player in Iraq, Yemen, Syria, and Lebanon; it had built a 2,000-mile "land bridge" running to the Mediterranean. Iran had intervened decisively, in concert with Russia, in the Syrian civil war, using that conflict to plus-up Hezbollah's already fearsome missile force and grab a position on Israel's frontier. It was in the process of outplaying Saudi Arabia and the UAE in a Yemeni civil war that served as a Persian Gulf proxy conflict. It was also providing its allies with the strategic succor that eventually helped Hamas mount an attack that killed 1,200 Israelis in October 2023—and then allowed the Huthis, Hezbollah, and other proxies to strike everything from Israeli cities to American military installations to commercial shipping amid the heightened tensions that followed. Perhaps most important, Iran was steadily building out its strategic partnerships with Moscow and Beijing; the Middle East, much as Americans hoped to escape it, was becoming the region where Washington's many geopolitical problems intersected. "Our cooperation can isolate America," Khamenei told Putin.[87] In the 1990s, the superpower had seemed unassailable. A generation later, there was trouble on every front.

*

BY THE THIRD DECADE OF THE TWENTY-FIRST CENTURY, THE WORLD WAS back in an old position: roiled by rivalry nearly from one end of Eurasia to the other. China, Russia, and Iran were making moves in the same regions that had been at issue in every major conflict of the modern era. As before, these gambits revealed much about the nature of global power and the current moment.

For one thing, these challenges confirmed a long-running theme of the Eurasian century: new technologies create new possibilities for power-projection. To be sure, distance has *not* become irrelevant; just ask the Chinese planners who mean to beat the U.S. military by knocking out its forward bases and making it fight from very far away. Nor has conquest become simple; just ask the troops Putin would soon send into Ukraine. But not for the first time, technological progress has made it easier to reach out and touch one's enemies.

Iran is a case study in the falling costs of power-projection: drones and missiles allow an impoverished nation, with a lackluster conventional military, to empower a regionwide network of proxies and punish its rivals at range. China's hypersonic missiles can enable prompt, precise conventional attacks on targets thousands of miles away.[88] Yet the most original forms of power-projection are in the digital domain.

In the next great-power conflict, cyberattacks on a country's networks will accompany physical attacks on its forces, which is why China has been laboring so assiduously to gain access to America's critical infrastructure. In competition short of war, digital operations are already ubiquitous. In 2021, Russian cyber-operators shut down an oil pipeline on America's East Coast, causing short-term economic havoc without setting foot on U.S. soil. In 2016, Putin's online ninjas used disinformation spread via social media to start at least one real riot between American political groups.[89] Welcome to the age of "virtual societal warfare"—the use of digital technologies as tools of destabilization.[90]

Virtual societal warfare is so threatening because of a second trend: the resumption of ideological rivalry. "The great struggles of the twentieth century . . . ended with a decisive victory for the forces of freedom," America's National Security Strategy proclaimed in 2002.[91] By 2005, there were over 120 democracies in the world. But then the global financial crisis of 2008–09 unsettled societies and caused an upsurge of illiberal populism. The balance of ideas, moreover, has always reflected the balance of power, so the reemergence of mighty autocracies has had ideological as well as geopolitical effects. The two decades since 2005 have been years of democratic recession.[92] That could become a depression, if illiberal rulers—aided by advanced technologies—have their way.

Domestically, China is shifting the balance by updating autocracy for the twenty-first century. From a competitive standpoint, the trouble with repression isn't that it is immoral but that it is economically irrational: jailing and killing your people en masse is awful for productivity. Now, however, the Chinese Communist Party is making a revolutionary bid to escape that constraint. China is pairing ubiquitous surveillance with artificial intelligence to instantly identify, and more precisely target, dissent. It is fusing AI, facial recognition, and big data in a "social credit" system that regulates behavior subtly, by tying political loyalty to the availability of loans, plane tickets, and other trappings of the good life. The system will "allow the trustworthy to roam everywhere under heaven," the government says, "while making it hard for the discredited to take a single step."[93]

Don't be fooled: this isn't a kinder, gentler tyranny. Big Brother will still be pervasive. And as China's Uighurs can attest, digital repression goes hand in hand with goon squads and prison camps. It *is* a bid to reduce the economic cost of repression without relinquishing one iota of political power—while using similar tools to weaken democracies in China's way.

Both Moscow and Beijing have long sought to rewire the system to favor illiberal rule, whether by touting the "virtues" of their regimes in global propaganda campaigns or offering an arsenal of assistance—surveillance gear, money, guns, training in the tactics of tyranny—to autocratic brethren.[94] These policies were initially defensive in nature; they were survival skills for dictators in an age of democratic dominance. Now the autocracies are taking the offensive.

Russia is using aggressive disinformation tactics to discredit and destabilize governments from North America to Africa. Beijing aggressively exports its free-speech restrictions by sanctioning democratic countries that criticize its human rights abuses. And just as Russia wages political warfare against its transatlantic rivals, China now employs an anti-democratic toolkit of friendly media outlets, bribes, and hackers to sow discord in democracies; it tries to poison the bloodstream of Taiwan and other free societies with constant injections of digital disinformation.[95] This aspect of virtual societal warfare is going to get much worse; as AI-enabled "deepfakes" expand the possibilities for digital manipulation, expect these destabilization operations to grow sharper still.[96]

This challenge relates to a third theme of the present era: an intensifying struggle for techno-primacy. Throughout history, geopolitical competitions have been technological competitions; the West has tended to win the former by winning the latter. A generation ago, America's technological lead was simply commanding. Things aren't so one-sided anymore.

Key "aspects of Chinese military modernization," the RAND Corporation wrote in 2015, "have come extraordinarily quickly by any reasonable standard."[97] Through technological theft and homegrown innovation, China has made huge strides in the air, sea, cyber, and space capabilities it would need to fight America in the Western Pacific. In areas such as hypersonic missiles, China is the global leader.[98] These breakthroughs are a sobering reminder that the technological gap has been narrowing—as the world undergoes an epochal burst of innovation.

The technologies that make up the "fourth industrial revolution"—AI, advanced robotics, quantum, synthetic biology, and others—build on the breakthroughs of the digital revolution and could have implications just as sweeping. By the mid-twenty-first century, countries that have mastered advanced robotics and AI may enjoy large productivity advantages over those stuck in an earlier era. On a twenty-first-century battlefield, AI-enabled drone swarms, AI-assisted targeting, and AI-aided decision-making could dramatically increase the speed and lethality of combat—and the disparity between those at the leading and lagging edges. Even outside of combat, whichever country leads in these sectors will gain economic and diplomatic followers around the globe.[99]

By most measures, America is still the world's technological superpower, in part because of advances accumulated over generations, and in part because autocratic regimes—like China's—often stifle the flows of information and capital required for broad, sustained success.[100] Yet China has a more dynamic innovation ecosystem than the Soviet Union did, because its quasi-capitalist economy is stronger than Moscow's was. Tyrannies can also steal ideas and goods unrepentantly, mobilize prodigious investments in key areas, and force private firms to share breakthroughs with the state—all of which Beijing has been doing in a bid to leap ahead.[101] America prevailed in the Cold War by outrunning the Soviet Union into the information age. Winning this rivalry will require winning the new technological race underway.

Cutting across these issues is a fourth theme: the fusion of deep insecurity with deep interdependence. Interdependence between antagonists is nothing novel, but post–Cold War interdependence was something different. Production itself became globalized. Critical technologies came to depend on intricate multinational supply chains. The U.S. and China became more financially intertwined than any two rivals in history. This complex globalization was supposed to bring global harmony. It became a conduit for coercion instead.

America was an early mover in "weaponized interdependence."[102] By the early twenty-first century, it was exploiting its centrality in global information networks to spy on rivals and its hold on financial networks to squeeze them. Successful innovation inspires emulation.

Under a strategy known as "dual circulation," China has been trying to slash its dependence on democratic countries for vital inputs such as computer chips and high-end sensors—while increasing control of key chokepoints, such as supplies of critical minerals, on which the world depends. "Western countries were able to hold sway over the world," Xi explains, "because they held the advanced technology." So China needs a "stranglehold" strategy of its own.[103] Think of this as "offensive decoupling"—not fully disconnecting from rival economies but limiting vulnerabilities while building positions of asymmetric leverage.[104] In an era where competition and interconnection are both intense, the global economy is a battleground.

Dual circulation is so important because it could limit America's coercive options in crisis. Which highlights a final point: the elemental aspects of rivalry endure, even as the global landscape never ceases to change.

Digital subversion is a new twist on an ancient tactic; political warfare and economic coercion were strategies Spykman understood well. China's multi-decade military buildup and Russia's serial aggression remind us that hard power has not gone out of style and great-power war may not be a thing of the past. Indeed, the tech competition is so important because it may determine who wins if conflict erupts. Most important, the policies of the revisionist powers are part of a larger, longer-running fight over familiar stakes: the Eurasian balance and the question of whether autocracies or democracies will run the world. It shouldn't be shocking, then, that another old theme is reemerging, as Eurasian ambitions produce expanding circles of hostility.

*

IT DIDN'T HAPPEN QUICKLY. FOR MUCH OF THE EURASIAN CENTURY, AMERica was a reluctant balancer; distance from dangers gave it the option of responding slowly to them. This was what made Washington's Cold War alliance system so important: it offered reassurance that the cavalry would arrive before it was too late. One might have expected, after the Cold War, that a superpower set on suppressing great-power competition would be fast to confront prospective rivals. That wasn't really the case.

Putin's malign potential was plain enough after he amputated parts of Georgia in 2008. Yet the Obama administration opted for diplomatic engagement, meant to "reset" the relationship, over neo-containment. After Putin invaded Ukraine in 2014, America initially refused to sell Kyiv weapons for fear that self-defense would somehow be escalatory.[105] If Putin felt so catastrophically free to use force in 2022, it was because he had gotten away with it before. In the Middle East, Obama was, prudently, combining coercion and negotiation to limit Iran's nuclear ambitions, while also, more perplexingly, largely ignoring its destabilizing activities.

In the Pacific, China was sprinting toward dominance of the South China Sea and becoming a first-rate economic challenger. But while Obama mounted a desultory "Pacific pivot," he banned the Pentagon from even talking about great-power rivalry and said he preferred a strong China to a weak one.[106] Hegemons aren't supposed to be this blasé about rising threats.

There were many reasons Washington wasn't rushing to resume great-power rivalry. Americans had gotten so rich trading with China that they refused to recognize what that country was becoming: engagement put golden fetters on Washington more than Beijing. They hoped moderates might take charge in Moscow and Tehran. They were ill-disposed to take on new challenges after two disillusioning wars and an enervating financial crisis. But in general, America had gotten high on its own supply. Accustomed to effortless superiority, it struggled to grasp the severity of the problems piling up.

It took a lot for that attitude to change. By 2017, Russia had invaded its neighbors three times, intervened in Syria, and meddled in a close-run U.S. presidential contest. Iran was stoking instability and terror against its enemies and surging to primacy in multiple nations of the Middle East. China was fundamentally changing the balance in Asia and competing for influence around the globe.

The subsequent COVID pandemic—which killed over one million Americans—then served as a coming-out party for a more belligerent Beijing. Hyper-confrontational "wolf-warrior diplomacy" and threats to weaponize scarce supplies of pharmaceuticals introduced the world to a China that was no longer biding its time.[107] The United States could not "speak to China from a position of strength," one of Beijing's top diplomats lectured his American counterparts in early 2021.[108] No one could credibly claim, after all this, that the bad old patterns of geopolitics were finished. The upshot was an overdue, and incomplete, hardening of U.S. policy.

"Great-power competition" became a bipartisan buzzword. Two very different presidents—Donald Trump and Joe Biden—declared that the world had entered a new era of rivalry.[109] The Pentagon started to refocus on China and Russia, rather than terrorists and insurgents; it began, albeit slowly, to beef up its posture on Eurasia's flanks. The Trump administration ditched the Iran nuclear deal and shifted to "maximum pressure" against Tehran; America took the offensive against Moscow's cyber-warriors and pushed back, periodically, against Russian influence in the Middle East. This wasn't a bloodless endeavor: In 2018, U.S. forces mowed down between two and three hundred Russian mercenaries who came too close for comfort in Syria.[110]

The pushback was most concerted in the Indo-Pacific, because China posed the starkest long-term threat. The Pentagon declared China its "pacing challenge" and oriented its plans and forces toward safeguarding the First Island Chain.[111] The U.S. Navy stepped up freedom-of-navigation operations in the South China Sea, as arms sales to Taiwan and other states increased. The Trump administration launched a tariff war against China; it temporarily hobbled Huawei, the telecommunications giant leading Beijing's 5G push, by restricting access to high-end semiconductors.[112] Biden then expanded those sanctions and made enormous outlays in U.S. semiconductor production to help the democratic world keep its edge. "A whole-of-government and whole-of-society campaign is being waged to bring China down," Xi's vice-minister of foreign affairs griped.[113]

It was worse than that, because the anti-China campaign was multilateral. America, Australia, Japan, and India revived the Quad—a "democratic security diamond," Japanese prime minister Abe Shinzo called it, connecting China's rivals on all sides.[114] In 2021, America inked the AUKUS partnership with Australia and the United Kingdom, in which countries from three continents joined hands to keep the Indo-Pacific military balance tilted against Beijing. Washington tightened bilateral alliances with Japan and the Philippines, while also increasing the interlinkages between those alliances; ties with New Delhi flourished after a deadly high-altitude dustup between Indian and Chinese troops in 2020. Chinese officials were soon lamenting the "NATO-ization" of Asia—the rise of overlapping security partnerships motivated by fear of a belligerent Beijing.[115]

That was going too far; a chief weakness of America's position in Asia was the lack of a single, multilateral alliance. But up and down the Western Pacific, countries were upgrading their militaries and pulling closer to Washington, while democracies as far away as France and the United Kingdom dispatched naval vessels to show solidarity with frontline states. Clubs of rich nations, namely the Group of 7 and NATO, were taking anti-China positions; advanced democracies were exploring, with Washington, supply-chain partnerships to pool their technological capabilities and enhance their collective position. America was "isolating China with a multilateral club strategy," rued one hawk in Beijing.[116]

Yet it wasn't fully *America's* strategy. The push to invigorate the Quad came mostly from Tokyo, where Abe had long feared the Western Pacific might become "Lake Beijing."[117] Australia led the way on Huawei and 5G. The initiative came from allies in other theaters, too: Poland and the Baltic states had been warning about a pugnacious Putin for years. Countries living in the shadow of Chinese or Russian power had the most to fear from Eurasian expansion, so they sought to pull a distant superpower into the fight.[118]

Even so, there was something halting about this response. Trump's Iran policy was a marvel of incoherence: in rejecting the nuclear deal, he rejected the one piece of Obama's policy that was actually constraining Tehran. In continually threatening to withdraw from the Middle East, he blew any credibility his more confrontational stance might have bought him with U.S. partners.

Similarly, the Trump *administration* was tough on Russia and China—but President Trump praised Putin, chased a "historic trade deal" with Xi, and tormented America's allies more than its enemies.[119] A would-be authoritarian himself, Trump baselessly alleged widespread fraud in the presidential election of 2020 and then whipped followers into an insurrectionary frenzy. He often seemed more hostile to the liberal order America was defending than he was to the tyrants testing it. Biden then declared that the world had reached an "inflection point" in an epic contest between autocracy and democracy. Yet he repeatedly proposed defense budget increases below the rate of inflation, even as Pentagon officials were warning that conflict with China could be just years away. Both presidents, meanwhile, talked about China as a century-defining challenge, but refused to back the single best initiative to counter Chinese economic influence in Asia: the Trans-Pacific Partnership trade deal. There was a bipartisan consensus on the return of great-power rivalry and a bipartisan failure to wage it effectively.[120]

Some allies weren't doing much better. Germany was becoming ever more dependent on Russian energy. Japan, Taiwan, and other Asian partners still weren't rearming with anything like the alacrity one might expect with a dragon at the door. "We will defend ourselves to the very last day," said Taiwan's foreign minister—at a time when his country was spending around 2 percent of GDP on defense.[121]

The most catastrophic success of the postwar, and now post–Cold War, order was that it convinced so many intelligent people that peace, prosperity, and democratic dominance were the natural order of things, rather than an always precarious set of achievements that was increasingly at risk of being destroyed. As during the late 1940s, it would take an unexpected crisis to show just how quickly things could collapse, and to reveal the era for what it was.

*

"I NEED AMMUNITION, NOT A RIDE," SAID VOLODYMYR ZELENSKYY.[122] THE Ukrainian president was answering an American query about whether he wished to flee for his life. Putin's troops had reached Kyiv's outskirts. Russian special forces were trying to kill Ukraine's leaders. Few Western analysts gave Ukraine much chance of survival; Zelenskyy's advisers were wavering.[123] But Zelenskyy stayed, beginning the former actor's transformation into an improbable wartime leader and making the Ukraine war into something different than Putin had expected.

It was natural that the gravest geopolitical crisis—so far—of the twenty-first century involved Ukraine, because that country figured prominently in prior rounds of Eurasian rivalry. Ukraine has a commanding position on the Black Sea, which offers Russia access to the Mediterranean and points beyond. It possesses some of the world's best agricultural land. Most profoundly, Ukraine connects the spacious Eurasian Heartland to the economically advanced European Rimland. Any European empire expanding eastward must go through Ukraine; any Eurasian giant thrusting into Europe must do likewise. In the world wars, Ukraine was the battlespace where empires collided. In the late Cold War, Ukraine's flight from the Soviet Union sealed that system's fate.[124] So it was one of history's tragic circularities that, in February 2022, Putin tried to make Russia a latter-day Eurasian superpower by breaking the Ukrainian state.

The invasion came at a global inflection point. After earlier wars against Ukraine and Georgia, as well as the de facto occupation of Belarus, Putin seemed well on his way to a post-Soviet empire. The Sino-Russian partnership made the two Eurasian giants look cohesive and unified. The ideological allure of democracy was fading following the attack on the U.S. Capitol—inspired by the country's own outgoing president—in January 2021. American power was recoiling after a humiliating withdrawal from Afghanistan. "If you can't beat the Taliban, how are you going to beat China?" one Indian official taunted.[125] Beijing's leaders, U.S. intelligence analysts reported, saw an "epochal geopolitical shift" underway.[126] The system was primed for another shock, which Putin aimed to provide.

The Russian leader had been trying to control Ukraine, by means violent or merely subversive, for two decades. He had been laying the groundwork for outright conquest since 2021. That year, Putin published a treatise "on the historical unity of Russians and Ukrainians"—a 7,000-word exposition of his earlier claim that Ukraine was "not even a country."[127] COVID-induced isolation, meanwhile, had left Putin fixated on his legacy. His three closest advisers, one subordinate quipped, were Catherine the Great, Peter the Great, and Ivan the Terrible.[128]

By early 2022, Russia's modern tsar saw his chance to act, because America appeared weak and distracted while Europe seemed unlikely to hit back hard given its reliance on Russian energy. Putin was also in a hurry, though, because his earlier aggression had only pushed Kyiv closer to the West.[129] A man of greater reflection might have asked what this indicated about Ukraine's instinct for survival. Putin instead became the latest tyrant to race through an apparent window of opportunity.

The game plan involved a brazen land-grab. Russian forces envisioned a shock-and-awe operation that would seize major cities, decapitate the government, and convince the country's surviving elites to switch sides. Kyiv would fall within days; conventional resistance would crumble; show trials, summary executions, and other atrocities would complete the subjugation of Europe's second-largest state. Moscow would simultaneously use the threat of nuclear escalation—of "consequences they have never seen," Putin blustered—to hold Western nations at bay.[130] Had this all come off as planned, the reverberations would have been global.

An occupied Ukraine would have been forcibly united with Russia and Belarus, restoring the Soviet Union's European core. Putin would have seized a position of power along the arc from Central Asia to Eastern Europe; insecurity would have pulsed up and down NATO's eastern front. A beleaguered America would have faced militarily ascendant rivals in Europe and Asia; successful aggression in one theater might have encouraged imitation in the latter. Admirers of autocracy would have lauded Putin's skill and cunning; doubts about U.S. staying power would have multiplied. A successful invasion of Ukraine would have thrown Western Eurasia into turmoil as instability radiated around the globe.

It wasn't a hopeless endeavor; the onslaught came uncomfortably close to success. Zelenskyy had hardly seemed like a latter-day Churchill in January 2022, when he breezily dismissed U.S. warnings of looming disaster. Once the attack began, ill-prepared Ukrainian forces faced as much as a twelve-to-one disadvantage on key fronts. Russian forces swept through the south and converged on Ukraine's major cities. Had Zelenskyy fled or Kyiv fallen, Ukrainian elites might indeed have wavered or defected. Yet Putin's blitzkrieg failed due to three crucial surprises.[131]

*

FIRST, INCOMPETENCE TEMPERED AGGRESSION. IN EARLIER WARS, PUTIN had pursued limited objectives with resources sufficient to achieve them. In the opening stages of the Ukraine conflict, there was a glaring gap between Moscow's grand objectives and its dismal execution.

Putin tried to do too much with too little; by spreading his troops over five separate axes, he reduced the odds of decisive gains on any of them. Making matters worse, a regime obsessed with secrecy, and suffused with sycophancy, never really stress-tested that plan or gave frontline units time to prepare for its execution. Most crippling of all, a president who had convinced himself that Ukraine was a fictitious state failed to anticipate the furious nationalism his invasion would elicit. Isolation— the product not just of COVID, but of two decades in power—made a long-tenured tyrant more belligerent and less effective.[132]

Second, as Russia stumbled, Ukraine stiffened. Its wartime performance made up for what its prewar preparations had lacked. Ukraine held key points on the road to Kyiv through desperate, courageous resistance; its military commanders deployed limited resources where Russian breakthroughs might have been most decisive. Most critically, Ukraine cohered rather than crumbled under attack—it was a real country, after all—allowing not just a whole-of-government but a whole-of-society defense.[133] That resistance bought time for Zelenskyy, in a virtuoso performance, to convince the world that Ukraine had a chance—and for the West to surprise Putin, and surprise itself, with the strength and rapidity of its response.

Prior to the assault, America was mostly preparing to supply a Ukrainian insurgency after the inevitable Russian victory. Despite blaring sirens from U.S. intelligence, many European states didn't even believe the invasion was coming.[134] But Putin's attack was a twenty-first-century analogue for the Korean War—an act of aggression so brazen it *demanded* a forceful riposte.

After 2014, it had taken Washington years to *sell* Ukraine 150 anti-tank missiles. In 2022, America and its allies simply *gave* Ukraine the weapons, from anti-aircraft missiles to guided artillery, that it used to blunt the Russian advance; the intelligence that helped it target Putin's forces; and the money that kept its economy afloat. From the earliest days of the fighting, when U.S. warnings helped Kyiv repel an airborne assault near the capital, this aid was a force-multiplier for Ukraine's own courage and creativity. It may not have been sufficient to allow Ukraine to win the war by clearing Russian troops from its territory. It *was* sufficient to prevent Ukraine from losing—and to inflict horrible damage on the country that was inflicting horrible damage on it.[135]

A splendid little war became a lethal trap for Putin's armies; Moscow lost more troops in a few months than it had lost in the entire Afghan war in the 1980s.[136] Putin lost his aura of invincibility, as well, when his own mercenaries—displeased with the war's conduct—turned against him in a bizarre, abortive march toward Moscow in June 2023. Meanwhile, Western sanctions cut Russia off from its own foreign reserve assets, international payments systems, and the advanced semiconductors that underpin economic and military power in the modern age. As Foreign Minister Sergey Lavrov lamented, "no one could have predicted" these consequences.[137] Certainly, it is hard to imagine all this happening in a world without U.S. leadership.

Only a superpower could so quickly scrounge up HIMARS, Javelins, artillery, and other critical capabilities from its stockpiles, or lean on allies to provide them. Only U.S. security guarantees, backed by U.S. nuclear weapons, could prevent Russia from coercing the countries that were helping Ukraine kill its troops in droves. Only America had the intelligence capabilities to warn the world what was coming. Only Washington had the convening power to unite dozens of countries, from multiple regions, in a global response.[138] One of the crucial differences between Ukraine in 2022 and, say, Czechoslovakia in 1938 was that America and the system it had established served as a rallying point for resistance at a vital moment. Which was why the war's global consequences were also so surprising.

Putin's conflict produced a larger, stronger NATO, reawakened to danger and recommitted to the collective defense. The alliance sent additional forces to Eastern Europe; it expanded by welcoming Finland and Sweden into its ranks. European countries hiked defense spending by 13 percent, the largest year-on-year increase since the Cold War; nations, namely Germany, that had grown addicted to Russian energy over decades mostly kicked the habit in months. Poland began to make itself a major military power, while Ukraine built a serious fighting force that was closely linked to the West.[139] In a more anarchic context, Putin's assault might have fractured his enemies. In a Europe steadied by U.S. power, it initially had the opposite result.

Something similar was happening in Asia. Here, the shock of Russia's invasion was compounded, in August 2022, by the biggest Taiwan crisis in a quarter century. After House Speaker Nancy Pelosi visited that island, Xi responded with calculated, demonstrative outrage, in the form of missile tests and military exercises that simulated a Chinese invasion or blockade. As Chinese planes raced across the Taiwan Strait, as Chinese ships circled the island, as Chinese missiles splashed down in vital sea lanes, the threat of war became tangible in the Western Pacific as well.

Japan reacted by pushing through plans to nearly double defense spending over a half decade, and to cooperate more closely with Washington to turn the Ryukyu Islands into a series of strategic strongpoints. Taiwan accelerated its defense reforms and raised military spending by 14 percent; the Philippines and Papua New Guinea opened new bases to U.S. forces. Tokyo established closer strategic partnerships with Australia and the Philippines; Japan and South Korea, long divided by historical enmities, began to mend ties. America started, still far too slowly, to build the stockpiles of munitions and the swarms of drones it would need for a war in the Western Pacific. Officials in Washington, Canberra, and Tokyo began whispering about a trilateral defense of Taiwan.[140] All these initiatives were aimed at China; all were catalyzed, in part, by Russia's example. "Ukraine today may be East Asia tomorrow," Japanese prime minister Kishida Fumio said.[141]

The Ukraine war strengthened free-world phalanxes on Eurasia's margins; it also fused them closer together. The coalition of countries that sanctioned Russia and supported Ukraine included South Korea, Taiwan, Japan, and Australia—Indo-Pacific actors that increasingly saw their own stake in Europe's security. By providing Ukraine with hundreds of thousands of rounds of vital artillery ammunition, South Korea did more than most European countries to keep Kyiv in the fight. The G-7 nations announced their commitment to peace in the Taiwan Strait and to fighting economic coercion by Beijing. In the fall of 2022, another geographically disparate group of democracies—America, Taiwan, Japan, and the Netherlands—cooperated to restrict China's access to high-end semiconductors and the tools to make them. This was the broadest, and potentially most devastating, shot in the technological cold war underway.[142]

The world, Biden declared after Putin's invasion, was witnessing another great clash "between democracy and autocracy, between liberty and repression, between a rules-based order and one governed by brute force."[143] A year later, a transregional coalition of democracies was starting the long process of rousing itself to the task.

"Starting" was the key word, though, because the process was nowhere near complete. European countries were rebuilding their militaries from the very low starting point post–Cold War cuts had produced. Some, like Germany, kept finding excuses to backtrack on even the remedial commitments they had made following Putin's assault. Most critically, in late 2023 and early 2024, the United States spent several agonizing months debating and dithering over whether to maintain military support for Ukraine, despite the obvious risk that a lapse in that assistance could still lead to an ugly Russian victory, with all the destabilizing global consequences and catastrophic effects for American credibility such a victory would bring. More than two years after Putin's invasion, Western countries were struggling to meet the demands of a long, grinding war of attrition in Ukraine—and to prepare themselves for what might come next.

On the other side of the supercontinent, Asia still lacked anything like the firm multilateral framework that had deterred aggression in Europe during the Cold War. The Pentagon was still short of munitions, submarines, and other critical capabilities in the Western Pacific; Taiwan was still moving too slowly to buy the capabilities and raise the manpower necessary for a robust defense. Discussions of blunting Chinese economic coercion remained mostly aspirational. In the Middle East, the perception America was withdrawing from the region was creating openings for Iran, Russia, and China. Meanwhile, the 10/7 terror attacks had revealed the potential for conflict to engulf multiple regions simultaneously. The escalatory pressures that ensued—featuring a violent back-and-forth between America and Israel, on the one hand, and Iran and its associated forces on the other—were a reminder of how pervasive strategic challenges remained in a region Americans would surely have preferred to forget. In short, the United States and its friends were acting with *more* purpose and energy—but certainly not enough.

The stage was therefore set for another high-stakes chess match, as America and its allies try to close off crucial vulnerabilities while their rivals seek to break the shackles on their ambitions. Complicating this task, from Washington's perspective, is a final dynamic: if the Ukraine conflict stirred greater unity among the existing order's defenders, it also produced a tighter coalition of autocracies. As Putin's war rallied the advanced democracies, it hastened construction of a Fortress Eurasia, manned by the free world's enemies.

*

FORTRESS EURASIA ISN'T THE MOST NATURAL SET OF ALIGNMENTS. DISagreements between the revisionist powers are many; trust and affection are scarce. Russia, China, and Iran have historically clashed where their imperial horizons meet. None of them can fully attain the geopolitical space they seek without impairing the interests, perhaps the survival, of the others. But those problems lie mostly in the past and, perhaps, the future. For now, the revisionists have much in common.

China, Iran, and Russia—as well as North Korea—have aspirations that require rolling back the American order. All desire a world in which autocracy is protected, even privileged. All understand that stability near the autocratic core of Eurasia enables stronger thrusts against the U.S.-led coalitions around the periphery. And while predatory powers aren't keen to commit suicide for one another, they know that if *any* of America's enemies are decisively defeated, the remainder will be dangerously exposed. As during prior eras of conflict, the world's expansionist states are banding together, for self-protection and strategic profit.[144]

This didn't happen overnight. North Korea and Iran have long shared missile technology and other means of mischief. Russia and Iran cooperated to win the Syrian civil war. China and Russia spent a generation building their partnership. The value of that alignment became clear in 2022, when Russia stripped its unthreatened Far East bare of military units to hurl at Ukraine. The subsequent war would strain Sino-Russian relations; Xi neither expected nor welcomed the blowback it created for Beijing. In late 2022, he publicly discouraged Putin from using nuclear weapons to escalate his way out a conventional conflict gone bad.[145] Nonetheless, by deepening the fundamental cleavage in global affairs—between the states defending the existing order and those assailing it—the war also produced a burst of Eurasian integration.

Fortress Eurasia is cohering militarily, through overlapping and mutually reinforcing defense ties. The Russia–Iran military relationship once consisted mostly of arms sales by Moscow. Now, it is becoming what CIA director William Burns called a "full-fledged defense partnership," featuring two-way flows—even coproduction—of weapons that strengthen those powers against their respective enemies.[146] Something similar is happening in the Russia–North Korea relationship—now a formal alliance—as Pyongyang provided Putin with artillery and missiles for use on Ukrainian battlefields, perhaps in exchange for assistance with its missile and nuclear programs. As the West sought to isolate Russia, in fact, Putin's navy was conducting exercises in the Gulf of Oman with Iran and China—a country that may not have intervened directly in Moscow's war but did provide money, microchips, drones, and other resources that kept its army fighting.[147] Meanwhile, the larger Sino-Russian defense relationship—the exercises in geopolitical hot spots, the defense-industrial collaboration to produce new capabilities and rebuild Moscow's heavily sanctioned defense-industrial base—

continued to race ahead. "Right now there are changes—the likes of which we haven't seen for 100 years," Xi told Putin at a summit in 2023, "and we are the ones driving these changes together."[148]

The revisionist powers are also restructuring international trade. Commerce that traverses Eurasia's marginal seas can be seized by globe-ranging navies. Economies that use the dollar for trade and finance are exposed to U.S. sanctions. A second aspect of Fortress Eurasia involves building trade and transportation networks that are safe from democratic interdiction.

Russia and Iran are expanding the International North–South Transport Corridor, a web of railroads, highways, and shipping routes that connect them via the landlocked Caspian Sea.[149] The war simultaneously impelled China to accelerate efforts to sanction-proof its own economy, as Beijing and Moscow enhanced cooperation in the Arctic—the least vulnerable maritime path between them.[150] By pushing Russia out of Western markets, in fact, the war fundamentally altered patterns of Eurasian trade; commerce in Russian oil, Chinese microchips, and other goods boomed. Hong Kong has become a destination for Russian firms seeking capital; Chinese buyers have scooped up Russian assets. And as Chinese technology pervades Eurasia, its currency proliferates, too. "Geopolitics will not, of course, lead to the global dethronement of the dollar any time soon," writes Russian scholar Alexander Gabuev. But it could forge a Sino-centric economic and technological bloc across much of the Old World.[151]

Finally, Fortress Eurasia is emerging intellectually. Eurasian themes are hegemonic in Moscow; a Russia severed from the West lacks other options. Iranian officials call Eurasian cooperation the antidote to U.S. "unilateralism"; they tout a "new world order" based on a strategic "triangle" with Russia and China.[152] And if a more globally integrated China doesn't have to go all-in on the supercontinent, its analysts agree that "whoever can guide the Eurasian process can lead the construction of a new world order"—one in which U.S. power is blunted, autocracy is supreme, and the world's largest landmass is laid open to neo-imperial designs.[153]

China intends to rule this domain. With time, Xi expects China to tower above its putative friends as well as its enemies.[154] Even in the near term, global tensions are hastening Russia's reduction to an economic and technological appendage of Beijing. Yet for military supplies, energy exports, and strategic solidarity, China still needs Russia. Xi can't defeat America in the Pacific if he faces insecurity on one of the longest land borders in the world.

Indeed, if the relationships that make up Fortress Eurasia are awkward, the benefits are real. There is already a perverse symbiosis between Russian and Chinese policies: Moscow's disinformation campaigns and Beijing's digital infrastructure projects undermine U.S. influence from Africa to the Balkans.[155] An Iran with tighter ties to Moscow and Beijing will be less susceptible to Western pressure in a crisis over its nuclear program or its support for a regional rogues' gallery, even if neither country provides all the backing Tehran might like. Commercial and technological synergies can reduce the reach of U.S. sanctions and the U.S. dollar, while enhancing the resilience of the illiberal bloc. Then there are the military effects.

The perennial question of whether Beijing and Moscow are "allies" is the wrong one, for it wouldn't take a formal Sino-Russian alliance to upend the military balance. Arms sales and deepening defense-technological cooperation are already turbocharging Beijing's challenge to the balance of power in Asia. If Russia provides China with its most advanced submarine-quieting technology or surface-to-air missiles, it could profoundly change the complexion of a war in the Western Pacific—just as provision of drones, artillery, and missiles by Iran and North Korea sustained Putin's forces in Ukraine.[156] If Beijing or Moscow sold Iran their most lethal missiles or fighter jets, the Persian Gulf would become a far more vexing place. If Russian technology or know-how boosts North Korea's missile and weapons of mass destruction programs, or if Moscow's diplomatic protection helps Pyongyang evade international scrutiny, those programs could mature far faster than U.S. analysts once expected. Eurasian defense relationships don't have to constitute some evil NATO to make a difference. They could simply be latter-day versions of the Rapallo Pact between Germany and the Soviet Union after World War I—agreements that sunder the status quo by promoting military-technological ties between dissatisfied states.[157]

Or the Eurasian powers could work together in a conflict against the United States. If Russia had the chance to bleed America by quietly supporting China in a war in the Western Pacific—through semi-covert cyberattacks against U.S. forces and infrastructure, for instance—does anyone doubt it would have the motivation? What would Washington do if Russian or Chinese ships showed up in the Persian Gulf during a crisis with Iran? Or if Moscow dialed up the pressure in Eastern Europe just as China was moving against Taiwan? This sort of collaboration wouldn't require a collective death-wish. It would just require creativity in posing dilemmas for an overstretched superpower that the revisionist states all detest.

After all, alignments between ambivalent friends—even future enemies—can pack a punch. Nazi Germany and imperial Japan never trusted each other, but their actions created cascading chaos both could exploit. Stalin and Hitler suppressed their mutual loathing long enough to set Europe ablaze. Today, a new pack of revisionist powers is reviving the nightmare of the twentieth century: a bloc of Eurasian autocracies that exerts pressure on the wider world.

*

THE UKRAINE WAR REVEALED A FRAUGHT, FRACTURING GLOBAL LANDscape. Yet it also highlighted a third cluster of states, those that aren't part of Fortress Eurasia or the free world but can affect the balance between them. The "global unity" that arose in response to the invasion was really the unity of a few dozen advanced democracies, with many other countries remaining on the sidelines. During the Cold War, the non-aligned aimed to survive and prosper by straddling the East–West divide. Today, another set of swing states will shape Eurasia's future.

Look at the Persian Gulf, where America's closest partners—Saudi

Arabia and the United Arab Emirates—spent much of the 2010s and early 2020s drawing steadily closer to Moscow and especially Beijing. Anti-communism once provided ideological glue in these countries' dealings with Washington; energy-for-security bargains underpinned the strategic relationship. No longer. U.S. military *capabilities* in the Middle East are unmatched, but the *commitment* of a superpower that has spent more than a decade trying to leave that region is more questionable. And modernizing autocrats have little use for the rhetoric of dictatorship versus democracy, because they have more in common politically with America's rivals than with America itself. It was telling that Saudi Arabia turned to China, not America, for help in restoring diplomatic ties with Iran in early 2023. To be sure, the Gulf monarchies still want the benefits of close ties to Washington—as Riyadh's subsequent bid for a formal U.S.–Saudi defense treaty demonstrated—but they are demanding that Washington pay much, much more to keep them onside in the contest with Beijing.

Or look farther west, where Turkey occupies the intersection of two seas and two continents. Under its long-ruling and increasingly illiberal president, Recep Tayyip Erdoğan, it has been playing a double game. Ankara enjoys NATO's protection while courting Russia; it took both sides in the war in Ukraine. Like Russia, China, and Iran, Turkey views itself as an ancient civilization with a rightful claim to empire. Under Erdoğan, it has pursued that vision by intervening in conflicts from the Caucasus to the Horn of Africa, often against U.S. interests.[158]

Then there is South Asia. Pakistan, once America's best frenemy, now leans toward China, which sees it as a conduit to the ocean and a cudgel against India. New Delhi, conversely, tilts toward Washington for safety against Beijing. Yet that partnership is selective and ambivalent; ideology and self-interest make India more comfortable exploiting rifts among the powers than siding fully with any of them. "We are one-fifth of the world's population," Minister of External Affairs S. Jaishankar declared in 2022. "We are entitled to weigh our own side."[159] As an India whose governance blends democratic practices with illiberal tendencies grows in power, it may also grow in its willingness to pursue policies—such as targeting dissidents on foreign soil—that challenge the very liberal order Washington aims to defend. In Egypt, Indonesia, and other key countries around the Eurasian periphery—as well as in Brazil, South Africa, and countries far beyond it—geopolitical alignments are no less fluid.

The swing states are diverse, but the commonalities are striking. None are among the rich, economically advanced democracies. All hold some resentment toward the West; all need trade, arms, and other benefits that the Eurasian autocracies, especially China, can offer. All prefer to maneuver between dueling coalitions, out of uncertainty about who will win and a desire to cut the best deals with both. All were diffident, at best, in responding to Putin's invasion of Ukraine, because they valued relations with Moscow and worried that a polarized world would preclude diplomatic flexibility. "Europe has to grow out of the mindset that Europe's problems are the world's problems but the world's problems are not Europe's problems," Jaishankar chided. And all can meaningfully affect the configuration of power around the world's central theater.[160]

Each of the swing states aided Putin's war effort by helping soften the blow of Western sanctions. Saudi Arabia did so spectacularly in late 2022, via oil production cuts that sent prices—and Putin's revenues—higher. Their choices have other critical implications as well.[161]

Saudi Arabia and the UAE will either smooth or obstruct Beijing's path to becoming a major diplomatic and military player in the Persian Gulf. A Pakistan closely bound to Beijing will make it easier for China to cinch the strategic noose tighter around India. Decisions in New Delhi will impact the global distribution of technological and manufacturing capacity, the balance of forces in the Indian Ocean, and how much trouble China faces on land as it pushes outward at sea. Turkey's positioning will affect the cohesion of NATO and the strategic setting from Central Asia to the Middle East. Decisions in Cairo, Jakarta, Pretoria, and other capitals will determine how successful the United States is in rallying broad diplomatic support amid crises in Ukraine, the Middle

East, and other hot spots that may flare in the years ahead. The competition for the swing states isn't just some global popularity contest. It will help determine whether the free world or Fortress Eurasia holds the upper hand.

*

THE PRESENT ERA THUS RESEMBLES THE COLD WAR, WHEN A CREW OF Eurasian powers confronted a flanking free-world community, while non-aligned—or multi-aligned—states maneuvered between. Or perhaps it resembles the run-up to World War II, when an axis of revisionists cratered the status quo. Or perhaps the analogy is World War I, when a liberal offshore superpower confronted an illiberal rival vying for primacy in two domains. The present era looks a bit like *all* the earlier instances of Eurasian rivalry. So expect this round to be ugly indeed.

America and its friends have a strong hand to play. Almost regardless of how one measures, the United States, its allies, and its close security partners command a preponderance of world GDP, a statistic that *understates* their share of accumulated wealth.[162] Regional military balances are changing, most alarmingly in the Pacific, but America retains global strengths any rival would need decades to match.[163] When the Israel–Hamas war erupted in October 2023, who else could have surged two carrier strike groups to the region to reassure allies and constrain enemies? Who else could, or would, have used its military power to protect the shipping of other nations from Huthi attacks? And whereas the autocratic coalition is still cohering, America's coalition features long-standing, firmly institutionalized alliances that create strength and stability in crisis. They make Eurasia more resilient to disruption than it was in an earlier, darker era.

There are other causes for optimism. China is the economic and manufacturing heavyweight of the revisionist coalition; in these areas, it may be America's most formidable foe yet. But China confronts serious challenges that are already slowing its advance: an approaching demographic implosion that could be one of history's worst; a dearth of arable land, clean water, and other vital resources; a neo-totalitarian political system that optimizes control by suffocating spontaneity; a maximum leader whose wisdom may not expand as his tolerance for dissent contracts.[164] The world began to wake up to a sluggish China in mid-2023, as Xi's economy struggled to escape its COVID-era doldrums. But the underlying problems run deeper, and raise grave doubts about the likelihood of reigniting the growth that once powered China's ascent.

This isn't the only weakness in the revisionist entente. Xi's ally in Moscow is an object lesson in how strategic misjudgment compounds structural problems. By draining Russia's military and isolating its economy, Putin's war—regardless of its ultimate outcome—has probably limited its long-term potential.[165] In Iran, too, ferocity masks frailty; the regime has become more aggressive even as it suffers recurring rounds of revolt. Like every autocratic coalition, this one is imposing and insecure.

That's no reason for complacency. America's alliances are formidable, but there's no guarantee they'll last forever. Global military strengths may not prevent the Pentagon from losing a war for preeminence in a vital region. If the United States veers into retrenchment or resentful unilateralism, its enemies could find room to roam. If America makes a habit of electing aspiring strongmen, it may not remain a democratic superpower. And don't think for a second that troubled autocracies can't bring a world of woe.

Russia surely hadn't won in Ukraine, as of this writing, but it was hardly guaranteed to lose there, either. Over the long term, that war may leave Russia less powerful than before—but in the medium term, it could simply make Russia angrier, less predictable, and more heavily militarized, as Putin regiments his economy and society for conflict. By mid-2024, in fact, Putin's regime was striking back against its Western enemies with an aggressive campaign of sabotage and destabilization in Europe. Similarly, a China that cannot overtake the United States economically could double down on coercion, going all-out for control of select industries and supply chains.[166] Or it could act more violently, trying to rupture the First Island Chain before America and its allies are able to prepare. "When bad folks have problems," Biden said of China in 2023, "they do bad things."[167] History also offers a final caution: even if the Eurasian autocracies can't overturn the existing order, they can still do grievous harm.

The best-case scenario, then, might be a new cold war between coalitions with antithetical views of world order. That contest would feature sustained efforts to shape geopolitical alignments and military balances from Eastern Europe, to the Levant and the Persian Gulf, to the Asian littoral. High-stakes crises and lethal proxy fights of the sort we are seeing today would be the cut-and-thrust of global politics; supply chains and chokepoints would be sites of economic warfare. If the original Cold War is any indication, the combatants would work assiduously to destabilize each other; competition would spill into overseas and flanking theaters. This phenomenon is already happening: just look at how Washington and Beijing are dueling over the potential placement of Chinese bases in the Persian Gulf and West Africa, and the technological choices of countries from Ethiopia to Brazil. The world would indeed go "back to the future"—to grim patterns of protracted competition—even as new rivalries reflect the characteristics of the modern age.

That's the *optimistic* scenario. If Eurasian autocracies resort to war in hopes of breaking the existing order, it wouldn't be the first time. Putin claims Russia is already fighting the West to stop the "dismemberment and enslavement of our Motherland."[168] Xi argues that America and its friends have "implemented comprehensive containment, encirclement and suppression against us"; he says China must prepare for "high winds, choppy waters, and even dangerous storms."[169] The former leader did use force to upend a key region. The latter could do likewise by attacking Taiwan, or by bloodying one of China's rivals—Vietnam, India, Japan, the Philippines—in hopes of cowing others.

This wouldn't lead anywhere good. A major Chinese assault in the Western Pacific could well bring war with the United States. That conflict would consume ships, planes, and munitions in quantities unlike anything since World War II. Precision-guided weapons and sophisticated "kill chains" would make the battlefield even deadlier. The war would turn the world's most vital sea lanes into shooting galleries and rip up technological supply chains. It might spread throughout the Western Pacific and into neighboring regions; it would spill into space and cyberspace, as the two sides target satellites and information networks. Homelands would not be sanctuaries; America could hit targets on the Chinese mainland, while Beijing would use cyberattacks and sabotage to weaken the United States. The escalation risks would be severe, given the sizable nuclear arsenals on both sides. And because any fight between America and China would be a fight for dominance, it could become a contest in attrition lasting years.[170]

A war in littoral Asia could even turn into a global conflict if it fused with crises in other regions, as happened in 1940–41, or tempted opportunistic aggression by Russia or Iran. This isn't some crazy hypothetical; in 2022, major crises occurred in Ukraine and the Taiwan Strait simultaneously. In May 2024, China carried out—again—aggressive military exercises around Taiwan at a time when Eastern Europe and the Middle East were already ablaze. A system racked by rivalry across Eurasia could be far more explosive than anything the world has seen in decades. And don't assume that the awful costs of great-power conflict will deter everyone from waging it.

In 1914, Germany went to war knowing it could lose if it didn't win quickly. In 1941, Japan struck Pearl Harbor despite the knowledge that it was risking its own destruction. Today, Chinese or Russian leaders could calculate that Americans won't want to die for countries located so far from their own shores. Or they might gamble on winning quickly, before America can intervene. Even if they were wrong, the price of the error would be ghastly.

A generation ago, leading experts believed great-power war was "literally unthinkable."[171] Today, a return of history's horrors is all too plausible. Americans, and democratic citizens everywhere, will need to learn the lessons of the first Eurasian century if they are to survive the second.

6

LESSONS OF THE PAST

I t is tempting, in every era, to think we live in a totally new world that demands totally new solutions. In reality, our problems are never as novel as they seem.

The Eurasian century was an age when new technologies and new forms of tyranny produced epic, earthshaking collisions. Three times, illiberal empires made bids to rule much of Eurasia as part of their larger quest for global power. Three times, this triggered conflict with grand coalitions anchored by overseas liberal states. These contests spread, spiraled, and consumed the energies of entire societies. Stark ideological rivalries made geopolitical tensions more total; aggressors reached new thresholds of immorality, while even democracies crossed ethical lines they might earlier have deemed absolute. None of this should surprise us in the slightest, given that Eurasian struggles put the future of humanity at stake.

History never repeats itself exactly. The threats posed by today's challengers are each, in their own way, unique. But anyone who witnessed the Eurasian century would recognize the pattern—and can visualize the world these powers mean to create.

In this world, China will physically possess Taiwan and the inner seas of the Western Pacific. It will dominate the economic and security affairs of maritime Asia while locking its rivals out of this vital region. Chinese influence will suffuse the supercontinent, whether through military coercion or means less violent but little less consequential. And as China settles accounts in its adjoining regions, its global horizons will expand—just as America's reach increased once its hemispheric primacy was secure.

The People's Liberation Army Navy will roam distant oceans, putting in at a global network of Chinese bases. Regions as remote as South America and the Arctic will become sharply contested zones. China's autocratic ethos will pervade international norms and bodies; the developing world will take its cues from Beijing. America's remaining allies, in Europe and the Indo-Pacific, will find themselves isolated and outgunned as China's position improves and its capacity to coerce matures. This, perhaps, is what the PRC's official news agency means when it says that "China is set to regain its might and re-ascend to the top of the world."[1]

Russia and Iran won't be fully comfortable in this future; they will find themselves in the shadow of a country that believes it has no equals. But as John Kennedy once remarked, "Caesar and Pompey and Antony and Octavius and the others did not fall out until they were successful."[2] For the time being, Moscow and Tehran will stand to profit from the fracturing of the order that binds them. So they will join China in exploiting this "new imperial moment," by pursuing the spheres of influence they desire.[3]

"It becomes clearer and clearer," another U.S. president, Franklin Roosevelt, remarked in 1940, "that the future world will be a shabby and dangerous place to live in . . . if it is ruled by force in the hands of a few."[4] Eurasia, Roosevelt understood, was the world's strategic hinge. Once the worst regimes had seized the most commanding positions, life would become awful for those they ruled—and precarious even for a mighty America an ocean away.

To be clear, neither Xi nor Putin is Hitler. Their expansion is modest, so far, compared to the malefactors who preceded them. But the Eurasian autocracies might become bolder once they have cast off their present constraints; greater strength rarely produces greater moderation by regimes that see power as a zero-sum game. It seems certain, moreover, that violence and brutality will cascade across areas where revisionist states hold sway. Just look at the mayhem Putin has sown in Ukraine. Or the atrocities that Hamas, Hezbollah, the Huthis, and other groups sustained by Iran have wrought across much of the Middle East. Or the quasi-genocidal program Xi has undertaken in Xinjiang. Or the way China has proclaimed its sovereignty over huge stretches of ocean and demanded that democratic states muzzle their citizens and mutilate their liberties as the price of friendly ties.[5] We have all the warning we need about what a world remade to the liking of the Eurasian powers would be.

This scenario—in which strategic real estate is apportioned among expansionist autocracies as illiberalism and coercion waft outward from the world's core—is what Washington fought two hot wars and one cold war to avert. The tools and techniques of competition evolve, but the consequences of Eurasian struggles are as weighty as ever before.

We are still, fortunately, a good distance from this reckoning. Although the parallels to 1938 or 1947 can be suggestive, we aren't yet living in a moment when history hangs by a thread. The greatest gift prior generations gave this one is a balance of power that favors the democracies, because America and its allies occupy positions of strength they built during and after the Cold War. Put differently, the fact that the front lines are in Ukraine and Taiwan, not Hawaii and the North Atlantic, is a testament to the success of the U.S.-led order—and a reminder of why China, Russia, and Iran are determined to lay that order low. The task for today's democratic policymakers is to prevent that from happening, by learning the lessons of the century before.

The great thinkers of the Eurasian century would have understood this charge. It is easy to take a dim view of geopolitics, because autocracies have often employed its insights for evil. "Kill! Kill! Kill!" Putin's favorite geopolitician, Aleksandr Dugin, once shrieked about Ukraine, adding: "This is my opinion as a professor."[6] But geopolitics is not inherently good or bad. It depends on the purposes to which the discipline is put.

Mackinder, Mahan, and Spykman sought to determine how societies that valued human freedom could prosper in a world where competition was becoming more vicious and tyranny more frightful. They understood that wielding power ruthlessly abroad might be the best way of serving societies that constrained its use at home. This democratic school of geopolitics balanced, and ultimately bested, doctrines of autocratic aggression—and thereby fostered an international system that was safer from the cruelties of global politics than ever before. This was the intellectual tradition that helped save the world during the twentieth century. It is the one from which defenders of a threatened order can draw their most potent insights today.

———

*

ONE LESSON IS THAT IDEOLOGY AND GEOPOLITICS ARE INSEPARABLE; EURasian struggles are fundamentally about what *type* of country will set humanity's course. A crowded, competitive landmass is a hard place for all its inhabitants. But not all Eurasia's inhabitants have sought security through sweeping conquest.

The countries that do are those that struggle to tolerate diversity abroad, just as they cannot abide it at home. They feature strong, centralized states that harness human energy in the service of expansion. They feel slighted by history and the prevailing order. They seek greatness in ways that existentially threaten those around them—and often cause human misery near and far.

It is ironic, in fact, that Americans see democracy as the endpoint of political evolution, because the modernization of tyranny is central to our age. The Eurasian century birthed geopolitical superpredators—totalitarian regimes that upheaved domestic society on the way to upheaving the larger world. These countries used the strengths of dynamic, industrialized nations to commit unprecedented crimes in the pursuit of unparalleled ambitions. Their leaders believed they were locked in mortal combat with democratic states. To be sure, the ideological divides were fluid; as Stalin and FDR, or Nixon and Mao, could attest, the dictates of survival sometimes led liberal and illiberal powers to find common cause. Some of the Eurasian century's aggressors were far more radical than others. But what was ultimately at issue in every competition was whether the world would be made safe for democracy or dominated by its enemies. So Eurasian struggles were, inescapably, tests of opposing political systems.

Coalitions led by liberal democracies compiled an impressive record. Their "decadence" didn't prevent them from making the sacrifices, mobilizing the resources, and orchestrating the alliances that carried the day. The habits of compromise, the decentralized decision-making, and other tendencies that made the democracies seem irresolute, even contemptible to their enemies also made them effective—eventually—in international affairs. The habits that made the autocracies so terrifying, conversely, also made them fallible.[7]

The racial and ideological extremism of the fascist states powered record-setting military rampages—but left them lousy at managing alliances, coopting foreign populations, and otherwise exerting global power. The experience of Germany during World War I, or the Soviet Union during the Cold War, showed how autocratic states could generate backbreaking amounts of geopolitical energy—until their backs indeed broke and their empires came crashing down. Ultra-personalized rule allowed Hitler to run the table for a time—but encouraged extreme risk-taking, an insensitivity to limits, and other flaws that doomed him in the end.

Today's challengers fit the pattern. China, Russia, and Iran are driven by deep historical grudges. They see a liberal, U.S.-led order as a stumbling block to their aspirations and an existential threat to their regimes. And while no one would mistake Russia and Iran for economic dynamos, a China that has become—in Spykman's phrasing—modern, vitalized, and militarized creates a more fundamental test for the ideological supremacy of democracy and the geopolitical balance of power.[8] Beijing has put a crucial question of the twentieth century back on the table: whether liberalism or illiberalism will rule the coming age.

It isn't clear, though, that China can evade the autocrat's dilemma. Xi's centralization of authority domestically will help him wield power more decisively and aggressively abroad. Yet it seems unlikely that China will become more vibrant or innovative as Xi enforces strict conformity. The example of Putin's miscalculations in Ukraine makes it doubtful that China's decision-making will improve, and its ability to win friends will increase, as an aging ruler entrenches himself in office and stifles dissent. Good judgment, after all, is a form of power, but dictators who silence debate and evade accountability get dumber over time.[9]

The rise and fall of Eurasian challenges is a study in the ferocity, and frailty, of illiberal regimes. If history and recent experience are any guide, Xi's rule may lengthen the odds of China bestriding the world in the long run. It could also make an already formidable country more bellicose, and more dangerous, between now and then.

*

SECOND, THE EURASIAN CENTURY WAS THE AMERICAN CENTURY: THE United States made its career as a superpower by keeping the supercontinent in balance. In an age of Eurasian consolidation, no combination of local powers could stop the strongest predators. In an age of industrial warfare, oceans provided less security than before. Thus, the country that had achieved, in its own hemisphere, what Mackinder feared might happen in Eurasia found itself repeatedly intervening to keep his nightmare from coming true.

America wasn't always a timely balancer. In both world wars, it nearly arrived too late. It was, however, a lethally effective balancer, which is why the likes of Wilhelm II and Hitler sought so desperately, through submarine warfare and other methods, to prevent its unmatched capabilities from crossing the seas. And America was, ultimately, a transformative balancer: the effect, once it engaged quasi-permanently in Eurasia's strategic affairs, was revolutionary.

Washington pacified, and made prosperous, Rimland regions that had been combat zones. It remade the geopolitics of Western Europe and East Asia by remaking the fascist societies that had terrorized those areas. It built a balance of power that favored stability, by forging coalitions that kept the Soviet Union in check. The combination of democracy, geography, and enlightened self-interest made the country that had once abjured allies remarkably good at winning them—and thereby adding, through attraction rather than aggression, their power to its own. American commitment was the answer—the only answer—to Eurasian anarchy, which is why the second half of the twentieth century was so different from the first.

The Eurasian century changed America just as thoroughly as America changed the Eurasian century. Discharging what Mahan had called the country's "duties to the world" required the United States to do things it had never done before: fielding a military of 12 million in World War II, erecting an unprecedented network of alliances, building the bureaucratic accoutrements of global power.[10] America's national identity—its sense of exceptionalism—came to reflect the country's unique, decisive role in world affairs, rather than its unique, happy distance from them.

The anti-interventionists always feared that a great power could not remain a great democracy. These fears weren't groundless, yet the United States managed to destroy its enemies without destroying itself. Whatever domestic compromises America made, whatever freedoms it transgressed, the country was a stronger and more inclusive democracy when the twentieth century ended than when it began—in part *because* global contests created virtuous pressures for the United States to become a truer version of itself. It is certainly hard to imagine America faring better had the emergence of a totalitarian Eurasia forced it to choose between inescapable, pervasive insecurity and the crushing onus of unilateral self-defense.

That's an encouraging precedent, because there's no more escaping America's centrality in this century than in the last. It's fashionable, these days, to herald the arrival of a "multipolar world." Neo-isolationists claim America can pull back and enjoy the benefits of international stability without the costs.[11] Don't fall for it.

Prior to 1945, the crucial regions of Eurasia were not models of self-regulating stability. They were incubators of aggression. Today, an Asia abandoned by America would be at China's mercy. Countries in the Middle East and Europe would struggle to stop their rivals without the backing, spine-stiffening, and coalition management Washington provides.[12] The consequence of U.S. retrenchment would be either the liberation of Eurasia's revisionists or the reemergence of a world in which key theaters become geopolitical hothouses because their residents must arm themselves feverishly—including with nuclear weapons—to survive.

The patterns of international politics changed dramatically once America committed to the supercontinent. Why wouldn't they change just as dramatically if America were now to depart? The next Eurasian century will be another American century—or it will be something far, far worse.

*

BUT WHERE SHOULD AMERICA APPLY ITS EFFORTS? EURASIA IS BIG. THE parts that are most important, and most endangered, have varied over time. "If anything happens in Western Europe," Dean Acheson commented, "the whole business goes to pieces."[13] As the Sino-American rivalry takes center stage, many strategists now say the same about Taiwan.[14] Taken to its extreme, this perspective implies that any minute, any dollar not spent to check the most formidable rival in the most dynamic region is wasted. The truth is not so simple. Even superpowers have their limits. Yet the interdependence, strategic and psychological, of the modern world makes it risky to treat Eurasia as anything but a coherent whole.

Before and during World War II, FDR prioritized Europe, because if the Allies lost there they might not win anywhere. But he never wrote off the Pacific, because serial setbacks in *any* major theater could have global effects. A decade later, Truman—like Acheson—knew that Western Europe came first. But he chose to fight a costly war in South Korea lest unchecked aggression shatter the free world's fragile confidence. This kind of thinking could go too far; the belief that security was truly indivisible helped usher Washington into Vietnam. Yet well-informed policymakers made that ghastly mistake because credibility *did* matter for a global superpower, and because defeats in peripheral settings *could* demoralize allies and destabilize positions that mattered more.

"No great state" can treat the world's continents as "water-tight compartments," Spykman wrote. The dilemma persists today.[15] China has the greatest ability to remake its region and, perhaps, the globe. Yet America can't simply focus on one theater and ignore the rest.

Europe still boasts the largest, most important concentration of liberal democracies; the Middle East remains a crossroads of competition due to geography and resources. Neither region is some trivial "distraction" that the disciplined strategist can safely set aside. One danger is that if America zeroes in on a single adversary, it will create openings that rivals in other vital theaters can exploit. Another is that if any important part of Eurasia slips into violent chaos, America will suffer not just there but far beyond.

An America that can't secure the Middle East against Iran and its proxies will also struggle to keep ambivalent Gulf monarchies aligned vis-à-vis Beijing. If Washington washes its hands of Europe, good luck convincing NATO allies that the security of the Western Pacific is their fight. Had the United States abandoned Ukraine to Russia's violent revisionism—as some Asia-firsters suggested—the shock waves might have washed over areas from the Baltic to the Taiwan Strait.[16] If Washington and its allies don't help Ukraine outlast Putin's assault, they risk sending the message—so harmful in so many regions—that decadent democracies will fade before their autocratic foes. A great benefit of America's security network is that Washington can rally global responses to local challenges. The corollary is that America can't regionalize its foreign policy without paying a hefty price.

This isn't an argument against prioritization. Recognition that the Pacific mattered coexisted with a Germany-first strategy in World War II. It isn't an argument against strengthening America's position in Asia; the need could hardly be more compelling. But as FDR or Truman could attest, sustaining order requires doing multiple things at once.

That may involve using urgency created by crises in one region to catalyze action in others, just as Truman used the Korean War to buttress Western Europe. It may mean using someone else's wars to jump-start preparations for one's own, as Lend-Lease aid invigorated the U.S. arms industry before World War II, and as the Ukraine war catalyzed investment in America's defense-industrial base. Fundamentally, though, this is a matter of how much energy America devotes to its many tasks.

The United States never really stopped reaping its post–Cold War peace dividend, which is why it has a one-war military at a time when it could face serious trouble in two or three regions simultaneously.[17] In this and so many facets of statecraft, an era of effortless primacy accustomed Americans to thinking that minimal effort could yield maximum effect. No longer. Not least of the decisions Washington faces in this harsh new era is whether to pay the rising cost of influence or risk becoming a regional player in an age of global turmoil.

*

AMERICA CAN HARDLY DO IT ALONE, OF COURSE. AS SPYKMAN, MACKINder, and Mahan all recognized, overseas powers can regulate Eurasia's affairs only by working with allies located close to the trouble. Aspirants to hegemony, for their part, can only subdue their neighbors by isolating them from support from abroad. Thus, a fourth lesson: Eurasian clashes are contests in coalition-making and coalition-breaking. Balancers must rally global alliances to beat back hegemonic threats—against aggressors that try cunning strategies, from subversion to submarine warfare, to sever the Old World from the New.

Coalition-making doesn't happen automatically; shared enmities don't automatically produce shared effort. It took the Allies several years, and several near-death experiences, to achieve the teamwork that finally overwhelmed imperial Germany. In World War II, Churchill and Roosevelt knew how fractious the Grand Alliance was, which is why they gave so much to keep it together. Cold War alliance management was a multi-decade exercise in what one U.S. diplomat called "gardening"—tending continuously to key relationships so they were vibrant at the crucial moment.[18] Success in the present struggle will require still deeper forms of solidarity, among countries whose total weight can dash Eurasian dreams.

Whether Washington can prevent aggression around the Eurasian periphery will hinge on its ability to cultivate coalitions that can wield overbearing power. Whether the democracies hold the high ground in the global economy will depend, in substantial part, on how effectively they integrate their markets and synchronize their innovation ecosystems. Blunting economic coercion and political warfare will take closer cooperation on intelligence, cyber-defense, and trade. From the military balance to the technological rivalry, meeting the challenge posed by a cohering Eurasia will require like-minded countries to lash themselves together more tightly than ever before.[19]

The hard core of this effort will be the advanced democracies that comprise America's key Eurasian alliance blocs. Those countries are tied to Washington by shared interests, shared values, and decades of institutionalized cooperation. Acting together, they can exert strong global pressure against any of Eurasia's revisionist powers.[20] Yet if the Ukraine war reinvigorated the free-world community, this coalition-making effort won't be quite like anything America has done before.

America's foremost challenge is in Asia, not Europe, so Japan may be Washington's most indispensable ally in this century, as London was in the last. Moreover, because Asia's security architecture is so fragmented—and because China's challenge spans so many issues— there won't be a single, all-encompassing coalition. The task, rather, will approximate "variable geometry"—arraying free-world nations into multiple smaller groupings that exert decisive influence in crucial areas, from semiconductor supply chains to undersea warfare.[21] If NATO was the model for alliance-building in the twentieth century, AUKUS is the model for the twenty-first. And as America pulls these coalitions together, its opponents have many tools for prying them apart.

Iran uses proxies and coercion to neutralize its regional enemies. Russia has long employed energy flows, political meddling, and intimidation to drive wedges between its foes. Yet China has by far the greatest coalition-rending potential, because it has an economic capacity to punish enemies and pay off fence-sitters that neither Nazi Germany nor the Soviet Union ever possessed. China's enemies are nonetheless coalescing; Eurasian challenges still elicit hostility near and far. But there won't be a historic "big bang" of coalition-building this time, as there was in the late 1940s. Building interlocking webs of resistance will be a harder, more gradual campaign—one that must include not just advanced democratic allies but also more diffident states.

In 1904, Mackinder saw India as the critical "bridge head" in a consolidating supercontinent.[22] As events subsequently showed, even a sea power that controls Eurasia's approaches needs allies on land to keep its rivals preoccupied. When Mackinder wrote, India was big and impoverished. Now, it is big and ever more dynamic. As a result, its choices will matter enormously on many issues, the most basic of which is whether China faces trouble in two domains or can focus on one.

As the Ukraine war demonstrated, alignment between India and America won't be easy or comprehensive. New Delhi prefers a multipolar world, in which India stands among the great powers, to a unipolar one in which America and its Western allies tower over the rest. "India is too big, has too much of a history and identity as a great civilization, to be attached to someone else," former foreign secretary Vijay Gokhale told me.[23] India is a democracy, all right, but one with eroding civil liberties and other troubling characteristics. Nonetheless, the basis for cooperation is there.

Because a unipolar Asia can only be under Chinese dominance, New Delhi and Washington share an interest in keeping that region in balance. Because America's goal is averting Chinese hegemony, it benefits from a stronger, more confident India, even one that remains proudly and stubbornly non-aligned. The process of building that cooperation, on military or technological issues, will be slow, painful, and selective— not to mention as vital as anything else America does to mold the Eurasian landscape in the years ahead.

*

COALITION-BUILDING, THEN, WILL BE MANY-FACETED AND MULTITIERED. America's closest, most reliable allies will be the advanced democracies that hold Eurasia's eastern and western margins. A second tier will include imperfectly aligned democratic partners, like India. The final tier will feature strategically important, illiberal governments who may simply share a common enemy with the free world, and whose cooperation will be most tenuous of all. There's ample precedent for such awkward arrangements. A fifth lesson is that strategy is the art of blending democratic solidarity with sordid compromises. Defeating one devil may require holding hands with another.

Two democracies, France and the United Kingdom, would have lost World War I had tsarist Russia not helped them keep Germany's attention divided. The Cold War flowed from the fact that Britain and America could beat Hitler only by using Stalin's Red Army to close the vise. During that long twilight struggle, the United States made some very thuggish characters members of the free world; it surrounded and defeated Moscow by mending ties with Mao.

It is facile to say that these and other transgressions by the democracies—blockading and bombing civilians, subverting Third World regimes—bankrupted their larger strategic endeavors. There is morality in keeping the world from being ruled by its most acquisitive, least humane regimes. Preserving a balance of power in which freedom can flourish may require illiberal actors and illiberal acts.

Today, there is no countervailing coalition in the Middle East without Saudi Arabia and the UAE, no strong southern flank of NATO without Turkey, no Southeast Asian bulwark against China without Singapore and Vietnam. There is no global strategy for countering Beijing that doesn't involve fighting for a "hedging middle" made up of ambivalent democracies and autocratic states.[24] Holding the Eurasian balance will require rallying the free world *and* buttressing an arc of authoritarians. If anything, this may prove harder than it was during the Cold War.

Then, America's illiberal friends were right-wing autocrats who loathed communism because they would be the first ones murdered if it triumphed. Now, America's enemies—especially Russia and China—traffic in an authoritarianism that seems less existentially threatening to other illiberal regimes, so the ideological gulf between the strongmen Washington needs and the strongmen it needs to thwart is less profound.[25] Add in that many countries outside the West are skeptical of an international order that was largely designed by the West, and the temptation to habitually hedge—or simply play one side off the other—becomes stronger still. America's challenge will be to maximize convergence with these awkward partners, through a mixture of patient relationship-building and utterly transactional, often amoral diplomacy, while minimizing divergence where it would upset the Eurasian balance the most. The United States might even consider a counterintuitive approach to cultivating—eventually—the most improbable relationship of them all.

For now, those who talk about driving wedges between Moscow and Beijing are dreaming. There simply isn't much the United States can do to reverse Sino-Russian alignment; Washington must therefore compete on multiple fronts. Yet proximity doesn't always bring amity. A China that comes anywhere close to achieving its objectives could threaten Russia more directly than it threatens America. Even short of that, a lot can go wrong between two giant-sized, expansionist neighbors that covet some of the same spoils. The best way of hastening the time when America's enemies turn on each other may be pushing them into a tighter embrace.

There's precedent for this, too. More than half a century ago, Washington contributed to the Sino-Soviet split by putting the weaker ally, Beijing, under great pressure, so that it would make demands its stronger ally, Moscow, was unwilling to meet.[26] The roles are now reversed—China is more powerful than Russia—but the logic still pertains. The more pressure the West exerts on Russia, the more Putin may have to ask Xi for aid he won't want to grant.[27] By assiduously isolating Moscow, the West can force it into a dependency on China that many Russian nationalists—if not Putin himself—will someday find quite trying. This may not matter so long as Xi and Putin, those brothers-in-arms, hold power. But after that, who knows? If America were, someday, to profit from Sino-Russian acrimony, it wouldn't be the first time geopolitics had made bedfellows that were very strange indeed.

*

IF THE STAKES, AND THE BASIC STRATEGIC GUIDELINES, OF EURASIAN struggles don't change, the methods do. In two world wars, revisionist states sought to violently fracture the Eurasian equilibrium. In a Cold War waged under the threat of nuclear annihilation, the Soviet Union relied mostly on military intimidation, subversion, and proxy forces. Today's revisionist toolkit is even more eclectic; it includes everything from ballistic missiles to telecommunications networks. Now as ever, attempts at Eurasian expansion match the characteristics of the moment and the shifting contours of global power. This means—a sixth lesson—that geopolitical competition *is* technological competition. The countries that rule in economic production and technological innovation tend to rule the world.

In the world wars, America and its allies didn't always wield the fanciest capabilities; they weren't the first to exploit the dive-bomber or the tank. But they dominated the mass-manufacturing that constituted the foundation of modern military power, and they mastered the technologies—from long-range bombers to maritime logistics—that delivered decisive force on a global battlefield. In the Cold War, the United States kept ahead of the Soviet Union in the epoch-defining nuclear rivalry, while using its unmatched wealth, technical expertise, and civilian technology to bring key regions back to life. By the 1980s, America was charging into the information age and leaving Moscow behind.

The Eurasian century was an American century because America had an unbeatable combination of technological prowess and economic heft—and because it applied those assets against the hardest strategic problems of the age. But now, as China looks to control key chokepoints and capture vital industries, the competition for techno-primacy has heated up again. History suggests that the best way to win this race is to run faster while slowing the other side down.

Yes, America must strengthen its innovation base with investments in areas—such as advanced computing, biotechnology, and clean energy—that will shape the global economy or act as force-multipliers across economic and military applications.[28] Yes, it needs alliances with like-minded nations: The global balance of R & D spending, and the distribution of influence in key supply chains, favors the advanced democracies, but only if they join hands.[29] What was true during World War II, when the British and Americans collaborated to break codes and build long-range fighters, remains true today: coalition-building is a technological imperative as well as a military one. But America and its allies shouldn't settle for being the best, most innovative versions of themselves.

To win World War II, the Allies didn't just build up their own capabilities; they systematically destroyed those of Germany and Japan. During the Cold War, the free world didn't just wait for a flawed Soviet system to expire; it used economic warfare and technological denial policies to limit the Kremlin's potential and hasten its demise. Beijing is far more globally connected than Moscow was, which makes any decoupling effort more painful. But if the world has really reached another "inflection point" in the struggle between opposing ways of life—if Xi and his allies really present a grave and growing threat to global order—how can the democracies justify *not* more aggressively taking the tech fight to their foes?[30]

The free world need not feel guilty about this. Decades of intellectual property theft, commercial espionage, forced technology transfer, and other mercantilist policies have underpinned China's industrial strategy. Xi Jinping has openly stated that his goal is to cut technological dependence on America while making foreign countries as dependent on China as possible.[31] Weakening China's innovation capacity by progressively restricting its access to the foreign money, markets, and materials it still needs to surge ahead is simply self-defense. Such a policy will intensify the struggle in technological coercion and counter-coercion; it will further fragment the global economy. It is also essential to preserving a technological landscape conducive to U.S. influence in peacetime competition—and America's prospects for victory should conflict erupt.[32]

*

AMERICA MUST "PAY THE PRICE FOR PEACE," SAID HARRY TRUMAN IN 1948, or it would "pay the price of war."[33] The ghastliest moments of the Eurasian century came when autocratic aggression ruptured the balance of power. Standards of morality went by the wayside in conquered regions. Autocratic spheres of influence became platforms for predation. Countervailing coalitions, thrown together under dire circumstances, had to claw their way back into hostile continents at horrid cost. This is why Truman's America, having paid the price of war twice in a quarter century, chose to continuously bolster the peace after 1945.

There was nothing simple about this. Preventing global war was arduous, morally troubling work. It required learning the apocalyptic absurdities of nuclear deterrence. It involved fighting bloody "limited" conflicts, going to the brink over Cuba and Berlin, and preparing incessantly for a confrontation America and its allies hoped never to fight. The "long peace" of the postwar era didn't just happen; it was the payoff of a decades-long effort to make the military balance favor the free world. A seventh lesson, then, is that a cold war is the reward for deterring a hot one.

As the citizens of Ukraine can attest, high-intensity warfare is not

some artifact of a receding past. As Israel has rediscovered, technological superiority is no guarantee against the most lethal forms of military
surprise. In a Western Pacific menaced by Chinese power, the peace
grows fragile. Don't assume that revisionist states won't simply try to
seize their objectives—or that democracies must always prevail in tests
of strength. The price of peace, in the present era, will be another long
military competition.

Deterrence on NATO's eastern front will require well-armed frontline states that can put up a real fight, forward-deployed alliance forces
that can slow a Russian onslaught, and a NATO that can surge power
into hard-to-access areas while keeping the Kremlin from using nuclear
coercion to impose a settlement on its terms.[34] That's difficult, but
doable, for the mightiest, most experienced alliance. The situation is
more daunting in the Pacific, where the U.S. has no region-wide alliance,
and where China's buildup is threatening to confront America with a
choice between fighting and losing a war to save Taiwan, and simply not
fighting at all.[35]

"Taiwan is like two feet from China," Trump remarked in 2019. "If
they invade, there isn't a fucking thing we can do about it."[36] Fortunately,
securing the peace in East Asia isn't as hopeless as the map might make
it seem. The fundamental asymmetry favoring China is proximity. The
fundamental asymmetry favoring its enemies is that denial is easier than
control, especially when control means projecting power over large bodies of water. Seizing Taiwan, with its oceanic moat and rugged terrain,
would take one of the most complex military operations in history.[37] The
outlines of a strategy for defeating—or better yet, deterring—such an
assault are readily apparent.

They include turning Taiwan into a prickly porcupine, bristling with
arms and ready to fight until the end; flipping geography against Beijing
by making the First Island Chain a series of strongpoints stocked with
anti-ship missiles and patrolled by lethal attack submarines, backed by a
Second Island Chain studded with American air power, logistical capabilities, and long-range precision-strike aircraft; ensuring that the Penta-

gon has ample magazines of the torpedoes, missiles, and other munitions needed to decimate a blockade squadron or invasion fleet; and preparing to cut off China's imports of energy and other key materials through a blockade centered on distant chokepoints that the U.S. Navy can control.

They include, also, knitting America's regional relationships into something more capable of, and explicitly committed to, a coalition defense; readying, with other advanced democracies, severe economic and technological punishments should Beijing attack; and integrating allied defense industrial bases into a twenty-first-century arsenal of democracy that can sustain a long conflict. Finally, and most uncomfortably, deterrence requires possessing a credible ability to fight a limited nuclear war in the Western Pacific, if only so that China doesn't feel emboldened, as its own arsenal matures, to use nuclear coercion to prevent America from intervening at all.[38]

This formula can deny China any easy victory, while exploiting U.S. advantages—alliances, global power-projection, economic and technological leverage—to make the conflict devastating, destabilizing, and existentially dangerous for Xi's regime. It all sounds awful, but preparing for the unthinkable is the best way of ensuring it never occurs. It is heartening, then, that Washington and other countries are making real, sometimes historic, progress in all these areas—and terrifying that they often seem to be moving in slow motion as Beijing races to ready for a fight.[39]

"For almost twenty years we had all of the time and almost none of the money," George Marshall wrote as Hitler steamrolled Europe. "Today we have all of the money and no time."[40] The United States will eventually pay to keep key regions out of hostile hands. Far better to balance early than to balance late.

---

*

ANY BALANCING EFFORT BEGINS AT HOME, SO IT HAS BECOME OBLIGATORY, in discussions of foreign policy, to say that America must get its own house in order. Like most clichés, it's partly true. One thing the anti-interventionists got right is that America's power is no greater than the vibrancy of its economy, society, and democracy. The twist is that if America had insisted on perfecting itself *before* going abroad, the world would be run by regimes less paralyzed by their imperfections. Global involvement can, in fact, be an impetus to domestic renewal: having enemies at the gates concentrates the mind on weaknesses within the walls.

This effect endures. Washington's turn toward great-power competition has already produced historic outlays in semiconductor manufacturing and other strategic priorities with domestic payoffs.[41] An eighth lesson, though, is that there's another, less-noticed aspect of "foreign policy begins at home": the Western Hemisphere is the forgotten, vital theater of Eurasian competition.

Mahan understood that America had to secure the Panama Canal and the Caribbean before it could patrol the oceans. Or, as Spykman put it, the United States eventually accrued "power to spare" for intervention in distant theaters because it was supreme within its own.[42] Hemispheric immunity and global activism went hand in hand. America's enemies understood this, too; from the Zimmermann telegram to the Cuban Missile Crisis, every struggle of the last century saw Eurasian powers stir the pot of political instability and anti-Americanism in Latin America, in hopes of putting Washington off-balance by putting it on the defensive in its own backyard.

Today's Eurasian powers know the playbook. Russia and Iran have supported illiberal populists around the Caribbean basin. China is inserting itself into Latin American economies, infrastructure, and technological networks, while laying the groundwork for a larger security presence from Argentina to Cuba.[43] One doesn't have to think it is October 1962 all over again to understand the implications.

Just as countries that dominate their home regions will have greater scope to reach into the Western Hemisphere, a presence in that hemisphere can distract and hobble a superpower used to ranging overseas. The logic of the Monroe Doctrine—the idea that America cannot let hostile powers or hostile ideologies hold sway in the Western

Hemisphere—remains as valid as ever, even if the language needlessly offends sovereign states to Washington's south.

Another epoch of competition foretells another effort to keep U.S. rivals from setting up shop there. Don't be shocked if America eventually uses some of the same sharp-edged tools, from economic coercion to covert intervention, that it deployed in the Cold War; even enlightened democracies resort to hard measures in hard times. Yet the more the United States can pursue a negative objective—strategic denial of the Western Hemisphere to its adversaries—with a positive program of regional cooperation, the more effective it will be.

A degree of deglobalization vis-à-vis China creates opportunities for deeper regionalization of trade and manufacturing in the Western Hemisphere.[44] Investments in sustaining the region's strained democracies, and rebuilding long-neglected relations with its militaries, are good value amid intensifying international tensions. Most ambitiously, a stronger North American community—in which America, Canada, and Mexico are increasingly fused together economically and technologically—can counterbalance China's forbidding heft.[45] That's an imposing, and politically challenging, agenda. But the tighter the bonds of integration within the Americas, the greater the power Washington can wield in a fragmenting world.

*

MUCH OF THIS PAINTS A GRIM PORTRAIT OF THE FUTURE—A FUTURE OF high-octane rivalry as far as the eye can see. The supercontinent's vital regions and waterways will see contests in "containment and counter-containment," as China's defense minister said in 2021.[46] The global economy will be reshaped by the threat of war and the pressures of competition. Proxy conflicts and crises will become more common; America and other defenders of the prevailing order will look to punish their rivals' missteps. Foreign policy will become a starker, more remorseless enterprise, as democratic societies rediscover that the only way to preserve a system that is liberated from the worst patterns of geopolitics is to master the ruthless practice of geopolitics in dealing with those who would bring about its demise.

That may not sound appealing. But remember: Eurasian struggles are opportunities for creation.

The twentieth century was a monument to humanity's worst impulses. It was also the cradle of the freest, most flourishing age humanity has known. The worst of times led directly to the best of times; the creation of the liberal order was how a global superpower and its allies wrenched history off its destructive path.

Today, old dangers are reappearing in new forms. The world no longer seems so safe from great-power war, autocratic ascendancy, the deliberate and large-scale victimization of civilians, and other scourges that characterized a long era of conflict. Keeping these specters at bay will demand another era of creation.

Most international orders are "orders of exclusion"; they suppress those on the outside by building norms, institutions, and architectures of cooperation among those within.[47] Whether the problem is deterring aggression, defeating political warfare, or foreclosing a future in which technology entrenches and empowers tyranny, the solution involves adapting and improving a system that has served so many countries so well.

A coalition that holds the line in crucial theaters will be one in which a globe-spanning group of countries has buttressed the norm against territorial conquest by pulling itself together—militarily, economically, diplomatically—as never before. A free-world alliance that outpaces its enemies technologically will be one that has reached new frontiers of innovation by pooling its resources and creativity in unprecedented ways. A group of democracies that defends its values will be one that has forged better methods for tackling transnational corruption and repression. A coalition that has competed effectively for global influence will be one that has embraced innovative forms of institution-building—of the sort seen with the Quad, AUKUS, and other initiatives—that adapt the architecture of international cooperation to match the most pressing modern challenges.

The presence of enemies, as Mackinder once wrote, can ultimately have "stimulative" effects.[48] The proper response to a world riven by conflict is not to junk the liberal order.[49] It is to strengthen that order against the actors trying to bring it down.

*

ACHIEVING ANY OF THIS MEANS HEEDING A FINAL LESSON: THERE IS NO such thing as destiny. The history of the modern era might make one think Eurasian gambits are doomed to fail—that seeking hegemony is tantamount to committing strategic suicide. After all, from Mackinder onward, every Eurasian challenger was defeated, because every challenger provoked a pack of enemies that killed its prey. The twentieth century led not, as Mackinder worried, to a nightmarish "empire of the world" but to a brighter existence for much of humanity.[50] The moral arc of the universe may be long, the saying goes, but perhaps it does bend toward justice.

It's a pleasing and profoundly dangerous notion. Each fight for Eurasia could have gone differently; the good guys didn't *have* to come out on top. A determined Germany might plausibly have defeated the Allies, and remade the system, in World War I. There were many moments when a different decision or personality might have changed the course of World War II. In the early Cold War, it wasn't fate but urgent, improvised policies that saved the day. There is no law of nature that expansion must fail and tyranny must be vanquished. There is no guarantee that history takes the path of progress.

Indeed, the idea of progress would have seemed absurd for much of the Eurasian century, when it appeared that modernity had produced ever worse forms of warfare and ever more toxic types of tyranny. Progress is the product of power, deployed for constructive purposes. The moral arc of the universe was exactly what America and its allies made of it—just as the outcome of this Eurasian struggle will hinge on their choices, their commitment, in years ahead.

There's no inherent reason that they can't find the winning formula. Eurasia's revisionist powers are already running into resistance; they are suffering from the pathologies of their rulers and regimes. The prospect that these countries may be traveling a road that ends in encirclement and exhaustion isn't lost on shrewd observers in autocratic capitals. Even Chinese military analysts admit that countries that take on America and its many allies typically pay an awful price. "Don't think of Imperial America as a 'paper tiger,'" writes one. "It's a 'real tiger,' that kills people."[51]

If Washington and its friends can consistently stymie this set of Eurasian ambitions, if they can bolster the order their enemies aim to weaken, if they can show that rivalry brings more pain than profit for revisionist regimes, then perhaps policies or politics in Moscow, Tehran, and Beijing will eventually mellow. As the resolution of the Cold War reminds us, countries—even ideologically radical ones—do sometimes reconcile themselves to realities they cannot change.

But don't take anything for granted. Outlasting the Soviet Union required a forty-year struggle pervaded by threats of Armageddon. Other aspiring hegemons did dreadful damage before they fell. Today's Eurasian powers will try to smash, subvert, or seduce the countries around them. They will hope an overseas superpower that has settled three prior confrontations stumbles in a fourth.

History suggests the odds are against them. But history also shows that surprises happen and democratic dominance is not assured. Geography shapes but strategy decides: that's the most crucial insight the Eurasian century offers.

ACKNOWLEDGMENTS

The acknowledgments section of a book is never sufficient to recognize, let alone discharge, the arrears an author incurs in the process of writing. That disclaimer notwithstanding, I am grateful to the Johns Hopkins School of Advanced International Studies and the American Enterprise Institute for providing me with delightfully stimulating intellectual homes while I wrote this book; to Jim Steinberg, Robert Doar, and Kori Schake for leading those fine institutions; to Cameron Abadi, Ravi Agrawal, Dan Kurtz-Phelan, Mattias Hesserus, Iain Martin, David Shipley, Stefan Theil, and—most of all—Toby Harshaw and Tim O'Brien at Bloomberg Opinion for tolerating my fascination with Mackinder and encouraging me to develop some of the ideas that informed my analysis; to John Glusman, Helen Thomaides, and the team at W. W. Norton for being such a pleasure to work with; and to Rafe Sagalyn for steering this project to Norton. As always, I am profoundly indebted to my family for all the love they offered during this project and many others. Finally, this book is dedicated to John Lewis Gaddis and Barton Bernstein. These two wonderful scholars and peerless mentors helped me understand what it means to be a historian. They supported me at critical stages along my intellectual and professional journey. I will be forever in their debt.

NOTES

APP: American Presidency Project, University of California Santa Barbara

CIA FOIA: CIA Freedom of Information Act Electronic Reading Room

CWIHP: Cold War International History Project

DBFP: *Documents on British Foreign Policy 1919–1939*, edited by E. L. Woodward and Rohan Butler (London: Her Majesty's Stationery Office, 1946–86)

DGFP: *Documents on German Foreign Policy, 1918–1945* (Washington, DC: U.S. Government Printing Office, 1949–83)

DNSA: Digital National Security Archive, United States

EHP: Edward House Papers, Manuscripts and Archives, Yale University

FDRL: Franklin D. Roosevelt Presidential Library

FRUS: *Foreign Relations of the United States*

GDD: Auswärtiges Amt, *German Diplomatic Documents, 1871–1914*, translated by E. T. S. Dugdale (New York: Harper, 1928–31)

LC: Library of Congress

PWW: Arthur Link, ed., *The Papers of Woodrow Wilson* (digital edition, University of Virginia Press, 2017)

RRL: Ronald Reagan Presidential Library

SMML: Seeley Mudd Manuscript Library, Princeton University

TNA: The National Archives, United Kingdom

INTRODUCTION

1. Quoted in John Milton Cooper, Jr., *Woodrow Wilson: A Biography* (New York: Knopf, 2009), 268.
2. Ambassador in Japan to Secretary of State, July 21, 1940, in *FRUS* 1940, vol. 4, 966.
3. Nicholas Spykman, *The Geography of the Peace*, edited by Helen Nicholl (New York: Harcourt, Brace, 1944), 34.
4. Report by the Joint Strategic Survey Committee, April 29, 1947, *FRUS* 1947, vol. 1, document 386.

5. David Crenshaw and Alicia Chen, "'Heads Bashed Bloody': China's Xi Marks Communist Party Centenary with Strong Words for Adversaries," *Washington Post*, July 1, 2021.

6. There is, technically, a difference between "Eurasia" (which includes the offshore islands) and "the Eurasian landmass" (which ends at the shores of continental Europe and continental Asia), just as the United Kingdom is part of the continent of Europe but not "continental Europe."

7. Halford J. Mackinder, *Democratic Ideals and Reality: A Study in the Politics of Reconstruction* [1919] (Washington, DC: National Defense University Press, 1942).

8. John Darwin, *After Tamerlane: The Global History of Empire since 1405* (New York: Bloomsbury, 2008).

9. Matthew White, *The Great Big Book of Horrible Things: The Definitive Chronicle of History's 100 Worst Atrocities* (New York: Norton, 2012), 563. Most observers agree that World War II was the deadliest war in history. Where World War I ranks depends on whether one is distinguishing between civil wars and interstate wars, how one deals with the issue of civilian versus military casualties, and whether one disaggregates the Second Sino-Japanese War from World War II, among other factors.

10. See Paul Chamberlin, *The Cold War's Killing Fields: Rethinking the Long Peace* (New York: HarperCollins, 2018).

11. Eric Hobsbawm, *The Age of Extremes: A Short History of the World, 1914–1991* (New York: Vintage, 1996).

12. There is a very useful, although somewhat specialized, literature on Mackinder and his contributions to the study of geopolitics. The most helpful sources are cited in the longer discussion of Mackinder in chapter 1.

13. Halford J. Mackinder, "The Geographic Pivot of History," *Geographical Journal*, April 1904, 421–37.

14. Mackinder was concerned, in 1904, about Russia and (to a lesser degree) Germany, two autocracies with modern or modernizing economies. The theme would be better developed in his later book, *Democratic Ideals and Reality*.

15. Richard Overy, *Why the Allies Won* (New York: Norton, 1997), 320.

CHAPTER 1: MACKINDER'S WORLD

1. The railway technically opened in 1903 but was still missing the final stretch of track, around Lake Baikal.

2. Paul Kennedy, *The Rise and Fall of British Naval Mastery* (New York: Penguin, 2017), 196.

3. Chris Miller, *We Shall Be Masters: Russian Pivots to East Asia from Peter the Great to Putin* (Cambridge, MA: Harvard University Press, 2021), 122.

4. Fritz Fischer, *War of Illusions: German Policies from 1911 to 1914*, translated by Marian Jackson (New York: Norton, 1975), 471.

5. Telegram from American Consul at Vladivostok to Secretary of State, November 8, 1917, Box 10, State Department Correspondence, Assistant Secretary of the Navy Files, FDRL.

6. Mark Edele, *Stalinism at War: The Soviet Union in World War II* (London: Bloomsbury, 2021), 68.

7. Albert Weeks, *Russia's Life-Saver: Lend-Lease Aid to the U.S.S.R. in World War II* (Lanham, MD: Lexington, 2004).

8. Carlotta Gall, "'Created to Scare the Population': How One Russian Brigade Terrorised Bucha," *Irish Times*, May 23, 2022; Andrew Roth, "Russian Ships, Tanks and Troops on the Move to Ukraine as Peace Talks Stall," *Observer*, January 23, 2022; Mark Krutov, "The Dead of the 64th: A Notorious Russian Army Unit and Its High Casualty Rate," Radio Free Europe/Radio Liberty, August 10, 2022.

9. Fred Pleitgen, Claudia Otto, and Ivana Kottasová, "'There Are Maniacs Who Enjoy Killing,' Russian Defector Says of His Former Unit Accused of War Crimes in Bucha," CNN, December 13, 2022.

10. Miller, *We Shall Be Masters*, 117.
11. Zachary Carter, *The Price of Peace: Money, Democracy, and the Life of John Maynard Keynes* (New York: Random House, 2020), 274.
12. Halford J. Mackinder, "The Round World and the Winning of the Peace," *Foreign Affairs*, July 1943, 595. See also Gerry Kearns, *Geopolitics and Empire: The Legacy of Halford Mackinder* (New York: Oxford University Press, 2009).
13. W. H. Parker, *Mackinder: Geography as an Aid to Statecraft* (New York: Oxford University Press, 1982), 2.
14. Leo Amery, *My Political Life*, vol. 1 (London: Hutchinson, 1953), 228; Parker, *Mackinder*, 21; Simone Pelizza, "Geopolitics, Education, and Empire: The Political Life of Sir Halford Mackinder, 1895–1925," PhD dissertation, Leeds University, March 2013, 35.
15. Geoff Sloan, "Haldane's Mackindergarten: A Radical Experiment in British Military Education?," *War in History*, July 2012, 323.
16. Brian Blouet, *Halford Mackinder: A Biography* (College Station: Texas A & M University Press, 2010), 134.
17. Amery, *My Political Life*, 228.
18. "World Tour in Thought. Mr. Mackinder, M.P., on the Duty of Democracy," *Observer*, March 13, 1910.
19. "Sir Halford Mackinder," *The Times*, March 17, 1947.
20. Mackinder, interestingly, rarely used the term "geopolitics," preferring "political geography."
21. Halford J. Mackinder, "On the Scope and Methods of Geography," *Proceedings of the Royal Geographical Society and Monthly Record of Geography*, March 1887, 143–44.
22. Halford J. Mackinder, "The Physical Basis of Political Geography," *Scottish Geographical Magazine*, 1890, 78–84.
23. Halford J. Mackinder, *Britain and the British Seas* (New York: Appleton, 1902); Halford J. Mackinder, *The Rhine, Its Valley and History* (London: Chatto, 1908).
24. Halford J. Mackinder, "The Geographical Pivot of History," *Geographical Journal*, April 1904, 422.
25. Kevin Narizny, "Anglo-American Primacy and the Global Spread of Democracy: An International Genealogy," *World Politics*, April 2012, 341–73.
26. Arnold Toynbee, *The Prospects of Western Civilization* (New York: Oxford University Press, 1949), 8.
27. Aaron Friedberg, *The Weary Titan: Britain and the Experience of Relative Decline, 1895–1905* (Princeton: Princeton University Press, 1988).
28. Henry Kissinger, *A World Restored: Metternich, Castlereagh, and the Problems of Peace, 1812–1822* (Boston: Houghton Mifflin, 1957).
29. T. G. Otte, "'A Very Internecine Policy': Anglo-Russian Cold Wars before the Cold War," in C. Baxter, M. Dockrill, and K. Hamilton, eds., *Britain in Global Politics, Volume 1: From Gladstone to Churchill* (New York: Palgrave Macmillan, 2013), 35.
30. Henry Kissinger, *Diplomacy* (New York: Simon & Schuster, 1994), 121, 128; Wolfgang Mommsen, *Imperial Germany 1867–1918: Politics, Culture, and Society in an Authoritarian State* (New York: St. Martin's Press, 1995).
31. Williamson Murray, "Strategy and Total War," in Hal Brands, ed., *The New Makers of Modern Strategy: From the Ancient World to the Digital Age* (Princeton: Princeton University Press, 2023), 522–44.
32. Richard Overy, *Blood and Ruins: The Last Imperial War, 1931–1945* (New York: Penguin, 2022), 3, 5.
33. Mackinder, "Geographical Pivot," 437.
34. Mackinder, "Geographical Pivot," 421–22.
35. Overy, *Blood and Ruins*, 6.
36. Mackinder, "Geographical Pivot," 421, 433.
37. Sheldon Anderson, "Metternich, Bismarck, and the Myth of the 'Long Peace,'" *Peace & Change*, July 2007, 301–28.
38. Mackinder, "Geographical Pivot," 422.
39. Mackinder, "Geographical Pivot," 432–33.

40. John Shelton Curtiss, *Russia's Crimean War* (Durham, NC: Duke University Press, 1979), 340, 419–20, 423, 529; Paul Kennedy, *The Rise and Fall of the Great Powers* (New York: Vintage, 1988), 174.

41. Geoffrey Wawro, *The Franco-Prussian War: The German Conquest of France in 1870–71* (Cambridge: Cambridge University Press, 2006).

42. Mackinder, "Geographical Pivot," 434.

43. Darwin, *After Tamerlane*, 322.

44. Mackinder, "Geographical Pivot," 434.

45. Mackinder, "Geographical Pivot," 434.

46. Mackinder, "Geographical Pivot," 436; Mackinder, *Democratic Ideals and Reality: A Study in the Politics of Reconstruction* [1919] (Washington, DC: National Defense University Press, 1942).

47. Mackinder, "Geographical Pivot," 428, 436.

48. Mackinder, *Democratic Ideals and Reality*, 106. Mackinder prefaced this dictum with "Who rules East Europe commands the Heartland," for reasons I explain in chapter 2.

49. Mackinder, "Geographical Pivot," 435–36.

50. Mackinder, "Geographical Pivot," 427–28.

51. See George Nathaniel Curzon, *Russia in Central Asia in 1889 and the Anglo-Russian Question* (London: Longman, Green, 1889).

52. Mackinder, "Geographical Pivot," 437.

53. Mackinder, "Geographical Pivot," 437–44.

54. Dennis Warner and Peggy Warner, *The Tide at Sunrise: A History of the Russo-Japanese War, 1904–05* (New York: Routledge, 2004).

55. Carl von Clausewitz, *On War*, edited and translated by Michael Howard and Peter Paret (Princeton: Princeton University Press, 1984), 102, 578.

56. Mark Zwonitzer, *The Statesman and the Storyteller: John Hay, Mark Twain, and the Rise of American Imperialism* (Chapel Hill, NC: Algonquin, 2016), 273.

57. Kori Schake, *Safe Passage: The Transition from British to American Hegemony* (Cambridge, MA: Harvard University Press, 2017), 157.

58. Halford J. Mackinder, "The Empire and Canada," *The Times*, December 15, 1908.

59. George Dangerfield, *The Awakening of American Nationalism, 1815–1828* (New York: Harper & Row, 1965), 4.

60. Washington Chauncey Ford, ed., *The Writings of John Quincy Adams*, vol. 4 (New York: Macmillan, 2015), 128.

61. Michael Hunt, *American Ascendancy: How the United States Gained and Wielded Global Dominance* (Chapel Hill: University of North Carolina Press, 2007), 24–31.

62. Frederick Jackson Turner, "The Significance of the Frontier in American History," 1893. See also Robert Kagan, *Dangerous Nation: America's Foreign Policy from Its Earliest Days to the Dawn of the Twentieth Century* (New York: Knopf, 2006).

63. Kent Calder, *Super Continent: The Logic of Eurasian Integration* (Stanford: Stanford University Press, 2019), xiv.

64. William Cowles to Theodore Roosevelt, July 29, 1907, Theodore Roosevelt Papers, LC.

65. Extracts from a letter from Rear Admiral Stephen Luce to the Secretary of the Navy, March 14, 1889, Reel 2, Alfred Thayer Mahan Papers, LC; Alfred Thayer Mahan, "Naval Warfare, Lecture II," Naval War College Lectures, Spring 1897, Reel 4, Mahan Papers, LC.

66. Alfred Thayer Mahan, *The Influence of Sea Power upon History, 1660–1783* (Boston: Little, Brown, 1890), ch. 1.

67. For one comparison of the two thinkers, see Paul Kennedy, "Mahan versus Mackinder: Two Interpretations of British Seapower," *Militärgeschichtliche Mitteilunger*, January 1974, 39–66. For an excellent article placing Mahan within the wider scope of geopolitical thought, see Sarah C. M. Paine, "Centuries of Security: Chinese, Russian and U.S. Continental versus Maritime Approaches," *Journal of Military History*, October 2022.

68. Mahan, *Influence of Sea Power upon History*, 25.

69. Alfred Thayer Mahan, *The Influence of Sea Power upon the French Revolution and Empire, 1793–1812*, vol. 2 (Boston: Little, Brown, 1892), 118.

70. Mahan, *Influence of Sea Power upon History*, 138.

71. Alfred Thayer Mahan, *The Interest of America in Sea Power, Present and Future* (Boston: Little, Brown, 1897), 124.

72. Alfred Thayer Mahan, *From Sail to Steam: Recollections of Naval Life* (New York: Harper, 1907), 324.

73. Sadao Asada, *From Mahan to Pearl Harbor: The Imperial Japanese Navy and the United States* (Annapolis: Naval Institute Press, 2006), 8; George Baer, *One Hundred Years of Sea Power: The U.S. Navy, 1890–1990* (Stanford: Stanford University Press, 1996), 14.

74. Albert Gleaves, *Life and Letters of Rear Admiral Stephen B. Luce* (New York: Putnam, 1925), 304; John Maurer, "Alfred Thayer Mahan and the Strategy of Sea Power," in Brands, ed., *New Makers of Modern Strategy*, 175–78.

75. Norman Angell, "'The Great Illusion': A Reply to Rear-Admiral A. T. Mahan," *North American Review*, June 1912, 772.

76. Jon Sumida, *Inventing Grand Strategy and Teaching Command: The Classic Works of Alfred Thayer Mahan Reconsidered* (Washington, DC: Woodrow Wilson Center Press, 1997), 92–94.

77. Alfred Thayer Mahan, "The Problem of Asia," *Harper's New Monthly Magazine*, March 1900, 546.

78. Alfred Thayer Mahan, *Mahan on Naval Warfare: Selections from the Writings of Rear Admiral Alfred Thayer Mahan*, edited by Allan Westcott (Boston: Little, Brown, 1918), 302.

79. Alfred Thayer Mahan, *The Problem of Asia and Its Effect upon International Policies* (Boston: Little, Brown, 1900), esp. 22, 24, 44.

80. Mahan, *Problem of Asia*, quoted at 62–63.

81. Alfred Thayer Mahan to Theodore Roosevelt, January 10, 1907, Theodore Roosevelt Papers, LC.

82. Robert Seager, *Alfred Thayer Mahan: The Man and His Letters* (Annapolis: Naval Institute Press, 1977), 500.

83. Mahan, *Mahan on Naval Warfare*, 319.

84. Alfred Thayer Mahan, *Mahan on Naval Strategy: Selections from the Writings of Rear Admiral Alfred Thayer Mahan* (Annapolis: Naval Institute Press, 2015), 336.

85. Mahan, *Interest of America in Sea Power*, 259; Mahan to Theodore Roosevelt, December 27, 1904, Reel 3, Mahan Papers, LC.

86. Robert Kaplan, *The Revenge of Geography: What the Map Tells Us About Coming Conflicts and the Battle against Fate* (New York: Random House, 1992), 105; Kevin McCrainie, *Mahan, Corbett, and the Foundations of Naval Strategic Thought* (Annapolis: Naval Institute Press, 2021).

87. Maurer, "Alfred Thayer Mahan."

88. Julian Corbett, *Some Principles of Maritime Strategy* (London: Longman, Green, 1918), 12.

89. See Sumida, *Inventing Grand Strategy and Teaching Command*, 30.

90. "Strategic studies" is a close cousin of a related discipline, "security studies," and the terms are sometimes used interchangeably. On their relationship, see Joshua Rovner, "Warring Tribes Studying War and Peace," *War on the Rocks*, April 12, 2016.

91. Franklin Roosevelt, "Quarantine Speech," October 5, 1937, Miller Center, University of Virginia; E. H. Carr, *The Twenty Years' Crisis, 1919–1939: An Introduction to the Study of International Relations* [1939] (New York: Harper Perennial, 1964).

92. David Ekbladh, "Present at the Creation: Edward Mead Earle and the Depression-Era Origins of Security Studies," *International Security*, Winter 2011–12, 107–41.

93. "American Military Policy and National Security, 1938," Records of the Office of the Director, Faculty Files, Box 6, Edward Mead Earle, Institute for Advanced Study Archives.

94. Edward Mead Earle, "American Security—Its Changing Conditions," *Annals of the American Academy of Political and Social Science*, November 1941, 191–92.

95. Ekbladh, "Present at the Creation"; Edward Mead Earle, ed., *Makers of Modern Strategy: Military Thought from Machiavelli to Hitler* (Princeton: Princeton University Press, 1943).

96. Edward Mead Earle to Franklin Roosevelt, January 7, 1942, Walter Lippmann Papers, Box 68, Manuscripts and Archives, Yale University.

97. Edward Mead Earle, "Studies of the Foreign Relations and Military Position of the United States," December 1941, Box 7, Edward Mead Earle Files, Institute for Advanced Study Archives.

98. Antero Holmila, "Re-Thinking Nicholas J. Spykman: From Historical Sociology to Balance of Power," *International History Review*, September–October 2020, 956. See also Or Rosenboim, *The Emergence of Globalism: Visions of World Order in Britain and the United States, 1939–1950* (Princeton: Princeton University Press, 2017), 58–93.

99. Nicholas Spykman, "The Study of International Relations," *Yale Alumni Weekly*, March 16, 1934, James Angell Records, Box 175, Manuscripts and Archives, Yale University.

100. Nicholas Spykman, *America's Strategy in World Politics: The United States and the Balance of Power* [1942] (New York: Routledge, 2017), 18, 7.

101. Nicholas Spykman, "Geography and Foreign Policy, I," *American Political Science Review*, February 1938, 29.

102. Spykman, "Geography and Foreign Policy, I," 43.

103. Spykman, *America's Strategy*, 89; also Kaplan, *Revenge of Geography*, 92.

104. Spykman, *America's Strategy*, 3. See also Spykman, "Geography and Foreign Policy, II," *American Political Science Review*, April 1938, 213–32.

105. Spykman, *America's Strategy*, 6–7.

106. Spykman, *America's Strategy*, 121, 154, 194, 196, 389.

107. Robert Kagan, "War and the Liberal Hegemony," *Liberties*, Summer 2022.

108. Spykman, *America's Strategy*, 444–45.

109. Albert Hirschman, *National Power and the Structure of Foreign Trade* (Berkeley: University of California Press, 1945), xv.

110. Spykman, *America's Strategy*, 34, 205–6, 267, 314. For a critique, see Robert J. Art, "The United States, the Balance of Power, and World War II: Was Spykman Right?," *Security Studies*, July–September 2005, 365–406.

111. Spykman, *America's Strategy*, 165, 460.

112. Spykman, *Geography of the Peace*, 41.

113. Spykman, *Geography of the Peace*, 29, 41–42, 43.

114. Spykman, *Geography of the Peace*, 47.

115. Edward Mead Earle, "Power Politics and American World Policy," *Political Science Quarterly*, March 1943, 94, 102.

116. George F. Kennan, "Measures Short of War (Diplomatic)," National War College Lecture, September 16, 1946, George F. Kennan Papers, SMML.

117. Spykman, *America's Strategy*, 11.

118. S. C. M. Paine, *The Japanese Empire: Grand Strategy from the Meiji Restoration to the Pacific War* (New York: Cambridge University Press, 2017); Andrew Lambert, *Seapower States: Maritime Culture, Continental Empires, and the Conflict That Made the Modern World* (New Haven: Yale University Press, 2018).

119. Mackubin Owens, "In Defense of Classical Geopolitics," *Naval War College Review*, Autumn 1999, esp. 66. On the origins, see also Jonathan Haslam, *No Virtue Like Necessity: Realist Thought in International Relations since Machiavelli* (New Haven: Yale University Press, 2013), esp. 176–78; Robert Strausz-Hupé, *Geopolitics: The Struggle for Space and Power* (New York: G. P. Putnam's Sons, 1942), 25–46.

120. Holger Herwig, "Geopolitik: Haushofer, Hitler, and Lebensraum," *Journal of Strategic Studies*, April–May 1999, 230.

121. Andreas Dorpalen, *The World of General Haushofer: Geopolitics in Action* (New York: Farrar & Rinehart, 1942), 29, 28, 42; Hans Weigert, "Haushofer and the Pacific," *Foreign Affairs*, July 1942, 738–40.

122. Dorpalen, *World of General Haushofer*, 142–43; Alfred D. Low, *The Men around Hitler: The Nazi Elite and Its Collaborators* (New York: Columbia University Press, 1996), 27; Derwent Whittlesey, "Haushofer: The Geopoliticians," in Earle, ed., *Makers of Modern Strategy*, esp. 398–410.
123. Parker, *Mackinder*, 173.
124. Herwig, "Geopolitik," 218.
125. OSS Reference Card, "Haushofer, Karl," undated, CIA FOIA, CIA-RDP82-00038R001000160005-0.
126. The best study is Holger Herwig, *Demon of Geopolitics: How Karl Haushofer "Educated" Hitler and Hess* (Lanham, MD: Rowman & Littlefield, 2016).
127. Herwig, *Demon of Geopolitics*, 83.
128. Herwig, *Demon of Geopolitics*, 137.
129. Herwig, "Geopolitik," 229.
130. Adolf Hitler, *Mein Kampf*, translated by Ralph Mannheim (Boston: Houghton Mifflin, 1943), 643.
131. Strausz-Hupé, *Geopolitics*, 139.
132. Herwig, "Geopolitik," 233–34.
133. See Karl Haushofer to Albrecht Haushofer, September 3, 1940, in *DGFP*, Series D, vol. 11, 15–18.
134. Low, *The Men Around Hitler*, 33.
135. Carlyle Morgan, "The Man Behind the Man Behind Hitler," *Christian Science Monitor*, March 12, 1947.
136. John Dunlop, "Aleksandr Dugin's Foundations of Geopolitics," *Demokratizatsiya*, Winter 2004; Aleksandr Dugin, *Last War of the World: The Geopolitics of Contemporary Russia*, translated by John Bryant (London: Arktos, 2015), 145; Waller Newell, *Tyrants: Power, Injustice, and Terror* (Cambridge: Cambridge University Press, 2019), 228.
137. Sergey Radchenko, "Daria Dugina Has Become a Martyr for Putin," *Spectator*, August 24, 2022.
138. Andrew Marshall to Donald Rumsfeld, May 2, 2002, Department of Defense Freedom of Information Act Electronic Reading Room.
139. Kaplan, *Revenge of Geography*.

CHAPTER 2: THE GREAT BLACK TORNADO

1. Correlli Barnett, *The Collapse of British Power* (New York: Morrow, 1972), 239.
2. J. S. Dunn, *The Crowe Memorandum: Sir Eyre Crowe and Foreign Office Perceptions of Germany, 1918–1925* (Newcastle upon Tyne, UK: Cambridge Scholars, 2013), 7; also T. G. Otte, "Eyre Crowe and British Foreign Policy: A Cognitive Map," in Otte and Constantine Pagedas, eds., *Personalities, War, and Diplomacy* (New York: Routledge, 1997).
3. Eyre Crowe, "Memorandum on the Present State of British Relations with France and Germany," January 1, 1907, WikiSource, accessed December 8, 2022.
4. Robert Massie, *Dreadnought: Britain, Germany, and the Coming of the Great War* (New York: Random House, 2012), 269.
5. Crowe, "Memorandum on the Present State of British Relations with France and Germany."
6. Kenneth Rose, *The Great War and Americans in Europe, 1914–1917* (New York: Routledge, 2017), 3.
7. A. J. P. Taylor, *The Struggle for Mastery in Europe 1848–1918* (Oxford: Oxford University Press, 1954), xxvii; Kennedy, *Rise and Fall of the Great Powers*, 210; Graham Allison, *Destined for War: Can America and China Escape Thucydides's Trap?* (Boston: Houghton Mifflin, 2017), 65.
8. GDD, vol. 3, 16; Taylor, *Struggle for Mastery*, 372–402; Fritz Fischer with Hajo Holborn and James Joll, *Germany's Aims in the First World War* (New York: Norton, 1967).
9. "Bernhard von Bülow on Germany's 'Place in the Sun,'" 1897, available at GHDI (German History in Documents and Images) website.

10. Imanuel Geiss, ed., *July 1914: Selected Documents: Outbreak of the First World War* (New York: Charles Scribner's Sons, 1967), 46.

11. Stephen Van Evera, "The Cult of the Offensive and the Origins of the First World War," *International Security*, Summer 1984, 66.

12. *GDD*, vol. 4, 314; Donald Kagan, *On the Origins of War and the Preservation of Peace* (New York: Knopf, 1996), 139–40.

13. Stephen Kotkin, *Stalin, Volume I: Paradoxes of Power, 1878–1928* (New York: Penguin, 2015), 139.

14. Annika Mombauer, *Helmuth von Moltke and the Origins of the First World War* (New York: Cambridge University Press, 2005), 18.

15. Max Hastings, *Catastrophe 1914: Europe Goes to War* (New York: Knopf, 2013), 7.

16. Mombauer, *Helmuth von Moltke*, 34.

17. Kennedy, *Rise and Fall of the Great Powers*, 213–14.

18. Volker Berghahn, *Imperial Germany: Economy, Society, Culture, and Politics* (New York: Berghahn, 2005), 265–66.

19. *GDD*, vol. 4, 126.

20. Taylor, *Struggle for Mastery*, esp. 427.

21. On the naval race, see Paul Kennedy, *The Rise of the Anglo-German Antagonism, 1860–1914* (London: Allen and Unwin, 1980).

22. Mombauer, *Helmuth von Moltke*; Jack Snyder, "Civil–Military Relations and the Cult of the Offensive, 1914 and 1984," *International Security*, Summer 1984.

23. Van Evera, "Cult of the Offensive," 69; David Stevenson, "War by Timetable? The Railway Race before 1914," *Past & Present*, February 1999, 179; Dale Copeland, *The Origins of Major War* (Ithaca, NY: Cornell University Press, 2001), 70.

24. Mombauer, *Helmuth von Moltke*, 172; Hew Strachan, *The First World War* (New York: Penguin, 2005), 70.

25. Sean McMeekin, *July 1914: Countdown to War* (New York: Basic Books, 2014), 20.

26. The Balkan angle is emphasized in Christopher Clark, *The Sleepwalkers: How Europe Went to War in 1914* (New York: Harper Perennial, 2014).

27. Stephen Van Evera, *Causes of War: Power and the Roots of Conflict* (Ithaca, NY: Cornell University Press, 1999), 204.

28. Henry Kissinger, *Diplomacy* (New York: Simon & Schuster, 1994), 198; Taylor, *Struggle for Mastery*, 508, 510, 527–28.

29. See *Die Deutschen Dokumente zum Kriegsausbruch 1914*, document 179, available at Brigham Young University website, accessed August 21, 2022.

30. Geoffrey Wawro, *A Mad Catastrophe: The Outbreak of World War I and the Collapse of the Habsburg Empire* (New York: Basic Books, 2014), 111; Imanuel Geiss, "The Outbreak of the First World War and German War Aims," *Journal of Contemporary History*, July 1966, 75–92; Copeland, *Origins of Major War*, 79–117.

31. Konrad H. Jarausch, "The Illusion of Limited War: Chancellor Bethmann Hollweg's Calculated Risk, July 1914," *Central European History*, March 1969, 48.

32. Geiss, ed., *July 1914*, 198–99.

33. Martin Gilbert, *The First World War* (London: Weidenfeld & Nicolson, 1994), 33–34.

34. Memorandum by Eyre Crowe, enclosure in No. 369, July 31, 1914, available at World War I Document Archive. See also Michael Howard, *The Continental Commitment: The Dilemma of British Defence Policy in the Era of the Two World Wars* (London: Ashfield, 1989).

35. Hastings, *Catastrophe 1914*, 81; Zara Steiner, *Britain and the Origins of the First World War: The Making of the 20th Century* (New York: St. Martin's Press, 1977).

36. Fischer, *Germany's Aims*, 101–6.

37. Fritz Fischer, *War of Illusions: German Policies from 1911 to 1914*, translated by Marian Jackson (New York: Norton, 1975), 547.

38. Mombauer, *Helmuth von Moltke*, 283.

39. Margaret MacMillan, *The War That Ended Peace: The Road to 1914* (New York: Random House, 2014), 596.

40. Van Evera, *Causes of War*, 204.

41. Nicholas Lambert, *Planning Armageddon: British Economic Warfare and the First World War* (Cambridge, MA: Harvard University Press, 2012), 232.

42. Michael Howard, *The First World War: A Very Short Introduction* (New York: Oxford University Press, 2007), 29–34; Daniel Yergin, *The Prize: The Epic Quest for Oil, Money and Power* (New York: Free Press, 1992), 168–69.

43. Lambert, *Planning Armageddon*; Geoffrey Bennett, *The Battle of Jutland* (Barnsley, UK: Pen & Sword Books, 2015), 157.

44. The critical developments were Serbia's defeat and Bulgaria's entry on the side of the Central Powers, which created a land corridor connecting Austria-Hungary and the Ottoman Empire.

45. *Official German Documents Relating to the World War*, translated by the Carnegie Endowment for International Peace, Division of International Law, vol. 2 (New York: Oxford University Press, 1923), 1119.

46. Lambert, *Planning Armageddon*, 325.

47. John Ellis, *Eye-Deep in Hell: Trench Warfare in World War I* (Baltimore: Johns Hopkins University Press, 1989), 93; Geoffrey Parker, ed., *The Cambridge History of Warfare* (New York: Cambridge University Press, 2020), 252–54.

48. Hastings, *Catastrophe 1914*, xvii–xviii.

49. MacMillan, *War That Ended Peace*, 596–97.

50. Kotkin, *Stalin*, 152; also Diana Preston, *A Higher Form of Killing: Six Weeks in World War I That Forever Changed the Nature of Warfare* (New York: Bloomsbury Press, 2014).

51. Niall Ferguson, *The Pity of War: Explaining World War I* (New York: Basic Books, 2000), xxiv.

52. Max Boot, *War Made New: Technology, Warfare, and the Course of History* (New York: Gotham, 2006), 198.

53. William McNeil, *Pursuit of Power: Technology, Armed Force, and Society since A.D. 1000* (Chicago: University of Chicago Press, 1984), 322; War Office of Great Britain, *Statistics of the Military Effort of the British Empire during the Great War, 1914–1920* (London: His Majesty's Stationery Office, 1922), 485.

54. David Reynolds, *The Long Shadow: The Legacies of the Great War in the Twentieth Century* (New York: Norton, 2015), xxv.

55. Howard, *First World War*, 60.

56. Secretary of the War Committee, "The General Review of the War," October 31, 1916, CAB 42/22/14, TNA.

57. Jonathan Bailey, "The First World War and the Birth of Modern Warfare," in MacGregor Knox and Williamson Murray, eds., *The Dynamics of Military Revolution, 1300–2050* (Cambridge: Cambridge University Press, 2001), 132–53.

58. Niall Ferguson, *The War of the World: Twentieth-Century Conflict and the Descent of the West* (New York: Penguin, 2006), 112.

59. Roger Long, "Introduction," in Roger Long and Ian Talbot, *India and World War I: A Centennial Assessment* (New York: Taylor & Francis, 2018), 4; Overy, *Blood and Ruins*, 14.

60. Strachan, *First World War*, 336.

61. Adam Tooze, *The Deluge: The Great War, America and the Remaking of the Global Order, 1916–1931* (New York: Penguin, 2015), 59; John Horne and Alan Kramer, *German Atrocities, 1914: A History of Denial* (New Haven: Yale University Press, 2022).

62. George Morton-Jack, *Army of Empire: The Untold Story of the Indian Army in World War I* (New York: Basic Books, 2018), 10.

63. Edward House to Woodrow Wilson, March 9, 1915, *PWW*.

64. Nicholas Mulder, *The Economic Weapon: The Rise of Sanctions as a Tool of Modern War* (New Haven: Yale University Press, 2022), 5.

65. *Official German Documents*, vol. 2, 1107.

66. Wolfgang Mommsen, *Imperial Germany, 1867–1918: Politics, Culture, and Society in an Authoritarian State* (New York: Bloomsbury, 2009), 209–12; Heinrich Winkler, *The Age of Catastrophe: A History of the West, 1914–1945* (New Haven: Yale University

Press, 2015), 10; Robert Kagan, *The Ghost at the Feast: America and the Collapse of World Order, 1900–1941* (New York: Random House, 2023).

67. John Keegan, *The First World War* (New York: Vintage, 2000), 82.

68. Paul Kennedy, "The First World War and the International Power System," *International Security*, Summer 1984, 25; Strachan, *First World War*, 312. Kennedy's statistics regarding percentage of world manufacturing were compiled using prewar production figures.

69. Meeting of Imperial War Cabinet, March 22, 1917, CAB 23/43, TNA.

70. Quoted in Ministry of Shipping, "The Shipping Crisis: June 1917," CAB 24/16/75, TNA.

71. George Cassar, *Lloyd George at War, 1916–1918* (London: Anthem Press, 2011), 253.

72. Wawro, *A Mad Catastrophe*, 371; Howard, *First World War*, 61.

73. Sean McMeekin, *The Ottoman Endgame: War, Revolution, and the Making of the Modern Middle East, 1908–1923* (New York: Penguin, 2016), 247.

74. Lloyd George, "Suggestions as to the Military Position," January 1, 1915, CAB 42/1/8, TNA.

75. David Stevenson, *1917: War, Peace, and Revolution* (New York: Oxford University Press, 2017), 384; Gilbert, *First World War*, 401.

76. Mulder, *Economic Weapon*, 62.

77. Ian Morris, *War: What Is It Good For? Conflict and the Progress of Civilization from Primates to Robots* (New York: Macmillan, 2014), 250.

78. Holger Herwig, *The First World War: Germany and Austria-Hungary, 1914–1918* (New York: Bloomsbury, 2009), 249; Michael Neiberg, "1917: Global War," in Jay Winter, ed., *The Cambridge History of World War I*, vol. 1 (New York: Cambridge University Press, 2014).

79. Herwig, *First World War*, 341; John Mosier, *The Myth of the Great War: How the Germans Won the Battles and How the Americans Saved the Allies* (New York: Harper Perennial, 2002).

80. Kennedy, *Rise and Fall of the Great Powers*, 260.

81. Mulder, *Economic Weapon*, 57.

82. Herwig, *First World War*, 254.

83. Robin Prior, "1916: Impasse," in Winter, ed., *Cambridge History*, vol. 1, 89; McNeil, *Pursuit of Power*, 323–24.

84. Roger Chickering, *Imperial Germany and the Great War, 1914–1918* (New York: Cambridge University Press, 2014), 83–86.

85. Beatrice Heuser, *The Evolution of Strategy: Thinking War from Antiquity to the Present* (New York: Cambridge University Press, 2010), 193.

86. Michael Geyer, "German Strategy in the Age of Machine Warfare, 1914–1945," in Peter Paret, ed., *Makers of Modern Strategy: From Machiavelli to the Nuclear Age* (Princeton: Princeton University Press, 1986), 548.

87. David Stevenson, *1917*, 368; Kotkin, *Stalin*, 186–89.

88. Political Intelligence Department, Foreign Office, "The Bolsheviks (II)," March–November 1917, CAB 24/47/50, TNA.

89. Elizabeth Greenhalgh, *Victory through Coalition: Britain and France during the First World War* (New York: Cambridge University Press, 2005), 102.

90. Gordon Craig, *Germany, 1866–1945* (New York: Oxford University Press, 1978), 369.

91. Ministry of Shipping, "The Shipping Crisis: June 1917," CAB 24/16/75, TNA.

92. Baer, *One Hundred Years of Sea Power*, 68.

93. Christopher Mick, "1918: Endgame," in Winter, ed., *Cambridge History of the First World War*, vol. 1, 147.

94. Greenhalgh, *Victory through Coalition*, 202, 205–7; David Stevenson, *With Our Backs to the Wall: Victory and Defeat in 1918* (Cambridge, MA: Belknap Press, 2011).

95. Halford J. Mackinder, "The Geographical Pivot of History," *Geographical Journal*, April 1904, 436.

96. Remarks by Secretary of State for War on the Chancellor of the Exchequer's Memorandum on the Conduct of the War, February 25, 1915, CAB 24/1, TNA.

97. Greenhalgh, *Victory through Coalition*, 70–71.

98. Robertson Memorandum, January 1, 1916, CAB 42/7/1, TNA.

99.   Memo Circulated by Prime Minister to Delegates at the Conference of the Allies, January 1917, G-106, CAB 24/3, TNA.
100. French view summarized in a meeting of the British War Council, January 13, 1916, CAB 42/7/5, TNA.
101. Meeting of the War Council, March 10, 1915, CAB 42/2/5, TNA; Nicholas Lambert, *The War Lords and the Gallipoli Disaster: How Globalized Trade Led Britain to Its Worst Defeat of the First World War* (New York: Oxford University Press, 2021).
102. McMeekin, *Ottoman Endgame*, 250–53; "A Canadian Soldier at Gallipoli (1915)," *Alpha History* online.
103. Halford J. Mackinder, *Democratic Ideals and Reality: A Study in the Politics of Reconstruction* [1919] (Washington, DC: National Defense University Press, 1942), 44.
104. Imperial War Cabinet, March 20, 1917, CAB 23/43, TNA; statistic from Anand Toprani, *Oil and the Great Powers: Britain and Germany, 1914 to 1945* (New York: Oxford University Press, 2019), 60–61.
105. Tooze, *Deluge*, 36–37.
106. Greenhalgh, *Victory through Coalition*, 109, 111–12.
107. Mulder, *Economic Weapon*, 28.
108. Strachan, *First World War*, 218.
109. Report of Cabinet Committee on War Policy, August 10, 1917, CAB 24/4, TNA.
110. Greenhalgh, *Victory through Coalition*, 42–43, 283.
111. *Official German Documents*, vol. 2, 1152.
112. Edward House, diary entry, April 1, 1919, EHP.
113. On this point, see Robert Kagan, "Woodrow Wilson and the Birth of Modern American Grand Strategy," in Hal Brands, ed., *The New Makers of Modern Strategy: From the Ancient World to the Digital Age* (Princeton: Princeton University Press, 2023).
114. See, for instance, Warren F. Kuehl, *Seeking World Order: The United States and International Organization to 1920* (Nashville: Vanderbilt University Press, 1969).
115. Edward House, diary entry, January 4, 1917, EHP.
116. Edward House to Woodrow Wilson, August 22, 1914, in Charles Seymour, ed., *The Intimate Papers of Colonel House*, vol. 1 (Boston: Houghton Mifflin, 1926), 284–85.
117. Lansing, "The President's Attitude toward Great Britain and Its Dangers," September 1916, Private Memorandum, Robert Lansing Papers, LC.
118. Kagan, *Ghost at the Feast*, 178.
119. Memorandum for the Prime Minister, January 27, 1916, CAB 42/8/9, TNA.
120. *Official German Documents*, vol. 2, 1061–64, 1086–1106. For a contrary argument, see Philip Zelikow, *The Road Less Traveled: The Secret Battle to End the Great War, 1916–1917* (New York: PublicAffairs, 2021).
121. Arthur Link, *Wilson: Campaigns for Progressivism and Peace, 1916–1917*, vol. 5 (Princeton: Princeton University Press, 1965), 28.
122. Justus Doenecke, *Nothing Less Than War: A New History of America's Entry into World War I* (Lexington: University Press of Kentucky, 2011), 45. Roughly $7 billion in lending came after U.S. intervention; over $2 billion came in private loans before April 1917. On private lending, see Richard van Alstyne, "Private American Loans to the Allies, 1914–1916," *Pacific Historical Review*, June 1933, 180.
123. War Committee Minutes, November 28, 1916, CAB 42/26/2, TNA.
124. Edward House to Woodrow Wilson, March 26, 1915, in Seymour, ed. *Intimate Papers*, vol. 1, 403–4.
125. Joseph Patrick Tumulty, *Woodrow Wilson as I Knew Him* (New York: Doubleday, Page, 1921), 232.
126. Doenecke, *Nothing Less Than War*; Ernest May, *The World War and American Isolation, 1914–1917* (Cambridge, MA: Harvard University Press, 1959); and Kagan, *Ghost at the Feast*, offer interpretations.
127. See Theodore Roosevelt to Kuno Meyer, January 7, 1915, Theodore Roosevelt Papers, LC.
128. Ross Kennedy, "Woodrow Wilson, World War I, and an American Conception of National Security," *Diplomatic History*, Winter 2001, 1–31, quoted at 4.

129. "An Address to His Fellow Passengers," July 4, 1919, *PWW.*
130. Wilson, "Address to a Joint Session of Congress Requesting a Declaration of War against Germany," April 2, 1917, APP.
131. *Official German Documents,* vol. 2, 1268.
132. *Official German Documents,* vol. 2, 1156.
133. May, *World War and American Isolation,* 414–15.
134. Chancellor of the Exchequer, "Our Financial Position in America," November 1916, CAB 42/22/4, TNA.
135. Seymour, ed. *Intimate Papers,* vol. 2, 471.
136. Senator William Norris in Victor L. Berger, *Hearing before the Special Committee, Appointed under the Authority of House Resolution No. 6 Concerning the Right of Victor L. Berger to Be Sworn In as a Member of the Sixty-Sixth Congress,* vol. 1 (Washington, DC: U.S. Government Printing Office, 1919), 470.
137. Wilson, "Address to a Joint Session of Congress."
138. Winston Churchill, *The World Crisis, 1911–1918* [1923] (New York: Free Press, 2005), 696.
139. Allan Millett, Peter Maslowski, and William Feis, *For the Common Defense: A Military History of the United States from 1607 to 2012* (New York: Free Press, 2012), 309; Mark Grotelueschen, *The AEF Way of War: The American Army and Combat in World War I* (New York: Cambridge University Press, 2006), 11.
140. Holger Herwig and David Trask, "The Failure of Imperial Germany's Undersea Offensive against World Shipping, February 1917–October 1918," *Historian,* August 1971, 619; Baer, *One Hundred Years of Sea Power,* 67.
141. Hindenburg's remarks, April 9, 1918, available at firstworldwar.com.
142. David Woodward, *Trial by Friendship: Anglo-American Relations, 1917–1918* (Lexington: University Press of Kentucky, 1993), 170.
143. Baer, *One Hundred Years of Sea Power,* 80.
144. Keegan, *First World War,* 407.
145. Hague to MilStaff, Washington, October 25, 1918, Woodrow Wilson Papers, WWP25324, LC; Gilbert, *First World War,* 434–48; Robert Zieger, *America's Great War: World War I and the American Experience* (Lanham, MD: Rowman & Littlefield, 2000), 98.
146. Baer, *One Hundred Years of Sea Power,* 70, 75–76.
147. Gilbert, *First World War,* 468.
148. Tooze, *Deluge,* is excellent on these issues.
149. Tasker Bliss to Newton Baker, July 22, 1918, Woodrow Wilson Papers, WWP25076, LC.
150. Howard, *First World War,* 51; Kagan, *Ghost at the Feast.*
151. Wilson, "A Flag Day Address," June 14, 1917, *PWW.*
152. Millett, Maslowski, and Feis, *For the Common Defense,* 314–15; Tooze, *Deluge,* 203.
153. George Noble, *Policies and Opinions in Paris, 1919: Wilsonian Diplomacy, the Versailles Peace, and French Public Opinion* (New York: Macmillan, 1935), 160.
154. That conventional wisdom is summarized and critiqued in Margaret MacMillan, *Paris 1919: Six Months That Changed the World* (New York: Random House, 2003).
155. MacMillan, *Paris 1919,* 480; Strachan, *First World War,* 333.
156. MacMillan, *Paris 1919,* 173; "Note sur le statut politique des pays de la rive gauche du rhin," December 15, 1918, in *Documents Diplomatiques Français: Armistices et Paix, 1918–1920* (Paris: Commission des Archives Diplomatiques, 2014), document 344.
157. MacMillan, *Paris 1919,* 480.
158. Political Intelligence Department, "Bolshevik Aims in the West and in the East," February 19, 1920, CAB 24/99/55, TNA.
159. "Effect of Secret Diplomacy on the Public Mind," April 4, 1919, Private Memorandum, Robert Lansing Papers, LC.
160. "Mantoux's Notes of Two Meetings of the Council of Four," March 27, 1919, *PWW.*
161. "Hankey's Notes of Two Meetings with the Council of Ten," January 15, 1919, *PWW;* "A Memorandum by David Lloyd George," March 25, 1919, *PWW.*

162.   Imperial War Cabinet, December 30, 1918, CAB 23/42, TNA.
163.   John Maynard Keynes, *The Economic Consequences of the Peace* (London: Macmillan, 1919), 38.
164.   John Thompson, *Woodrow Wilson: Profiles in Power* (New York: Longman, 2002), 229.
165.   Wilson, "Address to a Joint Session of Congress on the Conditions of Peace," January 8, 1918, APP.
166.   Imperial War Cabinet, December 30, 1918, CAB 23/42, TNA.
167.   Edward House, diary entry, October 28, 1918, EHP; Kagan, "Woodrow Wilson."
168.   Wilson, Address at the Metropolitan Opera House in New York City, September 27, 1918, *FRUS 1918*, vol. 1, supplement 1, document 258.
169.   Wilson, Address at Hotel Alexandria, Los Angeles, September 20, 1919, *PWW*.
170.   Noble, *Policies and Opinions in Paris*, 116; Wilson, Speech to Congress, January 22, 1917, *PWW*; Thomas Knock, *To End All Wars: Woodrow Wilson and the Quest for a New World Order* (Princeton: Princeton University Press, 1995).
171.   "Indications of an Explosion," March 28, 1919, Private Memorandum, Lansing Papers, LC.
172.   MacMillan, *Paris 1919*, 86.
173.   "Mantoux's Notes of a British–French–Italian Meeting," April 21, 1919, *PWW*; Tooze, *Deluge*.
174.   Colin Dueck, *Reluctant Crusaders: Power, Culture, and Change in American Grand Strategy* (Princeton: Princeton University Press, 2008), 51.
175.   John Milton Cooper, *Breaking the Heart of the World: Woodrow Wilson and the Fight for the League of Nations* (New York: Cambridge University Press, 2001), 375.
176.   Edward House, diary entry, January 1, 1919, EHP; Cooper, *Breaking the Heart of the World*, esp. 2.
177.   "Review of the Present Condition of the Peace Conference," January 22, 1919, Private Memorandum, Lansing Papers, LC.
178.   "Great Britain's World Responsibility," *Evening Telegraph*, June 18, 1920.
179.   Mackinder, *Democratic Ideals and Reality*, 18.
180.   Mackinder, *Democratic Ideals and Reality*, 45, 105.
181.   Mackinder, *Democratic Ideals and Reality*, 106.
182.   Mackinder, *Democratic Ideals and Reality*, esp. 17.
183.   Mackinder, *Democratic Ideals and Reality*, 49–50, 80.
184.   Mackinder, *Democratic Ideals and Reality*, 111–12.
185.   B. W. Blouet, "Sir Halford Mackinder as High Commissioner to South Russia, 1919–1920," *Geographical Journal*, July 1976, 228–36.
186.   "Report on the Situation in South Russia by Sir H. Mackinder, MP," January 1920, CAB 24/97/17, TNA; Mackinder to Curzon, November 21, 1919, FO-800-251, TNA.
187.   Halford J. Mackinder, "Notes of Points, Supplementary to His Memorandum of January 21, 1920," January 29, 1920, FO-800-251, TNA.
188.   "Report on the Situation in South Russia"; "Notes of Points."
189.   "Report on the Situation in South Russia."
190.   "Report on the Situation in South Russia"; "Notes of Points."
191.   Curzon to Keyes, February 9, 1920, *DBFP*, First Series, vol. 3, 814–15; Warsaw to Curzon, January 19, 1920, *DBFP*, First Series, vol. 3, 764; Foreign Office to Mackinder, February 20, 1919, FO-800-251, TNA.

CHAPTER 3: THE TOTALITARIAN ABYSS

1.   *DGFP*, Series D, vol. 13, 968.
2.   Gerhard Weinberg, ed., *Hitler's Second Book: The Unpublished Sequel to Mein Kampf*, translated by Krista Smith (New York: Enigma, 2006), 113; Richard Overy, *War and Economy in the Third Reich* (Oxford: Clarendon Press, 1995), 235.
3.   Saul Friedländer, *Prelude to Downfall: Hitler and the United States, 1939–1941* (New York: Knopf, 1967), 171.
4.   *DGFP*, Series D, vol. 13, 40–41.

5. "Atlantic Charter," August 14, 1941, Avalon Project, Lillian Goldman Law Library, Yale Law School.

6. Brendan Simms and Charlie Laderman, *Hitler's American Gamble: Pearl Harbor and Germany's March to Global War* (New York: Basic Books, 2021), 29; Klaus Schmider, *Hitler's Fatal Miscalculation: Why Germany Declared War on the United States* (New York: Cambridge University Press, 2021).

7. A good discussion of these leaders is Gerhard Weinberg, *Visions of Victory: The Hopes of Eight World War II Leaders* (New York: Cambridge University Press, 2005). See also Brendan Simms, *Hitler: A Global Biography* (New York: Basic Books, 2019), esp. 50.

8. *DBFP*, 98.

9. Richard Overy, *Blood and Ruins: The Last Imperial War, 1931–1945* (New York: Penguin, 2022).

10. James Crowley, "A New Asian Order," in Bernard Silberman and H. D. Harootunian, eds., *Japan in Crisis* (Princeton: Princeton University Press, 1974), 281–82; Michael Barnhart, *Japan Prepares for Total War: The Search for Economic Security, 1919–1941* (Ithaca, NY: Cornell University Press, 1988).

11. *DGFP*, Series D, vol. 1, 31.

12. James Crowley, *Japan's Quest for Autonomy: National Security and Foreign Policy, 1930–1938* (Princeton: Princeton University Press, 1966), 195.

13. Akira Iriye, *The Origins of the Second World War in Asia and the Pacific* (New York: Routledge, 1987), 61. See also S. C. M. Paine, *The Japanese Empire: Grand Strategy from the Meiji Restoration to the Pacific War* (New York: Cambridge University Press, 2017), 113; Walter LaFeber, *The Clash: U.S.-Japanese Relations throughout History* (New York: Norton, 1997), 155–62.

14. E. H. Carr, *The Twenty Years Crisis, 1919–1939: An Introduction to the Study of International Relations* [1939] (New York: Harper & Row, 1964), 230.

15. Seva Gunitsky, *Aftershocks: Great Powers and Domestic Reforms in the Twentieth Century* (Princeton: Princeton University Press, 2017), 101.

16. The Japanese model of fascism was significantly different from the German and Italian models, in part because of the role that the emperor played as divine authority.

17. John Gooch, *Mussolini and His Generals: The Armed Forces and Fascist Foreign Policy, 1922–1940* (New York: Cambridge University Press, 2007), 124; P. M. H. Bell, *The Origins of the Second World War in Europe* (New York: Longman, 1986), 53–87.

18. Adam Tooze, *The Deluge: The Great War, America and the Remaking of the Global Order, 1916–1931* (New York: Penguin, 2015), 513.

19. *DGFP*, Series D, vol. 8, 895.

20. Waller Newell, *Tyrants: Power, Injustice, and Terror* (Cambridge: Cambridge University Press, 2019); Giuseppe Finaldi, *Mussolini and Italian Fascism* (New York: Taylor & Francis, 2014).

21. Kenneth Scott, "Mussolini and the Roman Empire," *Classical Journal* 27 (1932): 652–53.

22. Kershaw, *The Nazi Dictatorship: Problems and Perspectives of Interpretation* (New York: Oxford University Press, 2000), 124; Weinberg, *Visions of Victory*.

23. *DGFP*, Series D, vol. 12, 760.

24. Henry Morgenthau to Franklin D. Roosevelt, October 17, 1938, Morgenthau Presidential Diaries, FDRL.

25. Felix Chuev, *Molotov Remembers: Inside Kremlin Politics: Conversations with Felix Chuev* (Chicago: Ivan R. Dee, 1993), 18.

26. Stephen Kotkin, *Stalin: Waiting for Hitler, 1929–1941* (New York: Penguin, 2017), 673, 769.

27. *DGFP*, Series D, vol. 11, esp. 554–59.

28. Kotkin, *Stalin: Waiting for Hitler*, 816–17.

29. Hal Brands and Charles Edel, *The Lessons of Tragedy: Statecraft and World Order* (New Haven: Yale University Press, 2019), 59; Donald Kagan, *On the Origins of War and the Preservation of Peace* (New York: Knopf, 1996).

30. Gabriel Gorodetsky, ed., *The Maisky Diaries: Red Ambassador to the Court of St. Jamess, 1932–1943* (New Haven: Yale University Press, 2015), 42.

31. Roosevelt, "Address at Chicago," October 5, 1937, APP.

32. *DBFP,* Third Series, vol. 1, 217.

33. Niall Ferguson, *The War of the World: Twentieth-Century Conflict and the Descent of the West* (New York: Penguin, 2006), 345.

34. The crisis has entered history as "the Munich crisis" because that is where the climactic meetings were held.

35. Williamson Murray, *The Change in the European Balance of Power, 1938–1939: The Path to Ruin* (Princeton: Princeton University Press, 1984); also Ferguson, *War of the World,* 363–66; Nicholas Mulder, *The Economic Weapon: The Rise of Sanctions as a Tool of Modern War* (New Haven: Yale University Press, 2022), 246–49.

36. *DBFP,* Third Series, vol. 1, 226.

37. *DGFP,* Series D, vol. 6, 379.

38. *DBFP,* Third Series, vol. 1, 221; Memorandum by the Secretary of State for Foreign Affairs, October 8, 1938, CAB 24/279/14, TNA.

39. Press Conference, June 5, 1940, Press Conferences of President Franklin D. Roosevelt, 1933–1945, Box 1, FDRL; Mackenzie King to Anthony Eden, July 6, 1937, FO 0954-4A-241, TNA.

40. See Michael Howard, *The Continental Commitment: The Dilemma of British Defence Policy in the Era of the Two World Wars* (London: Ashfield, 1989), esp. 118.

41. *DGFP,* Series D, vol. 10, 207.

42. Kotkin, *Stalin: Waiting for Hitler;* Roger Moorhouse, *The Devil's Alliance: Hitler's Pact with Stalin, 1939–1941* (New York: Basic Books, 2014).

43. Franklin Roosevelt, Excerpts from Press Conference, August 8, 1939, APP.

44. Kennedy, *Rise and Fall of the Great Powers,* 332.

45. C. A. MacDonald, *The United States, Britain, and Appeasement, 1938–1939* (London: Macmillan, 1981), 48; Anglo-French Conversations at Quai d'Orsay, November 24, 1938, *DBFP,* Third Series, vol. 3, 308.

46. *DGFP,* Series D, vol 1, 641.

47. John Clancy, *The Most Dangerous Moment of the War: Japan's Attack on the Indian Ocean, 1942* (Oxford: Casemate, 2015); Ronald Spector, *Eagle against the Sun: The American War with Japan* (New York: Free Press, 1985), chs. 2–7.

48. Williamson Murray, "May 1940: Contingency and Fragility of the German RMA," in MacGregor Knox and Williamson Murray, eds., *Dynamics of Military Revolution, 1300–2050* (New York: Cambridge University Press, 2001), esp. 155; Michael Geyer, "German Strategy in the Age of Machine Warfare, 1914–1945," in Peter Paret, ed., *Makers of Modern Strategy: From Machiavelli to the Nuclear Age* (Princeton: Princeton University Press, 1986).

49. See Ernest May, *Strange Victory: Hitler's Conquest of France* (New York: Hill & Wang, 2000).

50. Williamson Murray, "A Whale against an Elephant: Britain and Germany," in James Lacey, ed., *Great Strategic Rivalries: From the Classical World to the Cold War* (New York: Oxford University Press, 2016), 397; Gerhard Weinberg, *Hitler's Foreign Policy, 1933–1939: The Road to World War II* (New York: Enigma, 2005), 374–77.

51. Ferguson, *War of the World,* 367.

52. Gordon Wright, *The Ordeal of Total War, 1939–1945* (New York: Harper & Row, 1968), 117.

53. Speech by Prime Minister General Tojo Hideki to Assembly of Greater Asiatic Nations, November 5, 1943, available online at World Future Fund.

54. John Dower, *War without Mercy: Race and Power in the Pacific War* (New York: Pantheon, 1986), esp. 42–43.

55. Timothy Snyder, *Bloodlands: Europe between Hitler and Stalin* (New York: Basic Books, 2012), 163.

56. Volker Ullrich, *Hitler: Downfall, 1939–1945* (New York: Vintage, 2021), 267.

57. Winston Churchill, radio broadcast, August 24, 1941, in Martin Gilbert, ed., *The Churchill War Papers*, vol. 3, *The Ever-Widening War, 1941* (New York: Norton, 1993), 1103.

58. Tami Biddle, *Rhetoric and Reality in Air Warfare: The Evolution of British and American Ideas about Strategic Bombing, 1914–1945* (Princeton: Princeton University Press, 2002).

59. Hugh Trevor-Roper, *Hitler's Table Talk, 1941–1944* (London: Weidenfeld & Nicolson, 1953), 93.

60. Winston Churchill, "A Note on the War," December 25, 1939, in Gilbert, ed., *Churchill War Papers*, vol. 1, *At the Admiralty* (New York: Norton, 1993), 569.

61. Ian Kershaw, *Fateful Choices: Ten Decisions That Changed the World, 1940–1941* (London: Allen Lane, 2007).

62. Memorandum, "Economic Aid from the New World to the Old," June 16, 1940, CAB 66/8, TNA.

63. On Churchill's leadership, see Andrew Roberts, *Churchill: Walking with Destiny* (New York: Penguin, 2018).

64. Gorodetsky, *Maisky Diaries*, 352.

65. Gilbert, *Churchill War Papers*, vol. 2, *Never Surrender* (New York: Norton, 1993), 182.

66. Winston Churchill, Remarks in House of Commons, June 4, 1940, available at winston churchill.org.

67. Winston Churchill, Remarks in House of Commons, June 18, 1940, available at winston churchill.org.

68. Max Boot, *War Made New: Technology, Warfare, and the Course of History* (New York: Gotham, 2006), 273; Richard Overy, *The Battle of Britain: The Myth and the Reality* (New York: Norton, 2000), 81–88.

69. Winston Churchill to Franklin Roosevelt, December 7, 1940, in Warren Kimball, ed., *Churchill and Roosevelt: The Complete Correspondence*, vol. 1 (Princeton: Princeton University Press, 1984), 103–5.

70. "War Cabinet Plans to Meet a Certain Eventuality," Report by Chiefs of Staff Committee, June 11, 1940, CAB 66/8, TNA.

71. Winston Churchill to Joseph Stalin, June 25, 1940, in Gilbert, *Churchill War Papers*, vol. 2, 417.

72. Trevor-Roper, *Hitler's Table Talk*, 24.

73. *DGFP*, Series D, vol. 12, 1066.

74. John Lukacs, *The Last European War: September 1939–December 1941* (New Haven: Yale University Press, 2001), 139; Sean McMeekin, *Stalin's War: A New History of World War II* (New York: Hachette, 2021), 326–82.

75. Richard Overy, *The Dictators: Hitler's Germany, Stalin's Russia* (New York: Norton, 2006), 483.

76. Gorodetsky, ed., *Maisky Diaries*, 354.

77. Memorandum on Discussions with Stalin, July 31, 1941, *FRUS* 1941, vol. 1, document 752.

78. Simms and Laderman, *Hitler's American Gamble*, 36.

79. Simms, *Hitler*, 214.

80. Franklin Roosevelt, Fireside Chat on National Security, December 29, 1940, APP.

81. Franklin Roosevelt, Press Conference on National Defense, May 30, 1940, Roosevelt Press Conferences, FDRL.

82. Franklin Roosevelt, Fireside Chat, September 11, 1941, APP.

83. Franklin Roosevelt, Press Conference, June 14, 1940, Roosevelt Press Conferences, FDRL.

84. Franklin Roosevelt, Address at University of Virginia, June 10, 1940, APP.

85. Franklin Roosevelt, Fireside Chat on National Security, December 29, 1940, APP.

86. Charles Lindbergh, "Election Promises Should Be Kept: We Lack Leadership That Places America First," Address at Madison Square Garden, May 23, 1941.

87. Charles Kupchan, *Isolationism: A History of America's Efforts to Shield Itself from the World* (New York: Oxford University Press, 2020), 293; Mark Stoler, *Allies and Ad-*

versaries: *The Joint Chiefs of Staff, the Grand Alliance, and U.S. Strategy in World War II* (Chapel Hill: University of North Carolina Press, 2000), 13–14, 25.

88. Julian Zelizer, *Arsenal of Democracy: The Politics of National Security—from World War II to the War on Terrorism* (New York: Basic Books, 2010), 47.

89. Zelizer, *Arsenal of Democracy*, 43.

90. Warren Kimball, *The Most Unsordid Act: Lend-Lease, 1939–1941* (Baltimore: Johns Hopkins University Press, 1969); Robert Dallek, *Franklin D. Roosevelt and American Foreign Policy, 1932–1945* (New York: Oxford University Press, 1979).

91. Waldo Heinrichs, *Threshold of War: Franklin D. Roosevelt and American Entry into World War II* (New York: Oxford University Press, 1988), esp. 10.

92. William Leahy, diary entry, September 12, 1941, Reel 2, Leahy Papers, LC.

93. *DGFP*, Series D, vol. 10, 199.

94. Simms and Laderman, *Hitler's American Gamble*, 29; Schmider, *Hitler's Fatal Miscalculation*.

95. *DGFP*, Series D, vol. 13, 377; *DGFP*, Series D, vol. 12, 219–21.

96. Joseph Grew, *Turbulent Era: A Diplomatic Record of Forty Years*, vol. 2 (Boston: Houghton Mifflin, 1952), 1257; Michael Green, *By More Than Providence: Grand Strategy and American Power in the Asia Pacific since 1783* (New York: Columbia University Press, 2017), 182.

97. Paine, *The Japanese Empire*, 153.

98. Dallek, *Franklin D. Roosevelt*, 273–74.

99. Ernst Presseisen, *Germany and Japan: A Study in Totalitarian Diplomacy, 1933–1941* (The Hague: Martinus Nijhoff, 1959), esp. 242–43.

100. Grew to Roosevelt, December 14, 1940, *FRUS 1940*, vol. 4, document 493.

101. Heinrichs, *Threshold of War*, 7.

102. Eri Hotta, *Japan 1941: Countdown to Infamy* (New York: Vintage, 2014), 148.

103. Jeffrey Record, *Japan's Decision for War in 1941* (Carlisle Barracks, PA: Strategic Studies Institute, 2009), 25.

104. Heinrichs, *Threshold of War*, 183. See also Asada, *From Mahan to Pearl Harbor*, 241.

105. Dallek, *Franklin D. Roosevelt*, 242.

106. Roosevelt to Grew, January 21, 1941, *FRUS 1941*, vol. 4, document 5.

107. *Investigation of the Pearl Harbor Attack: Report of the Joint Committee on the Investigation of the Pearl Harbor Attack, Congress of the United States, 79th Congress, 2nd Session,* document No. 244 (Washington, DC: U.S. Government Printing Office, 1946), 177.

108. *GDFP*, Series D, vol. 13, 994.

109. Winston Churchill, *The Second World War*, vol. 3, *The Grand Alliance* (Boston: Houghton Mifflin, 1950), 539–40.

110. Richard Overy, *Why the Allies Won* (New York: Norton, 1997), 2; Adam Tooze, *The Wages of Destruction: The Making and Breaking of the Nazi Economy* (New York: Penguin, 2008), xxiii.

111. "Bohlen Minutes." November 28, 1943, *FRUS: The Conferences at Cairo and Tehran, 1943*, document 360.

112. Tooze, *Wages of Destruction*, 383.

113. Overy, *Why the Allies Won*, 4.

114. Henry Morgenthau, diary entry, November 26, 1941, Morgenthau Presidential Diaries, FDRL.

115. Gershom Gorenberg, *War of Shadows: Codebreakers, Spies, and the Secret Struggle to Drive the Nazis from the Middle East* (New York: Hachette, 2021), 296.

116. Daniel Yergin, *The Prize: The Epic Quest for Oil, Money and Power* (New York: Free Press, 1992), 376; George Baer, *One Hundred Years of Sea Power: The U.S. Navy, 1890–1990* (Stanford: Stanford University Press, 1996), esp. 194–96.

117. Francis Lowenheim, Harold Langley, and Manfred Jonas, *Roosevelt and Churchill: The Secret Wartime Correspondence* (New York: Saturday Review Press, 1975), 262; Jonathan Dimbleby, *The Battle of the Atlantic: How the Allies Won the War* (New York: Oxford University Press, 2016), esp. 336–40; Paul Kennedy, *Victory at Sea: Naval Power*

and the Transformation of the Global Order in World War II (New Haven: Yale University Press, 2021), 204–5.

118. King to Joint Chiefs of Staff, May 1942, Box 4, Safe File, FDRL.
119. *Fading Victory: The Diary of Admiral Matome Ugaki, 1941–1945*, translated by Masa-takaya Chihaya (Pittsburgh: University of Pittsburgh Press, 1991), 52.
120. Curtin to Casey, February 22, 1942, Australian Government, Department of Foreign Affairs and Trade, *Historical Documents, July 1941–June 1942*, vol. 5, document 358; S. C. M. Paine, *The Wars for Asia, 1911–1949* (New York: Cambridge University Press, 2012), 188–89.
121. Franklin Roosevelt, Fireside Chat, February 23, 1942, APP.
122. "Bohlen Minutes," November 19, 1943, *FRUS: Cairo and Tehran*, document 365.
123. Address to Joint Session of U.S. Congress, December 26, 1941, National Churchill Museum.
124. For Franco's position, see Andrew Buchanan, *American Grand Strategy in the Mediter-ranean during World War II* (New York: Cambridge University Press, 2014), 57–59.
125. Paul Kennedy, *Strategy and Diplomacy, 1870–1945: Eight Studies* (London: Allen & Un-win, 1983), 187.
126. Churchill to Roosevelt, April 16, 1942, FO-954-6C-568, TNA.
127. Roosevelt to Marshall, King, and Hopkins, July 15, 1942, Box 4, Safe File, FDRL. See also Gerhard Weinberg, *A World at Arms: A Global History of World War II* (New York: Cambridge University Press, 1994), 307–8.
128. Combined Chiefs of Staff Minutes, January 14, 1943, *FRUS: The Conferences at Washington, 1941–1942, and Casablanca, 1943*, document 337; Jonathan Parshall and Anthony Tully, *Shattered Sword: The Untold Story of the Battle of Midway* (Annapolis: U.S. Naval Institute Press, 2007).
129. British Chiefs of Staff, "American-British Strategy in 1943," January 3, 1943, *FRUS: Washington and Casablanca*, document 401.
130. Statistics from Robert Kagan, "Challenging the U.S. Is a Historic Mistake," *Wall Street Journal*, February 3, 2023; Christian Hartmann, *Operation Barbarossa: Nazi Germany's War in the East, 1941–1945* (New York: Oxford University Press, 2013), 42; James Shee-han, *Where Have All the Soldiers Gone? The Transformation of Modern Europe* (New York: Mariner, 2008), 128; Williamson Murray and Allan Millett, *A War to Be Won: Fighting the Second World War* (Cambridge, MA: Belknap Press, 2000), 543.
131. Sheehan, *Where Have All the Soldiers Gone?*, 128.
132. Phillips Payson O'Brien, *How the War Was Won: Air–Sea Power and Allied Victory in World War II* (New York: Cambridge University Press, 2015), 5.
133. "D-Day by the Numbers: Pulling Off the Biggest Amphibious Invasion in History," Miltary.com, June 5, 2019; Antony Beevor, *D-Day: The Battle for Normandy* (New York: Penguin, 2009).
134. "Stalin and Harriman Discuss the Military Situation," June 10, 1944, CWIHP.
135. William Hitchcock, *Bitter Road to Freedom: A New History of the Liberation of Europe* (New York: Simon & Schuster, 2008), 136.
136. Brendan Simms, "Strategies of Geopolitical Revolution: Hitler and Stalin," in Brands, ed., *The New Makers of Modern Strategy: From the Ancient World to the Digital Age* (Princeton: Princeton University Press, 2023), 629.
137. Arthur Herman, *Freedom's Forge: How American Business Produced Victory in World War II* (New York: Random House, 2013).
138. Allan Millett, Peter Maslowski, and William Feis, *For the Common Defense: A Military History of the United States from 1607 to 2012* (New York: Free Press, 2012), 387; Overy, *Blood and Ruins*, 530; Mark Harrison, "The Economics of World War II: An Overview," in Mark Harrison, ed., *The Economics of World War II: Six Great Powers in International Comparison* (Cambridge: Cambridge University Press 1998), 10.
139. David Kennedy, *Freedom from Fear: The American People in Depression and War, 1929–1945* (New York: Oxford University Press, 1999), 615.
140. Kennedy, *Freedom from Fear*, 731.

141. For good surveys, see Geoffrey Jukes, *The Second World War: The Eastern Front, 1941–1945* (London: Osprey, 2002); Chris Bellamy, *Absolute War: Soviet Russia in the Second World War* (New York: Knopf, 2007).

142. McMeekin, *Stalin's War*, 382–424.

143. Henry Morgenthau, diary entry, March 11, 1942, Morgenthau Presidential Diaries, FDRL.

144. Combined Chiefs of Staff Minutes, May 14, 1943, *FRUS: Conferences at Washington and Quebec, 1943*, document 35; Rana Mitter, *Forgotten Ally: China's World War II, 1937–1945* (Boston: Houghton Mifflin Harcourt, 2013), 5.

145. O'Brien, *How the War Was Won*.

146. Russell Weigley, *The American Way of War: A History of United States Military Strategy and Policy* (Bloomington: Indiana University Press, 1973), 280.

147. See Ian Toll, *The Conquering Tide: War in the Pacific Islands, 1942–1944* (New York: Norton, 2015).

148. Overy, *Why the Allies Won*, 18.

149. Kennedy, *Victory at Sea*; Millett, Maslowski, and Feis, *For the Common Defense*, 391–95.

150. On this subject, see Max Hastings, *Bomber Command* (New York: Dial, 1979).

151. O'Brien, *How the War Was Won*, 484.

152. Weigley, *American Way of War*, 240.

153. O'Brien, *How the War Was Won*, 317, 350–51; Overy, *Blood and Ruins*, 584–86; Conrad Crane, *American Airpower Strategy in World War II: Bombs, Cities, Civilians, and Oil* (Lawrence: University Press of Kansas, 2016), 48.

154. O'Brien, *How the War Was Won*, 373.

155. "Bohlen Minutes," November 30, 1943, *FRUS: Cairo and Tehran*, document 373.

156. Churchill to Eden, February 8, 1945, FO-954-10B-415, TNA.

157. Dallek, *Franklin D. Roosevelt*, 434.

158. Warren Kimball, *Forged in War: Roosevelt, Churchill, and the Second World War* (New York: Morrow, 1997), 11.

159. Michael Fullilove, *Rendezvous with Destiny: How Franklin D. Roosevelt and Five Extraordinary Men Took America into the War and into the World* (New York: Penguin, 2013), 100–101.

160. Winston Churchill, Press Conference, January 24, 1943, *FRUS: Washington and Casablanca*, document 395; Memorandum by the United States Chiefs of Staff, January 14, 1942, *FRUS: Washington and Casablanca*, document 121.

161. Kimball, ed., *Churchill and Roosevelt: The Complete Correspondence*; also Maurice Matloff and Edwin Snell, *Strategic Planning for Coalition Warfare, 1941–1942* (Washington, DC: U.S. Government Printing Office, 1959).

162. Roosevelt to Marshall, King, and Hopkins, July 15, 1942, Box 4, Safe File, FDRL.

163. Rick Atkinson, *The Guns at Last Light: The War in Western Europe, 1944–1945* (New York: Holt, 2013), 632.

164. Tami Davis Biddle, "Democratic Leaders and Strategies of Coalition Warfare: Churchill and Roosevelt in World War II," in Brands, ed., *New Makers*; Richard Leighton and Robert Coakley, *Global Logistics and Strategy, 1940–1943* (Washington, DC: U.S. Government Printing Office, 1955); Alan Bath, *Tracking the Axis Enemy: The Triumph of Anglo-American Naval Intelligence* (Lawrence: University Press of Kansas, 1998).

165. Paul Kennedy, "History from the Middle: The Case of the Second World War," *Journal of Military History*, January 2010, 35–51.

166. Weigley, *American Way of War*, 343.

167. See Milovan Djilas's Conversations at Stalin's Dacha, June 5, 1944, CWIHP.

168. Henry Morgenthau, diary entry, November 17, 1942, Morgenthau Presidential Diaries, FDRL; David Reynolds and Vladimir Pechatnov, *The Kremlin Letters: Stalin's Wartime Correspondence with Churchill and Roosevelt* (New Haven: Yale University Press, 2018), 13.

169. Biddle, "Democratic Leaders," 588.

170. Stalin to Roosevelt, June 11, 1943, Box 8, Map Room Papers, FDRL; Warren Kimball, *The Juggler: Franklin Roosevelt as Wartime Statesman* (Princeton: Princeton University Press, 1991), 30–33.

171. Maurice Matloff, *Strategic Planning for Coalition Warfare, 1943–1944* (Washington, DC: Center of Military History, United States Army, 1994).

172. "Bohlen Minutes," November 30, 1943, *FRUS: Cairo and Tehran*, document 373; Crane, *American Airpower*, 48.

173. Serhii Plokhy, *Yalta: The Price of Peace* (New York: Penguin, 2010); Vladislav Zubok, *Failed Empire: The Soviet Union in the Cold War from Stalin to Gorbachev* (Chapel Hill: University of North Carolina Press, 2007), 13.

174. *DGFP*, Series D, vol. 13, 869.

175. T. N. Dupuy, *A Genius for War: The German Army and General Staff, 1807–1945* (Englewood Cliffs, NJ: Prentice-Hall, 1977).

176. Overy, *War and Economy in the Third Reich*, 242; David Stahel, "The Wehrmacht and National Socialist Military Thinking," *War in History*, July 2017, esp. 355.

177. Keith Grint, "The Hedgehog and the Fox: Leadership Lessons from D-Day," *Leadership*, April 2014, 255.

178. Overy, *Why the Allies Won*, 305.

179. Jonathan Adelman, *Hitler and His Allies in World War II* (London: Routledge, 2007), 20.

180. Bernice Carroll, *Design for Total War* (The Hague: Mouton, 1968), see especially quote on 73; Wright, *Ordeal of Total War*, 61–62.

181. Overy, *Why the Allies Won*, 319; Toll, *Conquering Tide*, 515.

182. *DGFP*, Series D, vol. 12, 456.

183. Jonathan Fenby, *Alliance: The Inside Story of How Roosevelt, Stalin and Churchill Won One War and Began Another* (London: Pocket, 2008), 80; Weinberg, *A World at Arms*, 747–49.

184. *The Ciano Diaries, 1939–1943: The Complete, Unabridged Diaries of Count Galeazzo Ciano, Italian Minister of Foreign Affairs, 1936–1943*, edited by Hugh Gibson (Garden City, NY: Doubleday, 1946), 300. See also John Miglietta, *Hitler's Allies: The Ramifications of Nazi Alliance Politics in World War II* (New York: Routledge, 2022).

185. R. L. DiNardo, "The Dysfunctional Coalition: The Axis Powers and the Eastern Front in World War II," *Journal of Military History*, October 1996, 723.

186. Alton Frye, *Nazi Germany and the American Hemisphere* (New Haven: Yale University Press, 1967), 173.

187. Kai Bird and Martin Sherwin, *American Prometheus: The Triumph and Tragedy of J. Robert Oppenheimer* (New York: Knopf, 2007), 309.

188. Barton Bernstein, "Truman at Potsdam: His Secret Diary," *Foreign Service Journal*, July–August 1980, 34.

189. See Richard Rhodes, *The Making of the Atomic Bomb* (New York: Simon & Schuster, 1986).

190. Richard Frank, *Downfall: The End of the Imperial Japanese Empire* (New York: Penguin, 2001).

191. Crane, *American Airpower*, 65.

192. Franklin Roosevelt, Address to American Youth Congress, February 10, 1940, APP.

193. Marc Trachtenberg, *A Constructed Peace: The Making of the European Settlement, 1945–1963* (Princeton: Princeton University Press, 1999), 36.

194. Grew, *Turbulent Era*, vol. 2, 1446.

195. Henry Morgenthau, diary entry, August 19, 1944, Morgenthau Presidential Diaries, FDRL.

196. Roosevelt to Churchill, February 29, 1944, *FRUS 1944*, vol. 1, document 99; Churchill to Eden, May 11, 1945, CHAR 20/218/83, Winston Churchill Archive.

197. Halford J. Mackinder, "The Round World and the Winning of the Peace," *Foreign Affairs*, July 1943, 601.

198. Armstrong to Mackinder, December 21, 1942, Correspondence, "Halford Mackinder," Hamilton Fish Armstrong Papers, SMML.

199. Mackinder cable, May 27, 1943, Correspondence, "Halford Mackinder," Armstrong Papers, SMML.

200. Mackinder, "Round World," 601, 604–5.

201. Armstrong to Mackinder, October 8, 1943, Correspondence, "Halford Mackinder," Armstrong Papers, SMML.
202. Mackinder, "Round World," 604.

CHAPTER 4: THE GOLDEN AGE

1. W. Warren Wagar, *H. G. Wells: Traversing Time* (Middletown, CT: Wesleyan University Press, 2004), 272.
2. Uriel Tal, "Jewish and Universal Social Ethics in the Life and Thought of Albert Einstein," in Gerald Holton and Yehuda Elkana, eds., *Albert Einstein: Historical and Cultural Perspectives* (Princeton: Princeton University Press, 1982), 299.
3. Meeting of State–Defense Policy Review Group, February 27, 1950, FRUS 1950, vol. 1, document 64.
4. George Marshall, "Assistance to European Economic Recovery," *Department of State Bulletin*, January 18, 1948, 77, 71.
5. On the notion of the post–World War II era as a golden age, see also Eric Hobsbawm, *The Age of Extremes: A History of the World, 1914–1991* (New York: Vintage, 1996).
6. Harry S. Truman, Special Message to Congress, March 12, 1947, APP.
7. OSS, "Problems and Objectives of United States Policy," April 12, 1945, Declassified Documents Reference System; William Curti Wohlforth, *The Elusive Balance: Power and Perceptions during the Cold War* (Ithaca, NY: Cornell University Press, 1993), 121–22.
8. Vladislav Zubok, *A Failed Empire: The Soviet Union in the Cold War from Stalin to Gorbachev* (Chapel Hill: University of North Carolina Press, 2007), 19; John Lewis Gaddis, *We Now Know: Rethinking Cold War History* (New York: Oxford University Press, 1997), chs. 1–2.
9. Zubok, *Failed Empire*, 20.
10. Felix Chuev, *Molotov Remembers: Inside Kremlin Politics: Conversations with Felix Chuev* (Chicago: Ivan R. Dee, 1993), 63.
11. Smith to Secretary of State, FRUS 1946, vol. 6, document 517; Anne Applebaum, *Iron Curtain: The Crushing of Eastern Europe, 1944–1956* (New York: Knopf, 2012).
12. CIA, "The Possibility of Direct Soviet Military Action during 1949," May 3, 1949, CIA FOIA.
13. Norman Naimark, *Stalin and the Fate of Europe: The Postwar Struggle for Sovereignty* (Cambridge, MA: Harvard University Press, 2019).
14. Ambassador in France (Caffery) to Secretary of State, July 3, 1947, FRUS 1947, vol. 3, document 182.
15. British Embassy to State Department, March 11, 1948, FRUS 1948, vol. 3, document 37.
16. John Lewis Gaddis, *George F. Kennan: An American Life* (New York: Penguin, 2011).
17. David Mayers, "Soviet War Aims and the Grand Alliance: George Kennan's Views, 1944–1946," *Journal of Contemporary History*, January 1986, 68.
18. Kennan to Secretary, March 20, 1946, FRUS 1946, vol. 6, document 487.
19. Kennan to Secretary, February 22, 1946, FRUS 1946, vol. 6, document 475.
20. John Lewis Gaddis, *Strategies of Containment: A Critical Appraisal of American National Security Policy during the Cold War* (New York: Oxford, 2005), 386–87.
21. G. John Ikenberry, *After Victory: Institutions, Strategic Restraint, and the Rebuilding of Order after Major Wars* (Princeton: Princeton University Press, 2001), 167–68.
22. X (Kennan), "The Sources of Soviet Conduct," *Foreign Affairs*, July 1947, 576.
23. X, "Sources of Soviet Conduct," 582.
24. Wohlforth, *Elusive Balance*, 85; Telegram from Nikolai Novikov, September 27, 1946, CWIHP.
25. Kennan to Secretary, February 22, 1946, FRUS 1946, vol. 6, document 487.
26. Dean Acheson, *Present at the Creation: My Years in the State Department* (New York: Norton, 1969), 3–4.
27. Robert Beisner, *Dean Acheson: A Life in the Cold War* (New York: Oxford University Press, 2006); Wilson Miscamble, "Rejected Architect and Master Builder: George Kennan, Dean Acheson, and Postwar Europe," *Review of Politics*, Summer 1996.

28. Acheson, *Present at the Creation*, 219.

29. Gaddis, *George F. Kennan*, 254–55; Joseph Jones, *The Fifteen Weeks, February 21–June 5, 1947* (New York: Harcourt, Brace & World, 1964).

30. Harry S. Truman, Special Message to Congress, March 12, 1947, APP.

31. MemCon with Generalissimo Stalin, April 15, 1947, in Larry Bland et al., eds., *The Papers of George Catlett Marshall*, vol. 6 (Baltimore: Johns Hopkins University Press, 2013), 103.

32. Editorial Note, *FRUS 1947*, vol. 3, document 133.

33. William Hitchcock, *The Struggle for Europe: The Turbulent History of a Divided Continent, 1945 to the Present* (New York: Knopf, 2008), 63; Benn Steil, *The Marshall Plan: Dawn of the Cold War* (New York: Simon & Schuster, 2018).

34. Dean Acheson, "The Requirements of Reconstruction," *Department of State Bulletin*, May 18, 1947.

35. Takemae Eiji, *Inside GHQ: The Allied Occupation of Japan*, translated by Robert Rickets and Sebastian Swann (New York: Continuum, 2003), 7.

36. "Acheson Sets Path," *New York Times*, September 20, 1945; Tony Smith, *America's Mission: The United States and the Worldwide Struggle for Democracy* (Princeton: Princeton University Press, 2012), 155–67.

37. "Meeting of the Secretary of Defense and the Service Chiefs with the Secretary of State 1045 Hours," October 10, 1948, Box 147, James Forrestal Papers, SMML; Tony Judt, *Postwar: A History of Europe since 1945* (New York: Penguin, 2006), 145–49.

38. James Reston, "Atlantic Nations Sign Defense Pact," *New York Times*, April 5, 1949. Acheson had been out of government during the negotiations in 1948, but returned as secretary in time to preside over the signing.

39. John Lewis Gaddis, *The Long Peace: Inquiries into the History of the Cold War* (New York: Oxford University Press, 1986), 63. See also Timothy Sayle, *Enduring Alliance: A History of NATO and the Postwar Global Order* (Ithaca, NY: Cornell University Press, 2019).

40. See Paraphrase of Telegram from Bevin, April 9, 1948, *FRUS 1948*, vol. 3, document 67; Second Meeting of Washington Exploratory Talks, July 6, 1948, *FRUS 1948*, vol. 3, document 113.

41. Gaddis, *Strategies of Containment*, 393.

42. Beisner, *Dean Acheson*, 161–62; CIA 3–49, "Review of the World Situation," March 16, 1949, Box 178, NSC Files, Harry S. Truman Presidential Library.

43. William Stueck, *The Korean War: An International History* (Princeton: Princeton University Press, 1995); Kathryn Weathersby, "'Should We Fear This?' Stalin and the Danger of War with America," Cold War International History Project Working Paper 39, 2002.

44. Harry S. Truman, *Years of Trial and Hope* (Garden City, NY: Doubleday, 1956), 332–33.

45. Stueck, *Korean War*; Chen Jian, *China's Road to the Korean War: The Making of the Sino-American Confrontation* (New York: Columbia University Press, 1995).

46. Julian Zelizer, *Arsenal of Democracy: The Politics of National Security—from World War II to the War on Terrorism* (New York: Basic Books, 2010), 102.

47. See Melvyn Leffler, *A Preponderance of Power: National Security, the Truman Administration, and the Cold War* (Stanford: Stanford University Press, 1992); Hal Brands, *What Good Is Grand Strategy? Power and Purpose in American Statecraft from Harry S. Truman to George W. Bush* (Ithaca, NY: Cornell University Press, 2014), 47–53.

48. NSC-68, "United States Objectives and Programs for National Security," April 12, 1950, President's Secretary's Files (PSF), Harry S. Truman Presidential Library; "Estimated U.S. and Soviet/Russian Nuclear Stockpiles, 1945–94," *Bulletin of the Atomic Scientists*, December 1994, 59; Allan Millett, Peter Maslowski, and William Feis, *For the Common Defense: A Military History of the United States from 1607 to 2012* (New York: Free Press, 2012), 467–91.

49. Acheson, *Present at the Creation*, 378.

50. Annual Report of Supreme Allied Commander Europe, April 2, 1952, Box 278, Averell Harriman Papers, LC.

51. Acheson, *Present at the Creation*, xvii.

52. Beisner, *Dean Acheson*, 156; Acheson, "Soviet Reaction to Free World's Growing Strength," *Department of State Bulletin*, October 20, 1952, 597.

53. Discussion at the 229th Meeting of NSC, December 21, 1954, *FRUS 1952–1954*, vol. 2, part 1, document 143. See also Mira Rapp-Hooper, *Shields of the Republic: The Triumph and Peril of America's Alliances* (Cambridge, MA: Harvard University Press, 2020).

54. Richard Pells, *Not Like Us: How Europeans Have Loved, Hated, and Transformed American Culture since World War II* (New York: Basic Books, 2008), 69.

55. Heritage Foundation, "Global U.S. Troop Deployments, 1950–2003," October 24, 2004, and accompanying dataset; G. John Ikenberry, *Liberal Leviathan: The Origins, Crisis, and Transformation of the American World Order* (Princeton: Princeton University Press, 2011), 199.

56. Ikenberry, *Liberal Leviathan*; Douglas Irwin, *Clashing over Commerce: A History of U.S. Trade Policy* (Chicago: University of Chicago Press, 2017), 484–86.

57. Dean Acheson, "The Pattern of Leadership—A Pattern of Responsibility," *Department of State Bulletin*, September 22, 1952, 427.

58. Eisenhower to Churchill, March 29, 1955, Box 6, Eisenhower Diary, Ann Whitman File, Dwight David Eisenhower Presidential Library.

59. Zubok, *Failed Empire*, 102; Vladislav Zubok and Hope Harrison, "The Nuclear Education of Nikita Khrushchev," in John Lewis Gaddis, ed., *Cold War Statesmen Confront the Bomb: Nuclear Diplomacy since 1945* (New York: Oxford University Press, 1999), 157.

60. See "North Atlantic Military Committee Decision on M.C. 14/1: A Report by the Standing Group on Strategic Guidance," December 9, 1952, NATO Archive.

61. Dwight Eisenhower, Remarks at the National Editorial Association Dinner, June 22, 1954, APP.

62. "Measures to Implement the Strategic Concept for the Defense of the NATO Area," December 8, 1969, NATO Archive.

63. See Owen R. Cote, Jr., "The Third Battle: Innovation in the U.S. Navy's Silent Cold War Struggle with Soviet Submarines," U.S. Naval War College, Newport Papers 16, 2003.

64. Dwight Eisenhower, diary entry, January 23, 1956, *FRUS 1955–1957*, vol. 19, document 53.

65. "Estimated U.S. and Soviet/Russian Nuclear Stockpiles," 59; H. W. Brands, "The Age of Vulnerability: Eisenhower and the National Insecurity State," *American Historical Review* 94, October 1989, 963–89; David Rosenberg and W. B. Moore, "'Smoking Radiating Ruin at the End of Two Hours': Documents on American Plans for Nuclear War with the Soviet Union, 1954–1955," *International Security*, Spring 1983, 3–71.

66. NSC Meeting, December 3, 1954, *FRUS 1952–1954*, vol. 2, part 1, document 138; NSC Meeting, December 22, 1954, Box 6, NSC Series, Dwight David Eisenhower Presidential Library.

67. Henry Kissinger, *Nuclear Weapons and U.S. Foreign Policy* (New York: Council on Foreign Relations, 1957).

68. State to Ankara and Other Posts, December 23, 1964, Electronic Briefing Book (EBB) 31, National Security Archive (NSA).

69. State to NATO Capitals, June 11, 1980, EBB 390, NSA; Brendan Green, *The Revolution That Failed: Nuclear Competition, Arms Control, and the Cold War* (New York: Cambridge University Press, 2020).

70. Jonathan Haslam, *Russia's Cold War: From the October Revolution to the Fall of the Wall* (New Haven: Yale University Press, 2012), 304; Matthew Ambrose, *The Control Agenda: A History of the Strategic Arms Limitation Talks* (Ithaca, NY: Cornell University Press, 2018), 34–35.

71. MemCon, March 8, 1976, *FRUS 1969–1976*, vol. 35, document 73. See also Gordon Barrass, *The Great Cold War: A Journey through the Hall of Mirrors* (Stanford: Stanford University Press, 2009), 212–14.

72. Reagan–Mitterrand Meeting, March 22, 1984, Declassified Documents Reference System.

73. NSC Meeting, January 26, 1956, *FRUS 1955–1957*, vol. 20, document 103.

74. Norman Gelb, *The Berlin Wall: Kennedy, Khrushchev, and a Showdown in the Heart of Europe* (New York: Times Books, 1986), 3.

75. Embassy in Moscow to State, January 1, 1960, FRUS 1958–1960, vol. 9, document 63; Vladislav Zubok, "Khrushchev and the Berlin Crisis (1958–1962)," Cold War International History Project Working Paper 6, May 1993.

76. Sergei Khrushchev, ed., *Memoirs of Nikita Khrushchev*, vol. 3 (University Park: Pennsylvania State University Press, 2007), 436.

77. Chen Jian, *Mao's China and the Cold War* (Chapel Hill: University of North Carolina Press, 2001), 186.

78. Ernest May and Philip Zelikow, *Kennedy Tapes Concise Edition: Inside the White House during the Cuban Missile Crisis* (New York: Norton, 2002), xlvi.

79. Memorandum for Christian Herter, August 13, 1958, DNSA.

80. Discussion with Eisenhower, March 6, 1959, Declassified Documents Reference System; also TelCon with Eisenhower, November 22, 1958, DNSA; Richard Betts, *Nuclear Blackmail and Nuclear Balance* (Washington, DC: Brookings Institution, 1985), 86.

81. Roswell Gilpatric, Address, October 21, 1961, EBB 56, DNSA; Richard Ned Lebow and Janice Gross Stein, *We All Lost the Cold War* (Princeton: Princeton University Press, 1994), 37.

82. Steven Rearden, *Council of War: A History of the Joint Chiefs of Staff*, Joint History Office, Department of Defense, 2012, 220.

83. Taylor to Lemnitzer, September 6 and 19, 1961; Carl Kaysen to Taylor, September 5, 1961, EBB 56, DNSA.

84. On the crisis, see Serhii Plokhy, *Nuclear Folly: A New History of the Cuban Missile Crisis* (New York: Norton, 2021).

85. Thomas Zeiler, *Dean Rusk: Defending the American Mission Abroad* (Wilmington, DE: Scholarly Resources, 2000), 77.

86. Aleksandr Fursenko and Timothy Naftali, *One Hell of a Gamble: Khrushchev, Castro, and Kennedy, 1958–1964* (New York: Norton, 1998), ix, 244.

87. Central Committee Meeting, October 23, 1962, Digital Archive, CWIHP.

88. On close calls, see Scott Sagan, *The Limits of Safety: Organizations, Accidents, and Nuclear Weapons* (Princeton: Princeton University Press, 1993).

89. Kennedy to Khrushchev, December 28, 1962, FRUS 1961–1963, vol. 6, document 87.

90. Gaddis, *Long Peace*, 195–214.

91. Walter Lippmann, *The Cold War: A Study in U.S. Foreign Policy* (New York: Harper & Brothers, 1947), 21–23; also Ronald Spector, *A Continent Erupts: Decolonization, Civil War, and Massacre in Postwar Asia, 1945–1955* (New York: Norton, 2023).

92. Odd Arne Westad, *The Global Cold War: Third World Interventions and the Making of Our Times* (New York: Cambridge University Press, 2007), 54.

93. Hal Brands, *Latin America's Cold War* (Cambridge, MA: Harvard University Press, 2010), 23; Peter Rodman, *More Precious Than Peace: Fighting and Winning the Cold War in the Third World* (New York: Scribner, 1994).

94. John F. Kennedy, Address to Congress, May 25, 1961, APP.

95. Westad, *Global Cold War*; Piero Gleijeses, *Conflicting Missions: Havana, Washington, and Africa, 1959–1976* (Chapel Hill: University of North Carolina Press, 2002); Qiang Zhai, *China and the Vietnam Wars, 1950–1975* (Chapel Hill: University of North Carolina Press, 2005).

96. Paul Thomas Chamberlain, *The Cold War's Killing Fields: Rethinking the Long Peace* (New York: HarperCollins, 2018), 1.

97. Jeane Kirkpatrick, Remarks, March 21, 1981, Box 45, Richard Allen Papers, Hoover Institution Archives, Stanford University.

98. Address at Johns Hopkins University, April 7, 1965, APP.

99. Mark Atwood Lawrence, *The Vietnam War: A Concise International History* (New York: Oxford University Press, 2010), 99, 91; Zachary Shore, "Provoking America: Le Duan and the Origins of the Vietnam War," *Journal of Cold War Studies*, Fall 2015, esp. 100–101.

100. White House Meeting, September 9, 1964, *FRUS 1964–1968*, vol. 1, document 343.

101. Henry Kissinger, *White House Years* (Boston: Little, Brown, 1979), 64.

102. Odd Arne Westad, "Moscow and the Angolan Crisis, 1974–1976: A New Pattern of Intervention," *Cold War International History Project Bulletin* 8–9 (Winter 1996/97): 21.

103. Vladislav Zubok, "Soviet Foreign Policy from Détente to Gorbachev," in Melvyn Leffler and Odd Arne Westad, eds., *The Cambridge History of the Cold War*, vol. 3 (New York: Cambridge University Press, 2010), 101.

104. Christopher Andrew and Vasili Mitrokhin, *The World Was Going Our Way: The KGB and the Battle for the Third World* (New York: Basic Books, 2005), esp. 471.

105. Franklin Roosevelt, Address at Hyde Park, July 4, 1941, APP.

106. Harry S. Truman, Address on Mutual Security Program, March 6, 1952, APP.

107. Kennan to Secretary, February 22, 1946, *FRUS 1946*, vol. 6, document 475.

108. Arthur Schlesinger, Jr., *The Imperial Presidency* (New York: Houghton Mifflin, 1973), 299; Michael Hogan, *A Cross of Iron: Harry S. Truman and the Origins of the National Security State, 1945–1954* (New York: Cambridge University Press, 1998).

109. Robert Taft, *A Foreign Policy for Americans* (Garden City, NY: Doubleday, 1951), 5; Ellen Schrecker, *Many Are the Crimes: McCarthyism in America* (Princeton: Princeton University Press, 1998).

110. Gaddis, *Strategies of Containment*, 393.

111. Mary Dudziak, "Brown as a Cold War Case," *Journal of American History*, June 2004, 37.

112. Dwight Eisenhower, Address on Situation in Little Rock, September 24, 1957, APP.

113. Lyndon B. Johnson, Remarks on Voting Rights Act, August 6, 1965, APP.

114. CIA, "Restless Youth," September 1968, Declassified Documents Reference System; Jonathan Cole, *The Great American University: Its Rise to Preeminence, Its Indispensable National Role, Why It Must Be Protected* (New York: PublicAffairs, 2012).

115. Melvyn Leffler, *Safeguarding Democratic Capitalism: U.S. Foreign Policy and National Security, 1920–2015* (Princeton: Princeton University Press, 2017), 231.

116. Diane Kunz, *Butter and Guns: America's Cold War Economic Diplomacy* (New York: Free Press, 1997), 2; Margaret O'Mara, *The Code: Silicon Valley and the Remaking of America* (New York: Penguin Press, 2019).

117. National Foreign Assessment Center, "Soviet–American Relations: The Outlook of Brezhnev's Successors," November 1979, Box 59, William Odom File, Brzezinski Material, National Security Adviser File, Jimmy Carter Presidential Library.

118. Extracts from Brezhnev's Speech to Soviet Party Congress, February 24, 1976, Box 51, James Schlesinger Papers, LC. See also Raymond Garthoff, *Détente and Confrontation: American–Soviet Relations from Nixon to Reagan* (Washington, DC: Brookings Institution Press, 1985).

119. Lippmann, *Cold War*, esp. 18–23.

120. Editorial Note, *FRUS 1955–1957*, vol. 19, document 41.

121. Brent Scowcroft Oral History, November 12–13, 1999, Presidential Oral Histories, Miller Center, University of Virginia.

122. General Accounting Office, "Soviet Economy: Assessment of How Well the CIA Has Estimated the Size of the Economy," September 1991; Stephen Kotkin, *Armageddon Averted: The Soviet Collapse 1970–2000* (New York: Oxford University Press, 2008), 23–24.

123. Barry Watts and Andrew Krepinevich, *The Last Warrior: Andrew Marshall and the Shaping of Modern American Defense Strategy* (New York: Basic Books, 2015), 150–51; Robert Gates, *From the Shadows: The Ultimate Insider's Story of Five Presidents and How They Won the Cold War* (New York: Simon & Schuster, 1996), 318–19.

124. Anatoly Dobrynin, *In Confidence: Moscow's Ambassador to Six Cold War Presidents* (New York: Random House, 1995), 475.

125. Giovanni Arrighi, "The World Economy and the Cold War," in Leffler and Westad, eds., *Cambridge History of the Cold War*, vol. 3, 28.

126. See Herbert Meyer to William Casey, "What Should We Do About the Russians?," June 28, 1984, CIA FOIA.

127. Meeting of Kissinger, Fraser, and others, December 17, 1974, DNSA.
128. Leslie H. Gelb, "Foreign Affairs: Who Won the Cold War?," *New York Times*, August 20, 1992.
129. Mark Kramer, "Stalin, the Split with Yugoslavia, and Soviet–East European Efforts to Reassert Control, 1948–1953," in Timothy Snyder and Ray Brandon, eds., *Stalin and Europe: Imitation and Domination, 1928–1953* (New York: Oxford University Press, 2014), 295–315.
130. U.S. Minutes of Conversation, December 7, 1953, *FRUS 1952–1954*, vol. 5, part 2, document 353; Lorenz M. Lüthi, *The Sino-Soviet Split: Cold War in the Communist World* (Princeton: Princeton University Press, 2008).
131. Meeting of Nixon and CENTO Foreign Ministers, May 22, 1974, Box 4, MemCons, National Security Adviser File, Gerald R. Ford Presidential Library.
132. Nixon–Heath Meeting, December 20, 1971, Box 1025, Presidential–HAK MemCons, Richard M. Nixon Presidential Library.
133. Richard Javad Heydarian, *The Indo-Pacific: Trump, China, and the New Struggle for Global Mastery* (New York: Palgave Macmillan, 2020), 160.
134. Dobrynin to Foreign Ministry, March 8, 1972, *FRUS, Soviet–American Relations: The Détente Years*, document 267.
135. Ronald Reagan, Remarks at Moscow State University, May 31, 1988, APP; Chris Miller, *The Struggle to Save the Soviet Economy: Mikhail Gorbachev and the Collapse of the USSR* (Chapel Hill: University of North Carolina Press, 2016).
136. National Intelligence Council, "The USSR and the Vulnerability of Empire," November 27, 1981, CIA Records Search Tool (CREST), National Archives and Research Administration.
137. Watts and Krepinevich, *Last Warrior*, 119.
138. A. W. Marshall, "Long-Term Competition with the Soviets: A Framework for Strategic Analysis," RAND Corporation, R-862-PR, April 1972.
139. Harold Brown, *Department of Defense Annual Report, Fiscal Year 1982*, x.
140. National Security Planning Group Meeting, December 10, 1984, Box 91307, NSPGs, NSC Executive Secretariat File, RRL.
141. "The Russian Wheat Deal," October 1975, in Kiron Skinner, Annelise Anderson, and Martin Anderson, eds., *Reagan, in His Own Hand: The Writings of Ronald Reagan That Reveal His Revolutionary Vision for America* (New York: Free Press, 2001), 30–31.
142. "The Madrid Agreement," January 3, 1984, Box 4, Kampelman Papers, Minnesota Historical Society.
143. Richard Halloran, "Pentagon Draws Up First Strategy for Fighting a Long Nuclear War," *New York Times*, May 30, 1982.
144. Gordon Barrass, "U.S. Competitive Strategy during the Cold War," in Thomas Mahnken, ed., *Competitive Strategies for the 21st Century: Theory, History, and Practice* (Stanford: Stanford University Press, 2012), 85–86; David Walsh, *The Military Balance in the Cold War: U.S. Perceptions and Policy, 1976–1985* (New York: Routledge, 2008), 109–28.
145. NSDD-13, October 19, 1981, DNSA; George Wilson, "Preparing for Long Nuclear War Is Waste of Funds, Gen. Jones Says," *Washington Post*, June 19, 1982; Austin Long and Brendan Green, "Stalking the Secure Second Strike: Intelligence, Counterforce, and Nuclear Strategy," *Journal of Strategic Studies*, January–February 2015, esp. 48–56.
146. Ronald Reagan, Address on Defense and National Security, March 23, 1983, APP.
147. NSC Meeting, November 30, 1983, Box 91303, NSC Meetings, NSC ESF, RRL.
148. Reuters news dispatch, March 18, 1981, Richard Allen Papers, Hoover Institution Archives, Stanford University.
149. Nikolai Ogarkov, speech to Warsaw Pact Chiefs of Staff, September 1982, in Vojtech Mastny and Malcolm Byrne, eds., *A Cardboard Castle? An Inside History of the Warsaw Pact, 1955–1991* (Budapest: CEU Press, 2005), 467.
150. Ronald Reagan, Remarks to National Association of Evangelicals, March 8, 1983, APP.

151. NSC Meeting, May 24, 1982, Box 91284, ESF, RRL; also NSC Meeting, 12/21/1981, Box 91283, ESF, RRL; Seth Jones, *A Covert Action: Reagan, the CIA, and the Cold War Struggle in Poland* (New York: Norton, 2018).

152. Leslie Gelb, "Foreign Affairs; Who Won the Cold War?," *New York Times*, August 20, 1992.

153. Discussion on U.S.–Soviet Relations, October 11, 1983, Box 2, Jack Matlock Files, RRL; Ben Fischer, "The 1983 War Scare in U.S.–Soviet Relations," Center for the Study of Intelligence, 1996, EBB 426, DNSA.

154. Ronald Reagan, Speech at Westminster, June 8, 1982, APP.

155. Jeffrey Engel, *When the World Seemed New: George W. Bush and the End of the Cold War* (Boston: Houghton Mifflin, 2017), 375.

156. Anatoly Chernyaev, *My Six Years with Gorbachev* (University Park: Pennsylvania State University Press, 1996), 46; Archie Brown, *The Gorbachev Factor* (New York: Oxford University Press, 1996).

157. Mikhail Gorbachev, *Memoirs* (Garden City, NY: Doubleday, 1995), 401.

158. Special National Intelligence Estimate, "Gorbachev's Policy toward the United States," September 1986, CIA FOIA; Dobrynin, *In Confidence*, 570.

159. Carolyn Ekedahl and Melvin Goodman, *The Wars of Eduard Shevardnadze* (University Park: Penn State University Press, 1997), 100–101; Jack Matlock, *Autopsy on an Empire: The American Ambassador's Account of the Collapse of the Soviet Union* (New York: Random House, 1996), 57–67.

160. Ronald Reagan, "Gorbachev," October 13, 1985, Box 215, Donald Regan Papers, LC; Ronald Reagan, Remarks in West Berlin, June 12, 1987, APP.

161. Notes of Shultz–Gorbachev Meeting, April 14, 1987, Box 5, Don Oberdorfer Papers, SMML.

162. William Inboden, *The Peacemaker: Ronald Reagan, the Cold War, and the World on the Brink* (New York: Penguin, 2022).

163. U.S.–Soviet Meeting, October 12, 1986, EBB 203, DNSA.

164. Ronald Reagan, Address to the People of Western Europe, November 4, 1987, APP.

165. Politburo Meeting, February 26, 1987, EBB 238, DNSA.

166. William Odom, *The Collapse of the Soviet Military* (New Haven: Yale University Press, 1998), 134; Kiron Skinner, Annelise Anderson, and Martin Anderson, eds., *Reagan: A Life in Letters* (New York: Free Press, 2003), 384.

167. "Excerpts from Speech to U.N. on Major Soviet Military Cuts," *New York Times*, December 8, 1988; Gorbachev, *Memoirs*, 459–60.

168. James Mann, *The Rebellion of Ronald Reagan: A History of the End of the Cold War* (New York: Viking, 2009), 282–84, 305–6.

169. Scowcroft to Bush, November 29, 1989, Box 10, OA/ID 91116, German Unification Files, Scowcroft Collection, George H. W. Bush Presidential Library.

170. Gorbachev–Baker Discussion, February 9, 1990, in Svetlana Savranskaya, Thomas Blanton, and Vladislav Zubok, eds., *Masterpieces of History: The Peaceful End of the Cold War in Europe, 1989* (Budapest: Central European University Press, 2010), 683.

171. Anatoly Chernyaev, diary entry, January 18, 1986, EBB 220, DNSA. On this point, see also Robert Kagan, *The Jungle Grows Back: America and Our Imperiled World* (New York: Knopf, 2018), 70.

172. Samuel Huntington, *The Third Wave: Democratization in the Late Twentieth Century* (Norman: University of Oklahoma Press, 1991), 26, for the 1940s; Freedom House, *Freedom in the World 2013: Democratic Breakthroughs in the Balance*, 29, for 1990 and 2000.

173. World Trade Organization, *World Trade Report 2008: Trade in a Globalized World*, 15; Robert Kagan, *The World America Made* (New York: Vintage, 2012), 40–41.

174. Aaron Friedberg, *In the Shadow of the Garrison State: America's Anti-Statism and Its Cold War Grand Strategy* (Princeton: Princeton University Press, 2000), 341.

175. Chamberlain, *Cold War's Killing Fields*, 1.

176. John Lewis Gaddis, *The Cold War: A New History* (New York: Penguin, 2005), 2.

177. Baker, "Summons to Leadership," April 2, 1992, Box 169, Baker Papers, SMML.

178. Nicholas Spykman, *America's Strategy in World Politics: The United States and the Balance of Power* [1942] (New York: Routledge, 2017), 469.

179. Halford J. Mackinder, "The Geographic Pivot of History," *Geographical Journal*, April 1904, 437.

CHAPTER 5: THE SECOND EURASIAN CENTURY

1. "Joint Statement of the Russian Federation and the People's Republic of China on the International Relations Entering a New Era and the Global Sustainable Development," February 4, 2022.

2. "Russia, China Push Back Against U.S. and NATO in Pre-Olympics Summit," *PBS Newshour*, February 4, 2022.

3. Alexander [Aleksandr] Dugin, *The Last War of the World-Island* (London: Arktos, 2015), 145; Serhii Plokhy, *The Russo-Ukrainian War: The Return of History* (New York: Norton, 2023).

4. Hal Brands, *Dealing with Allies in Decline: Alliance Management and U.S. Strategy in an Era of Global Power Shifts* (Washington, DC: Center for Strategic and Budgetary Assessments, 2017), 13–14.

5. Jeane Kirkpatrick, "A Normal Country in a Normal Time," *National Interest* 21 (1990): 41–44.

6. James Baker, Remarks to Chicago Council on Foreign Relations, April 2, 1992, Box 169, Baker Papers, SMML.

7. Draft of FY 94–99 Defense Planning Guidance (DPG), February 18, 1992, EBB 245, DNSA; Patrick Tyler, "U.S. Strategy Plan Calls for Insuring No Rivals Develop," *New York Times*, March 8, 1992.

8. Steven Mufson, "China Blasts U.S. for Dispatching Warship Groups," *Washington Post*, March 20, 1996.

9. Robert Zoellick, "Whither China: From Membership to Responsibility?," Remarks to National Committee on U.S.–China Relations, September 21, 2005; Aaron Friedberg, *Getting China Wrong* (London: Polity, 2022).

10. See State to All Diplomatic Posts, September 23, 1993, Box 1, NSC Files, Speechwriting Office, William J. Clinton Presidential Library.

11. Introduction, *The National Security Strategy of the United States of America*, September 2002.

12. Meeting between Helmut Kohl and Lech Walesa, November 9, 1989, CWIHP.

13. John J. Mearsheimer, "Back to the Future: Instability in Europe after the Cold War," *International Security*, Summer 1990, 5–56.

14. See Michael Mandelbaum, *The Case for Goliath: How America Acts as the World's Government in the 21st Century* (New York: PublicAffairs, 2005); Stephen G. Brooks and William C. Wohlforth, *America Abroad: The United States' Global Role in the 21st Century* (New York: Oxford University Press, 2016).

15. John J. Mearsheimer, "Why Is Europe Peaceful Today?," *European Political Science*, September 2010, 387–97.

16. World Bank, "GDP (constant 2010 US$)"; and Stockholm International Peace Research Institute, Military Expenditure Database, "Data for all countries from 1988–2019 in constant (2018) USD."

17. A point made in Jonathan Holslag, *World Politics since 1989* (London: Polity, 2021), 283.

18. Michael McFaul, *Russia's Unfinished Revolution: Political Change from Gorbachev to Putin* (Ithaca, NY: Cornell University Press, 2015); Friedberg, *Getting China Wrong*.

19. The phrase comes from Draft of FY 94–99 Defense Planning Guidance.

20. FCO Cable, "Russian Foreign Policy," May 12, 1997, PREM-49-149-3, TNA. See also Mary Sarotte, *Not One Inch: America, Russia, and the Making of Post-Cold War Stalemate* (New Haven: Yale University Press, 2021).

21. Holslag, *World Politics since 1989*, 120. On the crisis, see also James Mann, *About Face: A History of America's Curious Relationship with China, from Nixon to Clinton* (New York: Vintage, 2000), 335–37.

22. Chua Chin Leng, "The Politics of Non Interference—A New World Order," *China Daily*, January 25, 2016.

23. Kimberly Marten, "Reconsidering NATO Expansion: A Counterfactual Analysis of Russia and the West in the 1990s," *European Journal of International Security*, November 2017, 135–61.

24. The alliance with the United States was traditionally viewed in Beijing as a "bottle cork." Adam Liff, "China and the U.S. Alliance System," *China Quarterly*, March 2018, 139.

25. Memorandum of Conversation—President Boris Yeltsin of Russia, November 19, 1999, William J. Clinton Presidential Library.

26. Samuel Kim, "Human Rights in China's International Relations," in Edward Friedman and Barrett McCormick, eds., *What If China Doesn't Democratize? Implications for War and Peace* (New York: M. E. Sharpe, 2000), 130–31; Wang Jisi and Kenneth Lieberthal, *Addressing U.S.–China Strategic Distrust*, Brookings Institution, March 2012, esp. 11–12.

27. Darya Korsunskaya, "Putin Says Russia Must Prevent 'Color Revolution,'" Reuters, November 20, 2014. See also Michael McFaul, *From Cold War to Hot Peace: An American Ambassador in Putin's Russia* (New York: Mariner, 2019), 57–75.

28. Michael O'Hanlon, "Is U.S. Defense Spending Too High, Too Low, or Just Right?," *Policy 2020*, Brookings Institution, October 15, 2019.

29. Barack Obama, "Remarks by the President on the Way Forward in Afghanistan," White House, June 22, 2011.

30. Kent Calder, *Super Continent: The Logic of Eurasian Integration* (Stanford: Stanford University Press, 2019), 100.

31. Toshi Yoshihara and Jack Bianchi, *Seizing on Weakness: Allied Strategy for Competing with China's Globalizing Military* (Washington, DC: Center for Strategic and Budgetary Assessments, 2021); Andrew J. Nathan and Andrew Scobell, *China's Search for Security* (New York: Columbia University Press, 2012).

32. Howard French, *Everything under the Heavens: How the Past Helps Shape China's Push for Global Power* (New York: Knopf, 2017); Michael Schuman, *Superpower Interrupted: The Chinese History of the World* (New York: PublicAffairs, 2020).

33. Elizabeth Economy, *The Third Revolution: Xi Jinping and the New Chinese State* (New York: Oxford University Press, 2018).

34. Evan Osnos, "The Future of America's Contest with China," *New Yorker*, January 13, 2020.

35. Liza Tobin, "Xi's Vision for Transforming Global Governance," *Texas National Security Review*, November 2018.

36. Daniel Tobin, "How Xi Jinping's 'New Era' Should Have Ended U.S. Debate on Beijing's Ambitions," Center for Strategic and International Studies, May 2020; Rush Doshi, *The Long Game: China's Grand Strategy to Displace the American Order* (Oxford: Oxford University Press, 2021); Elizabeth Economy, *The World According to China* (London: Polity, 2022).

37. See Minxin Pei, "China's Asia?," *Project Syndicate*, December 3, 2014; also Aaron Friedberg, *A Contest for Supremacy: China, America, and the Struggle for Mastery in Asia* (New York: Norton, 2022).

38. "China Won't Give Up 'One Inch' of Territory Says President Xi to Mattis," BBC News, June 28, 2018.

39. Ken Moriyasu, "For U.S., Pacific Showdown with China a Long Time Coming," *Nikkei Asia*, October 29, 2015.

40. Prashanth Parameswaran, "U.S. Blasts China's 'Great Wall of Sand' in the South China Sea," *Diplomat*, April 1, 2015; Jennifer Lind, "Life in China's Asia: What Regional Hegemony Would Look Like," *Foreign Affairs*, March–April 2018.

41. U.S. Department of Defense, 2022 *Report on Military and Security Developments Involving the People's Republic of China*; Noah Robertson, "China More Than Doubled Its Nuclear Arsenal since 2020, Pentagon Says," *Defense News*, October 19, 2023.

42. Michael Martina and David Brunnstrom, "CIA Chief Warns against Underestimating Xi's Ambitions toward Taiwan," Reuters, February 2, 2023.

43. Toshi Yoshihara and James Holmes, *Red Star over the Pacific: China's Rise and the Challenge to U.S. Maritime Strategy* (Annapolis: U.S. Naval Institute Press, 2018), 86.

44. Author's interview with Japanese official, November 2022; author's interviews with Australian officials, November 2022.

45. Yoshihara and Holmes, *Red Star*, 116–17; Geoffrey Gresh, *To Rule Eurasia's Waves: The New Great Power Competition at Sea* (New Haven: Yale University Press, 2020), 172.

46. Yun Sun, "Westward Ho! As America Pivots East, China Marches in the Other Direction," *Foreign Policy*, February 7, 2013.

47. See "Full Text of President Xi's Speech at Opening of Belt and Road Forum," Ministry of Foreign Affairs of the People's Republic of China, May 15, 2017.

48. Sheena Greitens, "Dealing with Demand for China's Global Surveillance Exports," Brookings Institution, April 2020; Daniel Markey, *China's Western Horizon: Beijing and the New Geopolitics of Eurasia* (New York: Oxford University Press, 2020); Sulmaan Wasif Khan, *Haunted by Chaos: China's Grand Strategy from Mao Zedong to Xi Jinping* (Cambridge, MA: Harvard University Press, 2018), 230–31.

49. Christina Garafola, Stephen Watts, and Kristin Leuschner, *China's Global Basing Ambitions: Defense Implications for the United States* (Santa Monica: RAND Corporation, 2022).

50. Markey, *China's Western Horizon*, 168.

51. Nadège Rolland, *China's Eurasian Century? Political and Strategic Implications of the Belt and Road Initiative* (Seattle: National Bureau of Asian Research, 2017), 143. See also Bruno Maçaes, *The Dawn of Eurasia: On the Trail of the New World Order* (New Haven: Yale University Press, 2018).

52. Niharika Mandhana, Rajesh Roy, and Chun Han Wong, "The Deadly India–China Clash: Spiked Clubs and Fists at 14,000 Feet," *Wall Street Journal*, June 17, 2020.

53. Jacob Helberg, *The Wires of War: Technology and the Global Struggle for Power* (New York: Simon & Schuster, 2021).

54. Elsa Kania, "'AI Weapons' in China's Military Innovation," Brookings Institution, April 2020; Julian Gewirtz, "China's Long March to Technological Supremacy," *Foreign Affairs*, August 27, 2019; Eyck Freymann, *One Belt One Road: Chinese Power Meets the World* (Cambridge, MA: Harvard University Asia Center, 2021).

55. Ross Andersen, "The Panopticon Is Already Here," *Atlantic*, September 2020.

56. Austin Ramzy and Chris Buckley, "'Absolutely No Mercy': Leaked Files Expose How China Organized Mass Detention of Muslims," *New York Times*, November 16, 2019.

57. Sean Roberts, *The War on the Uyghurs: China's Internal Campaign against a Muslim Minority* (Princeton: Princeton University Press, 2020), esp. 2, 174–75.

58. Max Seddon, "Putin's Made-for-TV Security Debate Gives Him Answers He Wants to Hear on Ukraine," *Financial Times*, February 21, 2022.

59. Steve Holland and Jeff Mason, "Obama, in Dig at Putin, Calls Russia 'Regional Power,'" Reuters, March 25, 2014.

60. Stephen Kotkin, "Russia's Perpetual Geopolitics: Putin Returns to the Historical Pattern," *Foreign Affairs*, May–June 2016, 3.

61. The best study of Putin is Fiona Hill and Clifford Gaddy, *Mr. Putin: Operative in the Kremlin* (Washington, DC: Brookings Institution Press, 2015).

62. Anna Borshchevskaya, *Putin's War in Syria: Russian Foreign Policy and the Price of America's Absence* (New York: Bloomsbury, 2021), 45.

63. Steven Lee Myers, *The New Tsar: The Rise and Reign of Vladimir Putin* (New York: Knopf, 2016), 266.

64. "Ukraine Conflict: Putin 'Was Ready for Nuclear Alert,'" BBC News, March 15, 2015; Defense Intelligence Agency, *Russia Military Power: Building a Military to Support Great Power Aspirations*, 2017.

65. Vladimir Putin, "A New Integration Project for Eurasia: The Future in the Making," *Izvestia*, October 3, 2011; Thomas Ambrosio, *Authoritarian Backlash: Russian Resistance to Democratization in the Former Soviet Union* (New York: Routledge, 2016).

66. Patricia Lewis, "Russian Treaty Proposals Hark Back to Post-Cold War Era," Chatham House, December 19, 2021.

67. Jeffrey Mankoff, *Russian Foreign Policy: The Return of Great-Power Politics* (Lanham, MD: Rowman & Littlefield, 2011), 46.

68. Heather Conley and Matthew Melino, "Russian Malign Influence in Montenegro: The Weaponization and Exploitation of History, Religion, and Economics," Center for Strategic and International Studies, May 14, 2019; Evan Osnos et al., "Trump, Putin, and the New Cold War," *New Yorker*, March 6, 2017.

69. "Minister: Russian Operation in Syria Stopped Chain of Color Revolutions in Middle East," TASS, February 21, 2017.

70. Michael Kofman, "Raiding and International Brigandry: Russia's Strategy for Great Power Competition," *War on the Rocks*, June 14, 2018; Julia Gurganus and Eugene Rumer, "Russia's Global Ambitions in Perspective," Carnegie Endowment for International Peace, February 2019.

71. Daniel R. Coats, "Worldwide Threat Assessment of the U.S. Intelligence Community," Senate Select Committee on Intelligence, January 29, 2019, 4.

72. Stuart Lau, "Why Xi Jinping Is Still Vladimir Putin's Best Friend," *Politico Europe*, March 20, 2023.

73. Kaplan, *Revenge of Geography*, 171.

74. Daniel Treisman, "Crimea: Anatomy of a Decision," in Treisman, ed., *The New Autocracy: Information, Politics, and Policy in Putin's Russia* (Washington, DC: Brookings Institution, 2018).

75. Daniel Treisman, "Putin Unbound: How Repression at Home Presaged Belligerence Abroad," *Foreign Affairs*, May–June 2022, 42. See also Robert Nalbandov, *Not by Bread Alone: Russian Foreign Policy under Putin* (Lincoln: University of Nebraska Press, 2016), 9–11.

76. Kathryn Stoner, *Russia Resurrected: Its Power and Purpose in a New Global Order* (New York: Oxford University Press, 2021), 216.

77. "Valdai International Discussion Club Meeting," Kremlin website, October 27, 2022; Lilia Shevtsova, "The Authoritarian Resurgence: Forward to the Past in Russia," *Journal of Democracy*, April 2015, 22–37.

78. "Creating Common Humanitarian, Economic Zone from Lisbon to Vladivostok Is Possible—Putin," TASS, October 27, 2022.

79. Seth Jones, *Three Dangerous Men: Russia, China, Iran, and the Rise of Irregular Warfare* (New York: Norton, 2021).

80. Ken Dilanian and Courtney Kube, "Airport Informants, Overhead Drones: How the U.S. Killed Soleimani," NBC News, January 10, 2020.

81. Anthony Lake, "Confronting Backlash States," *Foreign Affairs*, March/April 1994, 45–55.

82. Karim Sadjadpour, "Iran's Hollow Victory: The High Price of Regional Dominance," *Foreign Affairs*, March–April 2022, 30.

83. Afshon Ostovar, *Vanguard of the Imam: Religion, Politics, and Iran's Revolutionary Guards* (New York: Oxford University Press, 2016), 205.

84. Seth Jones, "War by Proxy: Iran's Growing Footprint in the Middle East," CSIS Briefs, March 2019, 6; Oded Yaron, "150,000 Missiles Aimed at Israel: How Far Does Hezbollah's Deadly Arsenal Reach?," *Haaretz*, October 23, 2023.

85. "Iran Launches Missile Attacks on U.S. Facilities in Iraq," Al Jazeera, January 8, 2020; Gawdat Bahgat and Anoushiravan Ehteshami, *Defending Iran: From Revolutionary Guards to Ballistic Missiles* (New York: Cambridge University Press, 2021).

86. Sadjadpour, "Iran's Hollow Victory"; Kim Ghattas, *Black Wave: Saudi Arabia, Iran, and the Forty-Year Rivalry That Unraveled Culture, Religion, and Collective Memory in the Middle East* (New York: Henry Holt, 2020).

87. "Iran's Khamenei Says Moscow, Tehran Cooperation Can Isolate U.S.—TV," Reuters, November 1, 2017.

88. Jeff Seldin, "US Defense Officials: China Is Leading in Hypersonic Weapons," Voice of America, March 10, 2023.

89. Scott Jasper, "Assessing Russia's Role and Responsibility in the Colonial Pipeline Attack," New Atlanticist, June 1, 2021; Alina Polyakova, "The Kremlin's Plot against Democracy," Foreign Affairs, September/October 2020, 142–43. It isn't clear whether Putin authorized the Colonial Pipeline attack or simply created an atmosphere in which it could occur.

90. Michael Mazarr et al., The Emerging Risk of Virtual Societal Warfare (Santa Monica: RAND Corporation, 2019).

91. Introduction, The National Security Strategy of the United States of America, September 2002.

92. Larry Diamond, "Facing Up to the Democratic Recession," Journal of Democracy, January 2015.

93. Simina Mistreanu, "Life Inside China's Social Credit Laboratory," Foreign Policy, April 3, 2018; Andrea Kendall-Taylor, Erica Frantz, and Joseph Wright, "The Digital Dictators: How Technology Strengthens Autocracy," Foreign Affairs, March–April 2020.

94. Hal Brands, "Democracy vs. Authoritarianism: How Ideology Shapes Great-Power Conflict," Survival, October–November 2018.

95. Christopher Walker and Jessica Ludwig, "The Long Arm of the Strongman: How China and Russia Use Sharp Power to Threaten Democracies," Foreign Affairs, May 12, 2021; Elizabeth Dwoskin, "How Russian Disinformation Toppled Government after Government in Africa," Washington Post, October 30, 2023; Alina Polyakova and Chris Meserole, "Exporting Digital Authoritarianism: The Russian and Chinese Models," Brookings Institution Policy Brief, August 2019. More broadly, see Larry Diamond, Marc Plattner, and Christopher Walker, eds., Authoritarianism Goes Global: The Challenge to Democracy (Baltimore: Johns Hopkins University Press, 2016).

96. Robert Chesney and Danielle Citron, "Deepfakes and the New Disinformation War: The Coming Age of Post-Truth Geopolitics," Foreign Affairs, January–February 2019.

97. Eric Heginbotham et al., The U.S.–China Military Scorecard: Forces, Geography, and the Evolving Balance of Power, 1996–2017 (Santa Monica: RAND Corporation, 2015), xxx. See also Christian Brose, The Kill Chain: Defending America in the Future of High-Tech Warfare (New York: Hachette, 2020).

98. Jeff Seldin, "US Defense Officials."

99. National Security Commission on Artificial Intelligence, Final Report (Washington, DC: National Security Commission on Artificial Intelligence, 2021).

100. David Shambaugh, China's Future (London: Polity, 2016); Kinling Lo, "Tech War: Beijing Will Come out of Decoupling Worse Off Than the US, Say Chinese Academics," South China Morning Post, February 1, 2022.

101. Michael Brown, Eric Chewning, and Pavneet Singh, "Preparing the United States for the Superpower Marathon with China," Brookings Institution, April 2020; Dan Blumenthal and Derek Scissors, "China's Technology Strategy: Leverage before Growth," American Enterprise Institute, June 8, 2023.

102. Henry Farrell and Abraham Newman, "Weaponized Interdependence: How Global Economic Networks Shape State Coercion," International Security, Summer 2019, 42–79.

103. Julian Gewirtz, "The Chinese Reassessment of Interdependence," China Leadership Monitor, June 1, 2020; also "China's 'Dual-Circulation' Strategy Means Relying Less on Foreigners," Economist, November 7, 2020; Chris Miller, Chip War: The Fight for the World's Most Critical Technology (New York: Scribner, 2022).

104. Matt Pottinger, Testimony, U.S.–China Economic and Security Review Commission, April 15, 2021. See also Mark Leonard, The Age of Unpeace: How Connectivity Causes Conflict (New York: Bantam, 2021).

105. "Obama: Ukraine 'Vulnerable' to Russian 'Military Domination' No Matter What U.S. Does," Radio Free Europe/Radio Liberty, March 10, 2016.

106. David Larter, "White House Tells the Pentagon to Quit Talking about 'Competition' with China," *Navy Times*, September 26, 2016; Jeffrey Goldberg, "The Obama Doctrine," *Atlantic*, April 2016.

107. Kurt Campbell and Mira Rapp-Hooper, "China Is Done Biding Its Time," *Foreign Affairs*, July 15, 2020.

108. "How It Happened: Transcript of the U.S.–China Opening Remarks in Alaska," *Nikkei Asia*, March 19, 2021.

109. *National Security Strategy of the United States of America* (Washington, DC: The White House, 2017); *National Security Strategy* (Washington, DC: The White House, 2022).

110. Nina Kollars and Jacquelyn Schneider, "Defending Forward: The 2018 Cyber Strategy Is Here," *War on the Rocks*, September 20, 2018; Thomas Gibbons-Neff, "How a 4-Hour Battle between Russian Mercenaries and U.S. Commandos Unfolded in Syria," *New York Times*, May 24, 2018.

111. Carla Babb, "Pentagon Launches Effort to Better Address China Challenge," Voice of America, June 9, 2021.

112. Chris Miller, "America Is Going to Decapitate Huawei," *New York Times*, September 15, 2020.

113. Steven Lee Myers and Chris Buckley, "Biden's China Strategy Meets Resistance at the Negotiating Table," *New York Times*, July 26, 2021.

114. Tanvi Madan, "The Rise, Fall, and Rebirth of the 'Quad,'" *War on the Rocks*, November 16, 2017; Abe Shinzo, "Asia's Democratic Security Diamond," *Project Syndicate*, December 27, 2012.

115. Ishaan Tharoor, "China and Russia Draw Closer, but How Close?," *Washington Post*, May 26, 2023.

116. Steven Lee Myers and Amy Qin, "Why Biden Seems Worse to China Than Trump," *New York Times*, July 20, 2021; Jacob Benjamin, "French Naval Activity in the South China Sea on the Rise," *Geopolitics*, July 7, 2021.

117. Michael Green, *Line of Advantage: Japan's Grand Strategy in the Era of Abe Shinzo* (New York: Columbia University Press, 2022), 3–4; Abe, "Asia's Democratic Security Diamond."

118. On this dynamic, see also Jakub Grygiel and A. Wess Mitchell, *The Unquiet Frontier: Rising Rivals, Vulnerable Allies, and the Crisis of American Power* (Princeton: Princeton University Press, 2016), esp. 86–88.

119. "Remarks by President Trump at Signing of the U.S.–China Phase One Trade Agreement," White House, January 15, 2020.

120. Michael Beckley and Hal Brands, "The Return of Pax Americana? Putin's War Is Fortifying the Democratic Alliance," *Foreign Affairs*, March 14, 2022.

121. "Taiwan Will Fight 'to the Very Last Day' If China Attacks," *Diplomat*, April 8, 2021.

122. Sharon Braithwaite, "Zelensky Refuses US Offer to Evacuate, Saying 'I Need Ammunition, Not a Ride,'" CNN, February 26, 2022.

123. Jim Sciutto and Katie Bo Williams, "U.S. Concerned Kyiv Could Fall to Russia within Days, Sources Familiar with Intel Say," CNN, February 25, 2022; author's discussion with U.S. officials, February 2023.

124. Serhii Plokhy, *The Gates of Europe: A History of Ukraine* (New York: Basic Books, 2017).

125. Author's discussion with Indian official, August 2021.

126. Office of the Director of National Intelligence, *Annual Threat Assessment of the U.S. Intelligence Community*, April 9, 2021.

127. Vladimir Putin, "On the Historical Unity of Russians and Ukrainians," July 12, 2021, Kremlin website; Mikhail Zygar, *All the Kremlin's Men: Inside the Court of Vladimir Putin* (New York: PublicAffairs, 2016), 153.

128. Max Seddon, Christopher Miller, and Felicia Schwartz, "How Putin Blundered into Ukraine—Then Doubled Down," *Financial Times*, February 23, 2023.

129. See Garrett M. Graff, "'Something Was Badly Wrong': When Washington Realized Russia Was Actually Invading Ukraine," *Politico*, February 24, 2023.

130. "Putin Warns Any Foreign Attempt to Interfere with Russian Action Would Lead to 'Consequences They Have Never Seen," Associated Press, February 23, 2022; Mykhaylo Zabrodskyi et al., *Preliminary Lessons in Conventional Warfighting from Russia's Invasion of Ukraine: February–July 2022*, Royal United Services Institute, July 2022; Greg Miller and Catherine Belton, "Russia's Spies Misread Ukraine and Misled Kremlin as War Loomed," *Washington Post*, August 19, 2022; author's discussions with U.S. officials, February–April 2022.

131. On the early days, see Hal Brands, "Ukraine and the Contingency of Global Order," *Foreign Affairs*, February 14, 2023; Liam Collins, Michael Kofman, and John Spencer, "The Battle of Hostomel Airport: A Key Moment in Russia's Defeat at Kyiv," *War on the Rocks*, August 10, 2023.

132. Frederick Kagan and Mason Clark, "How Not to Invade a Nation," *Foreign Affairs*, April 29, 2022; Paul Sonne, Ellen Nakashima, Shane Harris, and John Hudson, "Hubris and Isolation led Vladimir Putin to Misjudge Ukraine," *Washington Post*, April 12, 2022.

133. Zabrodskyi et al., *Preliminary Lessons*; Paul Sonne, Isabelle Khurshudyan, Serhiy Morgunov, and Kostiantyn Khudov, "Battle for Kyiv: Ukrainian Valor, Russian Blunders Combined to Save the Capital," *Washington Post*, August 24, 2022.

134. Shane Harris et al., "Road to War: U.S. Struggled to Convince Allies, and Zelensky, of Risk of Invasion," *Washington Post*, August 16, 2022; author's discussions with U.S. officials, April 2023.

135. Harris et al., "Road to War"; Julian Barnes and Helene Cooper, "Ukrainian Officials Drew on U.S. Intelligence to Plan Counteroffensive," *New York Times*, September 10, 2022; Jahara Matisek, Will Reno, and Sam Rosenberg, "The Good, the Bad and the Ugly: Assessing a Year of Military Aid to Ukraine," Royal United Services Institute, February 22, 2023.

136. Seth Jones, "The Bloody Toll of Russia's War in Ukraine," *Lawfare*, March 19, 2023.

137. Victor Jack, "Sergey Lavrov Admits Russia Was Surprised by Scale of Western Sanctions," *Politico Europe*, March 23, 2022.

138. European countries, namely Germany, surprised Washington with how far they were willing to go on sanctions. Yet these countries presumably would have been less willing to antagonize Russia absent U.S. security guarantees.

139. "Germany Says It Is No Longer Reliant on Russian Energy," BBC, January 18, 2023; "Poland Boosts Defence Spending over War in Ukraine," BBC, January 30, 2023; Stacy Meichtry, Alistair MacDonald, and Noemie Bisserbe, "Europe's Defense Dilemma: To Buy, or Not to Buy American," *Wall Street Journal*, July 10, 2023.

140. Author's discussions with officials in Tokyo and Canberra, November 2022; Mike Yeo, "New Japanese Strategy to Up Defense Spending, Counterstrike Purchases," *Defense News*, December 20, 2022; Samson Ellis and Cindy Wang, "Taiwan Plans 14% Boost in Defense Spending to Counter China," *Bloomberg*, August 25, 2022.

141. "'Ukraine Today Could Be East Asia Tomorrow': Japan PM Warns," France24.com, June 10, 2022.

142. Tessa Wong, "G7 Takes Stand against China's 'Economic Coercion,'" BBC, May 21, 2023; Gregory Allen, *China's New Strategy for Waging the Microchip Tech War*, Center for Strategic and International Studies, May 2023.

143. "Remarks by President Biden on the United Efforts of the Free World to Support the People of Ukraine," White House, March 26, 2022.

144. Parts of this section draw on Hal Brands, "The Battle for Eurasia," *Foreign Policy*, Summer 2023.

145. Stuart Lau, "Xi Warns Putin Not to Use Nuclear Arms in Ukraine," *Politico*, November 4, 2022.

146. "CIA Director Bill Burns on War in Ukraine, Intelligence Challenges Posed by China," PBS, December 16, 2022; Aamer Madhani, "White House Says Iran Is Helping Russia Build a Drone Factory East of Moscow for the War in Ukraine," Associated Press, June 9, 2023.

147. "Russia in Joint Naval Exercises with China and Iran in the Gulf of Oman," *Euronews*, March 16, 2023; Nathaniel Taplin, "How Russia Supplies Its War Machine," *Wall Street Journal*, March 10, 2023.

148. Alexander Gabuev, "What's Really Going On between Russia and China," *Foreign Affairs*, April 12, 2023; "China's Xi Tells Putin of 'Changes Not Seen for 100 Years,'" Al Jazeera, March 22, 2023.

149. Jay Solomon, "Iran Is Using the World's Largest Lake to Evade the U.S. and Ship Weapons to Russia," *Semafor*, June 6, 2023.

150. Trym Eiterjord, "Amid Ukraine War, Russia's Northern Sea Route Turns East," *Diplomat*, December 13, 2022.

151. Alexander Gabuev, "The Yuan Is an Unlikely Winner from Russia's Growing Isolation," *Bloomberg Opinion*, March 14, 2023; "Russia Overtakes Saudi Arabia as China's Top Oil Supplier," Al Jazeera, March 20, 2023; Nathaniel Taplin, "How Microchips Migrate from China to Russia," *Wall Street Journal*, February 25, 2023; Brian Kot, "Hong Kong's Technological Lifeline to Russia," Carnegie Endowment for International Peace, May 17, 2023.

152. "Iran Seeks to Expand Its Military Cooperation with China," Associated Press, April 27, 2022; Maryam Sinaee, "Iran Forms New Power 'Triangle' with Russia, China, Hardliners Say," *Iran International*, January 19, 2022.

153. Nadège Rolland, "A China–Russia Condominium over Eurasia," *Survival*, February–March 2019, 17.

154. Rolland, "China–Russia Condominium."

155. A good discussion of synergies is Andrea Kendall-Taylor and David Shullman, *Navigating the Deepening Russia–China Partnership* (Washington, DC: Center for a New American Security, 2021).

156. Kendall-Taylor and Shullman, *Navigating the Deepening Russia–China Partnership*.

157. Michael Kofman, "The Emperors League: Understanding Sino-Russian Defense Cooperation," *War on the Rocks*, August 2020.

158. Asli Aydintasbas, "Turkey Will Not Return to the Western Fold," *Foreign Affairs*, May 19, 2021; Jeffrey Mankoff, *Empires of Eurasia: How Imperial Legacies Shape International Security* (New Haven: Yale University Press, 2022).

159. Shreya Upadhyay, "BRICS, Quad, and India's Multi-Alignment Strategy," Stimson Center, July 12, 2022; author's discussion with Vijay Gokhale, October 25, 2022.

160. Sourav Roy Barman, "Europe Has to Grow Out of Mindset That Its Problems Are World's Problems: Jaishankar," *Indian Express*, June 4, 2022.

161. Hanna Ziady, "OPEC Announces the Biggest Cut to Oil Production since the Start of the Pandemic," CNN, October 5, 2022.

162. See Ash Jain and Matthew Kroenig, *Toward a Democratic Technology Alliance: An Innovation Edge That Favors Freedom*, Atlantic Council, 2022, esp. 9; also Stephen G. Brooks and William Wohlforth, *America Abroad: The United States' Global Role in the 21st Century* (New York: Oxford University Press, 2016).

163. Stephen G. Brooks and William Wohlforth, "The Myth of Multipolarity: American Power's Staying Power," *Foreign Affairs*, May–June 2023.

164. Hal Brands and Michael Beckley, *Danger Zone: The Coming Conflict with China* (New York: Norton, 2022).

165. Andrea Kendall-Taylor and Michael Kofman, "Russia's Dangerous Decline: The Kremlin Won't Go Down without a Fight," *Foreign Affairs*, November–December 2022.

166. Dan Blumenthal and Derek Scissors, "Breaking China's Hold," *Atlantic*, December 23, 2022.

167. "China a 'Ticking Time Bomb' Because of Economic Woes, Joe Biden Warns," *Guardian*, August 11, 2023.

168. Guy Faulconbridge, "Putin Escalates Ukraine War, Issues Nuclear Threat to West," Reuters, September 21, 2022.

169. Lingling Wei, "Xi Prepares for 'Extreme' Scenarios, Including Conflict with the West," *Wall Street Journal*, June 12, 2023; John Ruwitch, "China Accuses U.S. of Containment and Warns of Potential Conflict," NPR, March 7, 2023.

170. Hal Brands, *Getting Ready for a Long War with China: Dynamics of Protracted Conflict in the Western Pacific*, American Enterprise Institute, July 2022.

171. Robert Jervis, "Theories of War in an Era of Leading-Power Peace," *American Political Science Review*, March 2022, 1.

CHAPTER 6: LESSONS OF THE PAST

1. "Commentary: Milestone Congress Points to New Era for China, the World," Xinhua, October 24, 2017.

2. John F. Kennedy, "Remarks and Question-and-Answer Period at the Press Luncheon in Paris," June 2, 1961, APP. Kennedy invoked this analogy in reference to the Sino-Soviet pact.

3. Jeffrey Mankoff, "The War in Ukraine and Eurasia's New Imperial Moment," *Washington Quarterly*, Summer 2022.

4. Franklin Roosevelt, "Annual Message to the Congress," January 3, 1940, APP.

5. For instance, Jonathan Kearsley, Eryk Bagshaw, and Anthony Galloway, "'If You Make China the Enemy, China Will Be the Enemy': Beijing's Fresh Threat to Australia," *Sydney Morning Herald*, November 18, 2020. Among other things, Beijing demanded that Canberra cease funding certain think tanks engaged in "anti-China" research and otherwise censor domestic debate.

6. Charles Clover, *Black Wind, White Snow: The Rise of Russia's New Nationalism* (New Haven: Yale University Press, 2017), 327.

7. The general phenomenon is discussed in Matthew Kroenig, *The Return of Great Power Rivalry: Democracy versus Autocracy from the Ancient World to the U.S. and China* (New York: Oxford University Press, 2020).

8. Nicholas Spykman, *America's Strategy in World Politics: The United States and the Balance of Power* [1942] (New York: Routledge, 2017), 469.

9. Brian Klaas, "Vladimir Putin Has Fallen into the Dictator Trap," *Atlantic*, March 16, 2022; Hal Brands and Michael Beckley, *Danger Zone: The Coming Conflict with China* (New York: Norton, 2022).

10. Alfred Thayer Mahan, *The Interest of America in Sea Power, Present and Future* (Boston: Little, Brown, 1897), 259.

11. For useful critiques of these arguments, see Stephen G. Brooks and William Wohlforth, "The Myth of Multipolarity: American Power's Staying Power," *Foreign Affairs*, May–June 2023; Øystein Tunsjø, *The Return of Bipolarity in World Politics: China, the United States, and Geostructural Realism* (New York: Columbia University Press, 2018).

12. Hugo Meijer and Stephen Brooks, "Illusions of Autonomy: Why Europe Cannot Provide for Its Security If the United States Pulls Back," *International Security*, Spring 2021.

13. John Lewis Gaddis, *Strategies of Containment: A Critical Appraisal of American National Security Policy during the Cold War* (New York: Oxford University Press, 2005), 112.

14. Elbridge Colby, *The Strategy of Denial: American Defense in an Age of Great-Power Conflict* (New Haven: Yale University Press, 2022).

15. Spykman, *America's Strategy*, 165.

16. Elbridge Colby and Oriana Skylar Mastro, "Ukraine Is a Distraction from Taiwan," *Wall Street Journal*, February 13, 2022.

17. It is also why defense spending remains nearly as low, as a percentage of GDP, as at any time since 1945. On the one-war strategy, see James Mitre, "A Eulogy for the Two-War Construct," *Washington Quarterly*, Winter 2019.

18. George Shultz, *Turmoil and Triumph: My Years as Secretary of State* (New York: Charles Scribner's Sons, 1993).

19. This point was made to me repeatedly in discussions with U.S., Japanese, Australian, and British policymakers during conversations in these countries in November 2022.

20. Brooks and Wohlforth, "Myth of Multipolarity"; Jain and Kroenig, *Toward a Democratic Technology Alliance*.

21. Matthew P. Goodman, "Variable Geometry Takes Shape in Biden's Foreign Policy," Center for Strategic and International Studies, March 19, 2021.

22.   Halford J. Mackinder, "The Geographic Pivot of History," *Geographical Journal*, April 1904, 436.

23.   Author's discussion with Vijay Gokhale, October 25, 2022.

24.   The phrase is from "CIA Director Burns: What U.S. Intelligence Needs to Do Today—and Tomorrow," *Washington Post*, July 7, 2023.

25.   The exception is Iran, whose Shiite version of authoritarianism has historically seemed quite threatening to the Sunni regimes in the Gulf. On the broader dynamic, see Hal Brands, "Putin's Saudi Bromance Is Part of a Bigger Plan," *Bloomberg Opinion*, December 5, 2018.

26.   John Lewis Gaddis, *The Long Peace: Inquiries into the History of the Cold War* (New York: Oxford University Press, 1986).

27.   Case in point: China's refusal to provide lethal military aid to Russia in the opening stages of the war in Ukraine in 2022 for fear of triggering U.S. and European sanctions. "China Not Giving Material Support for Russia's War in Ukraine: U.S. Official," Reuters, June 30, 2022.

28.   "Remarks by National Security Advisor Jake Sullivan at the Special Competitive Studies Project Global Emerging Technologies Summit," White House, September 16, 2022.

29.   Andrew Imbrie et al., *Agile Alliances: How the United States and Its Allies Can Deliver a Democratic Way of AI*, Center for Security and Emerging Technologies, February 2020; Melissa Flagg, "Global R & D and a New Era of Alliances," CSET Data Brief, June 2020.

30.   As President Biden repeatedly remarked. See Jeremy Diamond, "Biden Can't Stop Thinking about China and the Future of American Democracy," CNN, April 29, 2021.

31.   See Matt Pottinger, Testimony before the United States–China Economic and Security Review Commission, April 15, 2021.

32.   For a more extended discussion, see Brands and Beckley, *Danger Zone*; Jonathan Hillman, *The Digital Silk Road: China's Quest to Wire the World and Win the Future* (New York: Harper Business, 2021).

33.   Harry S. Truman, "Special Message to the Congress on the Threat to the Freedom of Europe," March 17, 1948, APP.

34.   Robbie Gramer and Jack Detsch, "A (Mostly Secret) Revolution Is Afoot in NATO's Military," *Foreign Policy*, July 13, 2023; Sean Monaghan, "The Sword, the Shield, and the Hedgehog: Strengthening Deterrence in NATO's New Strategic Concept," *War on the Rocks*, August 23, 2022.

35.   Elbridge Colby, "America Must Prepare for a War over Taiwan," *Foreign Affairs*, August 10, 2022.

36.   Josh Rogin, "When Trump Caved to Xi and Threw Taiwan under the Bus," *Daily Beast*, March 8, 2021.

37.   Ian Easton, *Hostile Harbors: Taiwan's Ports and PLA Invasion Plans*, Project 2049 Institute, July 2021.

38.   See the discussion in Yukihiro Sakaguchi and Ryo Nakamura, "U.S. Nuclear Review Warns of Chinese 'Coercion' in Indo-Pacific," *Nikkei Asia*, October 28, 2022.

39.   On the Chinese buildup, see Department of Defense, *2022 Report on Military and Security Developments Involving the People's Republic of China*, November 2022. See also Michael Hirsh, "The Pentagon Is Freaking Out about a Potential War with China," *Politico*, June 9, 2023; Hal Brands, "Deterrence in Taiwan Is Failing," *Foreign Policy*, September 8, 2023.

40.   Larry Bland, Clarence Wunderlin, and Sharon Ritenour Stevens, eds., *The Papers of George Catlett Marshall*, vol. 2 (Baltimore: Johns Hopkins University Press, 1986), 274.

41.   Don Clark and Ana Swanson, "U.S. Pours Money into Chips, but Even Soaring Spending Has Limits," *New York Times*, January 1, 2023.

42.   Spykman, *America's Strategy*, 89.

43.   Ryan Berg, *Insulate, Curtail, Compete: Sketching a U.S. Grand Strategy in Latin America and the Caribbean*, Center for Strategic and International Studies, May 2023.

44.   See Shannon O'Neill, *The Globalization Myth: Why Regions Matter* (New Haven: Yale University Press, 2022).

45. Jorge Guajardo and Natalia Cote-Muñoz, "The Future of North America–China Relations," Working Paper, Woodrow Wilson International Center for Scholars, January 2022.

46. "Top China Generals Urge More Spending for U.S. Conflict 'Trap,'" *Bloomberg News*, March 9, 2021.

47. Kyle Lascurettes, *Orders of Exclusion: Great Powers and the Strategic Sources of Foundational Rules in International Relations* (New York: Oxford University Press, 2020).

48. Halford J. Mackinder, "The Geographical Pivot of History," *Geographical Journal*, April 1904, 427–28.

49. As some China hawks have suggested. See John Mearsheimer, "The Inevitable Rivalry: America, China, and the Tragedy of Great-Power Politics," *Foreign Affairs*, November–December 2021.

50. Mackinder, "Geographical Pivot," 436.

51. "Has the Wind Changed? PLA Hawks General Dai Xu and General Qiao Liang Release Odd Articles," GNews, July 11, 2020; Minnie Chan, "'Too Costly': Chinese Military Strategist Warns Now Is Not the Time to Take Back Taiwan by Force," *South China Morning Post*, May 4, 2020.

INDEX